Towa ― ―..
Inclusive Democracy

The crisis of the growth economy and the need for
a new liberatory project

Takis Fotopoulos

Cassell
London and New York

Cassell
Wellington House
125 Strand
London WC2R 0BB

127 West 24th Street
New York, NY 10011

First published 1997

British Library Cataloguing-in-Publication Data
A catalogue record for this book is available from the British Library.

Library of Congress Cataloging-in-Publication Data
Fotopoulos, Takis.
    Towards an inclusive democracy : the crisis of the growth economy
and the need for a new liberatory project / Takis Fotopoulos.
      p. cm.
    Includes bibliographical references and index.
    ISBN 0-304-33627-0 (hardback). — ISBN 0-304-33628-9 (pbk.)
    1. Democracy. 2. Capitalism. 3. Socialism. 4. Rationalism.
I. Title.
JC458.P48 1996
321.8—dc20   96-35201
                                     CIP

ISBN 0 304 33627 0 (hardback)
     0 304 33628 9 (paperback)

Typeset by York House Typographic Ltd, London
Printed and bound by Biddles Ltd, Guildford and King's Lynn

Contents

Acknowledgements   vii

Introduction   ix

Part I The Crisis of the Growth Economy

1   The Market Economy and the Marketization Process   **3**
From markets to market economies   4
The marketization process: the liberal phase   14
The marketization process: the statist phase   21
The marketization process: the neoliberal phase   33
Internationalization and the nation-state   46

2   The Growth Economy and 'Socialist' Statism   **62**
The rise of the growth economy   63
The fall of the 'socialist' growth economy in the East   73
The collapse of social democracy in the West   85
Why 'socialist' statism failed   100

3   The Growth Economy and the South   **110**
The failure of the growth economy in the South   111
The conventional approaches to development   117
The ecological dimension of development   129
Democracy and development   131

4   The Generalized Crisis of the Capitalist Growth Economy   **140**
A multidimensional crisis   141
The growth economy and the ecological crisis   149
Is there a way out?   157

Part II Towards a Confederal Inclusive Democracy

5   Towards a New Conception of Democracy   **171**
Democracy and the growth economy   171
Democracy, freedom and autonomy   175
Conceptions of democracy   185
The conception of an inclusive democracy   206

6   A Confederal Inclusive Democracy   **224**
Democracy and community   225
The preconditions of economic democracy   237
Outline of a model of economic democracy   255

7   From 'Here' to 'There'   **275**
A new kind of politics   276
The transition to economic democracy   289

CONTENTS

Part III Towards a Democratic Rationalism

8 How Do We Justify the Project for an Inclusive Democracy? 305
    The myth of objectivity: orthodox 'objectivity' 306
    The myth of objectivity: dialectical 'objectivity' 316
    Beyond 'objectivism', irrationalism and relativism 340

Epilogue 357

Select Bibliography 360

Name Index 375

Subject Index 378

Acknowledgements

I would like first to thank my colleagues on the editorial board of *Democracy and Nature* (formerly *Society and Nature*) in which some of the material in this book was first published. The constant theoretical discussions which I have been engaged in for the past four years with the editors of the English and Greek language editions of the journal, T. Papadopoulos, N. Raptis and P. Stavropoulos, were immensely stimulating and helped me in clarifying several important issues. Similarly, the perceptive comments of Murray Bookchin and Cornelius Castoriadis were of particular significance in the development of some of the ideas in this book. I should also like to thank Stephen Millett whose comments on the model of economic democracy were especially useful.

I am particularly grateful to Riki Matthews for her advice and scrupulous reading and copyediting of this book, as well as to Charlotte Ridings, Cassell's house editor and Alan Foster, Cassell's copyeditor, for their professional work. I would also like to express my gratitude to my editors Steve Cook and Jane Greenwood of Cassell for encouraging the publication of this book and for general advice throughout the preparation of the manuscript respectively. Last but not least there is my companion Sia and my son Costas, who have helped me with their valuable advice and support throughout the preparation of this book.

For the rest, the views I express in the following pages are entirely my own, and I therefore bear sole responsibility for any defects the book may contain.

T.F.
June 1996

For Sia and Costas

Introduction

The collapse of 'actually existing socialism' does not reflect the 'triumph of capitalism', as celebrated by its ideologues. Nor, of course, does it provide justification for a social system which, in its present universality, condemns to misery and insecurity the vast majority of the world population and threatens the planet with an ecological catastrophe. Furthermore, it does not herald the historical victory of Western 'socialist' statism over Eastern 'socialist' statism, as social democrats have hastened to declare. Social democracy, in the form that dominated the quarter of a century after World War II (state commitment to welfare state, full employment and the redistribution of income and wealth in favour of the weaker social groups), is dead and has been replaced by the present neoliberal consensus ('safety nets', flexible labour markets and the redistribution of income and wealth in favour of the privileged social groups). Therefore, what the dismantling of 'actually existing socialism' and the parallel collapse of social democracy have shown is the final disintegration of socialist statism, that is, the historical tradition that aimed at the conquest of state power, by legal or revolutionary means, as the necessary condition to bring about radical social transformation.

However, even before the actual dismantling of socialist statism (for reasons related to its own contradictions as well as to structural changes in the system of the 'market economy' that we shall pursue in the first part of this book), it was obvious that there was a fundamental incompatibility between the state socialist project and the demand for creating conditions of equal sharing of political, economic and social power among all citizens. State ownership and control of economic resources, even when it led to security of employment and to significant improvements in the distribution of income and wealth, proved utterly inadequate for creating economic democracy, namely the equal sharing of economic power, not to mention conditions for the equal sharing of political power. Furthermore, socialist statism did not make any significant progress in creating conditions of democracy in the social realm generally, that is to say the household, the workplace, the educational institutions and so on.

On the threshold of a new millennium, the development of a new liberatory project, which would represent both the synthesis, as well as the transcendence, of the major social movements for change in this century, is imperative. Therefore, the meaning of democracy today can only be derived from a synthesis of the two major historical traditions, namely, the democratic and the socialist with the radical green, feminist and libertarian traditions. The former define the political and economic content of democracy ('direct democracy' and 'economic democracy'), and the latter define its ecological and social content ('ecological democracy' and 'social realm democracy', i.e. democracy in the workplace, the household, etc.). So, the new liberatory project cannot be but a project for an inclusive democracy that would extend the public realm, beyond the traditional political domain, to the economic and broader social domains.

It is therefore obvious that an inclusive democracy implies the abolition of the unequal distribution of political and economic power and the related commodity and property relations, as well as the hierarchical structures in the household, the workplace, the education place and the broader social realm. In other words, it implies the elimination of domina-tion relations at the societal level, as well as the implied notion of dominating the natural world. It is equally clear that an inclusive democ-racy has nothing to do with what passes as 'democracy' today, that is the liberal oligarchies based on the system of the market economy and liberal 'democracy'. Furthermore, the inclusive democracy proposed in this book has very little to do with the various versions of 'radical' democracy promoted today by the 'civil societarian' Left. As I have tried to show in the book, the civil societarian approach is both a-historical and utopian in the negative sense of the word. It is a-historical because it ignores the structural changes which have led to the internationalized market econ-omy and the consequent impotence of autonomous (from the state) institutions and associations (unions, local economies, civic movements, etc.). It is utopian because, within the present institutional framework of the internationalized market economy and liberal 'democracy', which civil societarians take for granted, the enhancement of autonomous in-stitutions is only possible to the extent that it does not contravene the logic and dynamic of the market economy.

But, if a 'radical' democracy, under today's conditions of concentrated political and economic power, is utopian in the negative sense of the word, an inclusive democracy is definitely more than just a utopia, in the sense of an ideal society. A liberatory project is not a utopia if it is based on today's reality and at the same time expresses the discontent of significant social sectors and their explicit or implicit contesting of existing society. As the book attempts to show, the roots of the present multidimensional crisis (ecological, economic, political, social, cultural) lie in the non-democratic organization of society at all levels, in the sense that it is the concentration of power in the hands of various elites that marks the foundation of every aspect of the crisis.

Thus, it is the concentration of economic power, as a result of commodity relations and the grow-or-die dynamic of the market economy, which has led to the present economic crisis. This crisis is expressed, mainly, by the continuous expansion of inequality, the relentlessly growing gap, not only between the North and the South, but also between the economic elites and the rest of society within the North and the South. It is also the concentration of economic power in the hands of economic elites which fuels the social and cultural crisis, as expressed by the parallel spread of the dialectic of violence, both personal and collective, drug abuse, general social irresponsibility, as well as cultural homogeneity.

Furthermore, it is the concentration of political power in the hands of professional politicians and various 'experts' that has transformed politics into statecraft and resulted in a crisis of traditional politics, as expressed by the growing reluctance of citizens to participate in it as members of political parties, as voters, and so on.

Finally, the fact that the main form of power within the framework of the growth economy is economic, and that the concentration of economic power involves the ruling elites in a constant struggle to dominate people and Nature, could go a long way towards explaining the present ecological crisis. In other words, to understand the ecological crisis we should not refer simply to the prevailing system of values and the resulting technologies, nor just to production relations, but to the relations of domination that characterize a hierarchical society which is based on the system of market economy, and the implied idea of dominating the natural world. It is no accident that the destruction of the environment during the lifetime of the growth economy, in both its market economy and state socialist versions, goes far beyond the cumulative damage that previous societies have inflicted on the environment.

Therefore, the project for an inclusive democracy does not only express the highest human ideal of freedom in the sense 'of individual and collective autonomy, but it is also perhaps the only way out of the present multidimensional crisis.

In the first part of the book, the emergence of the system of the market economy and the nation-state in the last few centuries is discussed and the process that led from the liberal phase of the market economy to the present neoliberal internationalized phase is examined. It is shown that the present neoliberal consensus is not a conjunctural phenomenon but the completion of a process which started almost two centuries ago when the marketization of the economy was initiated, that is, the historical process that has transformed the socially controlled economies of the past into the market economy of the present. In this context, *statism* – the period of active state control of the economy and extensive interference with the self-regulating mechanism of the market aimed at directly determining the level of economic activity – was a historically brief interlude in the process of marketization which ended in the 1970s when statism became incompatible with the growing internationalization of the market economy (Chapter 1).

Next, an attempt is made to show that the rise in this century of the growth economy, that is, the system of economic organization which is geared, either 'objectively' or deliberately, towards maximizing economic growth, had, in both its capitalist and 'socialist' versions, different causes but a common effect. Thus, the rise of the capitalist growth economy was, mainly, a by-product of the dynamics of the market economy, whereas the emergence of its 'socialist' version was primarily related to the growth ideology and the post-Enlightenment partial identification of Progress with the development of productive forces. In both types of the growth economy the outcome was the same: a huge concentration of economic power within the old First and Second Worlds (Chapter 2) and between the North, in which the market/growth economy originated, and the South, which imported a bad copy of the same (Chapter 3).

The first part of the book concludes with a summarization of the findings of the first three chapters in an attempt to show that the main dimensions of the present multidimensional crisis (economic, ecological, political, social and ideological) not only are interconnected but that they may, also, be attributed in the last instance to the concentration of economic, political and social power that the institutional framework of the market economy and liberal 'democracy' implies. Finally, the Right's and the Left's proposals to deal with the crisis are assessed (Chapter 4).

The second part of the book develops a new conception of an inclusive democracy and compares and contrasts it with the historical conceptions of democracy (classical, liberal, Marxist) as well as with the various versions of 'radical' democracy currently in fashion (Chapter 5). This is followed by an outline of a model for a confederal inclusive democracy in general and for economic democracy in particular, which shows that it *is* feasible to design a system that transcends the inefficiency of both the market economy and central planning in covering human needs (Chapter 6). This part of the book concludes with a discussion of a transitional political and economic strategy towards an inclusive democracy (Chapter 7).

Finally, the last part of the book examines the moral and philosophical foundations of a democratic society and criticizes the attempts to ground the liberatory project on a 'science' of the economy and society, or on an 'objective' ethics. This leads to the conclusion that the project for an inclusive democracy can only be founded on a democratic rationalism that transcends 'objectivism' as well as general relativism and irrationalism (Chapter 8).

PART I

The Crisis of the Growth Economy

The Market Economy and the Marketization Process

Today, after the collapse of 'actually existing socialism', a very high degree of homogeneity characterizes the economic and political institutions of society. Thus, the system of the market economy and the consequent growth economy (defined as the system of economic organization which is geared, either 'objectively' or deliberately, towards maximizing economic growth) are universal. Also, the nation-state, usually accompanied by some form of liberal 'democracy', is still omnipresent, despite the fact that the present state's economic sovereignty withers away almost proportionately to the internationalization of the market economy. While both the market economy and the present form of statist 'democracy' are taken for granted, this has not always been the case. Both the nation-state and parliamentary democracy are historically recent phenomena. Also, although markets have existed for a very long time, the *system* of the market economy was established only two centuries ago.

The aim of this chapter is to show that economic *growth* and *marketization* (i.e. the historical process that has transformed the socially controlled economies of the past into the market economy of the present) are the fundamental pillars of the present system. The former is implied by the grow-or-die dynamic that characterizes market competition, whereas the latter is implicit in the pursuit of economic efficiency. A historical examination of the economic role of the state shows a clear connection between changes in its role and the main phases of the marketization process. First, the state played a crucial role in the establishment of the market economy two centuries ago and, also, during the first attempt to set up a liberal internationalized economy in the last century. The rise in this century of what I call *statism* — the period of active state control of the economy and extensive interference with the self-regulating mechanism of the market aimed at directly determining the level of economic activity — was a historically brief interlude to the process of marketization. The statist phase of this process lasted for only about half a century and was followed by the present rolling back of state control over the economy, within the framework of the neoliberal consensus. This clearly shows that once a market economy is established, its own dynamic tends to undermine any serious effort to create self-protective mechanisms for society against the hegemony of the market and transforms society itself into a market society.

In the last section to this chapter (see p. 46) the present debate about the 'globalization' of the market economy and the end of the nation-state is considered. Although in the last quarter of this century the right conditions for the completion of an internationalized market economy have been created (after the collapse of the first attempt in the first phase of marketization), this does not mean the complete phasing out of the nation-state, or the nationally based multinational corporation, as 'globalists' argue. However, the present successful internationalization of the economy does represent a higher stage in the marketization process; a stage which involves the effectual disappearance of the economic sovereignty of the nation-state. Therefore, contrary to modern social-democratic thinking, it is not just the effective social control of the *national* economy which is ruled out by the internationalization of the market economy. Equally impossible is any effective social control of the regional, continental or even planetary market economy.

From markets to market economies

A word of explanation is needed at the outset about the use of the term 'market economy', instead of the usual Marxist concept of 'the capitalist mode of production', which emphasizes production relations, or alternatively 'the capitalist world economy',[1] which focuses on exchange relations. The choice does not emanate from a need to comply with today's 'political correctness' which has exorcised the words 'capitalism' and – more conveniently – 'socialism'. It is a choice which is implied by my belief that although the concepts 'capitalist mode of production' and 'capitalist world economy' have provided important insights in the analysis of social classes and the world division of labour respectively, they are too narrow and outdated.

They are too narrow because they imply that power relations in general can be analysed in terms of (or be reduced to) economic power relations. It is a central premise of this book that economic power is only one form of power and if used as the central category in the analysis of social phenomena related to hierarchical relations (in the household, work, etc.), or issues of racial and cultural 'identity', it is bound to lead to inadequate or oversimplified interpretations.

They are outdated because in today's internationalized market economy, neither the class analysis implied by Marxist theory nor the concept of the world division of labour implied by the 'world-system' approach are particularly relevant. While these important topics are touched on in this book (see p. 36 regarding the new class structure that is emerging in the internationalized market economy, and Chapter 3, p. 131 about the new 'North–South' divide), to my mind, it is obvious that the present multi-dimensional crisis cannot be fruitfully discussed within the theoretical framework implied by the above concepts.

Of course, this does not mean that the central category used in this book, 'the market economy', is *per se* broad enough to interpret adequately social phenomena like the ones mentioned above. Still, the very fact that this category is used to explain only one part of reality, the economic realm, without claiming that this realm determines (not even 'in the last instance') the other realms does allow enough flexibility for the development of adequate interdisciplinary interpretations of social reality.

It is therefore obvious that the term 'market economy' is used here to define the concrete system that emerged in a specific place (Europe) and at a particular time (two centuries ago) and not as a general historical category of an approach aiming to show the evolution of the economic system throughout history, as the Marxist concept of the mode of production supposedly does. The methodological approach adopted in this book is based on the premise that it is impossible to derive 'general' theories about social or economic evolution which are based on 'scientific' or 'objective' views of social reality (see Chapter 8).

Finally, it should be noted that in this book the market economy is not identified with capitalism, as is usually the case. The *market economy* is defined here as the self-regulating system in which the fundamental economic problems (*what, how,* and *for whom* to produce) are solved 'automatically', through the price mechanism, rather than through conscious social decisions. Of course, this does not mean that in a market economy there are no social controls at all. Here, we should introduce an important distinction between the various types of social controls which will help us to interpret today's marketization and internationalization of the economy.

There are three main types of possible social controls on the market economy. There are first what we may call *regulatory controls*, which have usually been introduced by the capitalists in control of the market economy in order to 'regulate' the market. The aim of regulatory controls is to create a stable framework for the smooth functioning of the market economy without affecting its essential self-regulating nature. Such controls have always been necessary for the production and reproduction of the system of the market economy. Examples are the various controls introduced at present by the latest round of GATT, or by the Maastricht Treaty, which aim at regulating the world and the European markets respectively in the interest mainly of those controlling the respective markets (multinationals, big Europe-based national and multinational firms, etc.). Second, there are what we may call *social controls in the broad sense* which, although they have as their primary aim the protection of those controlling the market economy against foreign competition, yet may have some indirect effects that could be beneficial to the rest of society as well. A primary example of such controls is the various protectionist measures aiming at protecting domestic commodities and capital markets (tariffs, import controls, exchange controls, etc.). Finally, there are what we may call *social controls in the narrow sense* which aim at the protection of humans and nature against the effects of marketization. Such controls are usually introduced as a result of social struggles undertaken by those who are adversely affected by the market economy's effects on them or on their environment. Typical examples of such controls are social security legislation, welfare benefits, macro-economic controls to secure full employment, etc. In the rest of this book, unless otherwise stated, 'social controls' refers to this last category of social controls in the narrow sense. As shown later in this chapter, those controlling the neoliberal internationalized market economy aim at the abolition of social controls (both in the narrow and broad senses) but not of regulatory controls.

The market economy, as defined above, is a broader term than capitalism. The former refers to the way resources are allocated, whereas the latter refers to property relations. Thus, although historically the market economy has been associated with capitalism, namely, private ownership and control of the means of production, a market allocation of resources is not inconceivable within a system of social ownership and control of economic resources. The distinction drawn between capitalism and the market economy is particularly useful today when many in the self-styled 'Left', after the failure of the planned socialist economy, rediscover the merits of a 'socialist' market economy.[2] At the same time, several 'communist' parties in the South (China, Vietnam, etc.) have embarked on a strategy to build a 'socialist' market economy and are in the process of achieving a synthesis of the worst elements of the market economy (unemployment, inequality, poverty) and 'socialist' statism (authoritarianism, lack of any political freedom, etc.). As this book will, hopefully, make clear, the objective of a new liberatory project should not merely be the abolition of capitalist property relations but that of the market economy itself.

The first part of the chapter will discuss briefly the long historical period preceding the emergence of the market economy system. This will be followed in the second part by a discussion of the historical phases in the marketization process.

Pre-'market economy' markets

The process of marketization is one that, through the gradual lifting of social controls on the markets, tends to transform all goods and services into commodities and to convert citizens to mere consumers. Although the market today permeates all aspects of life, from family life to culture, education, religion, and so on, it can easily be shown that, despite the fact that markets have existed for a very long time, the marketization of the economy is a new phenomenon which has emerged in the past two centuries. Thus, as Karl Polanyi notes in his classic book *The Great Transformation*:

> *Previously to our time no economy has ever existed that even in principle was controlled by markets . . . [A]lthough the institution of the market was fairly common since the later Stone Age, its role was no more than incidental to economic life . . . [W]hile history and ethnography know of various kinds of economies, most of them comprising the institution of markets, they know of no economy prior to our own, even approximately controlled and regulated by markets* [3] *. . . . All economic systems known to us up to the end of feudalism in Western Europe were organised either on the principles of reciprocity or redistribution or householding (i.e., production for one's own use) or some combination of the three.* [4]

The motives, therefore, that ensured the functioning of the economic system derived from custom, law, magic, religion – but not gain. Markets, up to the end of the Middle Ages, played no significant role in the economic system. Even when, from the sixteenth century on, markets became both numerous and important, they were strictly controlled by society, under conditions that, as described ably by Pëtr Kropotkin, made a self-regulating market unthinkable:

> *The internal commerce was dealt with entirely by the guilds not by the individual artisans – prices being established by mutual agreement . . . [A]t the beginning external commerce was dealt with exclusively by the city and it was only later that it became the monopoly of the merchants' guild and later still of individual merchants . . . [T]he provisioning of the principal consumer goods was always handled by the city, and this custom was preserved in some Swiss towns for corn until the middle of the 19th century.* [5]

As a rule, both ancient and feudal economic systems were rooted in social relations, and non-economic motives regulated the distribution of material goods. The goods of everyday life, even in the early Middle Ages, were not regularly bought and sold in the market. This, combined with the fact that prior to the Industrial Revolution neither labour nor land was *commodified*, makes it clear that the marketization process had not begun before the rise of industrialism. Thus, it was only at the beginning of the last century that a self-regulating market was created which, for the first time in human history, established the institutional separation of society into an economic and a political sphere. Under neither tribal, feudal nor mercantile conditions was there a separate economic system in society.[6]

Still, economic liberalism projected backwards the principles underlying a self-regulating market onto the entire history of human civilization, distorting, in the process, the true nature and origins of trade, markets and money, as well as of town life. However, almost all anthropological or sociological assumptions contained in the philosophy of economic liberalism been refuted by social anthropology, primitive economics, the history of early civilization and general economic history. For instance, there is no evidence on which to base the assertions that to expect payment for labour is 'natural' for humans ('Even in the Middle Ages payment for work for strangers is [*sic*] something unheard of'[7]), nor that the motive of gain is 'natural'. The same applies to another crucial assumption of economic liberalism that markets, as well as money, would spontaneously arise if humans were left alone. In fact, both markets and money do not arise from within the community but from without.[8] Trade itself does not rely on markets, and even medieval commerce developed from the beginnings under the influence of export trade rather than local trade and was inter-communal in character rather than trade between individuals. Furthermore, local markets had no tendency to grow – a fact that implies that, contrary to liberal (and Marxist) received wisdom, there is nothing 'inevitable' about the marketization of the economy. Thus, as Henri Pirenne points out: 'It would be natural to suppose, at first glance, that a merchant class grew up little by little in the midst of the agricultural population. Nothing, however, gives credence to this theory.'[9]

Nation-states and markets
Similarly, there is no inevitability whatsoever concerning the related, and parallel to the marketization process, rise of the modern nation-state, which Marxists see as part and parcel of 'modernity' and progress. Thus, in the Marxist view, the nation-state is a stage in the historical development, a stage, which – by promoting the progress of industrialization – creates the necessary conditions for socialism. Marx himself supported fully the 'unity of great nations which, if originally brought about by political force, has now become a powerful coefficient of social production'.[10] But, in fact, as Bookchin observes:

If we bear in mind the large number of municipal confederacies that existed in Europe during the 11th century and in the centuries that followed it, the certainty so prevalent in modern-day historiography that the nation-state constitutes a 'logical' development in Europe out of feudalism can only be regarded as a bias.[11]

Thus, although the state appeared some 5500 years ago in Egypt, when the creation of an economic surplus made economic inequality possible, nation-states had not started to develop until the fourteenth to sixteenth centuries. In fact, it was not until the end of the seventeenth century that the present form of the nation-state emerged. And this was not without considerable resistance from the free cities of the era and rebellious villages.

The idea of a 'nation', as Bookchin also points out,[12] was alien to the ancient mind, and people owed their strongest allegiances to their kin group and to their community or perhaps region; a Greek 'nation', for instance, never developed among the Greek *polei*; similarly, the great empires of the ancient world were not 'nations' in any sense of the term. Even in the Middle Ages, as April Carter argues, although some monarchies did indeed have their national territories and made claims to sovereign power within them, these monarchies were just part of European Christendom, so that 'there was little of a national state – indeed there was little of any sort of state – in the territorial regnum of the Middle Ages; it was a paradise of Estates rather than the pattern of state'.[13]

The inescapable conclusion is that the concentration of power, which followed the rise of the nation-state and the market economy, had nothing inevitable about it. The rise of the former was, historically, the outcome of military violence, whereas that of the latter was the result of economic violence, that is, of the huge economic inequality which inevitably followed the drastic lessening of social controls over the market during the period of the emergence of mechanized mass production. In this way, a historic reversal took place regarding the role of the state and the market with respect to the process of concentration of power (political and economic) in the hands of the ruling elites. Before the start of the marketization process, it was mainly through political – in the broad sense – means (conquest, confiscation, expropriation, slavery, religious power) that power became concentrated. The role of the state in particular was decisive in this process, whereas that of the market was not significant. However, once the marketization process had been set in motion, it was mainly through economic means (the market itself) that power was accumulated, whereas the state largely legitimized this process.

The emergence of market economies

The crucial element that differentiates the market economy from all past economies (where markets were also self-regulating, since all markets tend to produce prices that equalize supply and demand) was the fact that, for the first time in human history, a self-regulating market *system* emerged – a system in which markets developed even for the means of production, that is, labour, land and money. The control of the economic system by the market, according to Polanyi, 'means no less than the running of society as an adjunct to the market: instead of economy being embedded in social relations (as in the past), social relations are embedded in the economic system'.[14] Competition, which was the motor force of the new system, ensured that the grow-or-die principle characterized its dynamics. These same dynamics imply that the market economy, once installed, will inevitably end up as an internationalized economy.

This does not mean, however, that some type of evolutionary process can explain the move from pre-'market economy' forms of economic organization to the present internationalized market economy, as Marxists attempt to do. In fact, the market economy itself did not actually 'evolve' out of a feudal era but literally exploded, particularly in England, during the eighteenth and especially the nineteenth centuries.[15] In other words, contrary to what liberals and Marxists assert, the marketization of the economy was not just an evolutionary process, following the expansion of trade under mercantilism. Here, however, we should distinguish between the three main forms of trade, that is, *foreign trade*, which involved the exchange of goods (usually luxuries) not available in a region; *local trade*, which involved the exchange of goods that were not worth transporting because of their weight, bulkiness or perishable nature; and *internal* or *national trade*, which involved similar goods from different sources offered in competition with one another. It was only the latter form of trade that was competitive in nature, in contrast to the other two which had a complementary character. Furthermore, it was national trade that played an instrumental role in the marketization process, since it was its expansion that resulted in the 'nationalization' of the market, rather than the expansion of local or foreign trade.

But, if modern markets did not evolve out of local markets and/or markets for foreign goods, the question arises as to what factors could explain the marketization process. Here, the nation-state, which was just emerging at the end of the Middle Ages, played a crucial role: (a) by creating the conditions for the 'nationalization' of the market (mercantilist phase); and (b) by freeing the market from effective social control (liberal phase of marketization).

The emergence therefore of the nation-state, which preceded the marketization of the economy, had the effect not only of destroying the political independence of the town or village community, but also of undermining their economic self-reliance. At the ideological level, the formation of national states was accompanied by the rise of nationalism: in other words, a new ideology, which attempted to create an identification between the individual and the abstract entity of the state, in place of the former identification of it with the community.

However, the fact that the state usually played a crucial role in the marketization process, and that, during the nineteenth century in particular, many of the newly formed nation-states were involved in a systematic effort to establish and protect a domestic market economy, does not imply a strict causal relationship; it would be wrong to attribute a cause and effect relationship to the rise of the nation-state and the rise of the 'national economy'. Although it is true that the victory of the nation-state over confederal forms of organization usually favoured the expansion of a market economy, in other cases, as Bookchin points out, it simply led to state parasitism and outright regression.[16]

As regards the role of the state in the mercantilist phase, it should be noted that before the commercial revolution, trade was not national but municipal or inter-community in character, bringing towns and villages together in regional networks and local markets but not in national ones. The newly emerging nations were merely political units consisting, economically, of innumerable self-sufficient households and insignificant local markets in the villages. The formation of a national or internal market was resisted by the fiercely protectionist towns and municipalities. Only wholesalers and rich merchants were pressing for it. No wonder that it was only by virtue of deliberate state action in the fifteenth and sixteenth centuries that the 'nationalization' of the market and the creation of internal trade were achieved.[17] As Kropotkin points out:

[T]he 16th century – a century of carnage and wars – can be summed up quite simply by this struggle of the nascent state against the free towns and their federations ... the role of the nascent state in the 16th and 17th centuries in relation to the urban centres was to destroy the independence of the cities ... to concentrate in its hands the external commerce of the cities and ruin it ... to subject internal commerce as well as manufacturers totally to the control of a host of officials.[18]

The 'nationalization' of the market was followed in the sixteenth and seventeenth centuries by further state action, the outcome of which was to undermine to an even greater extent the political and economic independence of the cities and to ruin village communes. This action involved the confiscation or 'enclosure' of communal lands – a process that was completed in Western Europe by the 1850s.[19] The effect was not only to destroy community links in towns and villages but also to create the foundations for the marketization of the economy, as both labour and land were now being released, in plentiful quantities, to be bought and sold in the emerging labour and land markets.

Nevertheless, mercantilism, with all its tendency towards commercialization, never attacked the institutional safeguards which protected labour and land from being *marketized*. The social controls on labour and land, which, under feudalism, had taken the form of custom and tradition, were simply replaced, under mercantilism, by statutes and ordinances. Therefore, the 'freeing' of trade performed by mercantilism merely liberated trade from localism; markets were still an accessory feature of an institutional set-up regulated more than ever by society. Up until the Industrial Revolution, there was no attempt to establish a market economy in the form of a big, self-regulating market. In fact, it was at the end of the eighteenth century that the transition from regulated markets to a system of self-regulated ones marked the 'great transformation' of society, that is, the move to a market economy. Up until that time, industrial production in Western Europe, and particularly in England, where the market economy was born, was a mere accessory to commerce. The use of machines in production and the development of the factory system reversed this relationship. The marketization of land, labour and money, which were crucial elements in the industrial process, was therefore, as Polanyi described it:

> . . . the inevitable consequence of the introduction of the factory system in a commercial society . . . [T]he fiction of their being produced as commodities became the organising principle of society . . . [H]uman society has become an accessory to the economic system . . . [T]he transformation implies a change in the motive of action on the part of the members of society: for the motive of subsistence that of gain must be substituted. All transactions are turned into money transactions . . . Prices must be allowed to regulate themselves.[20]

The marketization of labour and land were particularly significant. Under the guild system, working conditions as well as the wages of the workers were regulated by society, that is, by the custom and rule of the guild and the town. The same applied to land: the status and function of land was determined by legal and customary rules (whether its possession was transferable or not and if so under what restrictions, for what uses, etc.). The removal of labour and land from social control has led to the creation of new forms of domination and, at the same time, has destroyed the traditional fabric of the guild workers' communities, village communities, the old form of land tenure and so on. For instance, the principle of freedom from want was equally acknowledged in every type of social organization up until the beginning of the sixteenth century:[21] the individual in a primitive society was not threatened by starvation unless the whole community starved. Hunger, which was a necessary element of a self-regulating market, presupposed the liquidation of organic society. In fact, some argue that, contrary to popular and economic wisdom, people are relatively *less* well off now than they were in the Middle Ages![22]

One could therefore speculate that only a drastic change in the economic structure of Western European society at the time of the Industrial Revolution could have averted the marketization of society — a change that would have made the use of machines, in conditions of large-scale production, compatible with the social control of production. But such a change would have required a social revolution towards economic democracy to accompany the Industrial Revolution. As such a revolution did not materialize at the time, what followed was inevitable. Factories could not secure continued production unless the supply of means of production (especially, labour and land) was organized. But in a commercial society, the only way to organize their supply was to transform human activity and natural resources into commodities, whose supply did not depend on the needs of human beings and the ecosystem respectively, but on market prices. Therefore, the introduction of new systems of production to a commercial society, where the means of production were under private ownership and control, inevitably led (with the crucial support of the nation-state) to the transformation of the socially controlled economies of the past, in which the market played a marginal role in the economic process, into the present market economies.

Private control of production required that those controlling the means of production would have to be economically 'efficient' in order to survive competition, i.e. they had to ensure:

- the free flow of labour and land at a minimal cost. However, under conditions of private control of production, this flow has an inverse relationship to the social controls (in the narrow sense) on the market. Thus, the more effective the social controls on the market, and in particular on the markets for the means of production (labour, capital, land), the more difficult it is to ensure their free flow at a minimal cost. For instance, legislation to protect labour made the labour market less flexible and, consequently, the flow of labour less smooth or more expensive. Therefore, historically, those having private control of the means of production have always directed their efforts towards further *marketizing* the economy, that is, minimizing the social controls on the market;

- the continual flow of investments into new techniques, methods of production and products, in an effort to improve competitiveness, and the sales figures (a logic aptly expressed by the motto 'grow or die').[23] The outcome of this process is *economic growth*. Therefore, it is not a coincidence that 'the modern idea of growth was formulated about four centuries ago in Europe when the economy and the society began to separate',[24] although the *growth economy* itself emerged much later, after the market economy was initiated at the beginning of the nineteenth century, and only flourished in the post World War II period.

The rest of the chapter will examine the process of marketization, to be followed in Chapter 2 by a discussion of the growth economy. We may distinguish three main phases in the marketization process: (a) the liberal phase, which, after a transitional period of protectionism, led to (b) the statist phase; and (c) the present neoliberal phase.

The marketization process: the liberal phase

The move to a market economy represented a break of society with the economy. Once the two had been separated, the logic of the system created its own unstoppable dynamic. Those controlling production had to be 'efficient' (in terms of sales and cost) in order to survive the competition within a market-based system of production. Efficiency, in turn, depended, as we saw above, on investing in new techniques and products and the consequent massive expansion of production (i.e. economic growth) and on securing a free flow of 'labour' and 'land' at a minimum cost (i.e. marketization). The former fuelled the grow-or-die dynamic that has characterized market economy production and has led to the present multidimensional crisis. The latter implied the *commodification* of labour and land. But, as Polanyi points out:

> *labour and land are no other than the human beings themselves of which every society consists and the natural surroundings in which it exists; to include labour and land in the market mechanism means to subordinate the substance of society itself to the laws of the market.*[25]

To my mind, Polanyi's significant contribution was that he expressed the fundamental contradiction of the market economy system not in terms of an *economic* conflict between productive relations and productive forces (where the productive relations from forms of development of the productive forces 'turn into their fetters'), as Marx[26] assumed, but in terms of a broader social conflict between the requirements of the market economy and those of society; in particular, in terms of the conflict created by the fact that in a market economy labour and land have to be treated as genuine commodities, with their free and fully developed markets, whereas in fact they are only fictitious commodies.

Thus, as soon as a market economy was established, a ceaseless social struggle started. Schematically, this is the struggle between those controlling the market economy, i.e. the capitalist elite controlling production and distribution, and the rest of society. Those controlling the market economy aimed at marketizing labour and land as much as possible, that is, at minimizing – at best eliminating – all social controls on them, so that their free flow, at a minimum cost, could be secured. On the other hand, those at the other end, particularly the growing working class, aimed at maximizing social controls on labour and land, that is, at maximizing society's self-protection against the perils of the market economy, especially unemployment and poverty.

At the theoretical and political level, this conflict was expressed by the clash between *economic liberalism* and *socialism* (in a broad sense). Economic liberalism sought to establish a self-regulating market, using as its main methods *laissez-faire,* free trade and regulatory controls. On the other hand, socialism sought to conserve humans (although not nature, given the socialist identification of Progress with economic growth, see Chapter 2) as well as productive organization, using as its main methods social controls on the markets. This struggle constituted the central element of European history, from the Industrial Revolution to date. Thus, the emergence of early economic liberalism, under conditions not securing its continuous reproduction (liberal phase of marketization), was followed by the rise of *socialist statism*, defined as the historical tradition that aims at the conquest of state power, by legal or revolutionary means, as the necessary condition to bring about radical social change. Socialist statism was succeeded, in turn, by the present mature economic neoliberalism (neoliberal phase).

The advent of economic liberalism

Once the transition from socially controlled markets to a system of self-regulated ones was affected at the end of the eighteenth century (the institutionalizing of the physical mobility of labour in England in 1795 was a crucial step in this transition) then the conflict between those controlling the market economy and the rest of society started in earnest. Thus, almost immediately, a political and industrial working-class movement emerged and, as a result of its pressure, factory laws and social legislation were introduced. In 1824, for instance, the British Combination Acts of 1799 and 1800, which ruled that unions were a conspiracy against the public because they restricted trade, were repealed. However, all these institutional arrangements were incompatible with the self-regulation of the markets and the market economy itself. This incompatibility led to a counter-movement by those controlling the market economy in England, which ended up with the taking of legal steps to establish a competitive labour market (1834), the extension of freedom of contract to the land (between 1830 and 1860) and the abolition of export duties and reduction of import duties in the 1840s. In fact, the 1830s and the 1840s (not unlike the 1980s and the 1990s) were characterized by an explosion of legislation repealing restrictive regulations and an attempt to establish the foundations of a self-regulating market, that is, free trade, a competitive labour market and the Gold Standard – namely, the system of fixed exchange rates where the value of a currency was fixed to the value of gold.

As regards the Gold Standard in particular (which was adopted by Britain as early as 1821, to be followed by France and the United States in the 1850s and Germany in 1870, becoming universal in 1880), its supposedly automatic adjustment mechanism was a central element in this process. The aim of the Gold Standard was to create an international stable environment for world trade, similar to the domestic stable environment that had already been established for national trade; in other words, to create an internationalized market economy by fixing the value of currencies. A pure gold standard would require countries to give up central banking, as Ludwig von Mises advocated, since central banks' actions represented a form of intervention in the workings of a self-regulating system. This was particularly so if central banks, in their action, were guided by political (in the broad sense) criteria, expressing society's self-protection against the workings of the market mechanism. However, such a pure form was never applied. Instead, the system historically was associated with the creation of new token currencies based on the sovereignty of the central banks of issue. The national currency, in turn, played a crucial role in establishing the nation-state as the decisive economic and political unit. No wonder that only countries which possessed a monetary system controlled by central banks were reckoned sovereign states. Thus, both the currency and the central bank were not just expressions of a new nationalism but necessary prerequisites to cushion the effects of the gold standard on a country's income and employment.

The movement towards free trade reached its peak in the 1870s, marking the end of the system of privileged trading blocs and restricted commerce which characterized the growth of the colonial empires in the pre-1800 period. Although universal free trade was not attained during this time since, at the end, only Britain and Holland adopted policies of complete free trade, for a brief period in the 1860s and the 1870s the world came close to a self-regulating system, as envisaged by classical economic theory.[27]

So, the nineteenth century saw the first attempt at an internationalized market economy. This is shown by the massive expansion of the movement of commodities as well as capital and labour that took place during this period. This expansion was not, of course, an unexpected development, given that the precondition for the reproduction of the newly established market economy was its continuous growth, and this growth, in turn, necessitated the continuous expansion of the market, initially of the domestic market and later of the external market. Regarding the expansion of trade, it is estimated that the value of international trade doubled between 1830 and 1850, and at least trebled and may have nearly quadrupled in the period up to 1880, reaching a peak annual growth rate of 5.3 per cent in the period 1840–70.[28] As far as capital movements are concerned, from the end of the Napoleonic wars until the mid-1850s about $2000 million was invested abroad; by 1870 the value of these investments had trebled and by 1900 they totalled $23,000 million, reaching $43,000 million in 1914.[29] As for the movement of labour, between 1821 and 1915 the total recorded world immigration amounted to just over 51 million people.[30]

It is therefore obvious that international trade and the movement of capital and labour across frontiers played a major role in helping the newly emerged market economy to become a growth economy, although the extent to which the economic growth of individual countries was dependent on the existence of the international economy is still a matter for research. What is certain is that the pace of conversion differed from country to country, depending mainly on the availability of flexible markets[31] – a crucial factor in the failure of the first historical attempt towards a liberal internationalized market economy that we turn to next.

The rise of protectionism and nationalism

The attempt to establish a purely liberal internationalized market economy, in the sense of free trade, a competitive labour market and the Gold Standard, did not last more than 40 years, and by the 1870s and 1880s protectionist legislation was back. Thus, the aim to liberalize the markets in the first phase of the marketization process had the paradoxical effect of leading to more protection: either because of pressure by those controlling production to be protected from foreign competition, or because of pressure by the rest of society to be protected against the market mechanism itself. Both types of protectionism had the effect of undermining the marketization process, as we shall see in more detail in the next section.

As regards protectionism in favour of those controlling the market economy, the return to protectionism in the form of tariffs and other trade restrictions was evident in the 1880s and was reinforced by the parallel rise of nationalism. Protectionism gathered momentum in the entire period from 1880 to 1913 when in effect only Britain, Holland and Denmark adhered to free trade. However, trade continued expanding although not as fast as in the earlier period of 1840–70. Thus, in the period 1840–1914 world trade grew at an average annual rate of 3.4 per cent, significantly faster than the growth in production (2.1 per cent per annum). As a result, the ratio of international trade to production from barely 3 per cent in 1800 had, by 1913, reached 33 per cent.[32]

At the same time, protectionism in the form of social controls (narrow sense) on the market also intensified. Even British liberals had to legalize the activities of trade unions in 1871. It was also significant that not just England, but France and Prussia as well passed through a similar process: a period of *laissez-faire*, followed by a period of anti-liberal legislation with respect to public health, factory conditions, social insurance, public utilities and so on. Thus, 'At the end of the nineteenth century, across Europe and the US, governments legislated to limit the workings of *laissez-faire* – first by inspecting factories and offering minimal standards of education and later by providing subsistence income for the old and out of work.'[33] As a result, by the beginning of the twentieth century, social legislation of some sort was in place in almost every advanced market economy.[34]

If, therefore, at the beginning of the nineteenth century the ruling philosophy was internationalist, in the form of liberal nationalism (free trade, etc.), by the 1870s liberal nationalism started turning into national (or nationalistic) liberalism, with an emphasis on protectionism and imperialism abroad. The consequence of such protectionist pressures was that by the end of the Depression of 1873–86, which marked the end of the first experiment with pure economic liberalism, Germany had already established an all-round social insurance system and high tariff walls, whereas the United States had established even higher tariff walls, despite the commitment to free markets.

By the same token, both types of protectionism (i.e. tariffs and social controls) contributed to the rise of nationalism, a movement that was very much in ascendance during the second part of the last century, especially among the 'latecomers' to nationhood, Germany and Italy. The demand for nation-states did not just express the needs of those controlling the economy to get rid of the variety of commercial and industrial laws which had become an intolerable obstacle to their developing industry and expanding trade, as Engels argued in connection with the creation of the German nation-state:

> *The desire for a united 'Fatherland' had a very material foundation . . . it was the demand arising from the immediate needs of practical businessmen*

*and industrialists for the elimination of all the historically out-dated rubbish
which obstructed the free development of industry and trade.*[35]

In fact, the nation-state, after its historic victory over the alternative
confederal forms of organization, was seen as the only social form that
could provide effective protection not only for domestic capital against
foreign competition, but also for labour and land against the detrimental
effects of the domestic market. Therefore, the rise of nationalism cannot be
seen as separate from the emergence of the market economy and it was as
'inevitable' as the emergence of the nation-state and the market economy.
In other words, nationalism cannot be seen as an inevitable dimension of
modernity,[36] unless viewed within a specific problematic that assumes that
the only feasible course for history was the one that was actually taken.

Protectionism leads to statism

Protectionism, in both its forms considered above, undermined the market
economy that had been established in the nineteenth century and, in fact,
led to its near collapse in the twentieth. It undermined, first, the domestic
market economy by distorting the price mechanism and obstructing the
self-regulation of markets so that, eventually, 'unadjusted price and cost
structures prolonged depressions, unadjusted equipment retarded the
liquidation of un-profitable investments, [and] unadjusted price and income levels caused social tension'.[37] It undermined, secondly, the world
market economy by leading to colonial rivalry and competition for
markets still unprotected. As a result of protectionist policies, the world
economy, on which the nineteenth-century balance-of-power system had
rested, started disintegrating. This inevitably led to the near collapse of the
system itself because, as Polanyi has persuasively shown,[38] the '100 years'
peace' (1815–1914) crucially depended on two freedoms: the freedom of
trade and the freedom of capital. Therefore, once colonial rivalry started
having its effect on both freedoms, World War I became inevitable.

But it was not only the balance-of-power system that collapsed as a
result of protectionist policies. The Gold Standard system, on which the
stability of exchanges crucially depended, also could not stand the pressures
of protectionism. The precondition for its adjustment mechanism (i.e. the
mechanism which supposedly eliminates imbalances in the balance of
payments among the countries taking part in the system) to work efficiently was that adjustment should be achieved through changes in
'nominal' variables (prices, wages, interest rates) rather than through the
much more painful – socially and economically – changes in 'real' variables
(production, employment). However, protectionist measures, either in
favour of those controlling the market economy (tariffs, etc.) or in favour

of the rest of society (e.g. social insurance legislation, protection of trade unions, etc.) had the effect of distorting wages and prices and therefore obstructed the efficient functioning of the adjustment mechanism which had to rely on changes in income and employment to bring about the required adjustment.

In the 1920s, therefore, serious obstacles to the self-regulating function of the market mechanism were created,[39] not just on strict economic grounds (mainly, to protect the value of currencies) but also on political grounds, and in particular to reduce social tension in the aftermath of the 1917 Russian revolution. Wages became 'too rigid'. In Britain, for instance, as D. Moggridge points out: 'The General Strike (1926) removed the possibility of widespread reductions in money wages and costs, if only because attempts at reductions were too expensive socially and economically.'[40] The inevitable outcome was the collapse of the Gold Standard system in the 1930s − a crucial event for the rise of statism. In fact, the abandonment of the Gold Standard was a necessary condition for the expansion of the economic role of the state. This is so because deficit budget policies − a basic tool of statism − were not compatible with the Gold Standard which required the domestic economic policy to be subordinated to achieving an external balance. For instance, during the Great Depression, countries with deficits in the balance of payments were forced by the system to suffer further deflation in order to achieve external balance. This took place at the very moment that millions of people were unemployed, and domestic expansionary policies rather than deflationary policies were necessary to reduce unemployment!

The breakdown of the Gold Standard was, in effect, reflecting the world economy's disintegration, which had been in progress since the beginning of the century, as a result of the serious distortions introduced to the free functioning of the markets by anti-liberal legislation (factory laws, un-employment insurance), trade union activity and so on. To the extent that society's self-protection against the market economy was successful, the market economy itself was devitalized and eventually almost collapsed in the 1930s, during the Great Depression. Therefore, as Polanyi also stresses, it was the collapse of pure liberalism which set the foundations for the near collapse of the market economy itself in the 1930s and opened the way for the rise of statism. Thus, as Goldfrank describes Polanyi's thoughts on the matter:

> As nations became more enmeshed in the world market, the more powerful ones turned to social legislation, tariffs and other forms of protectionism to blunt the effects of unequal exchanges. From protectionism and imperialism it

was a short step to world war and from the misguided post-war attempt to restore the Gold Standard it was a short step to depression.[41]

The marketization process: the statist phase

The outcome of the disintegration of the world economy and of the collapse of the Gold Standard was that all major countries entered a period of active state interference to control the economy; in other words, they entered the period of statism – an event that marked a new phase in the marketization process which was, one may argue, the logical conclusion of protectionism which flourished during and after World War I[42] and reached its peak in the 1930s with the adoption of many direct restrictions on trade, such as import and export licensing, quotas and exchange controls.

The extreme example of statism was of course Stalinist Russia, where, for the first time since the establishment of the market economy in the nineteenth century, a 'systemic' attempt was made to reverse the marketization process. It was in the 1930s that the collectivization of farms removed land from the market. This development, in turn, may also be attributed to the disintegration of the world economy, resulting in its inability to absorb Russia's agricultural surplus and the consequent Russian inability to base industrial development on imports of machinery from the West. Furthermore, the introduction of the 5-year plans removed from the market most important economic decisions. Yet, these decisions did not come under the jurisdiction of society at large. As we shall see in the next chapter, the concentration of political and economic power at the hands of the communist party bureaucracy, in combination with the non-abandonment of the wage system, meant that the effect of socialist statism in Eastern Europe – from the viewpoint of the concentration of power – was just a change in the personnel of the ruling elite rather than the elimination of the elite itself. In other words, the place of capitalists in the ruling elite who had been controlling *indirectly* – through the market system, the economic process (i.e. what, how and for whom to produce), was simply taken over by bureaucrats, who controlled it *directly* – through the central planning system.

However, it was not just Russia (to be followed after World War II by several other countries on the periphery and semi-periphery of the capitalist system) that introduced statism. In the period between the mid-1930s and the mid-1970s, active state interference to control the market mechanism was the norm all over the capitalist world. Although the forms of statism in the West were not as comprehensive as in the East, and, of course, did not take the form of a 'systemic' change, the aim, especially in the post-World War II period, was similar. In other words, the aim was not just to help the private sector flourish under some minimal social controls (as, for example, is the case with Clintonomics, or the economics of the 'new' British Labour party under Tony Blair today) but rather to supplant the private sector itself, especially in the areas where the private sector has failed to cover the needs of the whole population – mainly, with respect to the provision of social services (health, education, social insurance, public utilities).

It may be useful to divide the statist phase of marketization into two major periods: first, the period from about 1933 up to and including the war period itself and, second, the post-war period, up to about the mid-1970s.

Pre-war statism

The foundation for statism was set in the interwar period during the Great Depression, which, following the 1929 crash, pushed the market economy into a general crisis. During this period, several countries introduced various degrees of statism to recover from the Great Depression. The most drastic form, within the market economy framework, was introduced in Nazi Germany. Well before the German economy was converted to a war footing, there was 'considerable supersession of the free market',[43] which took the form of budget deficit policies financed by the creation of new money (in fact, such policies were in place ten years before the rise of Hitler and had led to the German hyper-inflation), price and wage controls, state direction of private investment and so on. Even in the bastion of free enterprise, the United States, Roosevelt's New Deal involved actively promoting the devaluation of the dollar, state interference in determining prices and wages, large construction projects, as well as increased employers' contributions to the social security fund. The same pattern of drastic state intervention and interference with the pricing mechanism (in place of the relatively neutral state role in the economy – typified by balanced budget policies – that liberal orthodoxy required) was repeated in several other countries at the time (France, Sweden, etc.).

All cases of state interventionism in the pre-war period were successful in the broad objective of saving the market economy from collapse; still, the methods used were utterly anti-liberal, as their aims were not to enhance the marketization process but, instead, to constrain it. Furthermore, almost all cases were successful in the narrow objective of expanding production and employment without creating other problems, such as inflation. Was this proof that, after all, an effective social control of the market is feasible, as social democrats have always maintained? A further examination of the conditions under which the above success was achieved indicates that the answer to the question has to be negative.

One should not forget that the period under consideration was quite an exceptional one, that is, a period when the market economy itself was threatened with extinction. The fact, for instance, that 'business confidence' was at its lowest could go a long way in explaining the very tolerant attitude of those controlling production towards measures encroaching on their economic power and profits. In fact, it was only when – and as long as – state interventionism had the approval of those controlling production that it was successful, as the following examples clearly show.

In the United States, it was the initially tolerant stand of capital towards Roosevelt's budget deficit policies that resulted in the significant contribution of those policies to the early phases of the recovery (1934–36). It was, also, the US capitalists' change of mind, once recovery was under way, which resulted in a renewed pressure to balance the federal budget and, consequently, to a new recession (1937–38).[44]

In Germany, the significant success of Nazi economic policies (despite the much higher degree of statism involved, which included direct interference in the investment and pricing decisions of individual firms) was due to the fact that, as Bleaney puts it, 'the Nazis were accepted by business as infinitely preferable to revolution, a faith which they promptly justified by the abolition of trade unions and all other political parties'.[45]

On the other hand, in France, where the Popular Front Government of the Left attempted a drastic form of statism involving social reforms (cuts in working hours, mandatory paid holidays, etc.) and income redistribution in favour of the working classes, the attempt ended up in failure. Although unemployment was reduced drastically, inflation accelerated sharply, as those controlling production passed cost increases on to the consumers, and the government was unable to impose effective price controls. Furthermore, no significant recovery was achieved afterwards; as a result of the socialist nature of several of the reforms, the Front's policies were greeted by the familiar tactics of the flight of capital abroad and the refusal to invest domestically.

The conclusion is that the success or failure of pre-war statism did not depend on strict economic factors (as liberals and Marxists usually assume) but on political factors, that is, on whether the expansion of the state's economic role enjoyed the support of those controlling production, namely, what is euphemistically called 'business confidence', or not.

Though the Nazi form of statism and its implied attack against the market economy was to find an inglorious end under the ruins of the Third Reich, the form of statism that developed in the West was luckier: it flourished for another 30 years or so after the end of the war. And, in fact, there were significant differences between the Nazi and Western forms of statism. Thus, whereas the former was of a 'nationalist' character, mainly due to political and military considerations, the latter was much more internationalist – a conclusion derived also by Polanyi, in the context of a different problematic.[46] In effect, the post-war model of statism in the West was an evolution of the pre-war model.

During the war itself, statism, as one could expect, reached new heights. State planning, although necessitated by the war effort, had the side effect of showing the peacetime possibilities of conscious social control of the economy. This 'demonstration effect', combined with the radicalization of the electorate in the West (following the failure of the market economy in the 1930s and the defeat of fascism in the war) gave a new impetus to statism.

The social-democratic consensus

Britain, which, since the Industrial Revolution and up to date, has always played the role of the 'marketization barometer', set the foundation for the welfare state, that is, the form of statism that was to mark post-war history, up to the middle of the 1970s. The starting point in the establishment of the post-war welfare state was the Beveridge Report, whose explicit aim was 'to establish social security for all, from the cradle to the grave'.[47] It was published in 1942 and represented a conscious effort to check the side effects of the market economy, as far as covering basic needs (health, education, social security) was concerned. Two years later, a coalition government dominated by the Conservatives inaugurated what has been called the *social-democratic consensus* and published a White Paper on *Employment Policy*, which committed the government (a commitment observed by governments of all persuasions up to the rise of neoliberalism) to full employment policies through aggregate demand management, that is, through manipulation of the market. In effect, what this commitment meant was the formal recognition of the fact that the market was not capable of self-regulation, at least as far as the level of production and employment was concerned. Similarly, 'maximum employment' was recognized as the main policy objective by the US Employment Act of 1946. Comparable institutional changes took place all over the advanced capitalist world in the late 1940s, so that one may conclude that this period marks the beginning of the social-democratic consensus, which was to last into the 1970s.

However, the social-democratic consensus that emerged in the post-war period was not just a conjunctural phenomenon, as sometimes argued, but a structural change with significant implications at the economic, social, political and ideological/theoretical levels (that I will consider here) as well as at the cultural level.

At the political level, the social-democratic consensus was actively supported by social-democratic parties and trade unions and enjoyed the tolerance of capital and its political representatives. Thus, conservative parties were succeeding social-democratic ones, without changing in its essentials the new socio-economic role of the state with respect to the market. Despite some spasmodic privatizations of nationalized industries, particularly in Britain, governments all over the advanced capitalist world were following full employment policies and were expanding continually the welfare state and the public sector in general. The Old Left was also, explicitly or implicitly, part of this consensus, whereas parties and organizations that supported aims which were incompatible with the above institutional framework sought outlets in extra-parliamentary opposition, alternative cultures, or even in urban guerrilla tactics in a hopeless and self-contradictory attempt to function as catalysts for radical social change.

At the economic level, the social-democratic consensus was founded on modern industrial society, which, at its post-war peak, was characterized by mass production, big production units, bureaucratic organization and mass consumption. The state's economic role was crucial in a process of intensive accumulation that relied mainly on the enlargement of the domestic market. This involved not just an indirect role in influencing the level of economic activity through fiscal policy and the welfare state, but also direct action on the production side of the economy through nationalized enterprises and public investment. As the degree of internationalization of the economy during this period was relatively small and therefore the state's 'degrees of freedom' in implementing a national economic policy were much more significant than today, the new state role was both feasible and desirable. To the extent, therefore, that the post-war investment boom was continuing, the budget deficits, which inevitably followed, did not create any further problems in the accumulation process.

In fact, the period of the social-democratic consensus was associated with an unprecedented boom. The average annual rate of growth of per capita income in advanced capitalist countries rose from 1.4 per cent in 1820–1950 to 3.8 per cent in 1950–70. Also, capital accumulation increased from 2.9 per cent in 1870–1913 and 1.7 per cent in 1913–50 to 5.5 per cent in 1950–70.[48] Leaving aside the controversial issue of whether a causal relationship may be established between the expansion of the state's economic role and the boom,[49] there is little doubt that statism played a significant role in keeping unemployment at unprecedented low levels throughout the period under consideration. The low levels of unemployment were not simply due to budgetary deficit policies, as is sometimes wrongly argued. In fact, OECD governments were more or less in budget balance for the period of the social-democratic consensus as a whole.[50] A more fruitful way to explain the high levels of employment in that period would be to take into account the overall effect of statism on the economy and in particular the optimistic business expectations that counter-cyclical state intervention by itself creates,[51] as well as the various restrictions on the right of employers to sack employees, implemented particularly rigorously in the nationalized sector of the economy where overmanning was notorious. Thus, whereas the unemployment rate in the 16 more advanced capitalist countries was on the average 5.7 per cent in the 1870–1913 period and reached 7.3 per cent in 1913–50, it dropped to an average 3.1 per cent in 1950–70.[52] At the same time, the welfare state expanded rapidly, and by the early 1970s about one-fifth of the Gross Domestic Product (GDP) in advanced capitalist countries (apart from Japan) was spent on social expenditures.[53] Indicative of the rapid growth of the welfare state during this period is the fact that social expenditures in Britain, which had risen from 4 per cent of the Gross National Product (GNP) in 1910 to about 11 per cent in the interwar period, had reached an average of about 25 per cent in the early 1970s.[54]

At the social level, the social-democratic consensus had been associated with conditions of relative job security, enlargement of the labour market (following the mass entry of women into production during the post-war boom) and belief in a future of continuous economic growth and expansion of the welfare state. The above factors, combined with the fact that the working class was still numerically strong, had led to the emergence of a strong trade union movement which, through its bureaucratic leadership and particularly through its unofficial organizations (shop stewards' movement), exercised significant influence in controlling the market. Furthermore, within this climate, a series of strong liberation movements emerged among women, students and ethnic minorities. A crisis of social institutions was in progress, and large social groups were questioning the very foundations of the modern hierarchical society: the patriarchal family, the authoritarian school and university, the hierarchical factory or office, the bureaucratic trade union or party. In effect, all those movements were challenging the supposedly democratic character of society in the broader social realm.

The social consensus relied on the explicit or implicit agreement between capital and trade unions, and/or the political parties representing their interests, aiming at the reproduction of the *mixed economy*, that is, of the economic system that expressed the social-democratic consensus. The consensus involved a state commitment to secure high levels of employment and a 'social wage' (in terms of social services), in exchange for a trade union commitment to check workers' demands, so that the increase in real wages (increase in wages minus the rate of inflation) did not exceed the rise in productivity. The agreement was usually formalized in the form of *wage and price controls*, which, throughout the period of the social-democratic consensus, had played a significant role in checking inflation without encroaching on profits.

Finally, at the ideological/theoretical level, following the glorious post-war victory of Keynesianism (i.e. the social-democratic reformist trend within the orthodox economics profession) over the conservative neo-classical trend (i.e. the dominant economics paradigm during the earlier phase of the marketization process up to the war), the social-democratic consensus was firmly established among social scientists as well. The basis of the new orthodoxy, which covered both economic theory and economic policy, was state (macro-economic) control over the market in order to achieve the objectives of full employment, maximum economic growth and, to a certain extent, the redistribution of income in favour of weaker income groups.

In concluding, one could argue that what Polanyi meant by the term *Great Transformation* was to some extent achieved during the period of the social-democratic consensus. The market system, particularly labour and money, were put under significant social controls. Thus, as regards labour, not only the level of employment, but also the conditions of work and wages were left to be determined outside the market. This was done through fiscal policies and *wage and price controls* designed within the context of tripartite agreements between labour, capital and government. Also, as regards money, although neither investments nor savings were taken out of the control of the market, both directing investments and regulating the rate of savings became government tasks. This was done through aggressive monetary policies and controls, direct and/or indirect control of investment, and so on.

With the abandonment of the Gold Standard, whose adjustment mechanism was incompatible with any form of statism, in the 1930s the value of currencies was left to be determined by foreign exchange markets. The system of flexible currencies was more compatible with statism since, by leaving the value of currencies to the care of foreign exchange markets, it allowed more freedom for state interventionism in the economy. Nevertheless, as the system of flexible rates was thought to have negative repercussions on the expansion of foreign trade, because of the uncertainty it created in international exchanges, the system was promptly abandoned immediately after the war.

So, a new system of *managed flexibility* was established under the Bretton Woods Agreement of 1944. The new system was intended to match the requirements of both statism and free trade and was therefore designed as a compromise between the Gold Standard and the system of flexible currencies. In other words, the Bretton Woods system was intended to provide an international monetary system that would have constituted a compatible foundation for the international statist model that had already emerged in the pre-war period, by ensuring the economic sovereignty of nation-states with respect to domestic economic policies, as well as stability as regards the value of currencies. However, despite the fact that the Bretton Woods system initially succeeded in this aim, in the end, the contradictions within it, and especially the fact that it enshrined the dominance of the US dollar – an arrangement that at some stage became incompatible with the change in the world balance of economic forces as a result of the rise of Japanese and German economic power – brought about its downfall at the beginning of the 1970s. This fact contributed significantly to the demise of statism. Nation-states initially attempted to keep their economic sovereignty by reverting to a system of flexible rates, which, as long as capital and exchange controls were in place, could secure their economic sovereignty. However, as soon as these controls were abolished under market pressure, independent economic policies and statism itself became doomed.

The internationalization of the economy and the collapse of statism

Despite the expansion of statism at the *national* economic level, the marketization process at the *international* level (in the sense of gradual lifting of controls on the movement of commodities and later of capital), which was interrupted after the Great Depression and the explosion of protectionism that followed, was resumed. Thus, commercial rivalries between major capitalist nations and the consequent old nationalist rivalries, which characterized the first half of the twentieth century and led to two world wars, were swiftly overcome and replaced by a rapid expansion of trade (mainly between themselves). World exports increased by an average annual rate of 7 per cent in the period 1948–73 whereas global economic output grew at an average rate of 5 per cent.[55] As a result of these trends, by the early 1970s, one-sixth of manufacturing products consumed in Europe were imported from abroad. Thus, whereas import penetration (imports as a percentage of the domestic market for manufactures) within Europe was only 6 per cent in 1937 and 1950, it increased to 11 per cent in 1963 and 17 per cent in 1971, that is, at a level significantly higher than the 1913 level of 13 per cent.[56] Similarly, exports, as a percentage of the GDP, increased in Europe from an average of about 19 per cent for the entire first quarter after the war up to 1973, to almost 26 per cent in the period 1974–79.[57]

The post-war internationalization of the market economy was actively encouraged by the advanced capitalist countries particularly in view of the expansion of 'actually existing socialism' and of the national liberation movements in the Third World. However, the internationalization was basically the outcome of 'objective' factors related to the dynamics of the market economy and, in particular, to the expansion of multinational corporations' activity and the parallel growth of the Eurodollar market. The Eurodollar market provided a regulation-free environment where US dollars (and later other strong currencies like the yen, mark etc.) could be borrowed and lent free of any US regulatory and tax requirements. The growth of this new market, which simply reflected the growing needs of multinational corporations, was instrumental in the later lifting of exchange and capital controls. This is because the exchange controls of nation-states, particularly those in Britain where the Eurodollar market originated,[58] were put under severe strain, throughout the 1970s.

So, the institutional arrangements adopted in the post-war period to liberalize the markets for commodities and capital, at the planetary level (GATT rounds of tariff reductions), at the regional level (the European Economic Community (EEC), European Free Trade Association (EFTA)) and at the national level (abolition of capital and exchange controls in the US and Britain in the 1970s, etc.) mostly institutionalized rather than created the internationalized market economy. It was the market economy's grow-or-die dynamic that created it.

Growing internationalization implied that the growth of the market economy relied increasingly on the expansion of the world market rather than on that of the domestic market, as before – a fact that had very significant implications with regard to the state's economic role. During the period of social-democratic consensus, economic growth rested mainly on the growth of domestic demand which accounted for almost 90 per cent of total demand in advanced capitalist countries. In this framework, the state sector played an important part in controlling the size of the market through the manipulation of aggregate demand. The means used for this purpose were government spending and public investment, as well as the economic activity of nationalized enterprises. The necessary condition, however, for the economic system's efficient functioning was the relatively low degree of internationalization, that is, a degree which was compatible with an institutional framework relatively protective of the domestic market for commodities, capital and labour. It was precisely the negation of this condition, as internationalization of the market economy grew, that made the continuation of the social-democratic consensus impossible.

An indication of the above trends is given in Tables 1.1 and 1.2. Although the growth rate of exports is shown in Table 1.1 to be

Table 1.1 Average annual growth rates in OECD high income economies[1]

	Government spending[2]	Private consumption	Gross domestic investment	Exports of goods and services[3]	Gross domestic product
1960–70	4.8	4.3	5.6	8.4	5.1
1970–80	2.6	3.5	2.3	6.0	3.2
1980–93	2.1	3.0	3.4	5.1	2.9

1. This is the set of countries that are members of the Organisation for Economic Co-operation and Development (OECD) and which the World Bank classifies as 'high income economies', namely, the United States, Canada, Japan, Australia, New Zealand, the European Union (apart from Greece and Portugal), Switzerland and Norway.
2. Includes all current expenditure for purchases of goods and services by all levels of government.
3. The value of factor services such as investment income, interest and labour income is excluded.

Source: World Bank, *World Development Report* (1981 and 1995).

consistently higher than that of national income (GDP), this does not necessarily mean that exports had always been the engine of growth. In fact, the growth rate of exports historically has always exceeded that of income, and there is a variety of theoretical explanations for this phenomenon.[59] In other words, to assess the significance of a component of total demand, like that of exports or government spending, with respect to the overall growth rate of the economy, we have to compare not just growth rates but also the 'weights' of the respective components in total demand and income (Table 1.2). By a comparison of Tables 1.1 and 1.2 we can derive the following conclusions.

- First, although between the 1960s and the 1980s there is a general decline in growth rates, the fall in the growth rate of government spending is significantly higher than that of exports.
- Second, the proportion of income in advanced capitalist countries which is accounted for by exports increased by two-thirds in the last three decades, whereas the proportion of government spending, after reaching a peak in the last decade, seems to be declining in this decade, despite the extra government spending caused by the massive rise of unemployment and poverty.
- Third, as a result of these growth trends, whereas in the 1960s the ratio of government spending to income was significantly higher than that of exports to income, today exactly the opposite is the case.

Under conditions of growing internationalization, the size of the growth economy increasingly depends on supply conditions, which in turn determine trade performance, rather than on direct expansion of domestic demand. Supply conditions play a growing role with respect to

Table 1.2 Distribution of Gross Domestic Product (GDP) (%) in OECD high income economies

	Government spending[1]	Private consumption	Gross domestic investment	Exports of goods and services[2]
1960	15	63	21	12
1965	15	61	23	12
1970	16	60	23	14
1978	18	60	22	18
1987	18	61	21	18
1993	17	63	19	20

1. See notes in Table 1.1 for definitions of government spending and exports.
2. As import figures are not included in the table the sums in each row do not add up to 100.

Source: World Bank, *World Development Report* (various years).

accumulation and economic growth, since it is international trade that determines the size of each national growth economy, either positively (through an exports-led growth) or negatively (through an imports-led de-industrialization). In other words, competitiveness, under conditions of free trade, becomes even more crucial, not only with respect to an increasingly export-led growth, but also with respect to import penetration that ultimately leads to domestic business closures and unemployment. To put it schematically, the market economy, as internationalization grows, moves from a 'domestic market-led' growth economy to a 'trade-led' one.

In the framework of a trade-led growth, the prevailing conditions on the production side of the economy, in particular those relating to the cost of production, become critical: squeezing the cost of production, both in terms of labour cost and in terms of employers' taxes and insurance contributions, becomes very important. But squeezing the cost of production necessitated a drastic reduction in statism, since statism was responsible for a significant rise in the cost of production during the period of the social-democratic consensus, both directly and indirectly. Directly, because the expansion of the welfare state meant a growing burden on employers' contributions and taxes. In Britain, for instance, total taxes as a proportion of company profits (excluding National Insurance contributions) increased from about 44 per cent in 1955–59 to 48.6 per cent in 1967–70.[60] Indirectly, because, under the conditions of near-full employment which prevailed during the statist phase of the marketization process, organized labour could press successfully for wage rises that exceeded significantly the increase in productivity. This became a particularly painful problem (for those controlling the market economy) in the period

1968–73, when a massive strike movement, effectively autonomous from the trade union bureaucratic leadership, led to a fast rise in wages and a corresponding encroachment of profits. Thus, whereas in the period 1960–68 actual post-tax real wages and productivity in advanced capitalist countries increased at about the same rate (4 per cent), in 1968–73, the former increased by an average of 4.5 per cent versus a rise of 3.4 per cent in the latter.[61] As a result, the share of profits in business output fell by about 15 per cent in 1968–73.[62]

The cumulative effect of not letting the labour market – free of state intervention – determine the levels of wages and employment, as a market economy requires, was the crisis of the early 1970s. In other words, the crisis, contrary to the usually advanced view, was not mainly due to the oil crisis but to the fact that the degree of internationalization of the market economy achieved by then was no longer compatible with statism. This was because:

(a) the nation-state's effective control of the economy had become almost impossible in the framework of an increasingly free movement of capital (and commodities) across borders. Although international trade openness increased significantly in the post-war period, the lack of financial openness allowed governments to follow independent economic policies. However, as soon as the development of euro-currency markets significantly reduced the effectiveness of controls on financial markets, multinational corporations saw their power to undermine those national economic policies which were incompatible with their own objectives effectively enhanced;

(b) the expansion of statism itself had certain built-in elements leading to inflation and/or a profitability squeeze, which were both particularly troublesome within the competitive framework that the internationalized market economy has created. Such an element was the rapid rise of state spending – to finance the expansion of the state's social and economic role – which in some cases was faster than the rise of state revenue leading to an inflationary financing of the resulting budget deficits.[63] An even more significant element was the fact that employers, in order to minimize the impact on profits due to 'excessive' wage rises (i.e. wage rises exceeding the rises in productivity), successfully passed a significant part of the increased labour cost on to the consumers under the pretext of the oil crisis. However, the growing internationalization of the economy and the intensified competition which followed it made the passing of 'excessive' wage rises on to prices increasingly difficult. The result was that the profits squeeze mentioned above became even worse in the late 1970s. In

OECD Europe, for instance, profitability in terms of net profit share in manufacturing fell from 21.8 per cent in 1968 to 20.9 per cent in 1973 and to 17.4 per cent in 1979.[64]

The upshot was the 'stagflation' crisis of the 1970s which became inevitable once governments, to reduce the inflationary pressures created by the above trends and the oil crisis, embarked on traditional deflationary policies. Thus, not only did inflation not decelerate but also unemployment started rising significantly, as deflationary policies enhanced short-term unemployment, on top of the long-term unemployment which at that time was also expanding, as a result of the emerging information revolution.

In conclusion, the collapse of statism and the rise of neoliberalism we are going to discuss next have to be seen within the context of the growing internationalization of the market economy, which has made statism increasingly incompatible with it.

The marketization process: the neoliberal phase

The flourishing of the neoliberal movement
The economic crisis of the 1970s, which was exacerbated by the collapse of the Bretton Woods system and the return to the uncertainties of flexible currencies, led to the rise of the neoliberal movement. In contrast to the Liberal Old Right that was founded on tradition, hierarchy and political philosophy, the Neo-Liberal New Right's credo was based on blind belief in the market forces, individualism and economic 'science'.[65] Individualism has taken on a new meaning, since its aim is the citizen's liberation from 'dependence' on the welfare state. Thus, the liberatory demands of the 1960s for a society of self-determination are distorted by neo-liberals and reformulated as a demand for self-determination through the market!

The neoliberal movement, which first emerged among the economists in academia (the Chicago School, resurrection of Hayek and so on) and later on spilled over among professional politicians, especially in the United Kingdom and the United States, represented a powerful attack against social-democratic statism. However, what is interesting is the fact that neoliberal theorists attacked not just statism but 'excessive' democracy itself as the cause of the economic crisis, a sure indication of the incompatibility of the capitalist growth economy and democracy. Thus, several neoliberal critics of the social-democratic consensus, including Samuel Huntingdon, Daniel Bell and J.M. Buchanan, blamed 'excessive' democratic participation (i.e. the increasing influence of social controls over the market in the early post-war period and the consequent rise of the welfare state) as the main factor which has seriously undermined capitalist development.[66] For Huntingdon, the masses' mobilization and the uncontrollable democratic participation have led to a huge increase in state expenditure and the chronic fiscal crisis which undermines economic development. For Daniel Bell, the welfare state has led to the expansion of an uncontrollable hedonistic consumerism which downgrades the protestant ethic of austerity, saving and hard work, on which the development of Western capitalism was founded. Finally, for J.M. Buchanan, the political and state-bureaucratic elites, following a cost-benefit logic, keep expanding state provision as this expansion implies higher rewards with respect to the more corrupt parts of these elites and more political influence for the rest. No wonder that in a report to the Trilateral Commission (which had members from the three main economic regions, North America, Western Europe and Japan) Huntingdon *et al.* argued that the 'democratic surge' of the 1960s created an 'excess of democracy' which had increased demands on government for services, weakened its authority and generated inflation.[67]

It is therefore obvious that the target of the neoliberal movement was the social controls on the market that had been introduced during the statist phase of the marketization process. Social-democratic statism, in the form of nationalizations, full employment policies and the welfare state, has always been seen by the economic elites as undermining private capital's hegemony, through the creation of a tripartite system of economic power (the state, trade unions and capital). Once therefore a combination of economic and political factors made it possible, the attack against the social-democratic consensus became inevitable. The main economic factor was, as we have seen above, the internationalization of the economy which became incompatible with social-democratic statism. The political factors point to the decline of the Left, as a result of the expansion of the middle classes at the expense of the manual working class, and the parallel collapse of 'actually existing socialism'.

The ultimate neoliberal aim was, therefore, to enhance the power of those controlling the economy, through drastically reducing social control over the market. The main policies proposed by neoliberals and subsequently implemented first by the Thatcher/Reagan administrations and later by governments all over the world have been the following ones:

- **Liberalization of markets**. The *labour market* is the main target of liberalization. Thus, many important controls are being eliminated and others are being drastically amended with the explicit aim to make labour more 'flexible', that is, more amenable to market conditions ('hire-and-fire culture'). In fact, however, the aim is 'to turn labour into a commodity – not only in the way wages and conditions are set, but also the way labour is managed in the workplace'.[68] The weakening of these controls, combined with the abandonment of the full employment state commitment and the anti-trade union legislation, meant that the effects of the technological changes, which had led to structural unemployment, have not been offset by effective state action; instead, it was left to the market forces to sort out the unemployment problem. Furthermore, neoliberal policies, by restricting the state sector, have contributed directly to the rise of unemployment. As a result, unemployment has become massive, while poverty and inequality have also grown in proportion with the deregulation of the labour market. Thus, unemployment in advanced capitalist countries (the 'Group of 7' ('G7'), i.e., the seven more advanced capitalist countries: the USA, Japan, Canada, Germany, France, Britain and Italy) increased by 56 per cent between 1973 and 1980 (from an average 3.4 per cent to 5.3 per cent of the labour force[69]) and by another 50 per cent since then (from 5.3 per cent of the labour force in 1980 to 8.0 per cent in 1994).[70] Also, as regards the neoliberal myth about the creation of jobs following the deregulation of the labour market, recent studies show that most of the new jobs consist of low-paid work (usually contingency work) which replaces relatively well paid full-time employment. Thus, the fact is celebrated that in the model country of liberalization of the labour market, the USA, open unemployment is about half that in the European Union (5.6 per cent in 1995 versus 10.7 per cent).[71] What is usually not mentioned is that some 30 per cent of the labour force in the USA is now composed of contingency workers[72] and that the vast majority of 'new' jobs are paid much less than the old ones. Second, *capital markets* have also been liberalized, particularly international financial markets (lifting of exchange controls, etc.). The liberalization of capital markets has increased the opportunities for tax evasion, eroded the tax base required for the financing of the welfare state, made capital flight much easier and – more important – made impossible any kind of indicative planning and effective control of domestic aggregate demand. Thus, huge amounts of money move around in search of speculative gains and effectively undermine the ability of governments to follow macroeconomic policies which significantly diverge from those of their competitors. Finally, as we saw above, *commodities markets* have also been liberalized, mainly as a result of the latest GATT agreement. The overall outcome of these liberalization policies was that 'by the early 1990s, an almost fully liberal order has been created across the OECD region, giving market actors a degree of freedom that they had not held since the 1920s'.[73]

- **Privatization of state enterprises**. Privatizations are significant not only because they reduce the size of the state sector but also because they create new opportunities for private capital. Furthermore, the spreading of share ownership is promoted as a kind of 'popular capitalism', despite the fact that, as the British experience has shown, the concentration of capital is further enhanced by privatization. Thus, despite the fact that the number of shareholders tripled in the 1980s, after the massive privatizations of Thatcher's government, the proportion of shares held individually, rather than by capitalist firms and institutions, fell from 54 per cent in 1963 to 28 per cent in 1981 and to 20 per cent in 1988.[74]

- **Reduction of the welfare state into a safety net and parallel encouragement of the private sector's expansion into social services** (health, education, pension schemes and so on). This not only leads to the marketization of sectors of the economy that used to be under state control, but it also further reduces the 'social wage' and makes labour even more 'flexible' to market conditions.

- **Redistribution of taxes in favour of high income groups**. In Britain, for instance, the top income earners took the lion's share of the tax reductions engineered by the Thatcher governments between 1979–80 and 1990–91. Thus, the top earners (1.6 per cent of taxpayers) received almost 30 per cent of the total reduction in taxes, whereas the 11 per cent of income earners at the bottom received less than 2 per cent of the tax cuts.[75] The explicit aim of such tax cuts is to create 'incentives' for the economic elite to save and invest, whereas the implicit aim is to increase post-tax profits and spread the cost of the safety net. The inevitable outcome of neoliberal tax policies has been a further worsening in the distribution of post-tax income.

As a result of these policies, profitability, which had slumped at the end of the statist period, has been almost restored to the levels achieved at the peak of the post-war boom. Thus profitability in European manufacturing, which had reached a nadir 17.4 per cent in 1979, by 1989 increased to 23.7 per cent, not far from the 26 per cent achieved in 1952–66.[76]

The neoliberal consensus

The internationalization of the economy and the neoliberal policies coincided with significant technological changes (information revolution) marking the move of the market economy to a post-industrial phase. The combined effect was a drastic change in the employment structure which reduced massively the size of the manual working class. For instance, in the

G7 (minus Canada), the proportion of the active population employed in manufacturing fell by over a third between 1972–73 and 1992–93 (from an average of 31 per cent in 1972–73 to 20 per cent in 1992–93).[77] This fact had significant implications on the strength and significance of trade unions and social-democratic parties. Thus, in the US, trade unions have been decimated in just two decades, their membership falling from about 35 million to 15 million.[78] In Britain, 14 years of Thatcherism were enough to bring down trade union membership from 13.3 million in 1979 to under 9 million in 1993 and the proportion of union members (31 per cent) to the lowest level since 1946.[79] At the same time, in Britain again, the proportion of the active population in non-manual work increased from 12.8 per cent in 1951 to 31.9 per cent in 1978.[80] As a result of these trends, the structure of the British electorate changed drastically, with the proportion of the manual working class falling from a half to a third of the electorate within just 20 years (1964–83).[81]

Thus, a new class structure has emerged in the post-industrial internationalized market economy which, broadly, may be defined as follows. At the two extremes are what we may call the underclass and the overclass. The *underclass* consists mainly of the unemployed and those of the inactive (which do not consist merely of women staying at home as before, but, mostly, of men of working age and single parents) and the underemployed (part-timers, casual workers, etc.) who fall under the poverty line. People from the young age group, women, ethnic minorities and immigrants are disproportionately represented in the underclass. In Britain, it has been estimated that the 'absolutely disadvantaged' (a term defined similarly to the underclass) constitute about 30 per cent of the adult working population,[82] which, according to another study,[83] controls less than 14 per cent of income. At the other end of the scale is the new *overclass*, namely the upper middle class that has been created by the marketization process, which isolates itself in barbed wire enclosures[84] – luxury ghettos to match the misery ghettos of the underclass. The upper middle class, together with the upper class itself, constitute a very small percentage of the population but receive a disproportionately large part of income. In the USA, for instance, the top 1 per cent of family groups controlled in 1988 13.5 per cent of all income before taxes.[85]

Finally, between these two poles are the middle groups which constitute the vast majority of the population. If we take the British example again, these middle groups constitute about 70 per cent of the population. However, it is only the upper part of these middle groups, consisting of about 40 per cent of the population, which is, according to Hutton,[86] the *privileged* minority, and electorally, according to Galbraith,[87] the *contented electoral majority*. It is only this part of the population which is in full-time, well-paid and secure jobs and controls the bulk of income. In advanced capitalist countries, the top 40 per cent of the population on average control almost two-thirds of income[88] and, by their political and economic power, determine the electoral outcome. On the other hand, the lower part of the middle groups, consisting of about 30 per cent of the population, includes all those in low-paid, insecure and poorly protected jobs (the *marginalized* and the *insecure* according to Hutton). Most of the growing army of part-timers and occasional workers in low-paid jobs with no formal employment protection, as well as the traditional blue-collar low-skilled working class, belong to this category.

Therefore, the post-industrial neoliberal society is not even a 'two-thirds society' as it used to be described. It is in fact a '40 per cent society'. The social groups constituting this privileged minority are, basically, hostile to any expansion of statism and the welfare state and are increasingly attracted by the ideology of the private provision of services like health, education and pensions — although a significant part of this 'attraction' is forced by the neoliberal undermining of the state provision of these services. Their attitude towards statism and the welfare state is determined by the fact that public services and their financing by taxation have a disparate effect on the privileged minority and the underclass. In other words, it is, mainly, the privileged minority which has to finance, through taxation, public services in which they are not interested anymore (because of the deterioration in their quality as a result of neoliberal policies). As the privileged minority is also the electoral majority (because they take an active part in the electoral process, whereas the underclass mostly do not bother to vote, frustrated by the inability of political parties to solve their problems), the electoral outcome in advanced capitalist countries is determined by the attitudes of the privileged minority/electoral majority.

The inevitable result of the above changes in the class structure and composition of the electorate has been the rapid decline of traditional social-democratic parties and their attempt to capture a significant part of the vote of the privileged minority by 'modernizing' themselves, according to the guidelines of the neoliberal agenda. So, in the last 15 years or so, all major social-democratic parties, either in power (France, Sweden) or in opposition (Germany, Britain) have abandoned traditional social-democratic policies like the commitment to full employment and the welfare state and adopted, with minor variations, the essence of the neoliberal programme (privatizations, liberation of markets and so on), in the name of liberating the 'civil society' from statism! To all this, they usually try to add a 'social dimension'. The pathetic social-democratic attempt to add such a dimension to the new EU treaties is a case in point.

The upshot of these changes at the political level has been the 'Americanization' of the political process all over the advanced capitalist world. In place of the traditional contest between, on the one hand, social-democratic parties supporting the case for further expansion of the state's role and, on the other, conservative parties praising the advantages of the market economy and attempting to slow down statism, electoral contests have now become beauty contests between the leaders of bureaucratic parties, characterized by minimal programmatic differences and a common objective: state-craft, that is, the management of power. A neoliberal consensus has swept over the advanced capitalist world and has replaced the social-democratic consensus of the early post-war period.

Apart from the political implications, the neoliberal consensus has very important implications at the social, ideological, cultural and, of course, the economic level. Starting with the economic level, the new consensus does not imply that the state has no more economic role to play. One should not confuse liberalism/neoliberalism with *laissez-faire*. As I mentioned earlier, it was the state itself that created the system of self-regulating markets. Furthermore, some form of state intervention has always been necessary for the smooth functioning of the market economy system. The state is called today to play a crucial role with respect to the supply side of the economy and, in particular, to take measures to improve competitiveness, to train the workforce to the requirements of the new technology, even to subsidize (directly or indirectly) export industries. Therefore, the type of state intervention which is compatible with the marketization process not only is not discouraged but, instead, is actively promoted by the neoliberal consensus, especially by the 'progressive' elements within it (Clinton administration, social-democratic parties in Europe). So, it is not true that the neoliberal consensus has killed off the baby of the social-democratic consensus, that is, the mixed economy, as it is usually assumed. In fact, it did something worse. It redefined the content of the mixed economy so that it can better serve the interests of the economic elite and reproduce, on the threshold of the twenty-first century, similar conditions of inequality and social injustice to the ones that prevailed in the beginning of the nineteenth!

At the social level, the explicit 'one nation' aim of the social-democratic consensus is being replaced by the implicit '40 per cent society' aim of the neoliberal consensus. The neoliberal aim is associated with the fear of unemployment and uncertainty concerning the ability to cover adequately basic needs (health, education, housing). This uncertainty has contributed significantly to the retreat of radical currents within the feminist movement, the withdrawal of students from public life, the withering away of labour militancy and so on. At the same time, the hope invested in the Green movement has already faded, since the dominant trends within it do not challenge the fundamental institutions of the market economy but, instead, either adopt the social-democratic ideology of enhancing the civil society and resort to environmentalism (Europe) or, alternatively, turn to irrationalism and mysticism (USA). As a result, the status of hierarchical structures and institutions, which was challenged in the era of the social-democratic consensus, is now re-enhanced – although it never recovered. Still, as regards the social scope of the new consensus, there is a significant difference with respect to the scope of the social-democratic consensus. Thus, whereas the latter usually relied on the explicit agreement of capital and trade unions and frequently took the character of a broad social consensus, the neoliberal consensus usually is explicitly adopted only by the upper class and the majority of the '40 per cent society' (which directly benefit from it) and never takes the character of a broad social consensus.

At the cultural level, the marketization of culture and the recent liberalization and deregulation of markets has contributed significantly to the present cultural homogenization, with traditional communities and their cultures disappearing all over the world and people converted to consumers of a mass culture produced in the advanced capitalist countries and particularly the USA. In the film industry, for instance, even European countries with a strong cultural background and developed economies have effectively to give up their own film culture, unable to compete with the much more competitive US industry. Thus, in the early 1990s, US share of the films amounted to 73 per cent of the European market. Indicative of the degree of concentration of cultural power in the hands of a few US corporations is the fact that, in 1991, a handful of US distributors controlled 66 per cent of total cinema box office and 70 per cent of the total number of video rentals in Britain.[89]

In fact, the recent emergence of a sort of 'cultural' nationalism in many parts of the world expresses a desperate attempt to keep a cultural identity in the face of market homogenization. But cultural nationalism is devoid of any real meaning in an electronic environment, where 75 per cent of the international communications flow is controlled by a small number of multinationals.[90] In other words, cultural imperialism today does not need, as in the past, a gunboat diplomacy to integrate and absorb diverse cultures. The marketization of the communications flow has already established the preconditions for the downgrading of cultural diversity into a kind of superficial differentiation akin to a folklorist type.

Finally, at the ideological level, the neoliberal consensus is dominant. The conservative liberal tradition in the social sciences, particularly in economics, has now become the orthodoxy again – after a brief historical interval when the Keynesian statist ideas were prevalent. Social scientists have adopted *en masse* the liberal 'market paradigm', whereas most ex-Marxists, after the collapse of actually existing socialism, have adopted various forms of 'social-liberalism' which are fully compatible with the neoliberal consensus. Equally compatible with the neoliberal consensus is the post-modernist movement which, as is shown in Chapter 8, by assigning equal value to all traditions of social organization ends up with a general retreat to conformism and an implicit (if not explicit) acceptance of the marketization of society.

The internationalized market economy

The combined effect of the 'objective' (economic and technological) factors leading to further internationalization and the neoliberal policies to free the markets was that the internationalization of the market economy has accelerated sharply since the 1970s. Thus, as far as commodity markets are concerned, the degree of dependence of the growth economy on the growth of exports has increased significantly since the 1970s. In advanced capitalist countries, the average annual growth rate of exports was 1.8 times higher than that of the GDP during the period 1970–93 versus 1.6 in the period 1960–70.[91] No wonder that in just over 20 years, the ratio of world exports to GDP has grown by 50 per cent (from 14 per cent in 1970 to 21 per cent in 1992) and in the USA, the biggest market economy, this ratio has almost doubled in the same period – from 6 to 11 per cent – and is now higher than in Japan.[92] Also, the protection of domestic commodity markets has almost been eliminated within the two major economic blocs (European Union and North America-NAFTA) and will soon almost disappear worldwide, following the implementation of the new GATT agreement. The inevitable outcome of these developments has been that the average annual rate of growth of imports in the G7 increased by 41 per cent between the period 1965–80 and the period 1980–93 (from 3.9 per cent in 1965–80 to 5.5 per cent in 1980–90)[93] and, as a result, import penetration in the major European economies increased by over 60 per cent between the early 1970s and the end of the last decade.[94]

Also, as far as capital markets are concerned, the neoliberal abolition of exchange controls and restrictions to the movement of capital had a decisive influence on the internationalization of the market economy. In fact, according to some observers, the recent significant rise in foreign direct investment establishes a new trend where investment is tending to displace trade as the driving force of international integration.[95] Thus, foreign direct investment as a proportion of the advanced capitalist countries' GDP has nearly doubled in 20 years and now stands at more than 10 per cent.[96]

However, short-term capital movements may be even more important with respect to the loss of the nation-state's economic sovereignty. It has been estimated that one trillion dollars a day is changing hands on the world's foreign exchange markets and that only around 5 per cent of the deals struck are linked with foreign trade, whereas the rest are purely speculative.[97] In the early 1970s about 90 per cent of capital movements were linked to investment and trade and only 10 per cent were speculative. This fact alone may constitute a serious threat to the viability of the growth economy as Paul Volcker, former chairman of the Federal Reserve, implied, when he attributed about half of the 50 per cent decline in growth rates since the early 1970s to the huge growth of currency speculation.[98]

But, even if one accepts the counter-argument that short-term capital flows 'mainly redistribute success and failure around the system and add little to the structural capacity of economies to generate aggregate growth',[99] it cannot be disputed that the huge expansion of such capital movements has made it impossible for any nation-state (or even an economic bloc) to introduce, independently, any effective social controls on the markets. If we take into account the huge rise in international borrowing that took place in international capital markets since the liberalization moves of the 1970s[100] and the significant increase in foreign penetration of national central government bond markets,[101] it becomes obvious that no national government today may follow economic policies that are disapproved of by the capital markets, which have the power to create an intolerable economic pressure on the respective country's borrowing ability, currency value and investment flows. If we assume, for instance, that a social-democratic party adopts, against the trend, expansionary policies in order to reduce unemployment, it may easily be shown that under conditions of free capital mobility, 'very large depreciations could result'.[102] Thus, the lifting of controls has led to a situation where 'all Western countries have found that without capital controls they risk capital flight and an imposed hike in interest rates'.[103]

The increasing loss of economic sovereignty that the nation-state faces in the internationalized market economy is also reflected in the creation of huge economic blocs, within the context of which the economic role of the individual nation-state is being progressively downgraded in favour of supra-national institutions. This applies, in particular, with respect to the EU, where the relevant process has already begun. But it also applies to some extent with respect to the North American Free Trade Agreement (NAFTA). Each of those blocs has its core (Germany, the USA), a number of metropolitan countries in some degree of dependence with respect to the core country (Canada, France, the UK, Italy, etc.) and finally its periphery (Mexico, Mediterranean Europe). Furthermore, significant moves take place at the moment for the formation of new economic blocs out of existing regional associations. One could mention the Association of South-East Asian Nations (ASEAN), the Southern Cone Common Market in Latin America (MERCOSUR) and the Asia-Pacific Economic Co-operation zone (APEC) – which plans an enormous trans-Pacific free trade zone by 2020.

In fact, the same economic aims that brought about the emergence of the neoliberal consensus have led to the creation of these blocs. The basic aim is the improved competitiveness of the sections of capital which are based on each bloc. This improvement is expected to come about mainly on account of the enlargement of the size of the commodities market and in particular of the fact that the larger size makes improvements in productivity much easier, because of the possibility of pooling resources on research and development. However, once the integration has transcended the commodities market to include the capital and labour markets, as in the case of the EU, the advantages of forming economic blocs become even more significant. In that case, an economic bloc creates additional opportunities to squeeze the cost of production, especially labour cost, because of the possibility of greater movement of labour and capital. This is so because – contrary to what orthodox economic theory suggests – neither free trade nor capital and labour mobility eliminate wage differentials. For instance, in the EU, despite conditions of free trade, capital mobility and relative free movement of labour, the average gross hourly earnings of industrial workers (in purchasing power terms) in the periphery (Greece, Portugal) were still half of those at the centre at the end of the last decade,[104] with no signs of any significant closing in the gap.[105] Instead, mobility of capital creates opportunities to invest in areas of low cost, whereas mobility of labour puts pressure on the wages of high-income countries. Indeed, if integration within the tight framework of the nation-state has proved unable to eliminate strong regional differences, which still persist after decades of statehood (the income of the richest regions in France, Belgium, Spain, Germany and the Netherlands is double that of the poorest ones, whereas in Italy it is 2.5 times higher[106]) one could easily imagine the likely effect of integration within the framework of a much more loosely connected supra-national bloc.

In Europe, in particular, the complete liberalization of the commodities markets within the EU block, combined with the liberalization of labour and money markets, creates a vast economic area where an automatic system, similar to the Gold Standard system, could now function successfully. Indeed, this is the main aim behind the European Monetary Union (EMU). If we substitute the 'euro', the projected common EU currency, for gold, Europe will operate under a contemporary Gold Standard system when the EMU is completed. The reason why such a system is now in a better position to function more successfully than in the past is that the basic factor that led to the collapse of the Gold Standard has been eliminated, that is, the various restrictions on the markets for goods, labour and capital that have introduced various degrees of 'inflexibility' into them. Such restrictions, as we have seen, represented society's self-protection mechanisms against its marketization and led to the near collapse of the market economy itself. Since the neoliberal consensus has eliminated most of these restrictions, a historic opportunity has been created for the marketization process to be completed. The internationalized (neoliberal) phase has therefore much better chances of success than the first (liberal) phase. Of course, there is a price to be paid. The acceleration of marketization in countries like Thatcher's Britain has led to a dramatic increase in inequality and one can expect that exactly the same will happen at the bloc level, as some recent studies also confirm,[107] when advanced capitalist countries would share a common currency and a central bank with semi-peripheral ones.

With hindsight, it is therefore obvious that Polanyi was wrong in thinking that the rise of statism in the 1930s was evidence of the utopian character of the self-regulating market and of the existence of an 'underlying social process'[108] which leads societies to take control of their market economies. In fact, statism proved to be a relatively brief interlude in the marketization process. In this sense, statism was a transitional phenomenon related to the failure of the first attempt to create a system based on an internationalized self-regulating market economy. This failure was due not to the supposedly utopian character of the marketization of society, as Polanyi thought, but rather to the fact that the objective conditions for the completion of this process had not as yet been created during the first phase of marketization, in the nineteenth century.

On the other hand, today, the four institutions on which, according to Polanyi, the first attempt for a social system based on a self-regulating market relied, are being restored. Thus:

- *the self-regulating market*, which at the beginning of the century disintegrated (for the reasons we examined above), leading to the collapse of the first attempt for a system based on an internationalized market economy, is today more advanced than ever before in history. This is because of the present degree of freedom that capital and commodity markets enjoy, the retreat of statism everywhere and the universal enhancement of flexible markets for commodities, labour and capital. In other words, this is the outcome of the present degree of marketization of the economy, in the sense of phasing out all those social controls over markets which are not compatible with the interests of those controlling the economy;

- *the balance-of-power system*, which collapsed during the statist phase, is today being re-established, within the framework of a United Nations controlled by the major capitalist countries and the Latinamericanization of Russia which gave the USA an exclusive superpower status;
- *the liberal state*, a creation of the self-regulating market, which, during the statist phase of marketization, also collapsed in many parts of the world, both in the North and in the South, is presently omnipresent; and, finally
- *the international Gold Standard*, which could not survive the undermining of the self-regulated market, is today in the process of being restored and a version of it might reasonably be expected to be in place early in the next century. Thus, the projected establishment, within the next ten years, of a kind of European gold standard mechanism, in the form of a common currency, might be expected to induce, initially, movements for the establishment of some kind of fixed parities between the three major international currencies (euro, US dollar and yen), which, at the end, would logically result in some sort of an international version of the Gold Standard system, i.e. a global monetary system and possibly a single currency in a new interlinked economic space which would unify the richest parts of the world.

In concluding, it is obvious that the rise of neoliberalism is not a conjunctural phenomenon, as social democrats present it, but that it represents the completion of the marketization process that was inter-rupted by the rise of statism. Furthermore, the breakdown of 'actually existing socialism' in the East and the collapse of social democracy in the West – as a result, mainly, of the shrinking of its electoral clientele – have created the political conditions for the completion of the marketization process. So, the fact that neoliberal policies are supported today by both conservative and social-democratic parties, in government or in opposi-tion, and that the basic elements of neoliberalism have been incorporated into the strategies of the international institutions which control the world economy (IMF, World Bank), as well as in the treaties that have recently reformed the EU (Single Market Act, Maastricht Treaty), makes it plainly evident that we are faced with a new consensus founded on the neoliberal phase of marketization. This is a consensus that has replaced the defunct social-democratic consensus and which reflects the radical structural changes brought about by the development of the internationalized market economy.

Internationalization and the nation-state

Internationalization or globalization?
One issue that arose recently refers to the question whether what we face today is the internationalization of the market economy or, alternatively, its globalization. This is a very important issue because, as we shall see, the entire social-liberal case that the state can still play a significant role in controlling the economy rests on an attack against the globalization thesis.

First, we have to draw a clear line between the case of internationalization, as interpreted in this book, and that of globalization. Internationalization, in this book, refers to the case where markets become internationalized and as a result the economic policies of national governments and the reproduction of the growth economy itself are conditioned by the movement of commodities and capital across frontiers. On the other hand, globalization refers to the case where production itself becomes internationalized, in the sense that production units become stateless bodies operating in a borderless world with activities not primarily aiming at the country which is their national base and involving an integrated internal division of labour spanning many countries. Our thesis is that although globalization in the above sense is limited this does not contradict the argument that the accelerating internationalization, in combination with the end of statism, does represent a structural change – as was argued above – rather than just a conjunctural phenomenon.

The main objective of the elites which control today's market economy is, as it has always been, to maximize the role of the market and minimize social controls over it, so that maximum 'efficiency' and growth may be secured. Therefore, social controls in the narrow sense are universally phased out. The same applies to some significant social controls (broad sense) like import controls, tariffs, etc. which are also ruled out as hampering the expansion of the present internationalized market economy. However, this does not mean the elimination of all controls over the markets. Not only 'regulatory' controls remain in place and in some cases are expanded but even some social controls are not eliminated. Examples of social controls (broad sense) over today's markets are the various 'new protectionist' non-tariff barriers (NTBs), such as export restraints and orderly marketing arrangements, especially in steel, textiles and automobiles, which are implemented by many industrial sectors in advanced capitalist countries.[109] In fact, the various financial measures taken by the advanced capitalist countries (usually to subsidize their exports), have deprived the South of half a trillion US dollars a year, according to UN data.[110] Also, as regards social controls in the narrow sense, although the welfare state is basically left to decay, various 'safety nets' are kept in place in advanced capitalist countries, to check massive unrest. However, the safety nets, which target specific categories of people (very poor, etc.), not only imply the elimination of the basic characteristic of the welfare state, its universality, but, also, the institutionalization of poverty.

So, the present neoliberal form of the internationalized market economy may be seen as completing the cycle which started in the last century when a liberal version of it was attempted. Thus, after the collapse of the first attempt to introduce a self-regulating economic system, a new synthesis is attempted today. The new synthesis aims to avoid the extremes of pure liberalism, by combining essentially self-regulating markets with various types of safety nets and controls, which secure the privileged position primarily of the 'overclass' and secondarily that of the '40 per cent society', as well as the mere survival of the 'underclass', without affecting the self-regulation process in its essentials. Therefore, the nation–state still has a significant role to play not only in securing, through its monopoly of violence, the market economy framework, but also in maintaining the infrastructure for the smooth functioning of the neoliberal economy.

However, the supporters of social-liberalism assign a much more important (potential) role to the nation–state. A very recent example is the study by Paul Hirst and Grahame Thompson[111] who competently put the case for the continuing significance of the nation–state in the framework of the neoliberal internationalized market economy. Although the authors' explicit aim is to attack the globalization thesis, usually put forward by the nationalist Right, their study represents in effect an argument in favour of the sort of strategy and policies suggested today by the 'civil societarian Left'. Their argument can be summarized as follows:

(1) The present highly internationalized economy is not unprecedented and in a sense it is less open and integrated than the regime that prevailed from 1870 to 1914.
(2) Genuinely trans-national corporations appear to be relatively rare since most companies are nationally based.
(3) The world economy today is not genuinely global since trade, foreign direct investment and financial flows are concentrated in the 'Triad Countries', i.e. the countries in the three main economic regions (North America, the European Union and Japan).
(4) Therefore, the major economic powers 'have the capacity to exert

powerful governance pressures over financial markets and other economic tendencies. Global markets are by no means beyond regulation and control.'[112]

It is obvious that none of the above arguments, apart perhaps from (1), challenges the thesis put forward in this book about the present neoliberal internationalization of the market economy. Clearly, the internationalization thesis advanced in this book does not depend on a stateless, borderless trans-national corporation as globalizers assume. As it was argued above, a national base is still very useful to the trans-national corporations in gaining advantages against competitors, and this fact is perfectly compatible with the accelerating marketization of the economy. In fact, the thesis supported here, as regards the significance of TNCs with respect to internationalization, is very similar to the argument put forward by Suzan Strange that 'It is not the phenomenon of the trans-national corporation that is new but the changed balance between firms working only for a local or domestic market and those working for a global market and in part producing in countries other than their original home base.'[113]

The marketization thesis advanced here does not imply the elimination of the regulatory role of the state, let alone its physical disappearance at the political level. What it does imply is the loss of the state's economic sovereignty in the past quarter of a century or so. In fact, the authors themselves admit this when they christen as 'radical' even the objective of full employment in the advanced countries,[114] despite the fact that this used to be the main objective of social democracy throughout the period of the social-democratic consensus. It is therefore clear that when the authors argue that 'far from the nation-state being undermined by the processes of internationalization, these processes strengthen the importance of the nation state in many ways',[115] what they have in mind is not the social controls in a narrow sense, not even the social controls in the broad sense, but, mainly, what we called regulatory controls.[116] Their implicit assumption is obvious: the reproduction and stability of the market economy and its offspring, the growth economy, through the 'trickle-down effect' will help the poorer social groups.

It is noteworthy that even when the authors refer to the possibility of a 'new polycentric version of the mixed economy' for the achievement of 'ambitious' goals (like 'promoting employment') the only condition they mention for this is 'a highly co-ordinated policy on the part of the members of the Triad'.[117] However, what the authors do not explain is why the elites controlling the Triad will embark on policies to create a new global mixed economy. In fact, the only argument they produce to support this case is the old underconsumptionist thesis, namely, that the reproduction of the growth economy is not viable in the framework of high inequality, which inevitably leads to low demand.[118] Thus, the fact that as long as the '40 per cent society' expands its consumption, there is no problem for the growth economy to reproduce itself – as it has done in the past – is obviously ignored by the authors. Furthermore, the issue of whether a mixed economy is possible at all today is ignored by the authors who presumably feel that all is a matter of persuading the elites of the Triad (through some form of pressure 'from below') to adopt it!

It should therefore be clear that internationalization, as interpreted in this book, does not presuppose a 'genuine' global economy, nor the absence of the Triad. Instead, the economic significance of the Triad is explicitly acknowledged and the present degree of openness implies that social controls on the market economies of the Triad itself have to be homogenized. Since this homogenization, in a competitive framework, is based on the principle of the 'least common denominator' and given the present disparity of social controls in the Triad countries, any idea that the introduction of effective social controls (initiated by the state or the 'civil society') is still feasible becomes nonsensical.

The study by Hirst and Thompson, starting from an a-historical analysis of the present world economy, assumes that the present neoliberal inter-nationalized economy is a conjunctural phenomenon rather than a struc-tural change[119] and attempts to discard the thesis of 'globalizers' that the market economy today is not governable. However, the fact that the market economy is governable, in the narrow sense of regulation, is obvious to everybody, apart perhaps from some extreme 'globalizers'. The real issue is whether nation-states are still capable, in an internationalized market economy, of imposing effective social controls to protect man and nature, or whether instead such controls are not feasible any more either at the level of the nation-state or even at the level of the economic bloc (EU or NAFTA). If one accepts the non-feasibility thesis, then the possibility for such controls exists only at the global level. But this is just a theoretical possibility which ignores the historical dynamic of the market economy and the resulting political and economic power structures.

As regards the authors' argument that the present degree of openness of the market economy is not a new development, it should be clear that if the internationalized market economy of today is seen in its historical perspective, as this book attempts to do, then, the present degree of openness is surely not a new phenomenon but merely the latest stage in a historical process which started two centuries ago. Therefore, the issue is not whether the neoliberal internationalized economy is more or less open and integrated than the liberal one but whether it has higher chances of

Table 1.3 Trade openness[1] in advanced capitalist countries

	1913	1950	1973	1979	1989	1993
France	35.4	21.2	29.0	35.9	38.0	32.7
Germany	35.1	20.1	35.2	43.0	51.2	38.2
Japan	31.4	16.9	18.3	21.9	17.1	14.3
Holland	103.6	70.2	80.1	87.9	95.5	86.1
UK	44.7	36.0	39.3	48.3	48.7	47.3
USA	11.2	7.0	10.5	15.7	16.3	17.1

1. Ratio of merchandise trade (exports and imports combined) to GDP at current prices.

Source: Paul Hirst and Grahame Thompson, *Globalization in Question,* Table 2.5 (for the years 1913, 1950 and 1973) and estimates based on the World Bank's *World Development Report* (various years) for the years 1979, 1989 and 1993.

success in creating a self-regulating internationalized market economy than the first unsuccessful attempt.

Still, although it is true that the present degree of openness is not a new phenomenon, the evidence produced by Hirst and Thompson to support the case that the degree of openness today is less than that at the beginning of the century is highly disputable.

The main indicators the authors use to support the case of less openness today is the degree of trade and financial openness to the rest of the world. However, it is only with respect to trade openness that we may use reliable statistical indicators to measure it. And this type of openness, contrary to the evidence produced in this study, has increased significantly in the post-war period. Thus, trade openness has increased in all countries listed in Table 1.3 (apart from Japan) throughout the post-war period – with a slight decrease in the 1990s as a result of the recession in the major capitalist countries. Furthermore, trade openness in 1989 was significantly higher in four major trading countries (USA, Germany, UK and France) compared to 1913. As these four countries account for about three-quarters of the total trade in the six countries listed, it is obvious that the claim by Hirst and Thompson that there was a greater international openness in 1913 than today[120] (a claim which, curiously, is based on data up to 1973) is hardly supported by the facts. On the other hand, as regards financial openness, which, according to the data provided by the study, has decreased today compared to 1913, one may raise serious doubts about the statistical measure used for this purpose, which in the case of the country with the major reserve currency, the USA, yields nonsensical results.[121]

Withering away the nation-state?

As was argued earlier, the nation-state, contrary to the claims of the 'globalizers', still has a significant role to play in the neoliberal internationalized economy. However, this role does not involve any more the enforcement of social controls to protect society from the market. The state's role today is exclusively related to securing the reproduction of the market economy through its monopoly of violence and to creating the stable framework for the efficient functioning of the markets. So, in the same way that in the first phase of marketization, when the market economy was basically national, the nation-state was assigned the role of enforcing – through its monopoly of violence – the market rules, in today's internationalized market economy this role is assigned to the state as well as to international organizations like NATO, a capitalist controlled UN, etc. A clear indication of the new world order and the means it uses to enforce the rules of the internationalized market economy was given by the Gulf War.[122]

Thus, in the neoliberal internationalized economy the old Westphalian system of sovereign nation-states is replaced by a multi-level system of political-economic entities: micro-regions, traditional states and macro-regions with institutions of greater or lesser functional scope and formal authority and with world cities becoming the keyboards of the global economy.[123] Therefore, the crucial choice today is not, as in the past, internationalism versus nationalism. The real question is what form of association among peoples can provide the institutional framework for political, economic, social and cultural autonomy. The European case provides a very interesting example of the emerging trends in the present internationalized market economy.

In Eastern Europe, where the marketization process was violently interrupted by the advent of 'actually existing socialism', the state plays today the same role that it played in Western Europe in the past century, when it was involved in the process of establishing the system of free markets. Under these conditions, the role of the nation-state is critical and this fact could be a significant factor in explaining the much stronger influence of nationalism in these countries, particularly in Russia.

In Western Europe, there is a movement towards a federal supra-national state, which reflects the fact that the core EU countries have already entered the highest phase of the marketization process. The reality is that Western Europe is in a transitional period, which is, however, qualitatively different from that in the East. The present political conflicts with respect to the future organization of European integration arise out of the fundamental contradiction indicated by the fact that the economic structure of each nation-state has already been internationalized, whereas the political structure, formally at least, still bears the hallmarks of a nation-state. The main proposals for the European integration, excluding simple variations of these proposals, like the mainstream Green proposal for a 'Europe of regions', may be classified as follows:

(a) **The proposal for a commonwealth of nation-states.** This is supported by the European right wing, from the extreme nationalists of Le Pen in France to the Thatcherite nationalists in Britain. Their aim is the continuation of the nation-state within the framework of a bigger 'domestic' market. The supporters of this proposal are obviously unable to realize that today's transition to a new phase in the marketization process has created a fundamental incompatibility between the political structure of the nation-state, which characterized earlier phases of the marketization process, and the present internationalized economic structure.

(b) **The proposal for a confederation of socialist states.** This is supported by socialists who have remained outside the 'modernized' Left and still see that the old socialist ideal of social justice is completely incompatible with the institutional framework of the newly emerging Europe.[124] According to this view under today's conditions of internationalization, a confederation of states, in other words a form of loose concentration of political power, is the only form of unification that allows for the continuity, at the European level, of the welfare state and the commitment to full employment, without sacrificing national autonomy. Still, this proposal does not take into account the historical evidence, which conclusively shows that the attempt to concentrate political power, in order to reduce the market concentration of economic power (social democracy in the West) or eliminate it altogether (actually existing socialism in the East), has proved to be futile and totalitarian, respectively. In other words, those making this proposal cannot see that the response to the concentration of economic power is not a matching concentration of political power but a radical dispersion of both. Also, as this proposal identifies growth with Progress, it does not take into account the interdependence between the concentration of economic power and growth, which has led to the present rupture of society and Nature.

(c) **The proposal for a European federation.** This is supported by the political representatives of the neoliberal consensus, that is, by the liberal and social-democratic parties. Their aim is the federation of the present states and the concentration of political and economic power into the hands of federal organs (the European Commission, European Parliament, European Central Bank and so on). Although this proposal is more realistic than the commonwealth proposal, it should be stressed that it fully adopts the 'grow-or-die' dynamic of the market economy. In fact, the only aim of the liberals supporting this proposal is to create a political structure which is compatible with the internationalized economic structure – in other words, to create the best possible conditions for the cut-throat competition with the other economic blocs. On the other hand, social democrats (and those mainstream Greens who support this proposal), see in the federation the development of a kind of international statism, a European civil society that will protect society from the market. However, the same reasons which led to the failure of statism are bound to lead to the failure of the proposed international statism as well. The institutional framework that is being established by the Single Market Act and the Maastricht Treaty clearly incorporates all the fundamental principles of the neoliberal consensus.[125] Therefore, the market dynamic assigns an obviously utopian character to the social-democratic rhetoric on the civil society.

In view of the resistance to the proposal for a federal Europe and the practical difficulties involved in meeting the convergence criteria of the Maastricht Treaty it is possible that in the end the members of the EU may not adopt the full federalist solution and may opt instead for a compromise between proposals (a) and (c) above. It is therefore possible that at least in the short to medium term an institutional framework may be adopted which will semi-internationalize the European political structure to make it more compatible with its internationalized economic structure.

Is this the end of politics (as we know it)?

The trend towards the accelerating internationalization of the market economy has already led to a debate about the future of politics and democracy. Those who take for granted the present institutional framework of the market economy and liberal 'democracy' are divided as regards their reading of future trends. On the one hand, there are those who support the view that the present trends, in the long run, lead to the end not only of the nation-state but also of 'politics' and 'democracy', as these terms are defined within the existing institutional framework.[126] On the other hand, there are those in the 'Left' who, as we saw above, attempt to put a case that the nation-state is still the most appropriate engine for the reproduction of the growth economy and that the argument about globalization is hugely overstated.[127]

The supporters of the 'end of politics' thesis argue that the natural place for the general good, the political sphere, on which liberal democracy has rested, disappears in the present age of the networks. Politics, far from being the organizing principle of life, appears as 'a secondary activity, if not an artificial construct, poorly suited to the resolution of the practical problems of the modern world'.[128] This is because we have entered a period in which 'the gulf between the nation as a locus of identity and the nation as a locus of power is formidable'.[129] Thus, the present period leads to an 'imperial age' in the double sense that it describes a world which is at once unified and without a centre and, also, in the sense that the new age

> is succeeding the nation-state as the Roman empire succeeded the Roman republic: the society of men has become too vast to form a political entity. Its citizens constitute less and less of an entity capable of expressing a collective sovereignty; they are mere juridical subjects, holders of rights and subjected to obligations, in an abstract space whose territorial boundaries have become increasingly vague.[130]

I would have no difficulty in agreeing with the above thesis about the forthcoming end of 'politics' and 'democracy', provided, however, that these terms are meant to represent the present statecraft and liberal oligarchy which today pass for politics and democracy respectively. As I argue in Chapter 5, today's 'politics' and 'democracy' represent a flagrant distortion of the real meaning of these terms and are indeed in the process of being phased out, if not in form, at least in content. Just as in the past the 'nationalization' of the market led to the death of the communities, the free towns and their federations, one may reasonably expect that the internationalization of the market will lead to the death of nation-states and national politics. In fact, even if the present political institutions survive, in the future they will be devoid of any real content, remnants of the past, constituting a symbolic formality similar to the monarchies still existing in some Scandinavian countries.

But, the fact that one may agree with the hypothesis about the end of the nation-state and the consequent end of politics and democracy in their current meanings does not imply that s/he will have to agree also with the conclusions of the supporters of this hypothesis. In other words, although it is obvious that within the new institutional framework no meaningful politics and democracy is possible, this does not mean politics and democracy themselves are superfluous. What is obviously superfluous is the institutional framework which, however, both the supporters of the nation-state and those assuming its end take for granted!

Thus, Jean-Marie Guehenno, after criticizing any kind of political structure which obeys a territorial principle, including the federal form, proposes the 'building of "virtual communities" that will liberate us from the constraints of geography, and from the traditional political structures that have for so long framed our actions'.[131] But, one may counter-argue, no real politics and democracy are possible unless they are defined within a specific territory which, as will be shown in Chapter 6, has to be the area defined by the confederation of geographically defined communities. This does not mean localism and a return to primitive ways of living. What it does mean is the creation of *confederations of autonomous regions*, at the national, the continental and the planetary levels. This proposal starts from the belief that the only way to secure social and individual autonomy, at the political, economic, social and cultural levels, is by reintegrating society and economy, in other words, by creating institutions that would support an inclusive democracy (see Chapters 6 and 7).

What differentiates the above proposal for a confederation of regions from the usual Green proposal for a 'Europe of regions', or from the ecosocialist proposal of 'autonomous regions within a unified European continent'[132] is not that it assumes away the nation-state but rather that it assumes away the institutional framework which inevitably leads to the separation of the polity from the economy and the consequent concentration of power in the hands of various elites: the market economy and liberal democracy.

The very fact that, at present, some varieties of the confederal solution attract several 'identity movements' in Western Europe (from the Flemish to the Lombards and from the Scots to the Catalans) is not, of course, accidental. Despite the fact that these movements see the confederal solution as the best means to preserve their cultural identity, yet, they also express, *in a distorted way,* the demand for individual and social autonomy. The distortion arises from the fact that the marketization of society has undermined community values which historically marked the essence of communities (reciprocity, solidarity, co-operation) in favour of market values (competition, individualism). As a result, the demand for cultural autonomy is not founded today on community values but, instead, on market values, namely, values that encourage tensions and conflicts with other cultural communities. In this connection, the current neoracist explosion in Europe is directly relevant to the effectual undermining of community values by neoliberalism, as well as to the growing inequality and poverty following the rise of the neoliberal consensus.

The establishment of an inclusive democracy does not imply the automatic disappearance of cultural tensions, which could be expected to continue for a long period of time after the establishment of such a society. Still, one could reasonably assume that a society aiming at the elimination of the concentration of power will involve a significant qualitative change in the relations between communities, similar to the change to be expected in the relationships between individuals – a change that should be conducive to the minimization of cultural tensions.

In conclusion, the establishment of the market economy and a statist form of 'democracy' has led to the demeaning and inevitable superfluity of both politics and democracy, as we know them. Furthermore, the establishment of the market economy has led to the emergence of a growth economy which, as we shall see in the next three chapters, is in a state of crisis in the North as well as in the South.

Notes

1. See, e.g., Immanuel Wallerstein, *The Capitalist World Economy* (Cambridge, Massachusetts: Cambridge University Press, 1979), Ch. 1.
2. For a recent example, see Robert Pollin, 'Financial structures and egalitarian economic policy', *New Left Review*, No. 214 (Nov.-Dec. 1995).
3. Karl Polanyi, *The Great Transformation, the Political and Economic Origins of Our Time* (Boston: Beacon Press, 1944/1957), pp. 43–4.
4. Polanyi, *The Great Transformation*, pp. 55–6.
5. Pëtr Kropotkin, *Selected Writings on Anarchism and Revolution* (Cambridge, MA, and London: Massachusetts Institute of Technology, 1970), p. 231.
6. Polanyi, *The Great Transformation*, p. 71.
7. R.H. Lowie, quoted in Polanyi, *The Great Transformation*, p. 270.
8. For anthropological evidence, see Polanyi, *The Great Transformation*, pp. 274–6.
9. Henri Pirenne, *Medieval Cities,* quoted in Polanyi, *The Great Transformation,* p. 275.
10. Karl Marx and Friedrich Engels, *Selected Works* (Moscow: Progress Publishers, 1968), p. 293.
11. Murray Bookchin, *Urbanization Without Cities* (Montreal: Black Rose Press, 1992), p. 156.
12. Bookchin, *Urbanization Without Cities*, pp. 131–2.
13. Ernest Barker, quoted in April Carter, *The Political Theory of Anarchism* (London: Routledge, 1971), p. 30.
14. Polanyi, *The Great Transformation*, p. 57.
15. Bookchin, *Urbanization Without Cities*, p. 201.
16. Bookchin, *Urbanization Without Cities*, p. 146.
17. Polanyi, *The Great Transformation*, pp. 63–5.
18. Kropotkin, *Selected Writings*, pp. 245–7.
19. Kropotkin, *Selected Writings*, pp. 246–53.
20. Polanyi, *The Great Transformation*, pp. 41–2, 75.
21. Polanyi, *The Great Transformation*, p. 163.
22. K. Smith, *Free is Cheaper* (Gloucester: The John Ball Press, 1988) quoted in David Pepper, *Modern Environmentalism* (London: Routledge, 1996) p. 302.
23. The 'logic of growth' has been adequately analysed from both the liberal and the Marxist perspectives. For further analysis from the ecological standpoint, see, e.g., Michael Jacobs, *The Green Economy* (London: Pluto Press, 1991), pp. 3–49. Also, the chapter entitled 'Why capitalism needs growth' in Richard Douthwaite's book is useful, despite the deep ecology approach that it adopts; Richard Douthwaite, *The Growth Illusion* (Devon, UK: Resurgence, 1992), pp. 18–32.
24. Henry Teune, *Growth* (London: Sage Publications, 1988), p. 13.

25. Polanyi, *The Great Transformation*, p. 71.
26. Karl Marx, *A Contribution to the Critique of Political Economy* (London: Lawrence & Wishart, 1971), p. 21.
27. A.G. Kenwood and A.L. Lougheed, *The Growth of the International Economy, 1820–1980* (London: George Allen & Unwin, 1983), p. 74.
28. Kenwood and Lougheed, *The Growth of the International Economy*, pp. 79–80.
29. Kenwood and Lougheed, *The Growth of the International Economy*, p. 40.
30. Kenwood and Lougheed, *The Growth of the International Economy*, Table 6.
31. Kenwood and Lougheed, *The Growth of the International Economy*, p. 143.
32. Kenwood and Lougheed, *The Growth of the International Economy*, p. 91.
33. Will Hutton, *The State We're In* (London: Jonathan Cape, 1995), p. 174.
34. Nicholas Barr, *The Economics of the Welfare State* (London: Weidenfeld & Nicolson, 1987), Ch. 2.
35. Friedrich Engels, *The Role of Force in History* (New York: International Publishers, 1968), pp. 34–5.
36. E. Gellner, *Nations and Nationalism* (Oxford: Blackwell, 1983), p. 138.
37. Polanyi, *The Great Transformation*, p. 218.
38. Polanyi, *The Great Transformation*. See in particular pp. 233–4.
39. Polanyi, *The Great Transformation*, Ch. 1.
40. Quoted in Victor Argy, *The Postwar International Money Crisis* (London: Allen & Unwin, 1981), p. 17.
41. W.L. Goldfrank, 'Fascism and the great transformation', in Kari Polanyi-Levitt (ed.) *The Life and Work of Karl Polanyi* (Montreal: Black Rose Press, 1990), p. 90.
42. Kenwood and Lougheed, *The Growth of the International Economy*, pp. 185–6.
43. Michael Bleaney, *The Rise and Fall of Keynesian Economics* (London: Macmillan, 1985), p. 66.
44. Bleaney, *The Rise and Fall of Keynesian Economics*, pp. 41–52.
45. Bleaney, *The Rise and Fall of Keynesian Economics*, p. 75.
46. Polanyi, *The Great Transformation*, p. 245.
47. *UK, Social Insurance and Allied Services (The Beveridge Report), Cmd. 6404* (London: HMSO, 1942).
48. A. Maddison, *Phases of Capitalist Development* (London: Oxford University Press, 1982), p. 91.
49. For a discussion of the relevant evidence, see Bleaney, *The Rise and Fall of Keynesian Economics*, Ch. 4.
50. Andrew Glynn, 'Social democracy and full employment', *New Left Review*, No. 211 (May/June 1995), Table 1.
51. See R. Matthews, 'Why has Britain full employment since the war?', *Economic Journal*, Vol. 78, No. 3 (1968).
52. Bleaney, *The Rise and Fall of Keynesian Economics*, p. 92.
53. Ian Gough, *The Political Economy of the Welfare State* (London: Macmillan, 1979), Table 5.2, p. 79.
54. Ian Gough, *The Political Economy of the Welfare State*, Table 5.1, p. 77.
55. David Greenaway, *International Trade Policy: From Tariffs to the New Protectionism* (London: Macmillan, 1983), p. 153.
56. Philip Armstrong *et al.*, *Capitalism Since World War II* (London: Fontana, 1984), Table 10.3, p. 215.

57. Andrew Glynn, 'Social democracy and full employment', Table 2.
58. For an excellent description of the gradual lifting of capital controls in Britain under market pressure, see Will Hutton, *The State We're In*, Ch. 3.
59. See A.P. Thirlwall, *Balance of Payments Theory* (London: Macmillan, 1980), Ch. 11.
60. Andrew Glynn and Bob Sutcliffe, *British Capitalism, Workers and the Profits Squeeze* (Harmondsworth: Penguin, 1972), Table F. 1, p. 260.
61. Philip Armstrong et al., *Capitalism Since World War II*, Table 11.10, p. 260.
62. Philip Armstrong et al., *Capitalism Since World War II*, p. 246.
63. In Britain, for instance, total state revenue as a percentage of the GNP increased by 9 per cent between 1951 and 1975, whereas the corresponding figure for total state expenditures increased by 29 per cent in the same period; Ian Gough, *The Political Economy of the Welfare State*, Table 5.1, p. 77.
64. Andrew Glynn, 'Social democracy and full employment', Table 1.
65. Nick Bosanquet, *After the New Right* (London: Heinemann, 1983), p. 126.
66. See Yiannis Voulgaris, *Liberalism, Conservatism and the Welfare State, 1973–1990* (Themelio: Athens, 1994) (in Greek).
67. M.J. Crozier, S.P. Huntingdon and J. Watanuki, *The Crisis of Democracy: Report on the Governability of Democracies to the Trilateral Commission* (New York: New York University Press, 1975).
68. Will Hutton, *The State We're In*, p. 103.
69. Philip Armstrong et al., *Capitalism Since World War II*, Table 14.1.
70. OECD, *Economic Outlook*, No. 57, 1995; and European Commission, *European Economy*, No. 59, 1995.
71. European Commission, *Eurostatistics*, November 1995; OECD, *Economic Outlook*, No. 58, December 1995.
72. Hazel Henderson, *Resurgence* (May-June 1993), pp. 10–14.
73. Eric Helleiner, 'From Bretton Woods to global finance: a world turned upside down' in Richard Stubbs and Geoffrey R.D. Underhill, *Political Economy and the Changing Global Order* (London: Macmillan, 1994).
74. Christopher Johnson, *The Economy Under Mrs. Thatcher, 1979–1990* (London: Penguin, 1991) p. 168.
75. Johnson, *The Economy Under Mrs. Thatcher*. Calculations based on Table 27 data.
76. Andrew Glynn, 'Social democracy and full employment', Table 1.
77. International Labor Organization (ILO), *Yearbook of Labor Statistics* (Geneva: ILO, various years); and Frank Blackaby (ed.) *De-Industrialization* (London: Heinemann, 1979), Table 10.2.
78. Western, 'Union decline in 18 advanced capitalist countries', quoted by Frances Fox Piven 'Is it global economics or neo-laissez-faire?', *New Left Review*, No. 213 (Sept.-Oct. 1995).
79. Will Hutton, *The State We're In*, p. 92.
80. Nick Bosanquet, *After the New Right*, p. 126.
81. Bob Jessop et al., 'Popular capitalism, flexible accumulation and left strategy', *New Left Review* (Sept.-Oct. 1987).
82. Will Hutton, *The State We're In*, p. 106.
83. Alissa Goodman and Steven Webb, *For Richer, For Poorer* (London: Institute of Fiscal Studies, 1994), Figure 2.3.
84. Five million Americans live in barbed wire enclosures with their own private police and security arrangements (BBC *Panorama* 29 Jan. 1996).

85. John Kenneth Galbraith, *The Culture of Contentment* (London: Penguin, 1993), p. 15.
86. Will Hutton, *The State We're In*, p. 108.
87. Galbraith, *The Culture of Contentment*, p. 15.
88. World Bank, *World Development Report 1995*, Table 30; Goodman and Webb, *For Richer, For Poorer.*
89. The data about the film industry come from *Film and Television Handbook 1993* (London: British Film Institute, 1993), Tables 14, 16, 38.
90. As K. Gouliamos, a Canada-based professor on mass media, stresses, in the Athens weekly *To Vema* (9 Feb. 1992).
91. World Bank, *World Development Report 1995*, Tables 2, 13. (See Table 1.1.)
92. World Bank, *World Development Report 1994*, Table 9.
93. World Bank, *World Development Report 1995*, Table 13.
94. Import penetration in France, Germany, Italy, UK and Sweden has increased from 16 per cent in the early 1970s to 25.7 per cent in 1985–90; Andrew Glynn, 'Social democracy and full employment', Table 2.
95. Paul Hirst and Grahame Thompson, *Globalization in Question* (Cambridge: Polity Press, 1996), pp. 54–5.
96. UN-TCMD, *World Investment Report,* 1993.
97. *The Guardian* (7 March 1995).
98. Noam Chomsky, 'Rollback IV', *Z Magazine* (May 1995).
99. Hirst and Thompson, *Globalization in Question*, p. 51.
100. There was a tenfold increase in international lending between the 1970s and the 1980s: from about $96 billion in 1976–80 to $819 billion in 1993, Hirst and Thompson, *Globalization in Question,* Table 2.9.
101. Foreign penetration of national central government bond markets in advanced capitalist countries has increased by 50 per cent in the last decade (from 10 per cent in 1983 to 15 per cent in 1989); Hirst and Thompson, *Globalization in Question,* Table 2.11.
102. Andrew Glynn, 'Social democracy and full employment', p. 41.
103. Will Hutton, *The State We're In*, p. 61.
104. Eurostat, *A Social Portrait of Europe* (Luxembourg: Statistical Office of the European Communities, 1991), Table 6.13, p. 72.
105. A very recent comparison of the labour costs for producing a standard basket of goods with $100 shows that the labour cost in peripheral countries like Greece and Portugal is $50 versus $85 in Germany and Denmark; *OECD/The Observer* (10/9/95).
106. Eurostat, *Basic Statistics of the Community* (Luxembourg: Statistical Office of the European Communities, 1992), Tables 2.12–2.19, pp. 56–65.
107. See, for instance, Mica Panic, *European Monetary Union* (London: St Martin's Press, 1993).
108. Polanyi, *The Great Transformation,* p. 29.
109. Richard Stubbs and Geoffrey R.D. Underhill, 'Global issues in historical perspective' in *Political Economy and the Changing Global Order* (London: Macmillan, 1994), p. 156.
110. UN, *Development Report,* 1992.
111. Hirst and Thompson, *Globalization in Question.*
112. Hirst and Thompson, *Globalization in Question,* p. 3.
113. Suzan Strange, 'Rethinking structural change in the international political

economy: states, firms and diplomacy' in Stubbs and Underhill, *Political Economy and the Changing Global Order*, p. 104.

114. Hirst and Thompson, *Globalization in Question*, p. 6.
115. Hirst and Thompson, *Globalization in Question*, p. 17.
116. This becomes obvious from statements like the following: 'National governments have not proved powerless in the face of an overwhelming "globalization" of international finance. Indeed, they have joined together to organize an effective supervision of the new situation. This remains nevertheless the limited *supervision* of a market-led international economy. Regulation does not attempt to alter price fixing by markets in the direction of financial flows', Hirst and Thompson, *Globalization in Question*, pp. 134–5.
117. Hirst and Thompson, *Globalization in Question*, p. 152.
118. Hirst and Thompson, *Globalization in Question*, p. 163.
119. Hirst and Thompson, *Globalization in Question*, p. 15.
120. Hirst and Thompson, *Globalization in Question*, p. 27.
121. The statistical measure used by Hirst and Thompson (current account balance to GDP) is shown to be an obviously inappropriate measure of financial openness in the US case. The US current account surplus was reduced drastically from $32.3 billion in 1960–67 to less than $5 billion in 1968–81 (Phillip Armstrong *et al.*, *Capitalism Since World War II* (London: Fontana, 1984), Tables 10.7, 12.2 16.6). This should mean a corresponding decrease in the US's capital outflow and degree of financial openness. Yet, the outflow of direct investment from the USA to other advanced capitalist countries increased from 3.4 per cent of US total investment in the period 1960–69 to 4.4 per cent in 1970–79 (Grazia Ietto-Gillies, 'Some indicators of multinational domination of national economies', *International Review of Applied Economics*, Vol. 3, No. 1, 1989, Table 1) indicating exactly the opposite! The reason is obvious. The USA, as a country with a major reserve currency, does not depend on current account surpluses to finance its investment abroad – as non-reserve countries have to do. Therefore, the current account balance to GDP ratio cannot be used as a measure of financial openness in the case of a reserve-currency country like the USA, despite the country's enormous financial significance.
122. See Takis Fotopoulos, *The Gulf War: The First Battle in the North–South Conflict* (Athens: Exantas, 1991) (in Greek).
123. Robert W. Cox, 'Global restructuring: making sense of the changing international political economy' in Richard Stubbs and Geoffrey R.D. Underhill, *Political Economy and the Changing Global Order*, p. 53.
124. See, e.g., Eric Heffer, 'A rallying call for Eurosocialists', *The Guardian* (1 Nov. 1990).
125. See also Takis Fotopoulos, *The Neoliberal Consensus and the Crisis of the Growth Economy* (Athens: Gordios, 1993), Ch. 12 (in Greek).
126. Jean-Marie Guehenno, *The End of the Nation-State* (Minneapolis: University of Minnesota Press, 1995).
127. See, for instance, Robert Wade, *Globalization and Its Limits: The Continuing Economic Importance of Nations and Regions* (University of Sussex: Institute of Development Studies, 1994); Linda Weiss and John Hobson, *States and Economic Development: A Comparative Historical Analysis* (Cambridge: Cam-

bridge University Press, 1995); as well as the study by Hirst and Thompson, *Globalization in Question.*

128. Jean-Marie Guehenno, *The End of the Nation-State,* p. 19.
129. Jean-Marie Guehenno, *The End of the Nation-State,* p. 138.
130. Jean-Marie Guehenno, *The End of the Nation-State,* p. xii.
131. Jean-Marie Guehenno, *The End of the Nation-State,* p. 141.
132. Penny Kemp *et al., Europe's Green Alternative: A Manifesto for a New World* (London: Greenprint, 1992), p. 42.

CHAPTER 2

The Growth Economy and 'Socialist' Statism

The grow-or-die dynamic that was set in motion by the emergence of the market economy and the initiation of the marketization process, which we examined in Chapter 1, led to the creation of the modern growth economy. However, the advent of 'actually existing socialism' during this century created another type of growth economy in which economic growth was a deliberate objective rather than the outcome of the dynamics of the economic system itself. We shall define the growth economy as the system of economic organization which is geared, either 'objectively' or deliberately, to the maximization of economic growth. Therefore, the growth economy, historically, takes the form of either a 'capitalist' growth economy or a 'socialist' one. In both these versions, including the hybrid form of social democracy, the end-result is the same – the maximization of growth – but the means are different. In fact, it is the much lower degree of compatibility between ends and means in the socialist case than in the capitalist one which has already led to the eclipse of the socialist growth economy.

In the first part of this chapter an attempt is made to explain the rise of the growth economy in terms of the interaction between the dynamics of the market economy and the 'growth ideology'. Thus, contrary to the claims made by most currents in the Green movement, I would argue that it is not the 'growth ideology', in other words the system of values that emerged since the Industrial Revolution, which is the exclusive or the main cause of the emergence of the growth economy. The growth ideology has simply been used to justify 'objectively' the market economy and its dynamics, which inevitably led to the capitalist growth economy. In this problematic, concentration of economic power and ecological destruction are shown to be the inevitable consequences, as well as the fundamental preconditions, of economic growth. The implication is that the main issue today cannot be reduced to just a matter of changing our values, as some radical Greens naively argue, or even condemning economic growth *per se*. The crucial issue today is how we may create a new society where institutionalized domination of human being over human being and the consequent idea of dominating nature is ruled out. The search for such a system will lead us to the conclusion that it is not just growth ideology which has to be abandoned but the market economy itself.

In the second part of the chapter the 'socialist' version of the growth economy is examined, as well as the prospects of the market economy that has succeeded it, either of the capitalist type (East Europe) or of the 'socialist' type (China, Vietnam, Laos). In the third part, the collapse of the social-democratic growth economy in the West is discussed with particular emphasis given to the decline of social democracy in the countries of the European Union where it was born. The chapter concludes with a discussion of the causes of the fall of the 'socialist' growth economy and of socialist statism in general.

The rise of the growth economy

The two types of growth economy

Marketization and growth, fuelled by competition, constituted, historically, the two fundamental components of the system of the market economy, as we saw in Chapter 1. However, whereas the first component, the marketization process, had divided the intelligentsia of the industrial era and led to the two large theoretical and political movements, liberalism and socialism, no similar divide had arisen with respect to the second component, that is, economic growth. Economic growth became a central element of the *dominant social paradigm* (i.e. the system of beliefs, ideas and the corresponding values, which is associated with the political, economic and social institutions) in both the capitalist and the 'socialist' versions of the growth economy. Thus, economic growth became a liberal *and* a socialist objective, although it is intrinsically linked to the market economy and despite the commitment of the ruling elites in the countries of 'actually existing socialism' to substitute central planning for the market economy.

The distinction introduced in this book between the capitalist growth economy and the socialist growth economy is made on the basis of the way in which economic resources are allocated, and not in order to define the nature of the respective regimes. This is of particular importance with respect to the regimes of 'actually existing socialism', which can surely not be characterized as socialist, even by the standards of classical Marxism.[1] Therefore, in the capitalist growth economy, economic growth and the basic economic problems (what, how, for whom to produce) are left to the price mechanism, whereas in the socialist growth economy most of the corresponding decisions are taken through some form of central planning mechanism. Using this distinction, under the 'capitalist growth economy' label, we will classify the growth economies in the West, which mainly flourished in the post World War II period and took either a social-democratic form (at the beginning of the period) or the present neoliberal form. Under the 'socialist growth economy' label, we will classify the pre-1989 economic structures in the East, namely the countries of 'actually existing socialism'.

The above distinction is necessary because, although ownership – and particularly control of the means of production – was only formally social in the 'socialist' growth economy, the fact that the allocation of resources was achieved mainly through the central planning rather than the price mechanism constitutes an important qualitative difference. Thus, whereas in the capitalist growth economy (and the 'socialist market economy') the ultimate objective (growth), as well as the intermediate objectives (efficiency, competitiveness) are derived 'from within' the logic and dynamics of the system itself, in the 'socialist' growth economy, the same objectives are imposed 'from without', by the political decisions of the party bureaucrats who control the planning mechanism. In other words, it is conceivable that a planned economy may pursue different objectives from those that a market economy does. Although, obviously, a certain amount of development of productive forces will always be needed so that, at least, the basic needs of all citizens are satisfied, still, this does not imply a struggle to maximize growth in competition with the capitalist growth economy and everything this struggle involves in terms of the need to improve efficiency. So, whereas in the capitalist case, the growth economy is the *inevitable outcome* of the workings of the market economy at the micro-economic level, in the socialist case, it is simply the *selected objective* at the macro-economic level.

However, apart from this basic difference, the two types of growth economy share many common features and, in particular, two very important characteristics: concentration of economic power and eco-logical damage. These characteristics, in turn, follow from the fact that both versions share the intermediate objective of efficiency. Efficiency is defined in both systems on the basis of narrow techno-economic criteria of input minimization/output maximization and not on the basis of the satisfaction of human needs, which is supposed to be the aim of an economic system.[2] Therefore, although concentration of economic power in the socialist growth economy was mainly the outcome of the concentration of political power in the hands of the party elites, and not the outcome of the 'automatic' functioning of the economic system, still, the adopted objective to maximize growth and efficiency imposed the need to use the same methods of mass production in both the East and the West. Furthermore, given that the concept of economic efficiency, which both systems share, does not take into account the 'externalities' of the economic process and particularly the negative consequences of growth on the environment, the outcome is today's widespread environmental damage all over the planet.

The growth economy and the growth ideology

Perhaps a useful way to account for the rise of the growth economy, in both its capitalist and 'socialist' versions, would be to refer to the interaction between the 'objective' and 'subjective' factors which led to its emergence. The objective factors refer to the grow-or-die dynamic of the market economy, whereas the subjective factors refer to the role of the growth ideology. Nevertheless, as I will try to show, objective and subjective factors did not contribute equally in the emergence of the two types of the growth economy. Objective factors were particularly important with respect to the rise and reproduction of the capitalist growth economy, whereas subjective factors, the growth 'values', played mainly an ideological role, in the sense of justifying the emerging market economy. Conversely, subjective factors, in particular the Enlightenment's identification of Progress with the development of productive forces and the influence that the Enlightenment ideas had on the rising socialist movement, played a crucial role with respect to the rise and reproduction of the 'socialist' growth economy; on the other hand, the objective factors did not play any role in the emergence of the 'socialist' growth economy – although they were important with respect to its reproduction.

The *growth ideology* may simply be defined as the ideology founded on the social imaginary signification that 'the unlimited growth of production and of the productive forces is *in fact* the central objective of human existence'.[3] The growth ideology has been established for over 200 years, in the wake of the Industrial Revolution and the 'grow-or-die' dynamic that was set in motion by the market economy. Thus, from Adam Smith[4] to Karl Marx,[5] the fundamental problem was how humankind could, with the help of science and its technological applications, maximize growth. In fact, Marx was even more emphatic about the importance of rapid growth. As a recent Marxist study put it:

> The Marxist critique of capitalism has often appealed from one economic rationality to another, from a crisis-ridden growth process to one which would be crisis-free and therefore more rapid [my emphasis], from an inefficient

and wasteful allocation of productive resources to one which would rest on more accurate and comprehensive forms of calculation.[6]

This ideology has complemented the *liberal* ideology of the capitalist growth economy and the *socialist* ideology of the socialist growth economy. In this sense the growth ideology has been the ultimate ideological foundation for both the capitalist and the socialist growth economy, despite the different ways in which the hierarchical patterns of power concentration are structured in the two types of growth economy. Furthermore, the growth ideology has, in a sense, functioned as the 'ideology in the last instance', since it has determined which ideology will be dominant at the end. This is why the economic failure of the socialist growth economy (namely, the failure to create a Western-type consumer society) was the main reason that led to the collapse of this type of growth economy and to the present predominance of the capitalist growth economy and its own ideology (liberalism).

The common growth ideology can also account for the fact that both types of growth economy share a similar environmental degradation. Thus, to the extent that the present concentration of power cannot be simply reduced to capitalist production relations, as Marxists contend, to a similar extent, the ecological crisis itself cannot be merely reduced to capitalist relations and conditions of production, as eco-Marxists maintain.[7] It is, anyway, evident that an analysis of the ecological crisis on the basis of capitalist production relations fails to explain the presence of an even more serious ecological crisis in the countries of 'actually existing socialism', despite the absence of capitalist production relations, in the sense of privately owned means of production. Thus, just as it would be wrong to attribute the ecological crisis merely to the growth ideology, as the environmentalists and various *realos* within the Green movement do, disregarding the institutional framework of the market economy and the consequent power relations, it would be equally wrong to impute the crisis mainly to capitalist production conditions (as eco-Marxists are trying to do), disregarding the significance of the growth ideology on the theory and practice of socialist statism.

So, in order to provide an adequate interpretation of the ecological crisis, we should refer not just to the interplay of capitalist *production relations* with *conditions of production* (as eco-Marxists do), but to the interplay of ideology with the *power relations* that result from the concentration of power in the institutional framework of a hierarchical society. Historically, as Bookchin rightly points out:

> *The idea of dominating nature first arose within society as part of its institutionalisation into gerontocracies . . . and in patriarchies . . . not in any*

> *endeavour to control 'nature'. Various modes of social institutionalisation,*
> *not modes of organising human labour (so crucial to Marx) were the first*
> *sources of domination . . . hence, domination can be definitely removed only*
> *by resolving problematics that have their origins in hierarchy and status, not*
> *in class and the technological control of nature alone.*[8]

One could only add to this that although the idea of dominating nature is as old as social domination within hierarchical society, the first historical attempt to dominate nature *en masse* emerged with the rise of the market economy and the consequent development of the growth economy. Therefore, to explain the present ecological crisis we have to begin with the historical factors which led to the emergence of the hierarchical society in general, and continue with an examination of the contemporary form of hierarchical society, in which the elite draws its power mainly from the concentration of *economic* power.

In this context, the differentiated institutional framework of the two types of growth economy (capitalist and socialist) and the common ideological framework (growth ideology) will be equally important in the analysis of the objectives of those controlling the growth economy and the implications of those objectives with respect to the ecological consequences of growth. Thus:

- In the case of the capitalist growth economy, those controlling the means of production (capital, labour and 'land') have to aim, in the context of the marketization process, at the minimization of social controls on the respective markets – either these controls are designed to protect labour or the environment.
- In the case of the socialist growth economy, central planners are able, in theory, to take ecological factors into account when making their planning decisions; in practice, however, this would imply that growth and efficiency are not maximized, resulting in further lagging behind the capitalist growth economy.

It is therefore obvious that in both versions of the growth economy, the built-in logic of the system, which emanates from the objectives to maximize growth and economic efficiency, leads to either leaving the environment out of the calculations of the costs of growth, or to a straightforward attempt to use Nature as an instrument in the pursuit of the above objectives.

The growth economy and concentration of power

As we saw in Chapter 1, mechanized production under conditions of private ownership and control of the means of production implies, first, *marketization,* as the outcome of the effort of those controlling the market economy to minimize social controls on the markets and, second, *economic growth,* as the outcome of a process which, at the micro-economic level, involves the pursuit of profit through the continuous improvement of efficiency (by means of investments into new techniques, methods of production, products, etc.) and the sales figures. Both orthodox and Marxist economic theory could be used to show that the maximization of economic growth and efficiency crucially depend on the further division of labour, specialization and the expansion of the size of the market. This is why modern technology has always been designed to maximize economic efficiency (in the sense defined above) which implies further expansion of the division of labour and the degree of specialization, irrespective of the broader economic and social implications. Thus, economic growth, extension of division of labour and exploitation of comparative advantages imply a departure from the principle of self-reliance. But, this departure has considerable repercussions at the economic level (unemployment, poverty, economic crises in market economy), the cultural level (disintegration of social ties and values), the ecological level and, naturally, the general social level (drastic restriction of individual and social autonomy).

The inevitable consequence of the pursuit of profit, through maximization of efficiency and the size of the market, has been the concentration of economic power in the hands of the elites that control the economic process. It can be shown, as it has been confirmed by a recent study, that 'there is a robust positive relationship between industry profitability and market concentration'.[9] This is an indication that the pursuit of profit by those controlling the market economy does lead to concentration. At an early stage of marketization, the concentration of economic power was the outcome of the 'massification' of production, namely, the concentration of the production process in big production units that secured 'economies of scale' and economic efficiency. Today, capitalist companies, to survive competition in the internationalized market economy, have to 'produce small quantities of high quality, semi-customised goods tailored to niche markets, thereby displacing economies of scale as the central dynamic of competition'.[10] Thus, nowadays, the concentration of economic power coincides with a parallel process of 'demassification' of production and diversification, which is consistent with the requirements of the post-industrial society and modern technology. However, this 'demassification' of production, although it may influence the size of production unit, certainly does not affect the degree of concentration of economic power at the company level. This is indicated, for instance, by the fact that the top 500 trans-national corporations (TNCs) control today two-thirds of world trade (40 per cent of it carried out *within* TNCs) and that, excepting South Korea, *all* of them are headquartered in the North.[11]

Thus, contrary to the view held by classical, as well as some contemporary, anarchists,[12] in their effort to show that there are *natural* tendencies leading to a decentralized anarchist society (a similar claim is made today with respect to bio-regionalism by its advocates), it can be shown that there is a long-term market trend leading to the continual concentration of economic power, even when this trend is accompanied by a simultaneous physical decentralization of the production process, as is the case today. This increasing concentration can be shown at both the inter-country macro-economic level, and at the inter-company micro-economic level.

At the inter-country level, Kropotkin, on the basis of a declining British share in world exports, perceived at the end of the last century a continuous decentralization of manufacturing, leading to what he called a 'consecutive development of nations'.[13] However, with hindsight, we may now see that this consecutive development never materialized and that today, on the contrary, we see the largest concentration of economic power on record. As is well known, a historical gap has been created between the North and the South, since the time the market economy of the North started penetrating the traditional economies of the South. About 200 years ago, when the marketization process was just starting in the North, the average per capita income in the rich countries was only one-and-a-half times higher than that in poor countries.[14] About 100 years later, in 1900, it was six times higher, and by the time of the importation of the growth economy into the South in the early 1950s, it was 8.5 times higher. The gulf has increased dramatically since then, and by 1970 the per capita income in the North was 13 times higher than in the South.[15] Lately, this gulf has widened even further, as is indicated by the significant rise in the North's share of world output and exports in the last two decades; thus, its share of world output increased from about 74 per cent in 1970 to 79 per cent in 1992, whereas its export share increased from 65.5 per cent in 1979 to 75 per cent in 1992.[16]

Therefore, the internal reallocation, regarding the export shares of metropolitan countries noticed by Kropotkin, does not negate the fact that today wealth, income, production and exports are concentrated in the hands of less than one-seventh of the world's population. As regards trade itself, the economic elites of advanced capitalist countries dominate it directly or indirectly. Thus, the export share of the G7, which stood at about 52 per cent in 1953, was still about the same in 1993, despite the fact that a significant part of production by multinationals headquartered in the North had moved beyond the geographical boundaries of their bases.[17] In general, the 'Triad countries', which make up only 14 per cent of world population (1990), attracted 75 per cent of foreign direct investment in the 1980s (1980–91), accounted for 70 per cent of world trade and received about 70 per cent of world income.[18]

At the inter-company level, it is not difficult to establish a historical trend of increasing economic concentration. In Britain for instance, the top 100 manufacturing firms increased their share of total net output from 16 per cent in 1909 to 24 per cent in 1935, 32 per cent in 1958 and to around 40 per cent in the 1970s and 1980s.[19] Similar trends can be observed in other metropolitan countries.[20] Furthermore, the fact that the degree of concentration seems to be stabilizing lately is due more to the recent significant expansion of fragmentation strategies employed by large firms (multi-plant ownership, subcontracting, franchising, licensing agreements, and so on) rather than to any real slowdown in the concentration process. The same fragmentation strategies[21] may also explain, at least partly, the growth of small firms in the last decade, although the parallel expansion of the services sector has played a crucial role in this connection. Therefore, although it is true that the post-industrial society has brought a significant degree of diversification in the production process, this by no means implies a reversal of the trend towards increasing concentration of economic power. Finally, the huge concentration of investment power in a small number of capitalist firms is another indication of the degree of concentration of economic power. Thus, the largest 100 multinational corporations account for a third of the total foreign direct investment stock.[22] From this point of view, the various 'futurologists'[23] who talk about the world being 'de-massified' (in the sense of dispersion of power), after the second wave of industrialism and the diversity of the 'third wave' which is dawning, in fact, play the role of the apologetic of the present concentration of power.

However, concentration of economic power has not been the prerogative of the capitalist growth economy. A similar concentration took place in the socialist growth economy. Therefore, the difference between the two types of growth economy with respect to concentration is simply reduced to who owns the means of production and how they are allocated among different uses.

Thus, first, as far as the form of ownership of economic resources is concerned, both the private-capitalist and the state-socialist forms of ownership lead to the pursuit of *partial* interests. This is because, in both cases, the form of ownership assigns to a minority the right to control the production process: either *directly*, through private ownership, which gives a minority the right to control the means of production in a market economy, or *indirectly*, through state ownership, which assigns a similar right to the bureaucratic elite in control of the planning mechanism in 'actually existing socialism'. However, whereas in the capitalist growth economy concentration of economic power is realized through the workings of the market mechanism, in the socialist growth economy, concentration of economic power in the hands of the bureaucratic elite that controls the central plan is a direct result of the concentration of political power.

Second, as far as the mechanism for resource allocation is concerned, both the market mechanism and the planning mechanism result in establishing a few in privileged positions, at the expense of the many. In the market mechanism, this is brought about automatically through the unequal distribution of income that results from the mechanism's functioning, while in central planning this is accomplished through the institutionalization of various privileges in favour of the bureaucratic elite.

Therefore, to the extent that the 'socialist' concentration of power is 'accidental', when socialism takes the form of soviet 'democracy' at the political level and central planning at the economic level, to a corresponding extent the capitalist concentration of power is accidental when liberalism takes the form of parliamentary 'democracy' and the market economy respectively. In both cases, concentration is justified by the respective ideology, directly in Marxism and indirectly in liberalism. Thus, in the former, concentration of power is considered necessary in the 'transitional' period to communism, whereas in the latter, as long as it is 'legal', it is not considered to be incompatible with the fundamental liberal principle of the 'primacy of the individual', even though concentration negates the principle's universality. It is therefore clear that neither does 'actually existing socialism' lead to the liberation of human beings, nor does 'actually existing capitalism' affirm the 'primacy of the individual'.

Concentration of economic power does not, of course, constitute a new phenomenon. In all hierarchical societies, some concentration of wealth has always accompanied the concentration of political and military power in the hands of the various elites – a fact usually 'justified' through a system of social rules based upon religion. The new element in the growth economy is the fact that the reproduction of the social system itself, as well as of the power of the elite controlling it, crucially depends on the realization of the growth objective which, in turn, is 'justified' through its identification with Progress. So, economic growth functions not just as a fundamental social and economic goal, but also as a basic means to reproduce the structures of unequal distribution of economic and political power which characterize the modern hierarchical society, as well as a central element of the ideology that supports it. Therefore, the hierarchical society took a new form with the rise of the market economy in the West and of the planned economy in the East. In this new form, the elite draws its power not only (as in the past) from the concentration of political, military or, in general, social power, but, primarily, from the concentration of economic power, whether this concentration is brought about by the market mechanism, or through central planning.

However, the fact that the modern hierarchical society relies for its reproduction on the maximization of economic growth constitutes, also, its fundamental contradiction. This is not because, as is usually argued, the continuation of the growth economy has serious environmental implications, but because the necessary condition for the reproduction of the growth economy is the concentration of its benefits on a small section of the world population, i.e. the huge inequality in the distribution of world income. This is on two counts:

- First, it is simply not *physically* possible for the wasteful consumption standards, which are today enjoyed by the '40 per cent societies' in the North and the elites in the South, to be universalized and enjoyed by the world population. Thus, as was recently pointed out: 'It seems clear that the material consumption of industrial people cannot be universalized to encompass all humans on earth. The required increase in material production is large. To simply universalize the North's standard of living now, global industrial production would need to rise 130 times.'[24] It is also noteworthy that even this already untenable goal understates the problem by not including present growth and the short-term population growth projections.[25] In this sense, one may argue that the present rapid growth rate in countries like China (the Chinese GDP rose by an average rate of 9.6 per cent in 1980–93[26]) is physically sustainable only if the parallel huge increase in inequality continues.
- Second, a universalized growth economy is not *environmentally* sustainable, at the present state of technological knowledge and cost of 'environmentally friendly' technologies. In other words, the universalization of such technologies would not be possible, given their cost and the concentration of world income. Furthermore, it is at least doubtful whether after the universalization of such technologies their beneficial impact on the environment will remain the same.

Concentration and ecological disintegration do not simply constitute *consequences* of the establishment of the growth economy, but also *fundamental preconditions* for its reproduction. Contrary to the underconsumptionist 'civil societarians' who hope that the elites of the Triad, facing the threat of an inadequate demand because of growing inequality, will be induced to introduce a world mixed economy,[27] in fact, the opposite is the case. The growth economy in the North not only is not threatened by the growing inequality of the present internationalized market economy, but, instead, depends on it. Thus, just as the production of the growth economy is not possible without the plundering of nature, its physical reproduction is equally impossible without the further concentration of economic power.

In conclusion, it is obvious that the present concentration of economic, political and social power in the hands of the elites which control the growth economy is not simply a cultural phenomenon related to the values established by the industrial revolution, as significant currents within the ecological movement naively believe. Therefore, the realization of ecological balance is not just a matter of changes in value-systems (abandonment of the growth logic, consumerism, etc.) which would then lead to an eco-friendly way of living. In fact, the concentration of power constitutes the inevitable outcome of a historical process that started with the establishment of hierarchical social structures and the implied ideology of domination of human over human and Nature[28] and culminated in the last two centuries with the development of the market economy and its by-product, the growth economy.

The market/growth economy and concentration of economic power are opposite sides of the same coin. This means that neither the concentration of economic power nor the ecological implications of the growth economy are avoidable within the present institutional framework of the internationalized market/growth economy. But the increase in the concentration of economic power leads to the realization that Progress, in the sense of improvements in welfare through growth, has a necessarily *non-universal* character. Therefore, the moment of truth for the present social system will come when it will be universally acknowledged that the very existence of the present wasteful consumption standards depends on the fact that only a small proportion of the world population, now or in the future, will be able to enjoy them.

The fall of the 'socialist' growth economy in the East

A crucial part of the present multidimensional crisis is the crisis of socialist statism, namely, the historical tradition that aims at the conquest of state power, by legal or revolutionary means, as the necessary condition to bring about radical social change, i.e. as the precondition for employing our knowledge about nature and society in order to shape the natural environment and the course of social evolution. The socialist movement that emerged in nineteenth-century Europe and, of course, the Marxist movement, constituted the material manifestation of this view, which had become dominant in the wake of the Enlightenment. This view involved a course of linear (or dialectic) progress into the future. Politics could be grounded on science, on an effective knowledge, regardless of any collective, creative or self-instituting activity on the part of social individuals. The socialist statist view mainly flourished in the quarter of a century following the end of World War II, as a result of the vast geographic expansion of the socialist growth economy in East Europe and the takeover of power by social-democratic parties in West Europe.

Socialist statism, in its two main historical forms, namely 'actually existing socialism' in the East and social democracy in the West, has dominated the Left in the past 100 years or so, putting in second place the alternative form of socialism, libertarian socialism – a product of the autonomy tradition. Despite the significant differences between the social-democratic view, which involved the conquest of the bourgeois state in order to reform it, and the Marxist–Leninist view, which involved the abolition of the bourgeois state and its reconstitution into a proletarian state, both views involve a mechanism to achieve radical social change that implies the concentration of political and economic power. Lenin's[29] proletarian state or 'mini-state', which eventually withers away, involves a significant degree of concentration of power in the hands of the proletariat that could easily degenerate, as Bakunin[30] had predicted, into a huge concentration of power in the hands of an elite of ex-workers (avant-garde).

Today, the socialist statist view seems effectively demolished from the concentrated blows of the New Right and of the now emerging 'civil-societarian' Left, as well as of the new social movements. The socialist statist tradition itself is also in deep crisis, as indicated by the two major developments of the last 15 years: the eclipse of 'actually existing socialism' in the East and the parallel collapse of social democracy in the West. The crisis of socialist statism is, of course, understandable, considering that numerous socialist statist parties succeeded in their aim to seize state power. Thus, social-democratic movements in the First World, communist movements in the Second World and various self-styled socialist national-liberation movements in the Third World seized power, and they all failed to change the world, at least in accordance with their proclaimed declarations and expectations. In fact, even the very superstructures that these movements erected in the post-war period, which gave the impression of some change, have either been pulled down ('actually existing socialism' in the East) or are in the process of demolition (social democracy in the West). So, the failure of socialist statism refers to both the form of socialist statism in the East, which is associated in theory with Marxism and in practice with absolute state centralization, and to Western social democracy, that is, the statism which is associated in theory with Keynesianism and in practice with the welfare state and the mixed economy.

In what follows we shall examine the causes of the failure of socialist statism and the related forms of growth economy in both the East ('socialist' growth economy) and the West (the social-democratic version of the capitalist growth economy).

The causes of the fall of the 'socialist' growth economy

Socialist statism, in the form of 'actually existing socialism', did not even complete a full century of life before disintegrating under the pressure of its internal contradictions and the blows – mainly indirect – it received from international capitalism. However, regardless of the overall economic failure of 'actually existing socialism', it cannot be disputed that this system had in its record two achievements of major social significance and that it is exactly these achievements which today, following the rise of liberalism in these countries, are phased out.

The first achievement was to eliminate the insecurity created by open unemployment and the resulting marginalization of the individual. This was achieved, of course, at the expense of widespread 'disguised' unemployment (overmanning, etc.). But if, to the liberals, disguised unemployment was a symptom of economic inefficiency, to the socialists it was just an inevitable consequence of social policy. There is, however, no doubt that the attempt to disguise open unemployment in this way contradicted the very logic of the growth economy. This is why the ongoing full integration of these countries into the internationalized market economy has guaranteed the abandonment of the state's commitment to full employment – a commitment which had already been abandoned by Western social democrats. The inevitable result was bound to be widespread unemployment, as can be shown either through liberal Keynesian theory (where the free market is shown to be unable to ensure full employment, except under special circumstances and for a limited period of time[31]) or through Marxist theory (where unemployment – the 'reserve army of labour' – ensures that capital accumulation does not create a rising trend for wages[32]).

The second achievement was that the degree of inequality in the distribution of income was lower in the countries under 'actually existing socialism' than in Western countries at the same level of development, as was shown by reliable Western studies.[33] This, despite the considerable inequalities induced by the institutionalized privileges and various economic benefits enjoyed by the bureaucracy. It is not, therefore, surprising that the spreading of market mechanisms in these countries has led to a continually growing inequality. In 1990, according to Boris Saltykov,

Russia's vice-president responsible for education, those in the top 10 per cent of the social pyramid were three times as rich as the 10 per cent at the bottom; by 1992 they were ten to eleven times as rich![34] Furthermore, the prospects for the future look even gloomier, since their state machines will weaken in proportion to the degree of their further integration into the internationalized market economy; this implies that the state will be allowed even fewer degrees of freedom to intervene in order to reduce the market-generated inequalities.

To give an adequate interpretation of the phenomenon of the collapse of 'actually existing socialism', it is necessary to outline the causes of its economic failure. It was precisely the system's economic failure that, on the one hand, led to the spectacular U-turn of Soviet bureaucracy, which was expressed by Gorbachev's *perestroika*, and, on the other, functioned as the catalyst for the collapse of 'actually existing socialism' in the satellite countries. Economic failure manifested itself by a significant slowdown in the development of production forces which led, at the end, to stagnation. Indicatively, the growth rate of industrial output in the USSR fell from an average 7 per cent in the 1960s to 4 per cent in the 1970s and to 2 per cent in the 1980s.[35] Also, the average GNP growth rate fell from 7 per cent in the 1960s to about 5 per cent in the 1970s.[36] At the same time, serious shortages of consumer goods developed and the phenomena of techno-logical backwardness and low quality of production intensified.

There are three main interpretations of the economic failure of 'actually existing socialism' which originate in the three main political traditions: the liberal, autonomist and socialist-statist traditions. For the liberal approach, the ultimate cause of the failure lies in the attempt to substitute central planning for the market mechanism. Alternatively, for the autonomist approach, the cause of the failure lies in the lack of democracy that characterized the system. Finally, the socialist-statist approach usually occupies the middle ground between the other two approaches. Thus, the right wing of the socialist-statist tradition (social democrats in the West, *perestroika* leadership in the East) is closer to the liberal view, while the left wing (for example, Trotskyists) is closer to the autonomist view.

According to the liberal view,[37] in order to explain the economic inefficiency of 'actually existing socialism', we have to refer to what is called the system's 'planability', which is a function of the number of interrelated decisions to be taken during the planning process. This view maintains that supplanting the market will only lead to the most arbitrary and inefficient central decisions regarding the allocation of millions of products. This is so because 'plan-instructions are, so to speak, non-specific, defining an aggregate total, which may be in tons, roubles, square metres or whatever. *This* instruction is clear and binding, and so enterprises produce not what the user actually requires, but that assortment which adds up to required aggregate quantity'[38] – a process which inevitably induces the waste of materials and economic inefficiency.

Furthermore, according to the same view, the greater the multiplicity of possible alternative products and methods (which is a by-product of development) the less is the system's planability. In other words, the system's success at the early stages of development, manifested by the high growth rates, was a result of *extensive* development and of the use of previously unexploited production resources in the expansion of 'heavy industry'. Thus, in the last instance, this success was due to the fact that development was still at a very low stage – a fact which can explain the system's relative success in, for instance, the pre-war USSR or post-war Bulgaria. When the point was reached, however, that a higher stage of economic development demanded *intensive* use of production resources, through significant increases in productivity, and the production of technologically more advanced consumer goods, then the need for decentralization (which, to the liberals, can only be effective in a market system) inevitably arose. This point marked, also, the beginning of the countdown leading to successive economic crises and the final collapse of the system.

According to the alternative radical interpretation (reflecting views grounded on the autonomist tradition[39]), the basic cause of the system's inefficiency lies in the absence, first, of political democracy and, second, of democracy at the workplace in the sense of self-management of the production units. This lack of workers' participation in the decision-taking process, unavoidably, led to the alienation of direct producers, as a result of the total absence of work incentives.

The radical interpretation carries a lot of weight because it is true that the capitalist *economic* incentives were institutionally absent, whereas the socialist *ideological* incentives, which the bureaucratic elite tried to create in place of the economic ones, were doomed to fail. As regards the economic incentives, there are two main incentives provided by the capitalist growth economy: one positive, *consumerism,* and one negative, *unemployment.* Both were absent in the countries under 'actually existing socialism'. Consumerism was impossible, not only because of the bureaucratization of the economic process which had created an inefficient consumer goods sector, but also because these countries had to channel a relatively small proportion of their economic resources to the production of consumer goods. Given their lower level of development, compared with the advanced capitalist countries, this was their only way to cope with the exorbitant defence expenditures imposed on them by the Cold War.

Furthermore, the right to employment – usually inscribed in the constitution – not only led to widespread disguised unemployment, but also reinforced an attitude of 'minimal effort' and passivity. The consequences were inevitably disastrous, especially with respect to the efficiency of the information flow which is particularly significant for the adequate functioning of every mechanism of resource allocation.

As regards the ideological incentives (which were used mainly by Stalin and Mao in their effort to make up for the absent economic incentives), their failure was inevitable in a system characterized by the fundamental contradiction between an ideology based upon the principles of equality and social justice, and the reality of a blatantly unequal distribution of economic and political power.

The failure of 'actually existing socialism' to achieve the principal aim of creating an efficient socialist growth economy produced the following dilemma for the ruling elites: either socialist decentralization or decentralization through the market. The former involved the creation of an authentic socialist economy, through the institution of new structures for socialist self-management and a parallel struggle for the establishment of a new international division of labour based upon the principles of co-operation and solidarity. The latter involved the creation of a 'socialist' market economy and a full integration into the internationalized market economy, which is founded upon the principles of competition and individualism. The first option would entail the self-negation of the ruling elites (not to mention their exclusion from access to Western capital, while many of these countries were in deep debt), as well as the dissolution of the hierarchical structures they had established. On the other hand, the adoption of the second option was entirely consistent with the reproduction (with some changes in form) of the hierarchical structures and of the elites themselves (including most of their personnel).

Hence, the criteria used in selecting the form of decentralization were not economic (as presented by Western analysis and politicians), but *political*. The discourse used by the protagonists of *perestroika*, in order to justify it, was indicative. Thus, according to Alexander Yakovlev,[40] *perestroika* signified the substitution of the theory that universal human values transcend class interests for Marxist class theory. It is characteristic that among these 'universal' values the dominant value is considered to be the mixed economy and free competition!

Once the reformist elites embarked on a strategy to introduce a 'socialist' market economy, the dynamic that was set in motion was bound to lead to the transcendence not just of the 'socialist' growth economy but of 'actually existing socialism' itself. The soviet reformist elite in particular, unlike the Chinese elite, had to accompany the reforms (*perestroika*) with more openness (*glasnost*) in order to outmanoeuvre the strong hard-liner military-industrial faction in the establishment which did not wish to see any significant changes in the status quo. But, more openness gave the chance to the centrifugal forces, encouraged by the Western elites which had a vested interest in the restoration of the capitalist growth economy, to push for the fragmentation of the USSR and the overthrow of 'actually existing socialism'.

From a 'socialist' growth economy to a market economy

The collapse of the 'socialist' growth economy and its replacement by a market economy has become universal. From Russia to China and from Poland to Vietnam, the planned allocation of resources has either eclipsed or is in the process of doing so. The difference between East Europe and the Far East is that whereas the socialist growth economy in East Europe is being replaced by a capitalist market economy, in the Far East it is being replaced by a kind of 'socialist' market economy, where significant productive resources are still in state control.

The capitalist market economies in East Europe

In Eastern Europe, after the collapse of the political structures which, apart from Russia (and partially Yugoslavia and Albania), have been 'imported' by the Red Army, the new regimes, under the tutelage of the IMF, the World Bank, etc., embarked on a strategy to dismantle not just the system of planning in the allocation of resources but also the state ownership of the productive resources and replace both by a market economy and capitalist ownership and control.

The new elites that are currently being formed aim to create a new system of control and privileges based upon private ownership of the means of production, in place of the old system which was founded on party power and bureaucratic control. In fact, the new capitalist elites often consist of the same personnel as the old elites: thus, many members of the nomenclatura have already taken over the newly privatized companies, confirming Trotsky's[41] old prediction that bureaucrats can turn into capitalists. This is not surprising given that the ex-bureaucrats and black-marketeers, together with foreign capitalists, are the only ones able to command the funds and connections necessary to buy the productive resources on sale. Furthermore, the strings attached by the international capitalist organizations to the loans and 'aid' given to these countries were also designed to reinforce the capitalist market economy being established and to preclude any attempt towards a self-managed production structure.

The future of the market economies now emerging in Eastern Europe will be determined by whether it will be possible to build a successful capitalist growth economy in place of the 'socialist' growth economy that has just collapsed. This depends on two main factors: first, on whether the mass influx of Western capital, which is still awaited, will actually material-ize; and second, on whether some, at least, of the trade-flows within the former Eastern bloc, which are presently being dismantled in the process of integrating the bloc countries into the internationalized market economy, will be re-established. If these aims are generally accomplished, then the negative effects of marketization (drastic increase in unemployment, widening of inequality, downgrading of social services and so on) may be largely tolerable, provided that they do not acquire mass proportions.

However, the chances of these aims being achieved are small, although for some countries in central Europe they are considerably greater. Not only has the mass influx of Western capital not yet materialized but it seems all the more doubtful today whether it will ever do so. In the fierce competition among the countries of the 'extended' South to attract foreign investment, vast China possesses considerable comparative advan-tages (lower wages, political 'stability', and so on). The existing evidence up to now supports this hypothesis. The entire East European region has attracted very small flows of foreign investment, without macro-economic significance. In 1992 alone, China attracted more foreign direct invest-ment than the whole of the former Soviet bloc attracted between 1989 and 1993.[42] Furthermore, the flow of foreign investment in the region not only has been small but, in effect, was directed to buying the state industries which, with the collapse of the currencies in the region – particularly the rouble – were sold 'for a song'. In Hungary and Poland, for instance, the overwhelming bulk of privatizations (some 55,000 enterprises by the end of 1993) have gone to foreign buyers.

As regards the possibility of re-establishing trade links within the former Eastern bloc, the chances of these links acquiring in the future a quantita-tive significance similar to the old ones are almost nil. Particularly so, given Sachs's[43] plan's core objective of breaking-up the Comecon region. The parallel 'encouragement' (by the 'G7') of the revival of economic activity, on the basis of trade-led growth directed towards Western Europe,[44] further contributed to the break-up of the Comecon links. An immediate result of the Comecon break-up was that the traditional EU trade deficit with the region turned into a surplus.[45]

It may, therefore, safely be predicted that the more developed of these countries (the Czech republic, the Republic of Slovakia, Hungary, Po-land) will occupy a position in the semi-periphery of the internationalized market economy, while the remaining ones will constitute its periphery. So, the neoliberal policies imposed today by major Western capitalist countries, combined with the absence of the preconditions for the development of a strong domestic industry and technology, practically guarantee the 'Latin-Americanization' of Eastern Europe. Not surprisingly, a recent study found that, on current trends, most of the region will not regain their 1988 (pre-market economy) living standards even by the year 2010![46]

In regard to Russia, in particular, its present total integration in the internationalized market economy completes a process already begun in the previous century and abruptly interrupted by the rise of the Bolshevist regime to power. About 100 years ago, the tsarist reformist Sergei Witte complained that Russia was a country that exported raw materials and imported finished goods, that is, a country in the capitalist periphery. Today, the country returns to its former position, with regard to both the structure of production and, subsequently, the structure of its trade.

As far as production is concerned, the initiative for the required restructuring of the manufacturing sector, that would have created the conditions for survival in the competition with Western firms, should have come either from the managers of public corporations (supported by the state) or from private – domestic and foreign – capital. However, the first possibility was, from the start, ruled out by the Western financial backers of the reforms. The international organizations took pains to ensure that every single dollar of help to Russia would be 'linked' to market reforms.[47] Simultaneously, they pressed for the drastic reduction of public deficits and for the privatization of state companies which, following the dramatic devaluation of the rouble, offered particularly lucrative opportunities for Western capital. However, Western capital showed no particular desire to invest in Russian manufacturing. On the contrary, following its usual practice in the periphery, it turned to investments in the particularly profitable – due to the rich natural resources – energy (oil, gas) and timber sectors, as well as the mining of raw materials.[48] The result has been a continual decrease in production, industrial production in particular.

With regard to trade, the completion of Russia's integration into the internationalized market economy has resulted in the collapse of the traditional commercial links with the other countries of Eastern Europe and the former republics in the Soviet Union. According to M. Kaser, a distinguished sovietologist at Oxford University, in 1988, the final year of the Central Plan, Russian trade with the other republics constituted four-fifths of the total trade, representing 27 per cent of the Russian GNP.[49] The fragmentation of Comecon-region trade had a disastrous impact on industrial production as even an OECD report admitted: 'According to some calculations, this volume effect alone can explain most of the fall in output in Hungary and the former CFSR and about one-third of the decline in Poland.'[50] Today, trade with the other republics has collapsed, and Russia imports final products (essentially luxury consumer goods for the new elite) and exports raw materials, exactly as it did 100 years ago.

At the same time, the West, through various international organizations, imposes an increasingly stricter 'austerity' in order to 'stabilize' the Russian economy in its new place in the international division of labour. No wonder Sachs's shock therapy became famous for its three 'izations': liberalization, privatization, and stabilization. The effect of the above policies was a massive slump, which, according to the Russian State Committee for Statistics – the only reliable official source on the economy – reached a cumulative fall in industrial output approaching 50 per cent in the period 1991–93,[51] a decrease even greater than that which occurred in the United States during the Great Depression, in the wake of the 1929 crash! The human cost has been, inevitably, huge. According to a World Bank study, 37 per cent of the adult population and 46–47 per cent of the under 15s fell below the poverty line[52] in 1992. Not surprisingly, whereas the world crude death rate has fallen by a quarter between 1970 and 1993, in Russia it has *increased* by 44 per cent and almost all of this increase happened after 1989.[53] This is why even sections of the emerging new elite, which are interested in the development of a domestic manufacturing base, talk about the Latin-Americanization of Russia. Thus, Arkady Volsky, for instance, president of the Union of Russian Industrialists, states that Russia cannot possibly have a totally open economy, since only 16 per cent of its enterprises can withstand international competition.[54] In the same vein, Boris Kagarlitsky, leading cadre of the party of Labour, states that 'the government's economic policy does not aim to overcome the crisis but to make it work for the benefit of the new elite, which stands to profit from the country's Latin-Americanization'.[55]

At the political level, the most probable 'scenario' is a long period of instability which, in the long term, may initiate processes that will enhance radical and, most likely, extreme nationalist and fascist tendencies. In fact, the present resurgence of the communist party under Zyuganov expresses more a rising nationalism[56] and an effort to support 'the "good" – that is – paternalist nomenclature'[57] rather than any attempt to roll back the market economy, which is taken for granted by the reformed 'communists'.

In the meantime, the invasion of consumerism and the regime's objective inability to satisfy the consumer needs and, in particular, the expectations of large sections of the population, have led to an explosion of criminality, alcoholism and drug abuse. Notwithstanding, the trend favoured today by the rising new elites in Russia and the other Eastern countries is political liberalization, in the sense of 'democratization'. The same trend is actively supported by the West. In fact, the policy of 'democratization' has been advanced by the West since the early 1980s not only in Eastern Europe but throughout the capitalist periphery and semi-periphery, to which the Eastern bloc countries now belong. Thus, Ronald Reagan, in a speech to the British Parliament in 1981, announced that the US was about to throw its prestige and resources behind a programme to strengthen 'democracy throughout the world'.[58] The timing of this announcement was not accidental. The authoritarian regimes in the periphery could only survive as long as the 'alibi of growth', that is, the growth ideology, was still credible. However, at the beginning of the 1980s it was already clear that the 'development' that had taken place in the peripheral countries was based upon totally unstable foundations (mainly on foreign borrowing), and was unable to create a Western-type growth economy. At that point, democracy became 'a way of spreading and sharing responsibility', as B. Cumings[59] aptly commented. In reality therefore, 'democratic participation', which is celebrated today in the periphery and semi-periphery, is simply participation in misery. The system of *liberal oligarchy* now replacing the authoritarian regimes of the past cannot, by its nature, ensure citizens' true participation in decision-making – merely their collective apathy. This apathy, however, is today secured in a much more sophisticated way than in a Stalinist- or Pinochet-type of regime, which is not capable of creating the illusion of citizen participation. The average citizen is asked every four to five years to choose his or her masters, occasionally becomes involved in pressure groups, rarely rises to the elite itself, while 'by and large he does, and is expected to, remain relatively passive – in fact, the health of the system depends on it'.[60]

However, the crucial problem that the transplantation of liberal oligarchy to the periphery creates is that, whereas the Western liberal oligarchy is founded on the '40 per cent society', there is no chance, in the foreseeable future, for the peripheral liberal oligarchy to acquire a similar basis on which a system of institutionalized apathy could be built.

The 'socialist' market economies in the Far East

The Far Eastern 'socialist' growth economy (China, Vietnam, Laos) is being replaced not by a capitalist market economy as in Eastern Europe but by a 'socialist' one, in the sense that an attempt is made to keep most of industrial production under state control. However, the dynamic of the market economy that was set in motion by the reforms inevitably leads to a capitalist market economy in all these countries.

In China, the conversion to a market economy started in 1979. But, in contrast to the road taken in Eastern Europe, the massive public sector is still maintained not only in health, education, transport, tele-communications, banking and foreign trade but also in industry. Thus, socially owned enterprises (state, collective, etc.) still produce over 85 per cent of China's industrial output.[61] The obvious aim of the Chinese bureaucracy was to allow as much freedom as possible to the market forces at the micro-economic level of the state enterprise and keep for themselves overall control over the macro-economic allocation of resources, through state ownership and planning. This aim was obviously contradictory and the dynamics of the market economy at the micro level were bound to give an expanded role to the market, at the expense of planning, in the overall allocation of resources. Thus, as a study put it: 'functioning markets have come into being in Chinese industry and have become increasingly important in resource allocation . . . the growing importance of the market has been intimately linked with the decline of the resource allocation of planning'.[62]

The effect of the reforms, in terms of the conventional measures of 'success' of the growth economy, have been significant. The World Bank a few years ago was celebrating the fact that, as a result of the introduction of the market economy in China, the average annual growth rate since 1979 has been 8.8 per cent and per capita output has doubled in the period 1977–87.[63] However, it is very doubtful whether even this type of 'success' is sustainable, at least within the present institutional framework. Thus, as regards the state sector, most of the growth in it has not been 'intensive', namely due to improvements in productivity, but extensive, owing a lot to the huge reserves of surplus labour.[64] Also, as regards the growing private sector, the real engine of growth in it has been the foreign-invested industrial sector, most of which is concentrated in South-ern China. Not much analysis is needed to predict that the lower cost advantages of private enterprises (e.g. their ability to avoid paying any welfare benefits) will inevitably lead to the victory of private over col-lective enterprises, and of foreign-owned over local ones, as some studies also predict.[65] Thus, at the moment, a dual economy has been created in China and a corresponding dual structure of power, with the market gaining increasing control over the economy, at the expense of the bureaucracy which has to rely on repression to hold on to power.

The Chinese example is a perfect illustration of the impossibility, as well as the undesirability, of a 'socialist' market economy. Not only have the dynamics of it inexorably led to the elimination of the remnants of 'socialism'; they also, in the meantime, have already created the familiar effects of a market economy. Thus, despite the fact that social ownership is still the norm, inequality, unemployment and insecurity are now rampant in China. The fact that market-led investment, mainly foreign, is concentrated in the most profitable areas has led to huge disparities within China which at present are as great as those between Germany and the poorest countries of Eastern Europe.[66] Also, according to a very recent report, the per capita GDP of China's richest region, the Zhuhai Special Economic Zone, is now 86 times higher than that in the poorest area, Qinglong county in Guizhou.[67]

As regards unemployment, Chinese government officials estimate that 200 million peasants are presently without work, and the number is estimated to rise to 300 million by the year 2000.[68] A huge tidal wave of peasants, estimated at about 140 million (almost a third of the rural workforce), has already joined the 'blind flow' of migrant workers from inland farms searching for jobs in the 'booming' eastern seaboard. A report described graphically the plight of those people:

> [T]he 'lucky' few who get a job are easy prey for unscrupulous factory owners who put profit before safety and force them to work long hours in grimy sweatshops or fire cracker plants. On average, nearly 500 people die from industrial accidents in China each week, a dismal record that has attracted condemnation from the International Labour Organisation and international trade unions.[69]

At the same time, competition between the provinces to attract foreign firms has led to the creation of export zones where the concessions to foreign capital have created, as in other Asian capitalist miracles, 'a paradise built on remorseless exploitation of child labour, forced overtime, government strikebreaking and worse'.[70] No wonder death rates are rising, significant environmental problems are emerging and increasing income inequality is leading to social disruption and unrest.[71]

In China, as well as in Vietnam, as Gabriel Kolko points out in a postscript to his authoritative study of the Vietnam War, 'communist rulers are attempting to merge capitalist institutions and Leninist justifications for elite domination'.[72] In both countries, Professor Kolko argues, market-based reforms have created new categories of rich and poor, and widened the gap between town and country. Vietnam, he concludes, is quickly becoming a class society in the Western economic sense of the term.

The collapse of social democracy in the West

The move from social democracy to social liberalism
It is not, however, only 'actually existing socialism' that today has collapsed. Despite the absurd claims by many social democrats that the

collapse of the extreme form of socialist statism in Eastern Europe vindicated social democracy, in fact, the disintegration of the latter and of the related social-democratic version of the capitalist growth economy is no less conspicuous.

The main characteristic of the neoliberal consensus is the drastic alteration of the content of social democracy, that is, the radical shrinking, not just of statism in general, which we saw in Chapter 1, but of 'socialist' statism in particular. Thus, the fundamental structures of the neoliberal consensus are, above all, characterized by the minimization of social-democratic state interventionism; in other words, the type of interventionism which marked the post-war period of social-democratic consensus until about the mid-1970s. The central aims of social-democratic state interventionism were, as we saw in Chapter 1, first, to establish and maintain full employment; second, to create a comprehensive welfare state; and third, to achieve a fair distribution of income. The latter was supposed to be secured not only through the introduction of a 'social wage' system that was implied by the welfare state, but also through a progressive personal income tax system that would be used, in combination with public sector borrowing, to finance the welfare state.

In the event, the pursuit of these aims did have a relative success in improving the standard of living of the lower income strata, creating the image of a 'single-nation' society. Thus, at the ideological level, social democrats were able to claim that they had created a society which secured some social justice guarantees, without sacrificing every sense of individual freedom, that is, an 'actually existing capitalism with a human face' to counterbalance 'actually existing socialism'.

However, this type of socially credible capitalism – contrary to the claims of ex-Marxist intellectuals who have belatedly defected to social democracy – is either extinct (the United Kingdom), or is rapidly disappearing (Germany, Sweden, Norway). The abandonment of the state's commitment to full employment and the subsequent rise in unemployment and poverty, as well as the crippling of the welfare state, have led to the present '40 per cent society', which has taken the place of the 'single-nation' society. Today's social-democratic parties, rather than attempting to bring about drastic changes in the neoliberal market economy presently being established, realistically changed their ideology instead. As these parties therefore bear almost no relation at all to the traditional social-democratic parties of the 1950–75 period, they should more accurately be called 'social liberal' rather than social-democratic parties. In fact, the collapse of social democracy in the last decade or so has taken such dimensions that an old member of the 'New' Left in desperation asked:

Once, in the founding years of the Second International, [social democracy] was dedicated to the overthrow of capitalism. Then, it pursued partial reforms as gradual steps towards socialism. Finally, it settled for welfare and full employment within capitalism. If it now accepts a scaling down of one and giving up of the other, what kind of movement will it change into?[73]

This demeaning of the content of social democracy is due, as we have seen in Chapter 1, to fundamental changes in the structure of the market economy; changes that hardly permit the degree of statism in which the old social democracy flourished. Therefore, the substitution of social liberalism for social democracy is neither conjunctural nor temporary, as social liberals tend to assume. The present policies aiming at the constant curtailment of fiscal deficits and social expenditures, the dismantling of the welfare state and the abandonment of the full employment commitment are no longer a matter of choice; they are imposed on social liberals by the present degree of internationalization of the market economy, as it is expressed in particular by:

- the liberalized commodity markets which imply that growth depends to a significant extent on the continual improvement of competitiveness. This has reduced almost to zero the possibility of a state following a drastically different policy than its competitors on welfare state, employment, etc. As a recent study put it, today, 'labour standards are brought back into competition in trans-national markets. Consequently, trade acts to undermine the Keynesian welfare state and high labour standards linked to it'.[74]
- the liberalized capital markets which imply that the mere possibility of capital flight *en masse* has, to all intents and purposes, eliminated the political autonomy of the welfare state.[75]

So, under the structural constraints that the present internationalization of the market economy imposes and the electoral considerations prescribed by the change in class structure we saw in Chapter 1, the policies of social liberals are now hardly discernible from those of pure neoliberals. The same story repeats itself everywhere — from Australia, where the Labour Party had earnestly implemented privatization policies and taken drastic steps to cut budget deficits, to Sweden, where the social democrats, even before losing power in 1991, had embarked on a policy leading to the effective dismantlement of the employment system and the welfare state, which were the envy of social democrats around the world. Similarly in Norway 'the single most important goal of Labour's strategy, full employment, has been abandoned'.[76]

Let us consider, however, the case of Sweden in more detail, since it clearly demonstrates the causes of the collapse of social democracy. In

1990, Sweden's central bank was freed from its commitment to full employment and the crown was forced to follow the ECU's variations. The Swedish establishment, acknowledging that competitiveness played the primary role in economic growth, substituted the fight against inflation for the fight against unemployment as the main economic target. Within three years unemployment in Sweden increased more than five times (from 1.5 per cent in 1990 to 8.2 per cent in 1993). However, long before the commitment to full employment was abandoned, the institutional means for the attainment of this goal had already been dismantled. In fact, the institutional framework had begun to change as early as the mid-1980s, when the central bank abandoned controls on the other banks, thus beginning a process of market deregulation, comparable to the one observed by EU countries. The consequence was that the burden to control inflation fell exclusively onto the labour unions, which, however, were unable to press their members for low wages, particularly at a time of accelerating inflation caused by an uncontrollable bank credit creation.

As a study on the Swedish phenomenon[77] points out, deregulation was the main economic cause that destroyed the Swedish model. When, in the 1930s, Sweden established the statist model, the institutional framework of regulations and controls regarding the movement of capital, both within the country (bank borrowing, etc.) and between Sweden and other countries, was entirely different. Thus, the institutional framework at that time consisted of strict bank controls, severe foreign exchange regulations and a government committed to maintain domestic demand at a high level, in co-ordination with the central bank, which was committed to the full employment objective. Within this framework, the powerful Swedish labour unions were in a position to secure 'reasonable' wage raises, that is, not causing inflation. Today, however, the deregulation of money markets means that any attempt to base growth on government spending and budget deficits is doomed to fail, since it leads to speculative capital movements and currency instability. As a result, the Swedish model of social democracy has been falling to pieces recently, particularly since the autumn of 1992 when the neoliberal consensus was formalized. Then, in the middle of a serious crisis threatening the Swedish crown and the market economy itself, conservatives and social democrats agreed on a series of measures leading to a substantial downgrading of the welfare state.

The theoretical case in favour of social liberalism rests on an assortment of arguments according to which the present internationalized market economy is not necessarily incompatible with a 'redefined' social democracy. Some[78] argue, as we saw in Chapter 1, that the nation-state may still play an important role, not only in controlling the activities of nationally based multinational corporations, but also – in co-operation with other governments in the Triad – in controlling international markets. Others,[79] having abandoned the outdated Marxist class analysis, throw away the baby with the bath water and claim that today we live in a society of equality no longer characterized by vertical structures, where the government itself constitutes just one more organized social group, pursuing its own narrowly partisan interests! Still others, taking for granted the institutional framework set up by neoliberalism in the past decade (that is, the drastic enhancement of the market forces and competition, at the expense of social control on the economy), advance positions that hardly differ, in their essence, from the pure neoliberal positions. For instance, they reject the need to socialize the means of production (the British Labour Party in 1995 erased from its constitution the long-standing commitment to the socialization of the means of production), despite the fact that socialization has historically constituted a fundamental of socialism. Thus, a social-democrat sociology professor at the London School of Economics argues that 'what is of primary importance, is not the form of ownership, but the quality of control exercised by the state . . . that could ensure both quality of services and low prices'.[80] In this way, an obvious attempt is being made to evade the basic fact that no form of state control is possible, no matter how 'sophisticated', if it is in conflict with the fundamental principles of the market economy and the dynamics of competition.

No form of state control could, for instance, prevent a privatized public utility enterprise from discontinuing the supply of its services to those unable to pay. The British privatized water industry is a characteristic example. Since the privatization of the water companies and the drastic increase in water charges, there has been a dramatic increase in the incidence of water disconnections. Thus, between 1991 and 1993, water disconnections increased by 170 per cent. Disconnections were followed by a significant spread of disease, causing the reappearance of epidemics that had disappeared a century ago: cases of dysentery rose from 2756 in 1990 to 9935 in 1991 and 16,960 in 1992![81] Moreover, whereas the exclusive social control of public utility companies could ensure the reinvestment of their entire surplus in new technologies that would guarantee the modernization of their services, in the case of privatized companies it is taken for granted that a considerable portion of the surplus is bound for the shareholders' pockets.

Similarly, no form of state control could force the owners of companies covering basic needs to offer their services at prices affordable to the underclass, the thousands of unemployed, low-wagers and inactives that the institutional framework itself creates. In reality, as the British experience has shown, state control cannot even meet the aims set by social liberals, in particular low prices, for reasons related to the logic of the market[82] itself. Thus, a comparative study of telephone charges in 14 European countries showed that the privatization of British Telecom has not benefited individual customers. Britain was the only EU country where basic phone services were not in the hands of a state monopoly, and, at the same time, it was the EU country with the highest charges for local calls, yielding a profit margin of 74 per cent![83]

Finally, social liberals repudiate the universal character of the welfare state, blaming universality (the principle that social services are offered to every citizen irrespective of income and need) for the system's crisis.[84] Indeed, in their effort to support the case against universality, they do not even hesitate to invoke social justice, arguing that the universal system accentuates social inequalities because the middle classes are in a better position than the financially weaker – who are in real need – to benefit from social services (in education, health, insurance, etc.) According to the same view, the inequality of the system is further enhanced by the fact that the more affluent have many means at their disposal in order to evade direct taxation, through which these services are, mainly, financed.

However, though it is true that tax evasion flourishes among the affluent, this does not mean that there are no ways to tax them, on the basis not so much of their income – which is indeed easily concealed – but of their luxury consumption and property. Also, in regard to the argument that the middle classes can better claim social benefits, this constitutes the precise reason for which the abolition of the welfare state's universality would lead to a kind of charity 'safety net' for the destitute – exactly as was the case in turn of the century Europe. Thus, the various indirect ways proposed to abolish universality (which, typically, would force the affluent classes to return – usually through taxation – the value of the social services rendered them by the state) would merely provide an additional incentive for the privileged 'contended electoral majority' to withdraw from the *social* coverage of their basic needs, in favour of *private* coverage and to push professional politicians into further downgrading the quality of social services. It is therefore obvious that a system such as the one proposed by the European social liberals would easily end up resembling the American health and education system, which, with its extreme polarization between the high quality services provided by the private sector as compared to the misery of the state sector's services, must be the most socially unjust system among advanced industrialized countries. The only way in which the abolition of universality would not lead to such an outcome would be the parallel elimination of the private sector in the provision of social services – which is, of course, inconceivable in today's neoliberal market economy.

It is, therefore, obvious that the myth of the explosion in social expenditures is nurtured for other reasons and not because of the supposed financial crisis of the system, due to demographic or similar reasons. In Denmark, many hospitals have already established an age limit for admission (the present limit is 70), not because the proportion of elderly people in the population has increased, but because, in the framework of the neoliberal consensus, the number of hospital beds has been reduced by 25 per cent in the past 10 years.[85] Similarly, in Britain, it was recently revealed[86] that many hospitals have reduced the age limit for treatment of several diseases to 65! Therefore, the real reason for the savage cut in social expenditure is that, in the framework of an internationalized market economy, the higher a country's 'social wage' the lower its competitiveness. For EU countries in particular, in which the social wage has traditionally been – and still is – considerably higher than in the countries of the competitive economic regions (North America, the Far East), the problem has already become critical.

Universality, of course, does not eliminate inequalities, which are the main by-product of the market economy itself. However, within the present institutional framework (which is taken for granted by social liberals), universality helps to prevent the creation of a dual system, that is, a system in which the needs of a large portion (if not the majority) of the population are under-covered by a 'safety net', whereas the needs of the rest are over-covered by the private sector.

All the same, from a radical perspective, the real choice is not between a neoliberal system that *directly* abolishes universality and a social liberal system that *indirectly* achieves the same aim: both systems enhance the citizens' dependence on the state and/or the market in covering their basic needs. The real choice is between a system of social services that enhances this dependence and an alternative system that would strengthen the citizen's self-reliance and assign the system's control to the citizens themselves, through their communities.

The decline of social democracy in the European Union

The fate of social democracy in its cradle, Europe, is indicative of the failure of socialist statism's milder form. The substitution of the present neoliberal consensus for the social-democratic consensus is clearly discernible in the course followed by the European Union (EU), which by the end of the century may include most European states.

The process to create a single European market, which began in the 1950s with the Rome Treaty, accelerated in the past few years with the

Single Market Act that was put in effect in 1993, and the 1992 Maastricht Treaty, which replaced the Rome Treaty and will be in full effect by the end of the century. Accelerating the integration process was made imperative by the growing internationalization of the market economy and the intensifying competition with the other two parts of the Triad (North America and Japan). The supporters of the acceleration process maintained that, in the ultra-competitive internationalized market economy of the twenty-first century that is now dawning, only a market of continental dimensions could provide the security and the economies of scale needed for the survival of European capital. And indeed, during the past decade, the economic gap between the European countries and the rest of the Triad has widened considerably; a characteristic indication of the widening gap is the fact that the EU's world export share decreased by about 7 per cent between 1980 and 1994, the US's share fell by only 2 per cent, whereas the Japanese share increased by a massive 31 per cent.[87] The main cause of Europe's failure is the fact that its competitiveness has for long been lagging behind the competitiveness of the other regions. Thus, European competitiveness has fallen by 3.7 per cent since 1980, while US competitiveness has risen by 2.2 per cent and Japanese competitiveness (which for many years has been on top of the competitiveness league) increased by 0.5 per cent.[88]

The form that the integration has taken reflects, in various ways, the dominant neoliberal trend. Had, for instance, the acceleration of this process started in 1979 – when a European Commission's report was still foreseeing a European Union built on 'indicative planning' at the continental level[89] – a very different picture of European integration might have emerged. In fact, the European Commission's report was accurately reflecting the essence of the social-democratic consensus, which had just started breaking at the time. Its proposal amounted to a kind of 'European Keynesianism' that should have replaced national Keynesianism, which had already become – under conditions of increasingly free movement of capital – obsolete.

However, the collapse of the social-democratic consensus, following the flourishing of the neoliberal trend in the past decade, brushed aside the proposals for a European Keynesian strategy. Thus, the tendency that eventually prevailed in the EU was one that identified economic unification with the radical shrinking of national control on economic activity, without the parallel establishment of supra-national control – apart from monetary control. Consequently, the EU's executive power has been confined to creating a homogeneous institutional framework that allows for unimpeded entrepreneurial activity, while simultaneously providing for some minimal guarantees (those compatible with the neoliberal consensus requirements) regarding the protection of the environment and the social space.

The agreement for the single market rests on the main neoliberal assumption that the EU's economies are suffering from a lack of 'structural adjustment', that is, from structural deficiencies due to inflexibilities of the market mechanism and barriers to free competition. Such barriers that are mentioned in the Cecchini Report, on which the official ideology of the single market rests, are the various physical, technical and fiscal barriers that obstruct the flow of commodities, capital and labour.[90] As regards the capital market in particular, freeing this market from any controls, that is, the creation of conditions for the easy and unrestricted flow of capital between countries, is considered to be a basic requirement in this process. This is why the abolition of all foreign exchange controls has always been considered an essential condition for the 'Single European Market of 1993'.

However, the most important barriers are not the ones explicitly mentioned in the Report, but those implied by the emphasis it places on competition. These implied barriers are the 'institutional' barriers to free competition that had been introduced by the social-democratic consensus and which the agreement for the single market undertook to eliminate – a task brought to completion by the Maastricht Treaty. Such institutional barriers were the Keynesian type of state interventionism to secure full employment, the large welfare state that created fiscal problems, the labour unions' 'restrictive practices' and the public corporations, which did not always act on the basis of micro-economic criteria to raise economic efficiency. These barriers, as long as the degree of internationalization of the European economies was still relatively low, did not have a substantial negative effect on economic growth. However, once the growing internationalization of the economy and, in particular, the enlarged mobility of capital ceased to be compatible with the implementation of national macro-economic policies on Keynesian lines, their negative effect on growth became evident, as manifested by the stagflation crisis of the 1970s which hit particularly hard the European economies.[91]

Therefore, the Maastricht Treaty's basic aim was to attack the symptoms of these institutional barriers and, in particular, inflation and the huge public sector deficits caused by the expansion of statism. In keeping with this logic, the only economic criteria mentioned by the Treaty are stable prices, sound public finances and a sustainable balance of payments, whereas full employment and improving (or even maintaining) social welfare standards are not even mentioned as objectives! Article 3A of the Maastricht Treaty, which is presumably the most important article of the whole treaty, states clearly that:

> *The primary objective [of the single monetary and exchange rate policy] shall be to maintain price stability and, without prejudice to this objective, to support the general economic policies in the Community, in accordance with the principle of an open market economy with free competition . . . These activities of the Member States and the Community shall entail compliance with the following guiding principles: stable prices, sound public finances and monetary conditions and a sustainable balance of payments.*[92]

So, it is not surprising that Maastricht's 'social dimension' (which has been promoted by social democrats as a significant success) is, in fact, of very little significance, since it does not provide for any effective mechanisms – of equal significance, say, to the anti-inflation mechanisms it set up – in order to safeguard the right to work, the narrowing of inequalities, the eradication of poverty, etc. The treaty's Social Charter itself (for which the social democrats take great pride) aims at economic rather than social goals. Its real aim is to create homogeneous social structures within the EU so that the relatively affluent workers in the metropolitan countries can cope with the competition from peripheral countries, where the 'social wage' is much lower.[93] As one researcher observes on the subject, the Social Charter is not interested in people but in efficient and productive labour units. This is obvious, considering the fact that the Social Charter does not even mention the unemployed, those working at home caring for children, the elderly, the disabled, and that there is no provision in it with respect to the right to shelter, the right to education (apart from professional training), the right to health care for those out of work, or even general political rights.[94]

The Maastricht Treaty, therefore, simply confirmed the overtly neo-liberal character that the Community had begun to acquire with the Single Market Act. The improvement of competitiveness, through the reduction of inflation, remains the primary goal. To this goal belong the mechanisms to be established by the second and third phases of the Economic and Monetary Union (EMU). Thus, the EMU, as indeed the single market, signifies not the integration of peoples, or even the integration of states, but just the integration of free markets. Still, free markets mean not just the unimpeded movement of commodities, capital and labour, but also 'flexibility', that is, the elimination of barriers to the free formation of prices and wages, as well as overall curtailing of the state's control on economic activity. And this is, in fact, the essence of the neoliberal consensus that characterizes the EU's new institutional framework, i.e. the further marketization of the EU's economy. Thus, the aim of the new institutions is obvious: to maximize the freedom of organized capital, the concentration of which is facilitated in every way (as was attested, for instance, by the mass takeovers and mergers that took place in the late 1980s in view of the single market) and to minimize the freedom of organized labour, through any means available and, particularly, through the threat of unemployment.

It is indicative that national economic control on the level of economic activity and employment (which, in effect, is phased away through the abolition of fiscal freedom imposed by the 'convergence' criteria) is not replaced by a common European control of economic activity to secure full employment. Thus, whereas in the fight against inflation, which directly endangers the competitiveness and profit margins of European capital, there is provision even for the creation of a new supra-national institution (common central bank), the fight against unemployment is, in effect, left to the market forces, ensuring that, in the future, unemployment, underemployment and the consequent widening of inequality will be the rule. Of course, the possibility cannot be ruled out that a more flexible labour market might create new jobs, as happened in the USA in the last ten years or so. But the price to be paid to 'solve' the problem the 'American way' would be the acceleration in the rise of inequality and poverty.

Finally, the collapsing national welfare state is not being replaced by a common social policy that would guarantee the coverage of basic needs (health, education, social security, etc.) and a minimal income for all that would drastically reduce 'Euro-poverty'. Thus, in the interest of enhancing competitiveness to face America and Japan, the European ideal has degenerated today into a kind of 'Americanized Europe', where luxury and extreme poverty stand side by side and the comfortable life of the '40 per cent society' is a mirror image of the marginalization of the rest. Britain, which was the first European country to embark on neoliberal policies, now enshrined in the Maastricht Treaty, may be perhaps showing the future image of Europe. In Britain, the income share of the 10 per cent of the population at the bottom of the social pyramid fell, during the last years of Thatcherism, by over a third (from 4.65 per cent in 1979 to 3 per cent in 1991), whereas the share of the top 10 per cent rose by about 21 per cent (from 20.4 per cent to 25 per cent).[95]

Therefore, the institutional framework that is being established today in Europe consists of a model in which the continuation of growth depends on a process of further internationalizing its economy, through the destruction of local economic self-reliance and the continual expansion of exports to cope with a growing volume of imports. In this process, which takes place both between regions (the EU against the Japanese and American parts of the Triad) and inside each region, the victors will be the most competitive ones, who possess the production and technological bases that allow for the continual increase in productivity.

So, the social democrats are not to be blamed for 'betraying' the socialist ideals and consenting to the neoliberal content of the new Europe now emerging. Nor simply is the present recession to be blamed, which for some social liberals is due to the recessionary policies adopted by EU member states in their effort to meet the Maastricht convergence criteria. If we accept interpretations such as these, then the replacement of the neoliberal institutional framework is simply a matter for the 'true' socialists to gain power, who, in the context of economic recovery, would reinstate the institutional framework of the social-democratic consensus. In fact, there is no betrayal involved nor is the radical change of the institutional framework 'from within' possible in the future. In other words, if we take for granted what social democrats and their fellow travellers in the Green movement take for granted, that is, the internationalized market economy, as well as the need continually to improve competitiveness by freeing further the markets for commodities, capital and labour, then the content of social democracy must necessarily be the one supported today by social liberals.

The reason is that, within the framework of the internationalized economy, which constitutes the latest phase in the marketization process, the minimization of the state's social role does not constitute a choice but a precondition for European capital to compete effectively with Japanese and American capital, which, given the lack of a social-democratic tradition in the USA and the Far East, face much weaker institutional barriers. Today, therefore, social democracy has meaning neither at the national level nor at the supra-national level of post-Maastricht Europe, as we have seen in Chapter 1. Any attempt by European social democrats to change the present institutional framework in order to radically enhance the state's social role would make Europe less competitive than Japan or the USA and would result in a mass exodus of European capital. Also, a new, Europe-wide Keynesianism is not feasible, unless it was going to be combined with a self-reliant growth led by a highly protected internal market economy. But such a solution is in direct contradiction to the system's logic and dynamics. For the same reason, the proposals to renegotiate the Maastricht Treaty, in order to introduce social-democratic aims in the EU, are equally utopian in the negative sense of the word.

The issue, therefore, is not whether it will be neoliberal or, alternatively, social-liberal elites that will administer political power, with the TNCs administering economic power. The real issue is whether power will belong exclusively to the citizens and their communities, within an institutional framework entirely different from the present one. So, the true alternative solution would be to abandon the institutional framework of the market economy itself, whether social liberal or pure neoliberal, and to create a new institutional framework aiming to meet true needs, rather than the ones created by the market/growth economy. Such a system, based upon the political and cultural autonomy of the European regions, as well as their economic self-reliance, would be capable of providing a comfortable standard of living for all the citizens of a new and true European 'Community'.

A European 'social market': the new social-democratic myth

In the last few years a new 'vision' has been conquering European social democrats: the vision of a continent-wide 'social-market economy'. Thus, Michel Albert argues that 'capitalism is no monolithic structure, but an aggregate of tendencies out of which, in each case, two diverging currents, two broad "schools" emerge'.[96] These two models are what he calls 'the neo-American model' and the 'Rhineland' model of the social market (which includes primarily Germany, but also the Scandinavian countries and to some extent Japan). So, the author explicitly assumes the existence of differing national capitalisms which are characterized by different financial structures and – more important from our point of view – different systems of social protection: from almost complete lack of social protection in the USA, and rapidly diminishing social protection in the UK, to a significant level of social protection in Germany.

Thus, according to Albert, in the post-war period, a social market was created in Germany, a type of 'stakeholder' capitalism which reordered the institutional structure in a way that attempts to capture for the population as a whole the social returns of their contributions to production. A key element of this type of capitalism is its regulated labour market. Instead of the liberalized and deregulated labour markets, which thrive in the UK and the USA, the labour market in Germany still involves a lot of social controls: high redundancy payments, long notice periods, restrictive trade practices, long holidays, etc. Therefore, given the high economic performance of Germany in the post-war period up to the early 1990s, the conclusion could easily have been drawn that the Rhine model of capitalism not only is economically superior but should also be adopted because of its obvious social superiority.

However, it is now obvious that, in the competition between the USA/ UK model of liberalization and the Rhineland social market model, it is the former that is the clear winner. This is, of course, not surprising in view of the analysis in Chapter 1. The Rhine model is not a model for future capitalism but a remnant of the statist phase of marketization, which obviously cannot survive the present internationalization of the market

97

economy. Thus, as soon as marketization all over the world intensified in the 1990s, the Rhine model entered a period of crisis, giving the clear signal that no national capitalism is viable which has not 'homogenized' its social controls on the markets, in accordance with those of its competitors.

A clear indication of this crisis is given by such phenomena as the long-term slowdown in economic growth, the flight of capital and the explosion of unemployment. Thus, the average annual growth rate of the German GDP has fallen from 3.3 per cent in 1965–80 to 2.1 per cent in 1980–90.[97] Also, since 1990, German investment abroad has been five times higher than foreign direct investment in Germany.[98] In fact, shifting production to lower-cost countries has destroyed one million jobs in Germany since 1991.[99] This contributed significantly to unemployment, which rose by 50 per cent within the last three years whereas, at the same time, US unemployment fell by almost a quarter[100] (for the significance of the American 'solution' to the unemployment problem, see Chapter 4, p. 141). Today, official unemployment in Germany has already reached four million (10 per cent of the labour force) and the real number out of work may be nearer the six million mark.[101]

This crisis can be attributed directly to the various inflexibilities that the German 'social market' has introduced to the labour market, which meant that the unit labour cost in German manufacturing was the highest in the world in 1993: 50 per cent higher than in the USA and Japan, double that of Britain, five times higher than in the Asian Tiger countries and 46 times higher than in China or Russia![102] Furthermore, productivity growth in the early 1990s was falling significantly faster than wages, increasing unit wage costs even more and causing further deterioration in German competitiveness.[103] This development adversely affected both foreign investment, as companies were reluctant to invest in a high-cost country, and exports. Thus, Germany's share in world exports fell by 12 per cent in just four years according to the latest data.[104]

It is therefore not surprising that the German economic elite is already demanding the abolition of the system of collective bargaining and urging the strict implementation of the Maastricht criteria, so that the social market will wither away under the marketization pressures built into the system for European Monetary Union. At the time of writing (May 1996) the Kohl government has already announced a package of measures to liberalize the labour market and to restrict the welfare state, in effect signalling the end of the German 'social market' and, in the process, creating significant trade union unrest.

Still, European social democrats, faced with the fact that the adoption of the 'social market' is not feasible any more at the national level, are now proposing the Europeanization of the social market. Thus, Will Hutton argues:

> *The countries of EU together have the power to regulate the financial markets and control capital flows, and to play a part in compelling the US and Japan to regulate their relationship better, as part of a world deal . . . Europe can insist on common social rights across the continent so that MNCs cannot play one state off against another in an effort to bid down wages and working conditions. Europe can set common environmental standards and common rules of corporate governance, establishing the concept of the stakeholder company. Indeed social market Europe can formalise its rules and codes so that . . . a cooperative, more committed form of capitalism could be defended.*[105]

However, as it was argued in Chapter 1, the case for market controls can only stand if these controls are of the simple regulatory type. It is obvious that the USA and Japan will have no difficulty agreeing on the introduction of such controls that will make the functioning of the market economy smoother. But if these controls are of the type we called 'social controls in a narrow sense' – like the controls suggested in the above quote – neither Japan nor the USA will have any incentive (nor any pressure from their electorate given the weak social-democratic tradition in these countries) in agreeing to such controls that will deprive them of a significant comparative advantage over European, particularly German, industries. Therefore, the only possibility for introducing such controls at the European level will be through cutting off Europe from the internationalized market economy. In fact, the case for a 'new protectionism' to protect employment or the environment has gained ground lately among European socialists and environmentalists.[106]

But the fact that multinational corporations play a crucial role in the internationalized market economy and that their activities are not just intra-regional but inter-regional prescribes the fate of protectionist movements. Indicative is the fact that it was mainly inter-regional rather than intra-regional trade that benefited in the period of accelerating internationalization (1958–89). Thus, despite the growth in intra-regional trade, particularly within the EU, the largest increases in trade flows in the period 1958–89 were for inter-regional trade, i.e. trade between North America and the EU with Asia.[107] It is obvious that the grow-or-die dynamic of the market economy cannot be restricted within the boundaries of an economic bloc like those in Europe (the EU) or in North America (NAFTA), in the same way that it was never contained historically in the boundaries of the nation-state.

The demand for a new protectionism, if it takes for granted the existing

TOWARDS AN INCLUSIVE DEMOCRACY

framework of the market economy and competition (as is the case with protectionists either of the 'Left' – Green protectionists – or of the Right – Buchanan *et al.* in the USA, Goldsmith in the UK) is both a-historical and utopian, in the negative sense of the word. It is a-historical, because it ignores the structural changes that have led to the present neoliberal consensus and the internationalized market economy. It is utopian, because it disregards the fact that any effective attempt to intervene with the system of the market economy in the form of protectionism (either of the 'old' or the 'new' variety) is bound to be inefficient and non-competitive and, as such, against the logic and the dynamics of the system itself. Furthermore, it is utopian because it assumes that the 'greening' of trade, or the IMF/World Bank, or capitalism itself, is just a matter of persuading people about the evils of the free trade 'ideology'. Similarly, the proposal to minimize the role of the market ('the issue is not so much one of going "beyond" the market economy, but rather of reducing it to a minimal, functional level in our lives, putting it in its necessary place'[108]) easily brings to mind the wish to be 'a little pregnant'!

Why 'socialist' statism failed

In this last section I would like to argue that the fundamental reason for the historic failure of socialist statism in both its versions ('actually existing socialism' and social democracy) lies in its attempt to merge two incompatible elements: the 'growth' element, which expressed the logic of the market economy, with the social justice element, which expressed socialist ethics. This is so because whereas the growth element, as part of a growth economy, implies the concentration of economic power (whether as a consequence of the functioning of the market mechanism, or as a built-in element of central planning), the social justice element is inherently linked to the dispersion of economic power and to equality, i.e. to economic democracy. Thus, socialist statism, in its effort to make the benefits of growth accessible to everyone and lend universal meaning to Progress – which was identified with growth – attempted to create a socialist growth economy, disregarding the fundamental interdependence of growth and the concentration of economic power.

Moreover, the attempt to merge the growth element with the social justice element created a fundamental incompatibility between the ends and means. Thus, whereas the capitalist growth economy constituted the inevitable consequence of the market economy and, therefore, the means (market economy) and the end (growth economy) were perfectly compatible in this case, in the case of socialist statism, the end (growth economy) was not compatible with the means (social-democratic statism/central planning). In fact, the greater the degree of statism (as in the case of central planning), the greater the incompatibility between the means and ends, contributing even more to the failure of the system.

The role of growth, competitiveness and efficiency

The fact that both the capitalist growth economy and socialist statism shared the same goal, that is, economic growth, meant that the same principles played a decisive part in the organization of production and in economic and social life in general, irrespective of whether the production motive was private profit or some kind of 'collective' profit. This becomes obvious by the fact that the principles of economic efficiency and competitiveness mark both types of socialist statism. Thus, as regards economic efficiency, both the 'socialist' growth economy and the social–democratic version of socialist statism adopt it as a necessary condition for maximizing growth. Also, as regards competitiveness, it is either a direct consequence of an enterprise's integration into the *market economy* (nationalized industries in the case of social democracy), or an indirect consequence of a socialist growth economy's integration in the *world growth economy*.

In this problematic, it is hard to accept Gunder Frank's assertion that the countries of 'actually existing socialism' did not have any other choice but to submit to the competitiveness principle.[109] Competitiveness was not imposed on these countries by their integration into the *world market,* but because of their competitive participation in the *world growth economy* (let's catch and overtake America). In fact, the integration of these countries into the world market economy was never complete. This is shown, first, by the fact that Eastern Europe's trade with the West has historically represented a very small proportion of world trade: Eastern Europe's trade was less than 5 per cent of the pre-war world trade and about 10 per cent of the post-war trade.[110] Second, the fact that their internal price structure was very different from that of the world market has become evident after the collapse of 'actually existing socialism' and the very difficult problems that the Eastern European countries faced in adjusting to world price structures.

In more detail, with regard, first, to the principle of economic efficiency, this principle had always been the standard of assessing success with respect to the aim of developing the forces of production in the 'socialist' growth economy. The objective in designing technology and organizing production was, on the one hand, to maximize efficiency and, on the other, to ensure the maintenance and reproduction of hierarchical structures. This is the reason why a modern Soviet factory, even in Lenin's times (with his encouragement), in no way differed – in terms of internal functioning, hierarchical organization of production, etc. – from an equivalent capitalist one. This, of course, simply reflected the socialist-statist belief in the 'neutrality' of technology. Thus, in exactly the same way as technology was considered by socialist-statists as a neutral *means*, that could be used by *any* social system to achieve a specific aim, efficiency was also held as a neutral means, in achieving the growth objective. Moreover, the fact that the socialist growth economy adopted the same definition for economic efficiency as the capitalist growth economy (that is, a definition based upon narrow techno-economic criteria which did not include the ecological cost of growth) implied that the ecological consequences of growth were bound to be serious. Thus, despite the fact that in the socialist growth economy the growth process was not combined with the marketization of the economy, as in the West, it still resulted in significant ecological damage (in fact, greater than in the West, due to the lower level of technology in the East).

With regard, second, to the principle of competitiveness, this principle remained intact in Western social democracy, which simply tried to 'marry' statism with capitalist competition. For instance, nationalized industries never ceased to be a part of the market economy and were motivated in various ways to be competitive with other industries, private or public, domestic or foreign. In 'actually existing socialism' as well, despite the occasional official attacks against individualism, the material incentives (to produce 'more' and to produce 'better') to which these countries had long ago resorted as a substitute for socialist self-management, were but the confirmation of an implicit principle of competitiveness. So, the competitiveness principle, which is the basic organization principle of the market economy, was never abandoned as an explicit aim by Western social democracy, or as an implicit aim in 'actually existing socialism', despite the fact that both these two versions of socialist statism represented (each to a different degree, of course) an attempt to transcend the institutional framework of the market economy. However, competitiveness is incompatible with the economic self-reliance of social individuals and their communities, leading to an increasing division of labour and specialization and, subsequently, to the concentration of economic power in the hands of the elites controlling the economic process.

One may therefore argue that from the moment both versions of socialist statism showed that, in the last instance, they rested on the same fundamental principles as the market economy did and that they were, inevitably, leading to the reproduction of similar hierarchical structures, the countdown leading to the collapse of socialist statism itself, as well as the ideologies on which it rested (Marxism/Keynesianism), had begun. This was due to both subjective and objective factors.

The subjective factors refer to the widespread realization of the failure of socialist statism to lead to a new form of social organization, a new model of social life that would transcend the principles characterizing the system of the market economy. The economic crisis of socialist statism, combined with the inevitable enhancing of the bureaucratization of social life (inevitable, in the context of a form of socialism founded on the state and its bureaucracy), have been the essential factors that led to the credibility crisis of the socialist project in its statist form. For the average citizen it was obviously a better bet to choose the 'real thing', which might better 'deliver' in terms of consumer goods, rather than keep supporting a system that not only was failing in its socialist promises but in certain important aspects was a bad imitation of the market economy.

The objective factors refer to the fact that, as already mentioned, the pursuit of efficiency and competitiveness, which the growth objective implies, fundamentally contradicts the socialist aims. It is obvious that the criteria of social justice, on which the socialist aims are based, are much broader than the narrow economic criteria that define economic efficiency and competitiveness and as such are incompatible with them.

The conflict between the growth economy and socialist ethics

To conclude, as regards, first, 'actually existing socialism', its failure was due to the fundamental incompatibility between the requirements of the growth economy and the functioning of a centrally planned economy. Whereas in a market economy the market forces are comparatively free to secure the degree of concentration which is necessary for growth, in a planned economy the distorting interventions of bureaucrats and planning technocrats in the growth process, aiming at the contradictory merging of growth with social justice (for example, in the form of 'hidden unemployment'), inevitably led to economic inefficiency. Similarly, in a bureaucratically organized economic system, it was practically impossible to introduce new technologies and products, particularly in the consumer goods sector where a decentralized information system is a necessity.

From this viewpoint, one may assess as partly valid and partly insupportable Gunder Frank's thesis[111] that the history of the world system shows that as long as competition constitutes the basic 'fact of life' in the world, then 'socialism in one country' will not be possible and that 'world' socialism would not differ significantly from the present world. It is valid to the extent that it stresses that when an economy is part of the world market economy, then socialism (in the form of socialist statism – and, I would add, in the form of the autonomous civil society) is indeed not possible. This is why, as I will try to show in Chapter 6, the realization of the liberatory project is only possible within the framework of a new type of economy, which would be neither another version of the market economy, nor of the growth economy.

At the same time, Gunder Frank's thesis is insupportable when it claims that 'the *same* world system, and its essential structure and "mode" of operation, goes back for at least 5000 years'. The market economy, as a self-regulating *system*, where the basic economic decisions are taken through the market mechanism, is hardly 200 years old, as we saw in Chapter 1, and as has been convincingly shown, mainly by Polanyi.[112] Therefore, the fact that markets and competition preceded the Industrial Revolution does not negate the equally significant fact that their role in the past was marginal to the economic process. Thus, in the period before the emergence of the market economy, the forces of competition did not play any significant role, as far as price formation is concerned, nor were prices the basic way of allocating economic resources. The question, therefore, that arises is whether Gunder Frank, in (rightly) rejecting the Marxist theory of history, throws away the baby with the bath water and (wrongly) rejects any other interpretation of history, levelling out all the crucial differences between the present market society and previous societies, just because they all share some form of market.

Finally, as regards social democracy, it was the same attempt to merge growth with social justice that led to the collapse of the social-democratic consensus. The basic features of the social-democratic consensus also aimed at the decentralization of economic power – an aim that inherently contradicts the logic and dynamics of the market economy. To the extent therefore that the social-democratic consensus was successful in its aim, and brought about a change in the social balance of power, it was no longer compatible with the growing internationalization of the market economy. In this sense, the present predominance of the neoliberal consensus and the consequent concentration of economic power constitute the natural 'reaction' of the growth economy to the social-democratic 'action' and, at the same time, a stage in the completion of the historical process of marketizing the economy and society.

Notes

1. See Takis Fotopoulos, *Dependent Development: The Case of Greece* (Athens: Exantas Press, 1985, 1987), Ch. A (in Greek).
2. The usual definition of *economic efficiency* is in terms of *technical efficiency* (input minimization or output maximization for any given combination of inputs), *production efficiency* (which implies that no reallocation of resources could increase output) and *exchange efficiency* (which implies that no further exchanges could improve consumer welfare). However, this supposedly 'neutral' definition of efficiency assumes away distributional aspects so that it is perfectly possible for a particular allocation of resources to be 'efficient'

and, at the same time, not capable of meeting adequately (or not at all) the needs of many citizens.

3. Cornelius Castoriadis, *Philosophy, Politics, Autonomy* (Oxford: Oxford University Press, 1991), p. 184.

4. Adam Smith, *The Wealth of Nations* (Harmondsworth: Penguin, 1970), p. 104.

5. As Sean Sayers observes, drawing from Marx's *Capital*, Vol. 3, and *Grundrisse*, 'Marx regards the immense expansion of production to which capitalism has led as its progressive and "civilising" aspect'; Sean Sayers, 'Moral values and progress', *New Left Review*, No. 204 (Mar.-Apr. 1994), pp. 67–85.

6. John Grahl referring to the study by Elman Altvater, *The Future of the Market* (London: Verso, 1993), *New Left Review*, No. 214 (Nov.-Dec. 1995), p. 155.

7. See James O'Connor, 'Capitalism, nature, socialism', *Society and Nature*, Vol. 1. No. 2 (1992), pp. 174–202.

8. Murray Bookchin, *The Philosophy of Social Ecology* (Montreal: Black Rose, 1995), p. 142.

9. Martin J. Conyon, 'Industry profit margins and concentration: evidence from UK manufacturing', *International Review of Applied Economics*, Vol. 9, No. 3 (1995), p. 288.

10. P. Nolan and K. O'Donnell, 'Restructuring and the politics of industrial renewal: the limits of flexible specialisation' in A. Pollert (ed.) *Farewell to Flexibility?* (Oxford: Blackwell, 1991), p. 161.

11. Tim Lang and Colin Hines, *The New Protectionism: Protecting the Future Against Free Trade* (London: Earthscan, 1993), p. 34.

12. See, e.g., Pëtr Kropotkin, *Fields, Factories and Workshops Tomorrow* (London: Hutchinson, 1899); and the additional data and comments by Colin Ward in the 1974 edition of the book (London: Allen & Unwin). See also Kropotkin, *The Conquest of Bread* (Harmondsworth: Penguin, 1972), Ch. 16.

13. Pëtr Kropotkin, *Fields, Factories and Workshops Tomorrow*, pp. 32–4, 41–4.

14. P.J. McGowan and B. Kurdan, 'Imperialism in world system perspective', *International Studies Quarterly*, Vol. 25, No. 1 (March 1981), pp. 43–68.

15. Paul Bairoch, *The Economic Development of the Third World Since 1900* (London: Methuen, 1975), pp. 190–2.

16. Data calculated from the World Bank's *World Development Report 1994* and *World Development Report 1981* (Washington, DC: World Bank).

17. International Monetary Fund, *International Financial Statistics* (various years); World Bank, *World Development Report 1995*, Table 13.

18. Paul Hirst and Grahame Thompson, *Globalization in Question* (Cambridge: Polity Press, 1996), Tables 3.2, 3.3, 3.4.

19. Mike Campbell, *Capitalism in the UK* (London: Croom Helm, 1981), Table 3.2; and John Allen and Doreen Massey (eds), *Restructuring Britain: The Economy in Question* (London: Sage, 1988), Diagram 5.1.

20. Phillip Armstrong *et al.*, *Capitalism Since World War II* (London: Fontana, 1984), pp. 216–18.

21. John Allen and Doreen Massey (eds), *Restructuring Britain: The Economy in Question*, pp. 192–200.

22. Paul Hirst and Grahame Thompson, *Globalization in Question*, p. 53.

23. See, for instance, the interview of Alvin Toffler in *The Guardian* (13 Jan. 1996).

24. Michael Carley and Ian Christie, *Managing Sustainable Development* (Minneapolis: University of Minnesota Press, 1993), p. 50.
25. Andrew McLaughlin, 'What is deep ecology?', *Capitalism, Nature, Socialism,* Vol. 6/3, No. 23 (Sept. 1995).
26. World Bank, *World Development Report 1995,* Table 2.
27. Paul Hirst and Grahame Thompson, *Globalization in Question,* p. 163.
28. For a comprehensive analysis of this process, see the work of Murray Bookchin and, in particular, his works *Remaking Society* (Montreal: Black Rose, 1990), *The Ecology of Freedom* (Montreal: Black Rose, 1991) and *From Urbanization to Cities* (London: Cassell, 1995).
29. V. Lenin, *The State and Revolution* (Moscow: Foreign Languages Publishing House, 1917), p. 30.
30. G.P. Maximoff, *The Political Philosphy of Bakunin* (New York: The Free Press, 1953), p. 287.
31. See, e.g. Michael Bleaney, *The Rise and Fall of Keynesian Economics* (London: Macmillan, 1985), esp. Ch. 12.
32. See, e.g. Paul Sweezy, *The Theory of Capitalist Development* (New York: Monthly Review Press, 1942), pp. 87–92.
33. Michael Ellman, *Socialist Planning* (Cambridge: Cambridge University Press, 1979), pp. 267–8.
34. *The Guardian* (26 Nov. 1992).
35. Michael Barratt-Brown, *Models in Political Economy* (Harmondsworth: Penguin, 1984), p. 144.
36. A. Szymanski, 'The socialist world system', in *Socialist States in the World System,* C.K. Chase-Dunn (ed.) (London: Sage Publications, 1982), Table 2.3.
37. For an exposition of the liberal view, outside the extremist Right see, for example, the work of the prominent British sovietologist Alec Nove, *The Economics of Feasible Socialism* (London: Allen & Unwin, 1983). For a Left socialist-statist critique of Nove's work, see E. Mandel, 'In defence of socialist planning', *New Left Review,* No. 159 (Sept.-Oct. 1986).
38. Alec Nove, 'The Soviet economy: problems and prospects', *New Left Review,* No. 119 (Jan.-Feb. 1980), pp. 3–19.
39. Such views are expressed, e.g. by Cornelius Castoriadis, *Political and Social Writings* (Minneapolis: University of Minnesota Press, 1988), Vols 1-2, as well as by the East German Green, Rudolf Bahro – at the time he had not yet adopted the case for the 'Green Adolf' (see Janet Biehl, 'Ecology and the modernization of fascism in the German ultra-right', *Society and Nature,* Vol. 2, No. 2 (1994) – R. Bahro, *The Alternative in Eastern Europe* (London: Verso, 1978).
40. See the interview given by Alexander Yakovlev to *The Guardian* (20 Aug. 1991) and also his book, *The Fate of Marxism in Russia* (Yale: Yale University Press, 1993).
41. Leon Trotsky, *The Revolution Betrayed* (New York: Merit, 1965).
42. Peter Gowan, 'Neo-liberal theory and practice for Eastern Europe', *New Left Review,* No. 213 (Sept.-Oct. 1995), p. 40.
43. Jeffrey Sachs, 'What is to be done?', *The Economist,* 13 January 1990.
44. Peter Gowan, 'Neo-liberal theory and practice', pp. 6–7.
45. Peter Gowan, 'Neo-liberal theory and practice', p. 24.
46. J.M.C. Rollo and J. Stern, 'Growth and trade prospects for Central and

Eastern Europe', *The World Economy*, No. 199 (quoted by Peter Gowan, 'Neo-liberal theory and practice', p. 55).

47. Indicatively, Yeltsin and the Russian central bank, in order to receive a 1.5 billion dollar loan, had to promise the International Monetary Fund that they would drastically reduce state subsidies of Russian exports. All this, while the EU had refused to reduce tariffs on Eastern products, causing a further widening of the deficit in the Russian trade balance; *The Guardian* (26 May 1993).

48. *The Guardian* (24 Mar. 1993).

49. *The Guardian* (16 Mar. 1994).

50. OECD, *Integrating Emerging Market Economies into the International Trading System* (Paris: OECD, 1994) (quoted by Peter Gowan, 'Neo-liberal theory and practice', p. 17).

51. *The Guardian* (3 Dec. 1994).

52. Quoted by Peter Gowan, 'Neo-liberal theory and practice', p. 22.

53. World Bank, *World Bank Development Report 1995*, Table 26. According to a recent study, the crude death rate in Russia has gone up from 11.4 in 1991 to 14.4 in 1993 and 16.2 in the first quarter of 1994 (Michael Ellman, 'The increase in death and disease under "Katastroika"', *Cambridge Journal of Economics*, No. 18 (1994), p. 349).

54. *The Guardian* (16 Nov. 1992).

55. *The Guardian* (7 July 1993).

56. See Markus Mathyl, 'Is Russia on the road to dictatorship?', *Green Perspectives*, No. 34 (Dec. 1995).

57. Alexander Buzgalin and Andrei Kolganov, 'Russia: the rout of the neo-liberals', *New Left Review*, No. 215 (Jan.-Feb. 1996), p. 132.

58. Sheldon Wolin, 'What revolutionary action means today' in *Dimensions of Radical Democracy*, edited by Chantal Mouffe (London: Verso, 1995, 1992), p. 241.

59. B. Cumings, 'The abortive abertura', *New Left Review*, No. 173 (Jan.-Feb. 1989), pp. 5–32.

60. P. Bachrach, *The Theory of Democratic Elitism* (Boston, 1967), pp. 8–9.

61. Paul Bowles and Xiao-Yuan Dong, 'Current successes and future challenges in China's economic reforms', *New Left Review*, No. 208 (Nov.-Dec. 1994), Table 1.

62. W. Byrd, *The Market Mechanism and Economic Reform in China* (New York: Armonk, 1991), p. 219 (quoted by Paul Bowles and Xiao-Yuan Dong, 'Current successes and future challenges in China's economic reforms').

63. World Bank, *World Development Report 1991*, Fig. 1.1.

64. Richard Smith, 'The Chinese road to capitalism', *New Left Review*, No. 199, (May-June 1993), p. 69.

65. Richard Smith, 'The Chinese road to capitalism', pp. 96–7.

66. Paul Hirst and Grahame Thompson, *Globalization in Question*, p. 108. This conclusion is also supported by other studies which confirm that the spatial distribution of income has certainly become more unequal over the reform period: see, e.g., C. Brammal and M. Jones, 'Rural income inequality in China since 1978', *Journal of Peasant Studies*, Vol. 21, No. 1 (Oct. 1993).

67. Andrew Higgins quoting Hu Angang, a prominent Chinese economist at the Chinese Academy of Social Sciences, *The Guardian* (30 May 1996).

68. Simon Long quoting an article in the Chinese daily *Economic Information Daily, The Guardian* (8 Jan. 1994).
69. Catherine Field, *The Observer* (13 Feb. 1994).
70. Richard Smith, 'The Chinese road to capitalism', p. 95.
71. Paul Bowles and Xiao-Yuan Dong, 'Current successes and future challenges in China's economic reforms', p. 50.
72. Gabriel Kolko, *Anatomy of a War* (New York: The New Press, 1994) quoted by John Gittings, *The Guardian* (13 Jan. 1995).
73. 'Introduction', in P. Anderson and P. Camiller (eds), *Mapping the West European Left* (London: Verso, 1994), pp. 15–16.
74. Andrew Martin, 'Labour, the Keynesian welfare state, and the changing international political economy' in Richard Stubbs and Geoffrey R.D. Underhill, *Political Economy and the Changing Global Order* (London: Macmillan, 1994), p. 70.
75. Eric Helleiner, 'From Bretton Woods to global finance: a world turned upside-down' in Richard Stubbs and Geoffrey R.D. Underhill, *Political Economy,* p. 173.
76. Jan Fagerberg *et al.* 'The decline of social-democratic state capitalism in Norway', *New Left Review,* No. 181, May/June 1990, p. 88.
77. See Tom Notermans' article in the June 1993 issue of *Politics and Society.*
78. Paul Hirst and Grahame Thompson, *Globalization in Question.*
79. See, e.g., Martin Jacques, *Sunday Times* (18 July 1993).
80. See, e.g., Nicos Mouzelis, 'Four problems regarding modernization', *To Vima* (25 July 1993) (in Greek).
81. *The Guardian* (20 Dec. 1993).
82. See Will Hutton, *The Guardian* (18 Aug. 1993).
83. *European Consumers Bureau Report*/The *Guardian* (13 Feb. 1992).
84. See, e.g., the article of the LSE Professor Nicos Mouzelis, 'The future of the welfare-state', in the Athens daily *Eleftherotypia* (1–2 Jan. 1994).
85. *Le Monde* (8 Feb. 1994).
86. BBC, April 1994.
87. International Monetary Fund, *Financial Statistics* (various years).
88. *World Economic Forum* (1993).
89. See the European Commission, *The Challenges Ahead – A Plan for Europe* (Brussels, 1979).
90. Paolo Cecchini, *1992: The European Challenge* (London: Wildwood House, 1988), p. 4.
91. The average annual GDP growth rate of important European economies like Germany, the UK and Italy was significantly less than 3 per cent in the 1970s, whereas that of the USA was over 3 per cent and Japan's growth rate exceeded 5 per cent (World Bank, *World Development Report 1981,* Table 2).
92. European Commission, *Treaty on European Union* (Maastricht, 1992).
93. D. Piachaud, Professor at LSE, also reaches a similar conclusion; *The Guardian* (13 Nov. 1991).
94. F. Weber, 'Impact of the Social Charter', *Europe 1992* (Dublin, 1991), pp. 34, 37.
95. Alissa Goodman and Steven Webb, *For Richer, For Poorer* (London: Institute of Fiscal Studies, 1994), Fig. 2.3.
96. Michel Albert, *Capitalism Against Capitalism* (London: Whurr, 1993), p. 5.

97. World Bank, *World Development Report 1995*, Table 2.
98. Norbert Walter, 'German social market economy needs new lease of life', *The Guardian* (13 February 1995).
99. Mark Frankland, *The Observer* (24 December 1995).
100. German unemployment rose from 5.6 per cent in 1991 to 8.4 per cent in 1994 whereas US unemployment was reduced from 7.4 per cent in 1992 to 5.6 per cent in 1995 (European Commission, *Eurostatistics* (November 1995); OECD, *Economic Outlook*, No. 58 (December 1995)).
101. Ian Traynor, *The Guardian*, 25 January 1996.
102. David Kerr, 'British manufacturing is starting to score at the expense of inflexible European competitors', *The Guardian* (16 January 1995).
103. Indicatively, according to the latest *World Competitiveness Yearbook* (London: International Institute for Management Development, 1996) Germany fell from 6th to 10th place in the league of competitiveness between 1995 and 1996, whereas the USA remained at the top.
104. The German export share fell from 11.7 per cent in 1989 to 10.3 per cent in 1993; World Bank, *World Development Report,* 1991 and 1995, Table 13.
105. Will Hutton, *The State We're In* (London: Jonathan Cape, 1995), pp. 315–16.
106. Tim Lang and Colin Hines, *The New Protectionism: Protecting the Future Against Free Trade* (London: Earthscan, 1993).
107. Marc L. Busch and Helen V. Miller, 'The future of the international trading system: international firms, regionalism and domestic politics' in Richard Stubbs and Geoffrey R.D. Underhill, *Political Economy and the Changing Global Order* (London: Macmillan, 1994), Table 1.
108. Jeremy Seabrook, *The Myth of the Market* (Devon: Green Books, 1990) p. 33.
109. André Gunder Frank, 'Is real world socialism possible?', *Society and Nature,* Vol. 2, No. 3 (1994).
110. See Alan A. Brown and Egon Neuberger, *International Trade and Central Planning* (Berkeley: University of California Press, 1968), Table 1, and, also, *World Development Report* (World Bank, various years).
111. André Gunder Frank, 'Is real world socialism possible?'
112. See Karl Polanyi, *The Great Transformation* (Boston: Beacon Press, 1944). For a recent discussion of Polanyi's thesis, see also Kari Polanyi-Levitt (ed.), *The Life and Work of Karl Polanyi* (Montreal: Black Rose, 1990).

CHAPTER 3

The Growth Economy and the South

In this chapter I argue that the 'development problem' is not how to spread the growth economy of the North more efficiently to the South, as suggested by conventional approaches (liberal/Marxist/dependency/regulation theories). In fact, it is argued that it is the very spread of the growth economy to the South which is the main cause of the economic, social and ecological crises that affect the majority of the global population. The grow-or-die dynamic was bound to lead the market economy to spread itself all over the world, after its emergence in Europe, two centuries ago. But, whereas the indigenous market economy in the North led to the creation of a type of growth economy which thrives on a '40 per cent society', the imported market economy in the South led to a much more uneven development than in the North and to a bad copy of the latter's growth economy. So, the multidimensional crisis that affects the North today is mirrored by an economic, social and ecological near-catastrophe in the South.

The first part of this chapter begins with a discussion of the failure of the growth economy in the South and an assessment of the mythology about the economic 'miracles' of East Asia. This is followed, in the second part, by a discussion of the conventional approaches to development and their interpretations concerning the causes of the South's failure. These approaches are subject to the basic criticism that they all take for granted not only the desirability of the growth economy, as a general means to improve human welfare, but also the feasibility of its universalization. Although some of the radical approaches cast doubt on the possibility of the growth economy being universalized, they do so only with respect to its capitalist version.

In the final part of the chapter, after a brief discussion of the ecological implications of development, it is argued that the failure of the South is not, in fact, a problem of why the importation of the growth economy was not successful, not even a problem of 'development' at all, but a problem of democracy. The fact that the majority of the earth's population, mostly in the South but increasingly in the North as well, cannot satisfy even its basic needs is a clear indication that the dilemma 'growth economy' or 'steady-state' economy is a false one. North and South, which should be redefined to take into account the global character of today's market/ growth economy, share the same problem: how to create new political, economic and social structures securing an inclusive democracy that covers the collectively defined social, economic and cultural needs.

The failure of the growth economy in the South

The spreading of the growth economy

The post-war process of decolonization led to political 'independence' in the South; it also led to the spreading of the 'growth economy' – a process that continued and expanded the South's marketization initiated by colonialism. Depending on the class alliances formed in the newly independent countries of the South, the growth economy, following a similar process to that in the North, has taken the form of either a *capitalist growth economy* or a *'socialist' growth economy*. At the same time, the *growth ideology* and the implied ideology of domination over Nature have become the dominant ideologies in the South. The growth ideology, in a similar way as in the North, complements the *liberal* ideology in the capitalist growth economy and the *socialist* ideology in the socialist growth economy. However, despite the fact that communist parties still monopolize *political* power in some parts of the South (notably, China, Vietnam, Laos, etc.) the socialist growth economy in the South, as defined in Chapter 2, is effectively being phased out.

The spreading of the growth economy in the countries of the South has been a dismal failure. This failure has been basically due to the fact that the growth economy in the South did not develop indigenously, but was, instead, the outcome of two processes:

(a) the penetration of the market economy system, which was aggressively encouraged by the colonial elites; and
(b) the consequent emergence of the growth economy, which was 'imported' by the newly formed local elites in the post World War II period.

The failure of the growth economy in the South becomes obvious if we consider the present degree of concentration of world production in the North. We may roughly define the North as the set of those countries that are members of the Organization for Economic Co-operation and Development (OECD) which the World Bank classifies as 'high income economies', namely, the USA, Canada, Japan, Australia, New Zealand, the European Union (apart from Greece and Portugal), Switzerland and Norway. Today, the North, where only about 14 per cent of the world's population live, produces almost 79 per cent of the world's output and accounts for 75 per cent of the world's exports.[1]

Thus, the spreading of the growth economy in the South not only has failed to improve the welfare of most of the people there, but it also has led to a dramatic widening of the North–South divide. If, for instance, we use the typical measure that supporters of the growth economy use (i.e. the per capita gross national product), the growing gap between the North and the South becomes obvious. In 1978, the per capita income in the North was 40 times higher than that of the low-income countries in the South (where about 56 per cent of the world population lives) and six-and-a-half times higher than the per capita income of the middle-income countries in the South (where the remaining 30 per cent of the global population lives). By 1993 the gap had drastically widened: the per capita income of the North was almost 61 times higher than that in the low-income countries in the South and over nine times higher than the income of the middle-income countries. That means that within a relatively short period, the last 15 years, the North–South gap has increased by something between 34 per cent (North–low-income countries) and 31 per cent (North–middle-income countries)![2]

The above data imply that the system of the market economy is not *inherently* capable of transforming the South's economy into a type similar to the North's growth economy, that is, a type that produces a large consumerist middle class which extends fully to about 40 per cent of the population and partially to another 30 per cent (which is insecure but definitely in a better position than the vast majority of the population in the South). An indication of this fact are the poverty figures in the North and the South. As regards the South, even the World Bank, not a champion for the 'wretched of the Earth', had to admit that, in 1985, one-third of the total population in the South was poor.[3] On the other hand, in the North the poverty figure was about 13 per cent. Thus, the average poverty rate in the European Community (excluding Greece and Portugal) was 13.6 per cent in 1985.[4] Similarly, in the USA 13 per cent of the population lived below the official poverty line in 1988.[5] These data (the most recent comparative data available) refer to the middle of the last decade when the neoliberal consensus was not yet universal. Since then, all indications are that the situation has changed for the worse.

This means that the famous 'trickle-down effect' (i.e. that economic growth, in time, will generate additional national wealth that will then trickle down to all), even if it did (partially) work in the North, certainly is not working in the South. As Ted Trainer points out:

> [T]he 'indiscriminate growth and trickle down' approach to development has been accompanied by significant improvements in average life expectancy, infant mortality, literacy and GNP over the last few decades. But the distributions of the benefits have been extremely uneven ... A recent survey of the literature revealed about 120 statements to the effect that development has done little or nothing to improve the economic living standards of the poorest 40% or more of the Third World. Hardly any statements to the contrary were found.[6]

Indicatively, 10 per cent of the population in the poorest countries of the South take more than 33 per cent of the total income.[7] Also, according to the World Bank, one-fifth of the population in the South generally receives, on the average, almost half the total income.[8] And, of course, the evidence of the past two decades indicates that very little trickle-down has ever taken place. It has been estimated, for instance (on the basis of growth rates achieved between 1965–84, which include some of the best years of capitalism), that it will take over 300 years for the 28 poorest countries to rise from their present per capita average income to just *half* of the *present* average of the rich Western countries.[9]

But even in the North, the trickle-down effect has recently become significantly weaker than in the past, not just because of the recession, but mainly because of the intensification of the marketization process within the neoliberal market economy, which has further widened income inequality. This implies, as we shall see in the last section of this chapter, that a new 'North–South' divide, cutting across the traditional boundaries of the North and the South, has already been set into operation. In Britain, for instance, official data from the Department of Social Security (which for the first time included a breakdown of how all income groups fared during the growth process of the period 1979–1991/92) are revealing about the significance of the trickle-down effect. The poorest tenth of the population suffered a 17 per cent fall in real income, the people in the second decile saw no increase at all in their income, whereas the two top deciles had an increase in real income of 46 per cent and 62 per cent respectively. Overall, average incomes increased by 36 per cent during this period, but 70 per cent of the population had a below average increase in their income![10]

Of course, this does not mean that development towards a growth economy has not taken place in the South. It certainly has. In fact, today, a process of economic decentralization is in full swing within the world market economy system – a process in which financial and technological factors play a crucial role. Trans-national corporations (TNCs) now have the financial and technological capability of transferring stages within the production process (or sometimes the production process itself) to the South, in order to minimize production costs – particularly labour and environmental costs. This process has already contributed significantly to the creation of a handful of economic 'miracles' in the South which, however, can neither be universalized nor necessarily sustained, as we shall see in the next section.

The case of the 'economic miracles' in the South

The spectacular growth of countries like South Korea, Taiwan, Hong Kong, Singapore, Malaysia and Thailand have given rise to a new mythology, which is also adopted by parts of the self-styled 'Left': that the capitalist growth economy has, finally, proved capable of being universalized. Some[11] even talk about a radical shift in global wealth and output from the West to East Asia, if not from the North to the South. This new myth is based mainly on the much publicized fact that the average annual growth rate of the 'Asian Tigers' is much higher than that of advanced capitalist countries, closing fast the gap between the two groups of countries. And, indeed, the average growth rate of the above countries (minus Taiwan for which the World Bank does not provide data) was almost three times higher than that of advanced capitalist countries in the period 1970–93.[12] What is usually not mentioned is that, apart from the exceptional cases of the small 'city-states' (Singapore and Hong Kong), there is still a huge gap separating these countries from the North. Thus, in 1993, the per capita income of South Korea was still one-third, that of Malaysia one-seventh, and that of Thailand less than one-tenth of that of advanced capitalist countries! This fact implies that, even if the present spectacular growth rates could be sustained in the future, it will take a very long time indeed for the gap with the advanced capitalist countries to be closed.

But, in fact, the hypothesis about the sustainability of those growth rates is increasingly challenged, even by orthodox economists. As recent comparisons of the growth of the Asian Tigers with that of metropolitan countries during similar periods of growth have shown, the former have mainly advanced by mobilizing hitherto underutilized human resources and combining them with a massive employment of public and private investment, particularly in infrastructure.[13] In other words, the growth of these countries has been mainly of the 'extensive' rather than of the 'intensive' type. The former type depends on increases in the use of existing resources, which, at some stage, will inevitably be exhausted, whereas the latter type, which is the only sustainable one in the long run, depends on improvements in productivity. As the case of the countries in Eastern Europe has shown, the task of reproducing the growth economy through intensive growth is much harder than that of extensive growth. The historical experience therefore shows that the continuation of the expansion of the Asia 'miracles' is very doubtful.

In fact, if we take into account the foundations of growth in the 'socialist' growth economy versus those in East Asia, the doubts become even stronger. Economic growth in Eastern Europe was founded on central planning, whereas in East Asia it has been export-led. But it was not *laissez-faire* policies that induced their spectacular growth. As a number of studies have shown,[14] the expansion of the Asian Tigers was based on massive state intervention that boosted their export sectors, by public policies involving not only heavy protectionism[15] but even deliberate distortion of market prices to stimulate investment and trade.[16]

However, such a degree of statism, as we saw in the previous two chapters, is not possible any more in the context of today's internationalized market economy. This is particularly so if we take into account the much higher dependence of growth in these countries on the competitiveness of their exports than in advanced capitalist countries. Thus, the fact that the ratio of exports to income in the Asian Tigers has increased from an average of 53 per cent in 1970 to about 92 per cent in 1993 (versus a rise in advanced capitalist countries from 14 per cent to 20 per cent in the same period)[17] is a clear indication not only of the much higher vulnerability of East Asia's growth economy, compared to that of the North, but also of the asymmetry involved. It is clear that the reproduction of the growth economy in the Asiatic 'miracles' depends crucially on the North's demand, whereas the opposite is not true.

So, the Asian Tigers' 'miracle' does not represent 'the end of the Western world', as ex-Marxist social liberals argue,[18] since its reproduction crucially depends on the Western world. In fact, it seems that the view about the end of the West is a myth, even if in the East we include Japan, which, unlike the 'Tigers', has been one of the founder members of the capitalist club. The Japanese miracle seems to be fading away as the long-term growth rate of the country's per capita GNP has fallen from 9.4 per cent in 1960–79 to 3.4 per cent in 1980–93.[19] Furthermore, as capital seeks more flexible growth economies to invest in, unemployment, which was almost non-existent in the past, has been growing fast lately, with a rise of over 50 per cent in the last four years alone.[20]

Therefore, what the Asian Tigers do show, with their complete lack of welfare states and civil societies, is a glimpse of the future of political and economic democracy in the North. In an internationalized market economy, the requirements of competition homogenize not just the economy but society itself. One could therefore predict that the future of the market economy lies in a world model which would be the synthesis of the Anglo-Saxon liberal model with the Asian 'miracles' – a synthesis that would be characterized by an almost non-existent civil society, accompanied by various safety networks for the poor and expanded private health, education and insurance sectors for those of the rest that could afford to use them.

The growth economy and development

The fundamental question with respect to development is not why the growth economy in the South has not been as successful as in the North, but why the model of economy and society that was established in the North should be considered as a universally feasible and desirable societal model in the first place. As regards the feasibility of the model, as we saw earlier, there are strong grounds to believe that the chances of this model being universalized are close to nil. As regards the desirability of the model, the historical experience of the last 200 years has shown unequivocally that the flourishing of the market economy and its internationalization, as well as the consequent rise of the growth economy, have led to a huge concentration of economic power, to an ecological crisis that threatens to develop into an eco-catastrophe, the destruction of the countryside, the creation of monstrous mega-cities and the uprooting of local communities and cultures. In other words, it has now become obvious that this system of economic organization only partially, and for a small minority of the world population, serves the objective of satisfying human needs and improving human welfare, whereas generally it creates a new type of hierarchical society based on economic power, competition, greed and individualism.

However, both liberals and Marxists (including the related dependency and regulation approaches) explicitly or implicitly adopt the ideology of the growth economy and differ among themselves only on the question of whether capitalism, or, instead, some kind of socialist statism, is a better way to achieve it. Thus, these approaches, taking the feasibility and desirability of the growth economy for granted, ignore the fundamental issue of the power structures and relations implied by the growth economy. In other words, the conventional approaches ignore the fact that the concentration of power, that both the capitalist and the socialist growth economy involve, implies that the decisions about what the economic and other needs of a society are, as well as about the ways to cover them, are taken not by the people themselves but by elites who control the political and economic process. No wonder that the main focus of these conventional approaches is on whether a country has already achieved the status of a growth economy like those in the North (in which case it is classified as an 'advanced' country), or not ('underdeveloped' or, euphemistically, 'developing'). By analogy, the quantitative expansion of an advanced economy, measured in terms of increases in the real national income, is defined as *growth*, whereas the qualitative social and economic changes needed for its transformation into an advanced growth economy are defined as *development*.

Thus, the common characteristic in all definitions of development is that human welfare is identified with the expansion of individual consumption or, generally, the unlimited development of productive forces. For instance, a typical liberal definition defines development as 'a rise in the present value of average (weighted) consumption per head'.[21] Marxists identify development with the development of productive forces and define underdevelopment as a case of dominance of pre-capitalist modes of production, a case of backwardness.[22] Dependency theorists identify underdevelopment with dependence, which, in turn, is defined as 'a conditioning situation, in which the economies of one group of countries are conditioned by the development and expansion of others'.[23] Finally, the new regulation school defines the 'periphery' as 'that part of the world in which the regime of accumulation found in the most developed capitalist countries has not been able to take root'.[24] It is also revealing that even when orthodox and radical economists discuss the need to introduce alternative definitions and measures of development the issue of power structures and relations is, again, set aside. This is, for instance, the case with definitions that allow for the compositional aspects of development (the production of *what* is considered development) or the distributional aspects (the production *for whom* is considered development). Needs, the ways to satisfy them, as well as whose needs are to be met in the first place, are all issues that are supposed to be settled 'objectively' and not within an authentic democratic process. But what is meant by 'objectively' is that these crucial problems are 'solved' either through a 'rationing by the wallet' mechanism (market economy) or through the bureaucratic decisions of the planners (socialist statism).

A survey of the theoretical approaches to the causes of 'underdevelopment' reveals the narrow perspective taken by supporters of the growth economy in both the orthodox and the radical economics camps.

The conventional approaches to development

The classical approaches

The origin of modern growth theory can be found in the writings of *mercantilists* and *physiocrats*. It is not of course accidental that the problem of growth was central to eighteenth- and nineteenth-century thought, as it was during this period that the market economy and the consequent growth economy emerged.

Mercantilists, who aimed their analysis at the process of economic growth in the limited sense of an increase in *total* output rather than in per capita output, saw growth of the total labour force as the primary condition of economic progress and were strong supporters of active state intervention in promoting growth.[25] However, since the time of the physiocrats, and as the growth ideology and the ideology of the market economy have taken hold, the focus has shifted to capital accumulation and *laissez-faire*. But, whereas physiocrats see the motor of growth in capital accumulation in agriculture, as they think that it is only in this sector that economic surplus could be produced, liberal political economists of the classical school, since the time of Adam Smith, have assigned this role to capital accumulation in manufacturing. This was, of course, consistent with the requirements of the industrial revolution that set the foundations of the modern growth economy.

Thus, Adam Smith identified the sources of growth in terms, first, of technical progress and, second of capital accumulation. The former's importance arises from the fact that it increases productivity and the division of labour which, in turn, depends on the size of the market and the rate of capital accumulation. The significance of the latter originates in the fact that it not only provides the equipment to increase labour productivity, but that it also creates the employment opportunities which, in turn, determine the size of the market and the degree of division of labour.

David Ricardo provided the finest refinement of Smith's theory and of classical growth theory in general. Of particular importance was his description of the process through which the pressure of an expanding population on natural resources will eventually halt the growth process. Although he stressed the existence of counter-tendencies (mainly in the form of technical progress and foreign trade), which may significantly delay the process, yet he saw the arrival of the stationary state as inevitable.

However, it was mainly on Malthus's population principle that the classical belief that the growth process was an inexorable movement towards a stationary state was based. This principle was founded on the hypothesis that the pressure created by the population expansion on a limited stock of natural resources would eventually outrun the pace of technical progress, especially in agriculture. So, unless the 'preventative' checks (fewer marriages, sexual continence, etc.) could restrain this process, the 'positive' checks (massive poverty and starvation) would be set in motion. Thus, the Malthusian principle established a definite causality relationship between overpopulation and poverty, where the former was the cause and the latter the effect. However, the explanation provided for poverty by Malthus was based on the implicit adoption of the power structure of the growth economy and on the explicit blaming of the poor for their poverty. Thus, Malthus conveniently ignored the fact that it was the requirements (in terms of cheap labour) of the emerging growth economy which have led, with the decisive help of the enclosure movement (the fencing of land that used to be common), to the creation of a massive army of landless peasants and massive poverty. In fact, the enclosure movement, which began in England in the twelfth century but flourished mainly in the eighteenth and nineteenth centuries (1750–1860), had a two-sided economic effect: on the one hand, it gave wealthy landowners the opportunity to profit from either arable farming or raising sheep, and on the other, it compelled many small farmers to sell their property and move to the towns to work in the new factories.

Neo-Malthusians and the 'overpopulation' myth

Similarly, today, neo-Malthusians ignore the corresponding enclosure movement in the South, which marked the dismantling of the traditional economies in the area, after the successful penetration of the market and the growth economy. But, as Ted Trainer[26] points out: '[I]n Latin America 11% were landless in 1961, but by 1975 40% were ... [A]pproximately 80% of all Third World agricultural land continues to be owned by about 3 per cent of landowners.' Notwithstanding, neo-Malthusians support the thesis, which is also adopted by some eco-fascist currents within the Green movement, that the South's poverty should be blamed on its 'overpopulation'. Deep ecologists, as we shall see below, also adopt the neo-Malthusian thesis and argue that overpopulation created a 'population bomb',[27] which should be checked 'within an overall commitment to reduce the birth-rate, especially in third world countries'[28] – even by such methods as the cutting of aid to the Third World![29]

But, let us consider the facts behind the 'overpopulation' mythology. There is no doubt that the world population has increased rapidly in the past two centuries. It is not, however, accidental that the acceleration of the population growth coincides with the emergence and spreading of the market/growth economy all over the world. Thus, world population, which reached the 1 billion mark in the 1800s, doubled in the 1920s, doubled again in the 1970s, and is expected to double again by the 2020s.[30] However, it is at least doubtful whether the present population trends will continue into the next century. Within the very short time span of the last 20 years, the 'total fertility rates' (defined as the number of children that would be born to a woman if she were to live to the end of her childbearing years and bear children at each age in accordance with prevailing age-specific fertility rates) declined dramatically in the South. The 'total fertility rate' was almost halved during the last 20 years in most of the South. Thus, in 'low-income countries', where two-thirds of the total population in the South lives, the fertility rate fell from 5.9 in 1970 to 3.6 in 1993, and in the rest of the South, this rate fell from 4.5 to 3.0.[31] A significant part of this drastic decline is due to economic and physical violence used within the context of 'family planning' strategies which mainly affect unwanted baby girls (China, India). Indicatively, in India, between 1981 and 1991, the number of females per 1000 males declined from 934 to 929, according to the latest census, whereas in advanced capitalist countries there are 1060 females for every 1000 males.[32] Still, the expansion of contraceptive prevalence (the percentage of women using contraception) and television propaganda have played an equally important role in this process. It is not surprising therefore that on the very day the latest World Conference on Population and Development opened in Cairo – with the obvious objective of forcing a reduction in the South's fertility rates that supposedly were leading to a population explosion in the twenty-first century – the world's leading demographers announced (without attracting much publicity in the media) that their latest research showed an end to rising global numbers![33]

Furthermore, it can easily be shown that it is not the lack of capacity to produce food that causes hunger and the related diseases killing 40,000 people every day.[34] As David Satterthwaite of the International Institute for Environment and Development argues, it was 'land-owning structures and economic processes that excluded the "hungry" from the possibility of producing food or earning enough to buy it'.[35] And, of course, neither the depletion of resources (renewable and non-renewable) nor the degradation of the environment (manifested by such phenomena as the greenhouse effect and the damage to the ozone layer) could, by any stretch of the imagination, be blamed on population trends. Given the direct relationship that exists between consumption standards and environmental degradation and the fact that there is an inverse relationship between fertility rates and consumption standards (i.e. income groups with low fertility are usually those with high consumption levels), there is little doubt about the causes of the present crisis. Therefore, the concentration of income and wealth is not only the ultimate direct cause of poverty and starvation but, also, of the present environmental destruction; furthermore, it is the indirect cause of high fertility rates among low-income groups. In other words, it is the growth economy itself that has to be blamed for the present economic, ecological and demographic crisis.

We may therefore argue that the two main approaches which formed the backbone for the 20-year Programme of Action document approved at the Cairo population conference are equally irrelevant. According to the first approach, which we may call the *economic development approach,* the best way to tackle the 'population problem' is economic *'development',* that is, the continued expansion of the growth economy. This approach, which is based on the experience of the North, assumes that in a pre-industrial economy both birth and death rates are high, keeping the population roughly stable; as a country industrializes and living conditions (including hygienic conditions) improve, death rates fall, leading to a high population growth. However, the population explosion – the argument goes – is only temporary because soon, as better education and health conditions spread, birth rates tend to fall as well, leading to stable, moderate population growth. This was the population pattern in the North, and a similar pattern was expected for the South.

Still, although both death and birth rates have fallen in the South, fertility rates in the area are almost double those prevailing in the North. In 1993, total fertility rates were 5.5 in low-income countries (3.6 including China and India) and 3.0 in middle-income countries, versus 1.7 in the high-income countries of the North.[36] Furthermore, there is no serious expectation that in any foreseeable future these differentials will disappear. Today, it is almost generally accepted that overpopulation is the effect rather than the cause of poverty – a fact that was explicitly or implicitly accepted by those at the Cairo Conference who supported the economic development approach. According, for instance, to Julian Simon,[37] there is not much evidence that the rise in population makes countries poorer. Also, according to another report,[38] the most successful population control programmes in the last 25 years have been those that aimed at the decrease in poverty. This does not, of course, mean that poverty is the only cause of high fertility rates. Population trends depend on a multiplicity of factors: social (family planning, use of contraceptive methods, etc.), cultural (religion, tradition and so on), as well as economic. The main economic factor is, of course, poverty.

Poverty, defined in a broad sense, is determined by the distribution of income, unemployment and the quality of welfare services – especially health and education services. It can be shown that poverty is perhaps the most important explanatory factor of the differential fertility rates between countries. This fact becomes obvious, even if we use as a comparative measure of welfare the index used by the World Bank and other international institutions: the per capita income. The per capita income is, of course, a very inadequate measure of human welfare and has rightly been critized by radical economists of all persuasions. As a rule, however, significant differences in per capita incomes (like those reflected in the 1:61 ratio between low-income countries and high-income countries) do reflect significant differences in poverty in the broad sense (i.e. differences in employment, real incomes, welfare services, etc.) which, indirectly, affect the social and cultural factors that are relevant to population trends. Thus, a very strong correlation can be established between poverty and fertility rates: the higher the per capita income, the lower the fertility rate. Low-income countries (excluding China and India) with an average per capita income of $300, have a total fertility rate of 5.5 (a decline of 15 per cent since 1970). Middle-income countries, with an average per capita income of $2480, have a fertility rate of 3.0 (a decline of 32 per cent since 1970), whereas high-income economies, with an average per capita income of about $22,500, have a fertility rate of less than 1.7 (a decline of 26 per cent since 1970).[39] Therefore, given that income and wealth differentials, far from being reduced by the expansion of the growth economy, are further enhanced and that the 'trickle-down effect' has certainly proved invalid in the South, one may reasonably expect that the present significant fertility differentials will persist for many years to come – for as long as the huge income differentials remain.

The alternative to the *economic development* approach may be called the *social development* approach. This approach, which was promoted by the Cairo conference, emphasizes social rather than economic development and stresses the need to 'empower women', as the key to solving the 'population problem'. However, 'empowering women' in this context does not mean upgrading their general social position – which is anyway impossible under the present conditions of huge concentrations of power. It simply means, as a Green *realo* and prominent figure of the British establishment put it, 'empowering women to take control of their own fertility',[40] by improving access (from the social, economic and hygienic points of view) to contraceptives and abortions. The assumption on which this approach is based is that contraception, not 'development', is the best contraceptive, and that fighting poverty, as the same activist puts it, is not a 'realistic' target for addressing the problem. However, as I argued above, it is poverty in the broad sense that plays a critical role with respect to such crucial factors to population trends as infant mortality, which is over nine times as high in low-income countries compared with high-income countries,[41] or old-age security.

It is because of the obvious shortcomings of the alternate approach that even the liberal elites find it hard to rely exclusively on it and argue that 'development is not the only contraceptive, but, without it, no amount of condoms scattered on the pavement will help'.[42] The same shortcomings have obviously been grasped by Bill Clinton's National Security Council advisers who have identified the threat of peoples deprived of basic needs, such as food, water and shelter, as 'one of the main engines of world instability'.[43]

Neo-classical and Marxist/dependency approaches to development

In the last quarter of the nineteenth century, important methodological changes in economics, introduced independently by Jevons, Menger and Walras, started the *marginalist revolution*. This was not just a movement to convert classical political economy into a 'science' of economics. The revolution marked, also, a shift in emphasis from the problem of growth and development to the static problem of the allocation of resources under conditions of efficiency. Still, the world view of the neo-classical school that emerged out of the marginalist revolution remained typically classical; this was not of course surprising, given the expressed aim of neo-classicals just to refine and not to replace classical economics. It was a world view of harmony (all groups gain in the growth process), gradualism (development occurs through small, almost continuous steps), individualism (individual rational decisions secure a socially rational process) and *laissez-faire*.

Neo-classical economists though, unlike their classical predecessors, were optimistic about the long-term prospects of capitalist economies. They argued that technical progress would offset any natural resource barriers, and that, even if we assumed away technical progress, it would take a very long time for the stationary state to be reached. Thus, provided the market is left free to ensure adequate levels of saving (by boosting profits, through the depression of the cost of production, i.e. squeezing real wages, environmental cost, etc.) and investment (which feeds technical progress), economic growth could continue almost indefinitely.

On the radical side, Marx's economic interpretation of history was a perfect example of Euro-centrism; his criteria for assessing non-European societies were determined by the European experience and the ideology of the growth economy. Marx himself, not unlike the orthodox social scientists, identified progress and civilization with the unlimited development of productive forces ('the bourgeoisie, by the rapid improvement of all instruments of production, by the immensely facilitated means of communication, draws all, even the most barbarian nations, into civilisation').[44] Furthermore, the adoption of the growth ideology led him to dismiss all non-European forms of society under the blanket designation of 'a mere geographic terminology of the "Asiatic mode of production" which appears static, unchanging and totally non-dialectical'.[45] On the other hand, capitalism was seen as a dynamic system tending to generate economic development endogenously, through competition between capitals. Thus, the emergence of capitalism in a few metropolitan centres generates capital accumulation and development and opens up an initial lead over the rest of the world. Then, the dynamics of competition force capital to seek new methods of production, new markets, new sources of supply, etc., and set in motion forces leading to expansion, accumulation and economic development in the areas penetrated by capitalism. Capital, according to Marx, is going to create 'a world after its own image'.[46] The inevitable outcome of this process is the geographic spreading of the system, the internationalization of capital.

However, whereas orthodox social scientists saw the growth process within the context of a world view of harmony, gradualism, equilibrium tendencies and evolutionary change, Marx – through a dialectical analysis of social change – saw the same process within the context of a world view of conflict, contradictory forces and eventual revolution that would substitute the working class for the bourgeois class as the social agents of development. Still, for Marx, the fundamental contradiction in capitalism is found in the *social* character of modern production and the *private* appropriation of the economic surplus, rather than in the fact that economic growth itself necessarily leads to concentration of economic power and the destruction of the environment. In other words, the Marxist critique focuses its attention exclusively on the market economy and never touches the growth economy itself.

The post-war theories of 'development' were designed with the explicit aim of dealing with the problems created by the worldwide spreading of the growth economy of the North. These theories may be classified as either 'orthodox' or 'radical', the former denoting all development approaches belonging to the orthodox paradigm and the latter all those approaches belonging to the Marxist and dependency paradigms.

The *orthodox* paradigm includes all development theories in which the market economy is taken for granted and a world view of harmony is adopted, within an evolutionist process. Orthodox economic approaches to development may be broadly classified as 'neo-classical' and 'structuralist'. The so-called structuralist approaches to development (which are associated with the names of Paul Rosestein-Rodan, Ragnar Nurkse, Arthur Lewis, Hollis Chenery, Gunnar Myrdal and others) adopt Keynesian statism, whereas neo-classical approaches emphasize the role of free markets. Structuralists, like neo-classical economists, take the market economy for granted and use the traditional tools of orthodox economics in an attempt to show the existence of a process leading from a traditional, rural, underdeveloped economy to a modern, industrial one. But, unlike neo-classical economists, structuralists emphasize the role of structural rigidities and disequilibria in the transitional process towards a growth economy. Structuralists are, therefore, in favour of administrative action, and it is no wonder that their approach to development was very much in fashion during the statist phase of the marketization process. Similarly, it is not surprising that neo-classical approaches to development have come back into fashion with the present flourishing of neoliberalism, and that they have been aggressively promoted by the World Bank and the International Monetary Fund. The special World Bank report to mark its 50th birthday, for instance, is indicative of the 'new' orthodoxy in development: 'A new paradigm has emerged, one that emphasizes "market-friendly" approaches.'[47]

Radical approaches to development belong to the two main paradigms developed during the post-war period, that is, the Marxist and the dependency paradigms. The *Marxist* paradigm includes all those theories which adopt a world view of capitalism as a historical phase in the process of social evolution. In this problematic, development is primarily determined by each country's internal structure and specifically by the nature of the dominant *mode of production* (i.e. the forces and relations of production). In this context, underdevelopment is seen as a remnant of the past, as a pre-capitalist mode of production.

The *dependency* paradigm was developed in the post-war period, as a response to the failure of capitalist development in the Third World. It was, in fact, a theoretical reaction to the inability of both orthodox economics and classical Marxist theories of imperialism to explain this failure. This paradigm includes all those theories in which underdevelopment is seen as the outcome of specific power relations within the context of a world system. The dependency theories share with Marxist theories a world view of conflicting interests, instead of one of harmony, as in orthodox development approaches; a historical view of capitalist development, instead of the typical a-historical orthodox analysis; and finally, they adopt an internationalist approach emphasizing the integral nature of the world economy, instead of following the usual orthodox approach of concentrating on nation-states as the fundamental units of analysis.

However, the differences between the Marxist and the dependency approaches at the methodological, theoretical and political levels are equally important. The methodological differences refer to the fact that the central category in Marxist theory is that of the mode of production, whereas in dependency theories this role is played by the 'world-system' concept. Thus, capitalism is seen in the former within the context of class analysis, whereas in the latter it is seen within the conceptual framework of production for profit, in a world system of exchange and exploitation of some areas by others. This implies that the class structure (as well as underdevelopment) is the consequence of dependency relations, rather than the main determining cause, as in Marxist analysis.

Also, from the historical point of view, a crucial difference arises regarding the nature of the historical role of capitalism. Marxists assume that the role of capitalism in the development process is progressive and see capital accumulation as a process of continuous expansion. On the other hand, dependency theorists do not consider the historical role of capitalism as necessarily progressive; they see capital accumulation as a system of transferring the economic surplus from the periphery to the centre, rather than as one of continuous expansion. The implication is that Marxists see underdevelopment as a state of a pre-capitalist mode of production, as an earlier historical stage, whereas dependency theorists see it as the result of the imposition of a particular division of labour pattern on the periphery, that is, as the result of integration in the world system in a subordinate position. Finally, from the political point of view, whereas for orthodox Marxists development is not impossible within the capitalist system, since the expansion of capitalist relations could set the preconditions for a socialist revolution, for dependency theorists, development presupposes a break with the world-capitalist system.

Nevertheless, despite the significant differences between Marxists and dependency theorists, they all share a fundamental common characteristic: like orthodox social scientists, they never dispute the desirability of the growth economy itself, that is, of the unlimited development of productive forces. In fact, the main point of controversy in the famous debates (which raged in the 1970s) between Marxists, neo-Marxists and dependency theorists centres on one issue: why the growth economy in the South has not been as successful as in the North: in other words, why growth has not been rapid enough. In short, all the above approaches never blame the capitalist (or the socialist) growth economy as bound to lead to a huge concentration of economic power and the destruction of self-reliant economies. Nor do they ever stress that the growth economy, by undermining eco-communities, is the crucial cause of irreparable ecological damage. In a nutshell, they never criticize the system of the market economy for attempting to create a universal growth economy; instead, they criticize it for not doing so efficiently enough!

Thus, the main objective of radical theories has been to show the process through which the economic surplus of the South[48] is transferred to the North and how this process arrests the development of a successful growth economy in the former. The transfer process can be shown either within the theoretical framework of a chain of metropolis–satellite relations linking the international, national and local capitalist systems,[49] or within the context of a world system whose components (nation-states) are not closed systems, but integral parts of a totality characterized by a single division of labour.[50] The mechanism itself, through which the transfer of surplus takes place, is based either on the unequal exchange resulting from significant wage differentials between the North and the South,[51] or on the unequal specialization resulting from corresponding productivity differentials.[52]

Finally, the neo-Marxist 'modes of production' approach,[53] that was developed as a response to the 'unorthodox' dependency theories, examines the transitional process leading to a growth economy as a process of *articulation* of modes of production (capitalist and pre-capitalist ones) within a social formation. Again, not only is the desirability of the growth economy not disputed, but even its eventual universalization is taken for granted.

The regulation approach to development

Similar considerations apply with respect to the regulation approach,[54] which is currently fashionable among neo-Marxists, post-Marxists, ex-Marxists and others. Alain Lipietz[55] provides a typical example of the regulation approach to development – an approach that no one would deny represents a definite step forward as far as Marxist methodology is concerned. This is particularly true with respect to the regulationists' rejection of the crude functionalism that characterized some theories of imperialism and dependency. For instance, few would deny today the invalidity of propositions – central to the argument of many theories of imperialism and dependency – which asserted that the *function* of the periphery was to promote growth in the centre, through the various mechanisms of transfer of value from the periphery.

However, the regulation approach, like the neo-Marxist and dependency approaches, also aims to explain why the regime of accumulation found in the most developed capitalist countries did not grow roots in the South. In other words, the objective is, again, to answer the question as to whether a relatively independent capitalist development is possible in the periphery, so that the growth economy of the North can be transferred to the South, as predicted by classical Marxist theory. Thus, the desirability of 'independent capitalist development' is, again, taken for granted, and the only issue under discussion is the feasibility of reproducing it in the South.

This feasibility, according to the regulation approach, depends on internal class alliances: 'The development of capitalism in any given country is primarily the outcome of internal class struggles which result in embryonic regimes of accumulation being consolidated by forms of regulation that are backed up by the local state.'[56] This way, the regulation approach ends up by explicitly assuming that the huge concentration of economic power in the North is just the outcome of class struggles and alliances and the resulting role of the state; implicitly, the same is true regarding the concentration of power *within* the North and the South, as well as the consequent ecological damage. So, the actual 'International Division of Labour', which involves the unequal allocation between various countries of world labour and its products, is described as 'simply the outcome of various nations' attempts to control one another or to escape one another's control, of one or another class alliance's unremitting efforts to achieve or surrender national autonomy'.[57]

The implication is that the direct relationship between the grow-or-die dynamic of the market economy and the resulting concentration of economic power and ecological damage is simply relegated to 'the primacy of internal causes'; this is a position not very dissimilar to the liberal position, according to which it is not the market economy itself that has to be blamed for the misery and starvation in the South but its corrupt elites! Thus, it is simply ignored that the market economy and the consequent growth economy have a dynamic of their own, and that the marketization process and the parallel process of spreading the growth economy inevitably lead to the concentration of economic power and serious ecological damage. The implicit conclusion, which is promoted by the regulation approach, is that the state (at the centre, or the periphery) is capable of effectively controlling the market, even to the extent of creating, under certain conditions, 'independent capitalist development'; this is so because the state is 'the archetypal form of regulation [since] it is at the level of the state that the class struggle is resolved'.[58] All this, at the very moment when the internationalization of the market economy and the consequent withering away of the economic role of the nation-state is in full swing!

In conclusion, the problem with conventional theories of development (orthodox and Marxist paradigms) is that their problematic originated in the logic of the growth economy. Within this problematic, the issue of development is discussed in terms of the reasons why the countries in the South did not develop a growth economy similar to the one developed in the North. However, the type of approach needed to examine economic relations between the North and the South, and economic relations in general, is one that examines such relations in terms of power structures, rather than on the basis of 'objective economic laws', or 'general theories', Marxist or not. Therefore, the role of states and ruling elites (a 'subjective' element) is, indeed, important in this sort of analysis. But the role of the institutional framework, in the form of the market economy/growth economy (an 'objective' element) is equally important because it sets the 'degrees of freedom' that are available to the state and the ruling elites.

However, it seems that the regulation school, in its effort to throw away the Marxist 'objectivist baggage' (although, despite the rhetoric, this school does look just one more sophisticated attempt to develop a new 'general theory') has moved to the other extreme of almost ignoring the constraints imposed on the role of the state by the institutional framework!

The ecological dimension of development

In the 1980s, the appearance of the ecological crisis at the forefront added a new dimension to the development debate – a debate which up to then was just focused on the feasibility of reproducing the growth economy of the North in the South. The question of the ecological implications of development and implicitly the desirability of the growth economy itself became crucial. In the following, the orthodox economics approach to the ecological implications of development in the South will be discussed, whereas the general ecological approaches to growth/development in both the North and the South will be examined in Chapter 4.

For orthodox economists, the issue is whether 'development' is the cause of environmental damage, or whether it is the lack of development that is causing environmental problems. The World Bank has decided that some problems are associated with the lack of economic development; it specifically mentions inadequate sanitation and clean water, as well as indoor air pollution from biomass burning and many types of land degradation in the South as having poverty as their root cause. On the other hand, the same source argues: 'Many other problems are exacerbated by the growth of economic activity: industrial and energy-related pollution (local and global), deforestation caused by commercial logging and overuse of water.'[59]

Not surprisingly – in view of the fact that it is, after all, the proceeds of the ruling economic oligarchies from the functioning of the market economy that finance the activities of the World Bank and the salaries of its executives that draw up the relevant reports – the solutions suggested by the World Bank for both types of problems are consistent with the aim of maintaining and reproducing the existing institutional framework of the market economy. Thus, the proposed solution to the environmental problems is 'more development', but of a type that will not fail to 'take into account the value of the environment', so that a better trade-off between development and environmental quality is achieved. So, the environment is assumed to be something that can be 'valued', in a similar way that everything else is assigned a value within the market economy.

However, apart from the fact that there is no way to put an 'objective' value on most of the elements that constitute the environment (since they affect a subjective factor par excellence, i.e. the quality of life), the solution suggested, in effect, implies the extension of the marketization process to the environment itself. In other words, it implies the assignment of a market value to the environment (even if it is in the form of an imputed value), so that the effects of growth on it are 'internalized', either through the creation of new profitable 'green' business activities, or through 'corrective' state action on the workings of the market mechanism! Thus, not only is it conveniently ignored that it is the market mechanism itself which is the problem, because from the moment it incorporated an important part of the environment – land – it initiated the eco-damaging process, but it is also recommended that the marketization process has to be extended to the other parts of the environment (air, water, etc.) as well! The outcome of such a process is easily predictable: the environment will either be put under the control of the economic elites that control the market economy (if an actual market value can be assigned to it) or the state (if only an imputed value is possible). In either case, not only is the arrest of the ecological damage – at least – doubtful, but, also, the control over Nature by elites who aim to dominate it – using 'green' prescriptions this time – is perpetuated.

Furthermore, on the basis of all existing evidence, it is hard to reject the proposition that it is, mainly, *poverty as development* (i.e. poverty caused by development) that is causing the environmental degradation and not *poverty as underdevelopment*. This is particularly so, if we allow for the fact that it is the consumerist lifestyles of the rich that are causing environmental degradation rather than those of the poor. Thus, the 'Group of 7' richest capitalist countries in the world, where 12 per cent of the world population lives, is the cause of 38 per cent of global carbon dioxide emissions.[60] Still, the World Bank finds nothing wrong with the lifestyles of the rich and argues that:

> [F]or natural resources that are non-renewable, increases in consumption necessarily imply a reduction in the available stock. The evidence, however, gives no support to the hypothesis that marketed non-renewable resources such as metals, minerals and energy are becoming scarcer in the economic sense. This is because potential or actual shortages are reflected in rising market prices, which in turn have induced new discoveries, improvements in efficiency, possibilities for substitution, and technological innovations.[61]

Thus, the World Bank implicitly adopts the hypothesis we made earlier that concentration is not only a consequence but also a fundamental precondition for the reproduction of the growth economy. Thus, in the transitional period, 'rising market prices' would simply function as crude rationing devices which would benefit the privileged social groups. Also, even if rising market prices are followed by technological innovations, etc., it is at least doubtful whether the non-privileged social groups will be in a position to exploit them. It is therefore obvious that the World Bank simply celebrates the 'allocation by the wallet' of those global resources that are becoming scarce because of growth. Furthermore, there is no evidence that the new technologies, which are 'induced by higher prices', lead to some kind of 'sustainable growth'. In fact, the opposite might be the case. The UN Food and Agriculture Organization, for instance, states that 'Low-input production is probably the most environmentally-friendly system and has been practised since time immemorial; still, during the development process, every country has abandoned this practice because of its low productivity and its inability to meet the food require-ments of an ever increasing population.'[62] Inevitably, the abandonment of this practice has meant the creation of farmers' dependency on chemical companies. Furthermore, farmers, to finance the purchase of chemicals, usually produced by trans-nationals, become dependent on export crops.

Democracy and development

Towards a new 'North–South' divide

In the context of today's neoliberal internationalized market economy, it is doubtful whether the old distinction between North and South makes much sense any more. If, for instance, we use the familiar – and almost meaningless – per capita GNP indicator to classify countries in the North–South divide, we ignore the fact that the rapidly widening gap between privileged and non-privileged social groups has already reproduced huge 'South' enclaves in the heart of the North. For instance, in Britain, between 1979 and 1993, poverty increased from 8 per cent to 24 per cent among couples with young children and from 19 to 58 per cent among lone-parent families.[63] Also, if we use alternative indicators concerning the degree to which essential needs are covered for various segments of the population, irrespective of whether they live in the 'North' or the 'South', the question arises as to which group a country like the USA belongs to when one in five US children live in poverty and eight million of those children lack health care. Similarly, according to a UNICEF report,[64] compared to their per capita income, the USA and Belgium in the 'North' perform far worse in child survival, nutrition and education than Jordan, Syria, Poland, Romania, Bulgaria and Kenya in the 'South'. Furthermore, according to the same report, if we rank the countries of the world in terms of the well-being of their people – and particularly children – then, at the top of the list we find such countries as Vietnam, Sri Lanka, Nepal, Cuba and Burma (Myanmar), which have far lower infant mortality rates and better records of junior school attendance than would be expected from their per capita GNP.

The above discussion raises not only the issue of whether the old distinction between 'North' and 'South' makes sense; it also raises the issue of the indicator itself that can be used for such a classification. In particular, the question arises whether it is feasible or desirable to develop a common indicator to classify countries with very different cultural and economic needs. A common indicator, even a complex one, implies not only the same economic and cultural needs but also that societies could be classified, on the basis of it, in a hierarchical order that justifies the use of similar means, the same 'experts', aid, etc., so that those at the bottom could reach those at the top. Furthermore, a common indicator implies that the 'development' achieved in the countries at the top is desirable, whereas alternative models of need satisfaction should be avoided; in other words, it implies common values. Thus, for example, when modern agribusiness maximizes output of a single crop through monoculture and, as a result, productivity improves and competitiveness increases, then this becomes an obviously preferable method of farming to expand per capita GNP, even if it is eroding biodiversity.

However, despite the obvious problems of measurement involved, it may still be useful to keep the 'North–South' distinction, provided that we redefine our terms. Thus, the 'New North' could be defined as all those social groups that benefit from the marketization process, whether they live in the old North or South.[65] In general, we may say that this New North consists of the '40 per cent society' in the old First World and a small minority in the old Second and Third Worlds. In the old First World, the beneficiaries from the marketization process do not just include those in control of the means of production, which constitute the bulk of the ruling elite, but also the large middle classes that have flourished in this process (professionals, skilled workers, etc.). Similarly, in the old Third World the beneficiaries include not just the ruling elites (big landowners, importers and so on), but also a rudimentary middle class of professionals, top state employees, etc. Finally, in the old Second World the beneficiaries include the new ruling elite, which has been emerging in the marketization process (usually ex-members of the old party nomenclatura) and a very small middle class of professionals.

Development or democracy?

Today, increasing numbers of people do not have access to the political process (except as voters), to the economic process (except as consumers) or to the environment (except as conditioned by their roles in the economic and political process, defined by the market economy and the parliamentary system respectively). Thus, at the political level, it is the elites of professional politicians who take all significant political decisions. Similarly, at the economic level, what is produced in a country is not determined by the democratic decisions of its citizens but by property relations and the income distribution pattern. Finally, the sort of 'protection' the environment is entitled to have is effectively determined by the political and economic elites which control the market/growth economy. Moreover, a process leading to the further concentration of power at all levels is in full swing.

The reaction to this state of affairs usually takes two forms. On the one hand, as their environments are destroyed or degraded, their power eroded or denied and their communities threatened, millions are now demanding a halt to the kind of development associated with the growth economy. As the social activist Gustavo Esteva writes: '[i]f you live in Rio or Mexico City you need to be very rich or stupid not to notice that development stinks'.[66] On the other hand, a whole series of recent initiatives and struggles has developed in both the South and the North, which represent, in their many and various ways, 'attempts by local people to reclaim the political process and to re-root it within the local community. The central demand made by group after group is for authority to be vested in the community – not the state, local government, the market or the local landlord, but those who rely on the local commons for their livelihood'.[67]

These attempts, in effect, express an understanding – which is some-times subconscious – that it is the institutional framework itself, in other words, the market economy and the liberal nation-state, which alienates people from the political and economic process. The market economy, as we have seen in Chapter 1, did not arise through some kind of 'automatic' mechanism in Europe, but through the crucial role played by the nation-state. Similarly, the penetration of the system of the market economy in the South (i.e. its economic integration within the world market economy system) was also 'a result of a conscious and often violent intervention by the government'.[68] In fact, it could be argued that it was the spreading of the growth economy in the South that has led to the global reproduction of the power pattern that characterizes the capitalist growth economy. In other words, it is the lack of control over domestic resources by the vast majority of the population, because of the lack of political and economic democracy, which is the ultimate cause of the kind of 'development' taking place in the South.

In this problematic, it is neither colonial exploitation – which, however, played a significant role in the violent destruction of the economic self-reliance of many countries – nor simply the corruption of elites in the

South or the conspiracies of those in the North that have led to the failure of the growth economy in the South. Contrary to classical Marxist thought, which saw colonialism as a 'necessary evil' because it contributed to the development of capitalism in the periphery,[69] I would argue that the fundamental cause of this failure is an inherent contradiction in the process of spreading the growth economy.

The growth economy can only survive through its continual reproduction and extension to new areas of economic activity. One way to achieve this is through the creation of new areas of economic activity, as a result, mainly, of technological changes, in mature growth economies. A second way is through a process of geographical expansion that, in fact, implies the destruction of the economic self-reliance of every community on earth. But, from the moment economic self-reliance is destroyed, either violently (colonialism), or through the market, and, as a result, two parties with unequal economic power (in terms of productivity, technology and income differentials) come in direct economic contact, then the automatic functioning of the market mechanism secures the reproduction and extension of inequality between the two parties. The essence, therefore, of the South's failure lies in the hugely uneven control over incomes and productive resources, which inevitably follows the establishment of a market/growth economy. It can easily be shown that in a market economy system, dominated by the growth ideology and personal greed, 'maldevelopment' is a matter of the automatic functioning of the system itself, since it is the purchasing power of the high income groups in the North and of the elites in the South that determines *what, how* and *for whom* to produce.[70] In other words, what is true for a 'domestic' market/growth economy, which, barring any effective social control of the market forces, can only be grounded on inequality in the distribution of economic power and unevenness in the development of various economic sectors, is equally (if not more) true for an internationalized market/growth economy.

From this perspective, it is surprising to see important theoreticians in the autonomy tradition adopt the view that the basic cause for the non-'development' of the South has been the fact that

> *this extraordinary spreading of the West had to face societies with completely different imaginary institutions which, as a result, have created anthropological types of a very different type than the type of the Western citizen, as described by the Declaration of Human Rights, or the type of the industrial worker and entrepreneur.*[71]

It is obvious that such an approach ignores the catastrophic impact of the spreading of the market economy and the subsequent growth economy on the self-reliant communities of the South and, in effect, exonerates the system of the market economy itself, in order to blame the 'imaginary significations' that developed in the South! No wonder that in this problematic the way out of the present global crisis can only emerge in the West ('I think that only a new development of the liberation movement in the West could change the parameters of the problem, i.e. could in some way ease the penetration – at least up to the point required – of the traditional institutions and traditional religious imaginary significations that today are dominant in most of the countries of the Third World').[72]

It is clear that this approach confuses the causes of the failure of the growth economy to spread to the South with the causes of the South's present predicament. Although it is true that 'traditional institutions and traditional religious imaginary significations' are significant explanatory factors for the failure of the spreading of the growth economy into the South, the present situation in the South is exclusively due to the penetration of their traditional economies and societies by the market/ growth economy of the North. Had the traditional structures of the South not been penetrated by the North's market economy, the former might have developed into a very different kind of world than it is today. A different world, but not the world of a failed growth economy, with all the unevenness, inequality, individualism and greed that characterize it.

Finally, the above discussion of development in terms of democracy should not be confused with the currently fashionable trend in the North (as André Gunder Frank[73] points out) of moving from the massive support of 'development' in the past, to the support (even backed by military invasions – see the recent US invasion in Haiti) of 'democracy' now. It is clear that 'development' and 'democracy' are used by the North as ideologies, in the sense of the 'objective' justification of the status quo. Thus, in the same way that the ideologies of the market economy and export-led growth were used in the past to justify the 'development' that was going on in the Third World, today it is the ideology of liberal democracy that is called to play the same role. In this context, the economic oligarchy of the 500 trans-national corporations (TNCs) which control the world economy (70 per cent of world trade, 80 per cent of foreign investment and 30 per cent of world GDP)[74] is presented as a 'market democracy', that is, a kind of economic democracy, whereas the control of the political process by political elites is presented as a political democracy. Together, free market and liberal democracy are 'fashionably identified as though they were inseparable if not indistinguishable',[75] ignoring the fact that, although TNCs are nationally based, still, they are not committed to any given community but to their worldwide networks. Therefore, both democracy and the environment are easily expendable in their calculations.

To conclude, what is needed is the development of a new approach that aims at the self-determination of individuals and communities, at the economic, social and political levels. Such an approach should be based on the formation of new political, economic and social structures that secure citizens' control over their own resources. Human needs do not have to be conditioned and infinitely expanded by a growth-oriented system; they could therefore be constantly adjusted and limited by the community itself. Furthermore, the needs of the significant part of the population that belongs to the non-privileged social strata in the North do not differ significantly from the needs of most of the population in the South. The problem therefore is how the 'New South', that is, the non-privileged social groups in the North and the South which constitute the vast majority of the world population, would force the 'New North', in other words, the small (but powerful, because of its monopolization of all effective means of power) minority, to realize the simple fact that the fundamental cause of the present economic, ecological and social crisis is the oligarchic political and economic structures that secure the maintenance and reproduction of its privileges.

The problem of 'development' is not therefore one of how the South could install a properly functioning market/growth economy, as the conventional approaches to development assert. It is not even a problem of how the growth economy could be replaced by a 'steady-state economy', as deep ecologists and others (usually belonging to the 'New North') argue. The problem is how a new inclusive democracy could determine collectively the basic needs of the population and find ways to meet them that minimize harm to the natural world.

Notes

1. Data calculated from the World Bank's *World Development Report 1995* (Oxford: Oxford University Press, 1995), Tables 1, 3, 13.
2. Data calculated from the World Bank's *World Development Report 1995, 1980*, Table 1.
3. World Bank, *Poverty: World Development Report 1990* (Washington, DC: World Bank), p. 28.
4. Eurostat, *Poverty in Figures* (Luxembourg: Office for Official Publications of the European Communities, 1990), Table B7.
5. Worldwatch, *Poverty and the Environment* (Washington, DC: Worldwatch Institute, 1989), p. 24.
6. Ted Trainer, 'A rejection of the Brundtland Report', *IFDA Dossier* 77 (May-June 1990), pp. 77–8.
7. Ted Trainer, *Developed to Death* (London: Green Print, 1989), p. 9.
8. *World Development Report 1992* (World Bank), Table 30.
9. Ted Trainer, *Developed to Death*, p. 39.
10. *Households Below Average Income* (London: HMSO, 1994).

11. *The Economist* (1 October 1994) (quoted by Paul Hirst and Grahame Thompson, *Globalization in Question* (London: Polity Press 1996), p. 99).

12. The average annual growth rate in South Korea, Hong Kong, Singapore, Malaysia and Thailand was about 8 per cent in 1970–93, versus 3 per cent in high income OECD countries (data calculated on the basis of the World Bank's *World Development Report 1995).*

13. See, for instance, A. Young, 'Lessons from the East Asian NICs: a contrarian view', *European Economic Review,* Vol. 38, Nos 3/4 (April 1994), pp. 964–73; and Paul Krugman, 'The myth of Asia's miracle', *Foreign Affairs* (Nov.-Dec. 1994), pp. 65–73.

14. 'D. Rodrick emphasizes the crucial role of the governments in these countries in engineering a rise in investment: this involved a range of strategic interventionary measures including investment subsidies, administrative guidance and the use of public enterprises' (quoted by Paul Hirst and Grahame Thompson, *Globalization in Question,* p. 114). See also Robert Pollin and Diana Alarcon, 'Debt crisis, accumulation and economic re-structuring in Latin America', *International Review of Applied Economics,* Vol. 2, No. 2 (June 1988); and Takis Fotopoulos, 'Economic restructuring and the debt problem: the Greek case', *International Review of Applied Economics,* Vol. 6, No. 1 (1992).

15. 'South Korea has been a protectionist island in the hegemonic free trade sea since the 1940s . . . it has had particularly strong neo-mercantilist tendencies since the early 1970s', Bruce Cumings: 'The abortive abertura: South Korea in the light of Latin American experience', *New Left Review,* No. 173 (Jan.-Feb. 1989), p. 13.

16. See A.H. Amsden, *Asia's Next Giant: South Korea and Late Industrialization* (Oxford: Oxford University Press, 1989), Ch. 6.

17. World Bank, *World Development Report 1995,* Table 9.

18. Martin Jacques, 'The end of the Western world', BBC2, 12 and 19 May 1996.

19. World Bank, *World Development Report* 1981 and 1995, Table 1.

20. Japanese unemployment rose from 2.1 per cent of the labour force in 1991 to 3.1 per cent in 1995, and it is forecast to rise to 3.4 per cent in 1996, OECD, *Economic Outlook* (December 1995).

21. Ian M.D. Little, *Economic Development: Theory, Policy and International Relations* (New York: Basic Books, 1982), p. 6.

22. Anthony Brewer, *Marxist Theories of Imperialism: A Critical Survey* (London: Routledge & Kegan Paul, 1980), p. 18.

23. T. Dos Santos, 'The crisis of development theory and the problem of dependence in Latin America' in *Underdevelopment and Development,* Henry Bernstein (ed.) (Harmondsworth: Penguin, 1973), p. 76.

24. Alain Lipietz, *Miracles and Mirages* (London: Verso, 1987), pp. 29–30.

25. See, e.g., Phyllis Deane, *The Evolution of Economic Ideas* (Cambridge: Cambridge University Press, 1978), Ch. 3.

26. Ted Trainer, *Developed to Death,* p. 17. For further evidence about the enclosure movement in the South during the colonial and post-colonial period, see *The Ecologist,* Vol. 22, No. 4 (July-Aug. 1992).

27. Paul Ehrlich, *The Population Bomb* (New York: Simon & Schuster, 1990).

28. Bill Devall, *Simple in Means, Rich in Ends: Practising Deep Ecology* (London: Green Print, 1990), p. 16. Similarly, Arne Naess, the father of deep ecology,

stresses that 'the flourishing of non-human life requires such a decrease' (of the human population); Arne Naess, 'Deep ecology and ultimate premises', reprinted from *The Ecologist* in *Society and Nature,* Vol. 1, No. 2 (1992) p. 114.

29. For a comprehensive critique of the neo-Malthusian trends within the Green movement, see Murray Bookchin, 'The population myth' in *Which Way for the Ecology Movement?* (Edinburgh: AK Press, 1994).

30. World Bank, *World Development Report 1995,* Table 25; and *Whitaker's Almanack* 1991.

31. World Bank, *World Development Report 1995,* Table 26.

32. *The Guardian* (11 Jan. 1996). Similarly, a TV documentary in UK, that caused a lot of stir, documented the brutal tactics used in Chinese orphanages to get rid of thousands of unwanted, mainly female, babies, within the context of the Chinese 'one child' population policy; Channel 4, 'Dying rooms' (9 Jan. 1996). See, also, Human Rights Watch/Asia (HRWA), *Death by Default* (1995).

33. International Union for the Scientific Study of Population (IUSSP), quoted in *The Guardian* (5 Sept. 1994).

34. *Washington Post/The Guardian* (9 June 1994).

35. *The Guardian* (2 Sept. 1994).

36. *World Development Report 1995,* Table 26.

37. *US National Academy of Sciences Report* (Washington, DC: US Government Printing Office, 1986).

38. *The Guardian,* 29 April 1992.

39. World Bank, *World Development Report 1995*, Table 26.

40. Jonathon Porritt, 'Birth of a new world order', *The Guardian* (2 Sept. 1994).

41. In 1993, the infant mortality rate (per 1000 live births) was 64 in low-income countries (89, if we exclude China and India) versus seven in high-income countries. The corresponding rates for those children under five were 103 (144 excluding China and India) versus nine! *World Development Report 1995,* Table 27.

42. Editorial in *The Guardian* (3 Sept. 1994).

43. *The Observer* (4 Sept. 1994).

44. Karl Marx and Friedrich Engels, *Manifesto of the Communist Party* (Moscow: Progress Publishers, 1952), p. 46.

45. Shlomo Avineri (ed.), *Karl Marx on Colonialism and Modernization* (New York: Anchor Books, 1969), pp. 5–6.

46. Karl Marx, *The Revolutions of 1848* (Harmondsworth: Penguin, 1973), p. 71.

47. The World Bank Group, *Learning from the Past: Embracing the Future* (Washington, DC: World Bank, 19 July 1994).

48. For a definition of the economic surplus see Paul A. Baran, *The Political Economy of Growth* (New York: Modern Reader, 1957), Ch. 2.

49. See André Gunder Frank, *Capitalism and Underdevelopment in Latin America* (New York: Modern Reader, 1967, 1969).

50. See Immanuel Wallerstein, *The Modern World System* (New York: Academic Press, 1974), and *The Capitalist World Economy* (Cambridge: Cambridge University Press, 1979).

51. Arghiri Emmanuel, *Unequal Exchange, A Study of the Imperialism of Trade* (New York: Monthly Review Press, 1972).
52. See Samir Amin, *Accumulation on a World Scale* (New York: Monthly Review Press, 1974).
53. See, for instance, John G. Taylor, *From Modernization to Modes of Production, A Critique of the Sociologies of Development and Underdevelopment* (London: Macmillan, 1979).
54. For an introduction to the regulation approach in general, see Robert Boyer, *La théorie de la régulation* (Paris: Editions La Découverte, 1986).
55. Alain Lipietz, *Miracles and Mirages*.
56. Alain Lipietz, *Miracles and Mirages*, p. 19.
57. Alain Lipietz, *Miracles and Mirages*, pp. 25–6.
58. Alain Lipietz, *Miracles and Mirages*, p. 19.
59. World Bank, *Development and the Environment* (Oxford: Oxford University Press, 1992), p. 7.
60. Data calculated on the basis of the *World Development Report 1994*; and Richard Douthwaite, *The Growth Illusion* (Bideford, Devon: Green Books, 1992), p. 195.
61. World Bank, *Development and the Environment*, p. 37.
62. UNFAO, *Sustainable Crop Production and Protection: Background Document* (UNFAO: 1991), p. 2.
63. Barry Hugill, *The Observer*, (3 March 1996).
64. UNICEF Report 1994, *The Guardian* (22 June 1994).
65. In a similar vein, John Holloway of Edinburgh University argues in *Capital & Class* that we live in a world where 'exploitation is not the exploitation of poor countries by rich countries but of global labour by global capital'; quoted in William Keegan's column, *The Observer* (6 Feb. 1994).
66. Gustavo Esteva, 'The right to stop development', NGONET UNCED *Feature* (13 June 1992), Rio de Janeiro.
67. See 'Reclaiming the commons', *The Ecologist*, Vol. 22, No. 4 (July-Aug. 1992), p. 202.
68. Gustavo Esteva, quoted in *The Ecologist*, Vol. 22, No. 4 (July-Aug. 1992), p. 174.
69. See Shlomo Avineri (ed.), *Karl Marx on Colonialism and Modernization*.
70. See Ted Trainer, *Developed to Death*.
71. Cornelius Castoriadis, 'The West and the Third World' in *The Broken World* (Athens: Upsilon, 1992), p. 91.
72. Cornelius Castoriadis, *The Broken World*, p. 96.
73. André Gunder Frank, 'Development, democracy, and the market', *Society and Nature*, Vol. 3, No. 1 (1995), pp. 1–25.
74. *The Ecologist*, Vol. 22, No. 4 (July-Aug. 1992), p. 159. For more data, see Tim Lang and Colin Hines, *The New Protectionism* (London: Earthscan, 1993), Ch. 3.
75. André Gunder Frank, 'Development, democracy, and the market', p. 12.

CHAPTER 4

The Generalized Crisis of the Capitalist Growth Economy

It has now become generally acknowledged that contemporary society, which presently takes everywhere the form of a market/growth economy, is undergoing a profound and widespread crisis. It is precisely the universal character of this crisis that constitutes the determining factor differentiating it from other crises in the past, while, simultaneously, it calls into question practically every structure and 'signification' that supports contemporary hierarchical societies in East and West, North and South. Thus, the present crisis calls into question not just the political, economic, social and ecological structures that came into being with the rise of the market economy, but also the actual values that have sustained these structures and particularly the post-Enlightenment meaning of Progress and its partial identification with growth.

In the first part of the chapter the many dimensions of the present generalized crisis are discussed (economic, political, social, ideological). In the second part the focus is on the ecological crisis and the approaches developed to interpret it, which, in fact, represent a synthesis of the classical traditions that emerged with the rise of the market economy (liberalism, socialism) and the ecological paradigm. The premises of three other approaches, which, in various degrees, may be considered as not belonging to this synthesis (deep ecology, 'sustainable' development and 'appropriate' development approaches) are also discussed.

In the final part, the Right's and Left's proposals to deal with the multidimensional crisis are examined and it is argued that the proposal of the former for further marketization is bound to worsen the crisis whereas that of the latter for the enhancement of the 'civil society' is both a-historical and utopian in the negative sense of the word. The conclusion is that the need for a new vision, which will transcend both the neoliberal market economy and socialist statism, is, in the context of the present generalized crisis, more pressing than ever.

A multidimensional crisis

The economic dimension

As regards, first, the economic crisis, the North has yet to recover from the crisis that surfaced in the mid-1970s as a result of the fundamental contradiction that was created, as we saw in Chapter 1, by the internationalization of the market economy and the parallel expansion of statism, in the sense of active state control aiming at determining the level of economic activity. In an effort to resolve this contradiction, a process of shrinking the state's economic role and of parallel freeing and deregulating markets was initiated by neoliberals and social liberals which has already had devastating consequences on the majority of the population in the North.

Thus, the drastic reduction in statism has been at least partly responsible for the vast expansion of open unemployment. However, it seems that the present period of massive unemployment in the North is a transitional period which will move the market economy from the relative full employment conditions of the period of the social-democratic consensus to a new period of massive low-paid employment and under-employment. This development would be the outcome both of the liberalization of labour markets and of a determined effort by the political elites to reduce open unemployment, which carries a high political cost and completely discredits the market/growth economy. A recent analysis of US Labor Department numbers is revealing about present trends. Between 1979 and 1995 more than 43 million jobs had been lost in the USA and, as the analysis puts it (although most of these jobs have been replaced),

> the sting is in the nature of the replacement work. Whereas 25 years ago the vast majority of the people who were laid off found jobs that paid as well as their old ones, Labor Department numbers show that now only about 35 per cent of laid-off full-time workers end up in equally remunerative or better-paid jobs . . . the result is the most job insecurity since the Depression of the 1930s.[1]

Furthermore, the effect of the liberalization of markets in the USA has been the drastic worsening of the distribution of income. The real wages of two-thirds of American workers have dropped considerably (weekly wages fell by 18 per cent between 1973 and 1990), causing a significant widening of inequality.[2] Thus, although average household income climbed 10 per cent between 1979 and 1994, 97 per cent of the gain went to the richest 20 per cent.[3]

The USA trends are sure to be reproduced soon all over the North, particularly after the collapse of the alternative 'Rhineland' model of 'social market' capitalism. The fierce competition among the countries in the Triad can safely be predicted to create conditions, not so much of massive *open* unemployment, but of low-paid employment in the context of 'flexible' labour markets. The OECD General Secretary was explicit about this at the April 1996 Lille jobs summit of the 'Group of 7': 'Tomorrow, the third way between unemployment and insecurity will be closer to the Anglo-Saxon rather than to the "European" model . . . it is the Anglo-Saxon countries which, as a result of the greater flexibility of their economies, are able to create more jobs'.[4]

However, to my mind, the crisis of the market/growth economy in the North does not constitute the decisive element in the economic crisis. As long as the '40 per cent' society is somehow reproduced, the system may be stabilized when it moves to a new equilibrium resting on the exploitation of the technological advantages of the North and the low production cost of the new South. I think the decisive element in the economic crisis consists of the fact that the system of the market economy is not *inherently* capable of transforming the market economy of the South into a self-sustaining growth economy, similar to the one already established in the North. This is demonstrated by the fact that the gap between North and South has widened dramatically since the start of the peripheral marketization process – that is, since the market economy of the former began to penetrate the traditional economies of the latter – and it is still rapidly increasing. The result of the universalization of the market/growth economy is the marginalization of a very significant part of the world population. Thus, according to the ILO, in the early 1990s, 120 million people were unemployed and 700 million people were underemployed living below subsistence level.[5] In other words, about 30 per cent of the world's population which is capable of working do not have enough work for subsistence, a crisis correctly described as worse than in the 1930s. Furthermore, according to the latest UN Human Development Report (1996), the total wealth of the world's 358 billionaires equals the combined income of 2,300,000,000 people, the poorest 45 per cent of the world population. These facts, by themselves, are calling into question the entire economic and social basis of the market economy.

The inherent incapability of the North to create self-sustaining consumer societies in the South emanates from the fact that the concentration of economic power and the parallel increasing inequality all over the world are not just consequences but also, as was shown earlier, preconditions for the reproduction of the market/growth economy. The earth's natural resources simply do not suffice for the standards of living enjoyed today by the privileged in the North to be universalized. In other words, there is an absolute natural barrier that makes impossible the globalization of the North's capitalist type of growth economy.

Thus, even if world population was going to remain at the present level in the next century, the universalization of the North's growth economy would imply the quadrupling of the annual world production of energy for per capita energy consumption levels presently enjoyed by the high income countries to be globalized (or a sixfold increase for everybody to enjoy the American consumption standards). But, of course, the world population is bound to increase significantly in the next century. If we assume, for example, that the world population rises sometime in the next century to 11 billion – a reasonable estimate on the basis of presently available data – then, for the inhabitants of our planet to reach the per capita energy use rates that those living in the rich countries enjoy now, world energy production would have to be eight times as great as it is at present (or 12 times as great for everybody to enjoy the US consumption standards).[6] However, on the basis of existing estimates of all potentially recoverable mineral and energy resources (including all the deposits we are ever likely to find), 'there is no chance that everybody in the world can rise to anywhere near the per capita use rates that the few in rich countries enjoy now . . . nor is there any foreseeable way of deriving such enormous quantities of energy from alternative sources such as the sun, wind or tides'.[7] If, alternatively, we try to globalize the present Western energy consumption standards using nuclear energy, then, as the same study stresses, on the basis of the world population reaching 11 billion in the next century, we would need to build 200,000 giant nuclear reactors, i.e. one thousand times the world's present nuclear capacity.

For all that, despite the huge 'objective' crisis, which means that the present economic system cannot meet even the basic needs of at least one-fifth of the world's population,[8] the world market economy is not widely questioned. It is obvious that the recent collapse of the 'socialist' growth economy and the consequent integration of the 'Left' into social-liberalism has functioned as a decisive pacifying factor at the subjective level. This makes the need for a new liberatory project, which will transcend both the market economy and 'socialist' statism, even more imperative.

The political dimension

The phenomenon known as the 'crisis of politics', which is today under-mining the foundations of parliamentary democracy, provides a character-istic indication of the political dimension of the crisis. The growing crisis of traditional politics is expressed today by several symptoms which frequently take the form of an implicit or explicit questioning of funda-mental liberal democracy institutions (parties, electoral contests, etc.). Such symptoms are the significant and sometimes rising abstention rates in electoral contests, the diminishing numbers of party members, the fact that the respect for professional politicians has never been at such a low level (the very frequent financial scandals of late in Italy, France, Spain, Greece and elsewhere have simply reaffirmed the belief that politics, for the vast majority of the politicians – liberals and social democrats alike – is just a job, i.e. a way to make money), etc. Within this context of a general crisis of traditional politics, it does not seem surprising, as we shall see below, that Left politics suffers particularly badly.

As regards the general crisis of traditional politics, a historical cause of the present mass apathy is the fact that 'the last two centuries have proved the fundamental incompatibility of both liberal democracy and of Marxist–Leninist "socialism" with the project of autonomy'.[9] However, the question still remains why this crisis has become particularly acute in the last decade or so. To my mind, the answer has to be found in the cumulative effect of the structural changes which have affected the market economy since the mid-1970s:

- The growing internationalization of the market economy that has undermined effectively not only the state's power to control economic events but, by implication, the belief in the efficacy of traditional politics.
- The acute intensification of the struggle for competitiveness among the countries in the Triad (EC, USA, Japan) which, in turn, has resulted in the collapse of social democracy, the establishment of the 'neoliberal consensus' and the consequent effective elimination of ideological differences between political parties.
- The technological changes which have led to the present post-industrial society and the corresponding changes in the structure of employment and the electorate, which, in combination with the massive unemployment and underemployment, have led to the decline of the power of the traditional working class.

Today's electoral contests are in effect decided by the '40 per cent' contended electoral majority, whereas the 'underclass', which was created by neoliberalism and automation, mostly does not take part in such contests. Therefore, the growing apathy towards politics does not mainly reflect a general indifference regarding social issues, as a result of consumerism, but a growing lack of confidence, especially of weaker social groups, in traditional political parties and their ability to solve social problems. It is not accidental that the higher abstention rates in electoral contests usually occur among the lower income groups, which fail to see anymore any significant difference between liberal and social-democratic parties. Another part of the growing indifference with traditional politics, especially among young people, is due to the growing disillusionment with socialism, which has led to the myth of 'the end of ideologies' and further enhanced the spreading of the culture of individualism that has been promoted by neoliberalism.

However, if the worsening of the crisis in politics may be attributed to the above factors, the crisis itself is chronic and embraces all citizens (apart from a very small minority) who feel alienated from a process which in reality they do not control. This, in turn, puts into question liberal democracy, a system that allows a social minority (professional politicians) to determine the quality of life of each citizen.

Left politics has been particularly affected by the general crisis of traditional politics. The usual explanation of this phenomenon goes back to the challenge to the system posed by the rise of the New Left in the late 1960s which, once it withered away, was inevitably followed by the ruling elite's backlash which led to a general shift to the Right in the West. But, I think that the structural changes mentioned above were bound to particularly affect Left politics, backlash or no backlash. The collapse of social democracy was not only the inevitable outcome of the drastic reduction of the state's economic power, and in particular its power to secure high levels of employment in an internationalized economy, but also because Keynesian policies undermined the profits and competitiveness of capital, as they pushed real wages to rise faster than productivity.

The abandonment of the full employment commitment, combined with the gradual dismantling of the welfare state (in order to create better conditions of competitiveness through the drastic reduction of the 'social wage' which was putting a significant burden on the cost of production), fatally undermined the political appeal of social democracy and led to the present crisis of social-democratic politics. Still, social democrats pretend that there is no 'neoliberal consensus' and that their policies are significantly different from those of the neoliberals. All this, despite the fact that the fundamental neoliberal principle, that is, the maximization of the role of the market in the economy and society, has already been enshrined in their own governmental or political programmes. However, the neoliberal consensus, which in Europe has already been institutionalized through the Maastricht Treaty, is not merely a temporary phenomenon but, as we have seen above, represents the political consequence of structural changes in the market economy system that lead to the completion of the market – a historical process that was merely interrupted by the statist phase.

Finally, the collapse of 'actually existing socialism' played a crucial role with respect to the decline of Left politics, since it contributed significantly to a further disillusionment with the socialist project and provided the moral cover, for those that needed it, for individualist values. The massive shift of many ex-socialist intellectuals towards liberalism is a clear indication of this. The fact that the regimes in the East were not authentically socialist in the first place did not play any significant role in modifying the general pessimism created by their collapse. This may be explained on the grounds either that the average supporter of the Left in the West was not in a position to assess the true nature of these regimes, or that the very failure of the experiment for radical social change in a sense 'proved' the inapplicability of socialist ideals. Thus, the collapse of 'socialist' statism in the East, instead of functioning as a catalyst for the development of a new non-authoritarian conception of politics – in other words, a general movement to an authentic Left – simply led to a general movement to the Right. This movement to the Right refers not just to the '40 per cent' privileged minority which benefits from the neoliberal consensus but also to a significant part of the middle groups between this minority and the underclass, which hope to benefit from the neoliberal consensus. The rest, including most of the underclass who are the main victims of the neoliberal internationalized economy, have fallen into political apathy and an unconscious rejection of established society which usually has taken the form of an explosion of crime and, sometimes, violent riots. And this takes us to the social dimension of the crisis.

The social dimension

The present social crisis is in fact a continuation of the crisis that started in the 1960s when the hierarchical relations between social individuals in contemporary society (between bosses and workers, men and women, parents and children, teachers and pupils and so on) were questioned. Fundamental traditional institutions, like marriage, the family, etc. which for many years had regulated some of these relations, have since then been faltering, despite the conservative backlash that accompanied the rise of the neoliberal consensus. This crisis in social relations reflects, also, a crisis of identity, in the sense that people no longer have well-defined socially predetermined roles with which they may identify. Such predetermined roles are collapsing daily, creating confusion in social relations and shaking society's internal structure. At the same time, the crisis of identity manifests itself, lately, at the cultural level as well, leading to the well-known ethnic conflicts (e.g. in the former Yugoslavia).

The social crisis has been aggravated by the expansion of the market economy into all sectors of social life, in the context of its present internationalized form. It is, of course, well known that the market is the greatest enemy of traditional values. It is not, therefore, surprising that the social crisis is more pronounced in precisely those countries where marketization has been well advanced. This becomes evident by the fact that neither campaigns of the 'back to basics' type (Britain), nor the growth of religious, mystic and other similar tendencies (USA) have had any restraining effect on the most obvious symptom of the social crisis: the explosion of criminality.

In Britain, for instance, it took 30 years for the crime rate to double, from 1 million incidents in 1950 to 2.2 million in 1979. However, in the past ten years, the crime rate has more than doubled, and it reached the 5 million mark in the 1990s. The ruling elites respond to the explosion of crime by building more jails, despite the fact that, as a Home Office study in Britain (reflecting similar research from the USA and Germany) has shown, the prison population has to increase by 25 per cent to cut the annual crime rate by 1 per cent![10] Thus, in the USA the prison population has tripled in the last 15 years (from 330,000 in 1980 to 1.5 million in 1995) with the black population being the most hard hit (one in three black males aged 20–30 is either in prison or on probation) and in Britain increased by 30 per cent in the last three years.[11] In fact, the explosion of crime, as Martin Woolacott points out, tends to take the form of an insurgency in urban conglomerations all over the world and is treated as such by the ruling elites.[12]

So, the marketization of the economy has not only increased the economic privileges of the privileged minority; it has also increased its insecurity. This is why the new overclass increasingly isolates itself in luxury ghettos. At the same time, marketization, and in particular the flexible labour market, has increased job insecurity – a phenomenon that today affects everybody apart from the very few in the upper class. In Britain, for instance, 'five million people have been made redundant in the 1990s and although the great majority soon found another job, their experience of work has been transformed'.[13] No wonder that a very recent poll showed that only one person in six nowadays finds it easier than it was a few years ago to plan the future with confidence; and almost three times as many people, 45 per cent, find it harder.[14] Similarly, in the USA three-quarters of all households have had a close encounter with layoffs since 1980, according to a poll by the *New York Times* and, in a reversal from the early 1980s, workers with at least some college education make up the majority of people whose jobs are eliminated and better paid workers account for twice the share of the lost jobs that they did in the 1980s.[15] The very fact that full-time jobs have been disappearing fast in the last 20 years is significantly contributing to the feeling of insecurity. In Britain, again, the proportion of the adult population in full-time tenured jobs fell from about 55 per cent in 1975 to 35 per cent in 1993.[16]

For all that, the growth economy has already created a *growth society*, the main characteristics of which are consumerism, privacy and the subsequent disintegration of society's cohesion as citizens are converted into consumers. In this sense, the growth society heralds the 'non-society', that is, the substitution of atomized families and individuals for society. It is the increasingly atomized character of the growth society that, at the subjective level, allows its reproduction, despite the fact that given the present potentialities, it is a dismal failure.

The ideological dimension
The generalized crisis manifests itself, also, at the ideological level, with a parallel crisis regarding the credibility of science. This crisis, which surfaced about 25 years ago, has systematically undermined many 'truths'[17] and especially those on the basis of which we used to justify our 'certainty' concerning the 'scientific' interpretation of social and economic phenomena. But, as science plays a double role with respect to the reproduction of the growth economy, this crisis is particularly significant. Thus, first, science plays a functional role in the material reproduction of the growth economy through its decisive contribution to the effort to dominate the natural world and maximize growth. Second, science plays an equally important ideological role in justifying 'objectively' the growth economy. Just as religion played an important part in justifying feudal hierarchy, so does science, particularly social 'science', play a crucial role today in justifying the modern hierarchical society. In fact, from the moment science replaced religion as the dominant world view, it had 'objectively' justified the growth economy, both in its capitalist and socialist types.

However, the realization of the effects of economic growth upon Nature and, subsequently, upon the quality of life, called into question the functional role of science in advancing Progress. When, on top of this, the credibility of scientific truths themselves was challenged, whether those truths originated in orthodox social science[18] or in the alternative 'science' of socialism, Marxism,[19] then, the moment of truth for the growth ideology had come. Today, the central imaginary signification of the growth economy, that is, the identification of Progress with growth and the implied idea of human domination over Nature, is, for the first time after the Enlightenment, under massive fire.

At the same time, the collapse of socialist statism and the rise of neoliberalism had the effect that the radical critique of 'scientific' socialism, statism and authoritarian politics did not function as a catalyst for further development of the non-authoritarian Left thinking. Instead, the critique of scientism was taken over by post-modernist theoreticians and was developed into a general relativism, which inevitably led to the abandonment of any effective critique of the status quo and to the theorization of conformism.[20]

But, as will be stressed in Chapter 8, it is not science itself and rationalism in general that have to be blamed for the present multidimensional crisis, as irrationalists of various types usually assert. Like technology, applied science is not 'neutral' to the logic and dynamic of the market economy. Science belongs to the autonomy tradition from the point of view of the methods it uses to derive its truths and, sometimes, even from the point of view of its content (e.g. demystification of religious beliefs). Therefore, what is needed today is not to jettison rationalism altogether in the interpretation of social phenomena but to transcend 'objective' rationalism (i.e. the rationalism which is grounded on 'objective laws' of natural or social evolution) and develop a new kind of democratic rationalism.

The growth economy and the ecological crisis

A major component of the present multidimensional crisis is the ecological crisis, namely the crisis which concerns mainly not the relations between social individuals, as the other dimensions of the crisis, but our interaction, as social individuals, with the environment. The upsetting of ecological systems, the widespread pollution, the gradual exhaustion of natural resources and, in general, the rapid downgrading of the environment and the quality of life have made the limits of economic growth manifestly apparent in the past 30 years.

Despite the efforts of 'eco-realists'[21] to give a rosy picture of the growth economy, it cannot be denied that carbon dioxide concentrations (the main contributor to the greenhouse effect) which have remained almost stable for the entire millennium, that is up to the emergence of the market economy, have since then taken off, increasing by almost 30 per cent.[22] As a result, in the period since the beginning of this century, a long-term trend of warming in the lowest layer of the atmosphere can be established[23] and all the recent evidence points to a significant rise in temperatures in the last decade or so.[24] Also, the fact cannot be denied that half of the world's tropical forests, home to a third of the world's plants and animals, have disappeared in this century alone and that recently this process accelerated. Thus, in the last 10 years (1980–90) the annual rate of felling of tropical forests rose by 36 per cent and, today, a forest area approximately the size of Austria disappears every year![25] Finally, no one can deny the fact that, as a result of intensive farming – another direct result of the emergence of the growth economy – and its effects on agroecosystems, animal rearing, etc., the natural world, including human health, is seriously damaged.

The case of the 'mad cow disease' (Bovine Spongiform Enceph-alopathy – BSE) is illustrative because it is directly related to both the main elements of the market economy: marketization and growth. BSE has taken on massive proportions in Britain during this decade and because of the possible link with Creutzfeldt-Jacob disease (CJD), today, hundreds of thousands of human lives may be in danger. The very fact that this massive crisis happened in Britain is not of course accidental. As we saw in Chapter 1, Britain was pivotal in the launching of the present neoliberal phase of marketization. Thus, in the context of the deregulations and lifting of social controls on markets that followed the neoliberal rise to power in 1979, animal feed procedures were fatally relaxed.[26] As a result, British farmers, in their struggle to minimize costs – as the market economy dictated – moved to less safe cow feed procedures, initiating the present crisis. This was not because British farmers were more greedy but because they were more exposed to market forces than their counterparts elsewhere. Farmers everywhere, in order to survive in a market/growth economy, have to keep minimizing the production cost, intensifying production and increasing the size of their holdings. Thus, as farmers become more and more dependent on inputs (chemicals, seed, etc.) sold to them by the agrochemical industry, they have to grow in order to survive. In Britain, for instance, a dairy farmer in the 1950s could earn a living with 15 cows; by the 1980s to have the same real income he needed 75 cows.[27] At the same time, as small farmers are thrown out of their farms, unable to survive in the grow-or-die competition with agribusiness, concentration increases: the number of farms in Britain fell from 454,000 in 1953 to 242,300 in 1981.[28]

The realization of the ecological implications of the growth economy has led, particularly in the last quarter of the century, to the development of various 'ecological' approaches. I am not going to deal here with the differences between environmentalism and ecologism[29] and, generally, the controversies among Green thinkers about what constitutes 'ecological' thought. As far as this book is concerned any approach dealing with the environmental implications of the growth component of the market economy can be classified under what we may call the 'ecological paradigm'. It is therefore obvious that I include in the ecological paradigm the approaches which aim to 'green' the growth economy, as well as those aiming to jettison it altogether. In the former category belongs, for instance, the 'sustainable development' approach (see next section) and liberal environmentalism,[30] whereas in the latter belong the social ecology[31] approach, which sees the causes of the present ecological crisis in terms of the hierarchical structures of domination and exploitation in capitalist society, eco-socialism,[32] which emphasizes the significance of production relations, the 'appropriate development approach' and the deep ecology approach.

Some of the above approaches explicitly attempt a synthesis between one of the classical traditions which focus on the marketization element of the market economy and an analysis of the ecological implications of growth; other approaches do not aim, at least explicitly, at such a synthesis. As regards the former, one may, for instance, classify under the 'synthesis' label the approaches of liberal environmentalism, eco-socialism and social ecology, which represent an explicit attempt for a synthesis with liberalism, socialist statism (usually Marxism) and libertarian socialism respectively. As regards the latter, the case par excellence is of course that of 'deep ecology', which focuses almost exclusively on the ecological implications of the growth economy. However, the 'appropriate development' and 'sustainable development' approaches may also be classified in this category because, although they do deal with both the marketization and growth components of the market economy, it would be inaccurate to classify them as an attempt at an explicit synthesis with any of the old traditions.

In the sections that follow, these three approaches will be discussed in more detail.

The sustainable development approach

The 'sustainable development' approach, which was promoted by the Brundtland Report,[33] and embraced by the Green *realos* all over the world, aims at achieving sustainable development. This is defined as 'development that meets the needs of the present without compromising the ability of future generations to meet their own needs'.[34]

The Report is founded on three fundamental principles, according to which, the continuation of growth:

(a) is the key to social justice, since it can eliminate poverty;[35]
(b) is the key to environmental protection;[36]
(c) 'could be environmentally sustainable, if industrialized nations can continue the recent shifts in the content of their growth towards less material and energy-intensive activities and the improvement of their efficiency in using materials and energy'.[37]

As regards (a), one may point out that there are two main ways in which economic growth may reduce poverty: either through the trickle-down effect (as neoliberals argue) and/or through some kind of redistributive government action (as statists hold). Leaving aside the inefficacy of the trickle-down effect which was considered earlier, it is obvious that effective redistributive government action in favour of the underclass is by definition excluded within the framework of the neoliberal internationalized market economy, which is taken for granted by the Report. In fact, as we have seen in Chapter 1, the redistribution of income that takes place in this framework is against the underclass, not in favour of it!

As regards (b) what the Report implies is the possibility of a 'green capitalism'. But this assumed possibility ignores the fundamental contradiction that exists between the logic and dynamic of the growth economy, on the one hand, and the attempt to condition this dynamic with qualitative criteria on the other. Thus, the contradiction that emerged in the past, when an attempt was made by socialist statism to introduce socialist criteria (equity and social justice) in the growth process, is certain to emerge again at present, if a similar attempt is made to introduce ecological criteria (e.g. sustainability and enhancement of the resource base) into the same process.

Finally, as regards (c), although one would agree that some gains have been made in pollution control and the efficient use of energy and resources, there is no sign that the ecological problems have become, as a result, less serious or threatening. Instead, the opposite seems to be the case with respect to all major ecological problems, that is, the greenhouse effect, acid rain, salinity, ozone depletion, forest loss, desertification, soil loss and so on.[38]

One may therefore conclude that the fact that this approach ignores the phenomenon of the concentration of power, as a fundamental consequence and also a precondition for growth, is not irrelevant to the essential solutions proposed by it: more growth, more effort and better policies, laws and institutions, as well as increasing efficiency of energy and resource use. It is therefore obvious that the real aim of this approach is not to propose ways to achieve sustainable development but, instead, ways to create an 'eco-friendly' market/growth economy – a contradiction in terms.

The deep ecology approach

Supporters of the sustainable development approach are not the only ones who see the way out of the ecological crisis in contradictory terms, that is, in terms of a growth economy subject to qualitative prescriptions of sustainability. Deep ecologists fall into a similar trap. Deep ecology attributes equality to all forms of life ('biocentric equality') and suggests that relations with the natural world will have to change first, in order to change social relations, and not vice versa. Thus, supporters of this approach argue that the ultimate cause of the ecological crisis should be found in the historical identification, since the Enlightenment, of progress with economic growth. Consequently, the way out of the crisis is to abandon notions of progress so that the present growth economy can be replaced by a 'steady-state economy' or even a 'declining-state economy'.[39] Similarly, others see sustainable development in terms of 'a development path towards a stable state', which necessitates a 'stable population'[40] – a clear indication that the deep ecology approach adopts fully the overpopulation myth that we considered earlier.

It is obvious that deep ecology sees the causes of the ecological crisis as the direct outcome of an *anthropocentric* approach to the natural world, which sees human values as the source of all value and aims at the use of nature as an instrument in the satisfaction of human wants. It is also clear that the deep ecology approach considers the present non-sustainable development as a cultural rather than as an institutional issue, as a matter of values rather than as the inevitable outcome of the rise of the market economy, with its grow-or-die dynamic, which has led to the present growth economy.

However, it would be hardly justifiable to blame anthropocentrism for the present global ecological damage. Anthropocentrism, after all, was around – especially in the West – long before the process of massive ecological destruction started about two centuries ago. One could there-fore argue that it is not anthropocentrism as such that has led to the present crisis but the fact that the market economy and the subsequent growth economy had to be founded on an ideology that justified the human domination of nature *en masse*. If this is so, then, the way out of the ecological crisis is not just a matter of changing our values to put nature on an equal footing with treasured human values. No one could seriously expect that a new culture involving a non-domineering approach towards nature could have a chance of appealing to the vast majority of the earth's population who are faced with the dilemma of jobs versus the environ-ment. It is therefore obvious that the dilemma 'growth economy' versus 'a steady-state economy' is a false one and is usually put by people who do not face, as a result of their social position, the above genuine dilemma.

Furthermore, changing our values with respect to our relationship to nature will not, by itself, force the market economy or the state to wither away. It is therefore naive to suggest, as deep ecologists do, that 'if everyone consumed significantly less, the world market economy would probably collapse'.[41] It does not require a deep historical knowledge or knowledge of economics to realize that a significant decline in sales, far from leading to a collapse of the market economy, may simply induce a slump leading to even more massive unemployment at the economic level which might easily be accompanied by the rise of totalitarian regimes at the political level (perhaps of the eco-fascist variety this time).

Similar considerations could be expressed with respect to another version of deep ecology which stresses the 'Euro-centric' character of the growth economy and the need for sustainable development to be based on 'knowledge and technologies that originate from an intimate under-standing of the natural world [and] . . . the revival of a very ancient cultural gaiocentric tradition of considering the earth as a goddess and mother of all life'.[42] According to this version, land reform, a return to traditional

cultures and the abandonment by industrial countries of their fatal attraction to the fossil fuel technologies and culture is the solution to the
problem of unsustainable development – a problem which is created by
capitalism, defined as 'primarily the politics of acquiring and holding
wealth for a small ruling class'.[43]

But capitalism, or better, the market economy/growth economy, is not
just a matter of policy or ideology. It is a historical structure, a form of social
and economic organization. Therefore, the enclosure of land in the South, as
well as the kind of technologies developed within the market economy, are
not just matters of policy, or of 'aping the white culture', but part and parcel
of the market economy system itself. Similarly, competition and integration
in the world economy are not simply cultural issues but inevitable outcomes
of the institutional framework defined by the market economy. Hence, the
root of the problem is not that 'the entire capitalist culture . . . is ecologically
illiterate and, therefore, dangerous and unsustainable'.[44] The capitalist culture
is a culture that has developed in consistency with the fundamental organizational principles of the market economy and the growth economy, that is,
efficiency and competition. It is the establishment of the market economy
that required its own culture and not vice versa. People (I do not mean those
controlling the means of production) did not wake up one fine morning and
decide to be efficient and competitive. It was the destruction of their own
livelihood by, for instance, the enclosure movement in Britain, or by
colonialism in the colonies, which forced them – in their struggle to survive
– to join the market economy system and adopt the principles of competitiveness and efficiency.

This is the main reason why sustainable development is not just a
cultural issue, or a matter of changing policies, but a matter of changing the
entire institutional framework and replacing it with institutions which
negate the concentration of power, that is, with a marketless and moneyless economy based on an inclusive democracy. Then, and only then, can
one seriously hope that the culture based on the growth ideology and the
subsequent idea of dominating nature will wither away. In other words,
concentration of power within the context of the growth economy is the
necessary condition for the present set of cultural values which involve an
ideology of dominating nature. Although simply negating the concentration of power is not a *sufficient condition* for the development of a new set of
values with respect to our relationship to nature, it is definitely the *necessary
condition* for a radical change in cultural values.

Finally, it is not the industrial society itself or technology as such that
should be blamed for the present ecological crisis, as deep ecologists usually
assert. Technology has never been 'neutral' with respect to the logic and the
dynamics of the market economy. For all that, environmentalists as well as

socialist statists explicitly, or usually implicitly, assume that technology is socially neutral and that we only have to use it for the right purposes in order to solve not just the ecological problem but the social problem in general. It is obvious that this approach ignores the social institutionalizing of science (see Chapter 8) and technology and the fact that the design, and particularly the implementation of new techniques, is directly related to the social organization in general and the organization of production in particular.[45] In a market economy, as in any society, technology embodies concrete relations of production, its hierarchical organization and, of course, its primary aim which, in the case of a market economy, refers to the maximization of economic growth and efficiency (defined on the basis of narrow techno-economic criteria) for profit purposes. So, technology is always designed, or at least those designs are adopted, which best serve the objectives of the market/growth economy.

Similarly, it is not industrialism in general that created the present eco-damaging form of economic organization but the specific type of industrial society that developed in the last two centuries in the framework of the market/growth economy. Therefore, the ultimate causes of the ecological crisis are the market economy and its offspring, the growth economy, and not its symptoms, namely, the present type of technology and industrial society (see p. 278).

The 'appropriate development' approach

This approach, although it starts from a valid critique of the market/growth economy, ends up with conclusions which are not much different from those of deep ecologists. The central argument of this approach is summarized as follows by its main exponent:

> *There has been a great deal of development.* The trouble is that it has been highly inappropriate development. *It has been development in the interests of the rich − the Third World upper classes, the transnational corporations, and the rich countries ... market forces have a powerful tendency to produce inappropriate development.*[46]

The type of 'appropriate' development suggested by this approach implies the creation of a 'conserver' society that would involve 'non-affluent lifestyles, high levels of local self-sufficiency and co-operation, smallness of scale, decentralization and a zero growth'.[47] Still, this approach, contradicting its explicit critique of the foundations of the market economy, proposes that appropriate development would involve an economy that 'could retain much free enterprise in the form of small firms and co-operatives'.[48] Also, the localist character of this approach, which takes for granted the existing oligarchic political and economic structures, becomes obvious from the proposals for 'devolution of many functions from the state to the neighbourhood level [which] would reduce the need for bureaucracy'.[49]

It is obvious that this approach, by not placing power relations at the centre of the analysis, ends up with a 'third way' beyond capitalism and socialism, which seems not to be in fundamental contradiction with either the market economy or liberal democracy. This impression is confirmed by the proposal that this approach makes to regulate the market with the aim of reversing the present concentration of economic power.[50] Clearly, such a proposal ignores the fact that any serious attempt to regulate the market in order to decentralize economic power is today both a-historical and utopian. It is a-historical because it does not see that the present deregulation 'mania' is, in fact, part and parcel of the current phase of the 'marketization' process, i.e. of the internationalized phase of the market economy; and it is utopian because it ignores the grow-or-die dynamic of the market economy.

But *utopianism* (in the negative sense of the word) is not the only trap into which the appropriate development approach falls – a utopianism which is inherent in any conception of compatibility between 'appropriate development' and the present institutional framework. The same could be said about the trap of *localism*, which is implied by the notion of 'local self-sufficiency'; and, finally, the trap of *objectivism*, which is innate in any notion of 'basic needs' that are not defined democratically.

So, this approach, by attempting 'to hold open the possibility of a rather non-Marxist transition which attends to the cultural problem (value change) now rather than after the "revolution" '[51] derives identical solutions to those of deep ecology, i.e. that capitalism will die if enough people change their values and lifestyles.[52] This is not surprising, in view of the fact that neither this approach nor the deep ecology approach can see that the *dominant* social values which determine mass consciousness cannot change until the present political and economic structures change. Still, this does not mean that we should wait for the 'revolution' so that values might change. As I will attempt to show later, what is needed is the development of a strong political and social movement that explicitly aims at replacing the present oligarchic political and economic structures, created by liberal democracy and the market economy respectively, with institutions of political and economic democracy. It is only within a process of establishing such democratic structures that one could seriously hope that the present cultural values of dominating nature, which emerged as a by-product of the concentration of power generated by the growth economy, will wither away.

Is there a way out?

Several, if not all, of the above dimensions of the present crisis are acknowledged by both the Right and the Left. Not surprisingly, in terms of the above analysis, the proposals made by both ends of the political spectrum, despite appearances, do not differ significantly between them, as both the Right and the Left take for granted the existing institutional framework of the market economy and liberal democracy. But let us consider in more detail the relevant proposals and counterpose them to the requirements of a new liberatory approach.

The Right's proposal: further marketization

On the part of the Right, the New Right's[53] solution to overcoming the present multidimensional crisis is further marketization. But, if we consider the possible effects of further marketizing the economy, it becomes obvious that none of the aspects of the multidimensional crisis that we considered is amenable to market solutions. Therefore, the Right's proposals for freeing completely the market forces, privatization and a minimal state amount to nothing less than the rational organization of inequality.

Thus, as regards, first, the economic crisis, in the sense defined above, the enhancement of the marketization process could confidently be expected to aggravate the crisis, since it is bound to increase the concentration of economic power, both in the sense of further widening the North–South gap and in the sense of widening the gap between the 'new' North and the 'new' South.

As regards the North–South gap, it can easily be shown that it is not competition that has historically led to some advances in the production efficiency and international competitiveness of late developers, but protectionist/interventionist policies.[54] The significant widening of the North–South gap in the last 15 years, which marked the worldwide liberalization of markets, is a clear indication for the future. This means that the intensification of marketization, far from helping the growth economy to be universalized, is in fact a crucial factor in further concentrating economic power in the Triad countries.

As regards the 'new' North–'new' South gap, i.e. the distribution of income, the evidence is overwhelming concerning the negative effects of further marketization. Thus, a recent OECD study found that in the 1980s, when the neoliberal market economy started flourishing, the income gap had widened in many of the 25 OECD member states, particularly the models of neoliberalism, the USA and the UK.[55] Also, according to UN data, the gap between the richest 20 per cent and the poorest 20 per cent of the world's population increased eightfold in the

1980s, measured in per capita incomes.[56] No wonder that the global income distribution presents a pattern where the richest 20 per cent of the population receives 85 per cent of world income and the 20 per cent at the bottom receive just 1.4 per cent of it.[57] Thus, the New Right's claim that the liberalization of markets brings about a decentralization of economic power is obviously false. In fact, the opposite is true: the more liberalized the markets are, the greater the concentration of economic power in terms of income and wealth. The fact that the USA has always been the model of a market economy is not irrelevant to its also being 'the most unequal industrialized country in terms of income and wealth'[58] – a fact confirmed by Federal Reserve figures from 1989 (the most recent available) which show that the wealthiest 1 per cent of households owns nearly 40 per cent of the nation's wealth! Also, a comparative study of income distribution trends in countries characterized by different degrees of marketization found, not surprisingly, that the more 'liberal' an economy is the greater the increase in income inequality.[59]

Finally, as regards the ecological and social crisis, the freeing of markets, which is advocated by the New Right, inevitably leads to a deepening of both crises. As the historical experience of the last 200 years has shown, when the rise of the market economy and the subsequent growth economy led to the greatest ecological damage in the history of humankind, the market economy had neither any inherent mechanism to avert the ecological damage nor any effective social controls compatible with its logic and dynamics. Also, as regards the social crisis, it is unavoidable that the marketization of society would further undermine traditional and community values deepening the crisis. Similarly, the marketization of culture inevitably undermines it by homogenizing cultural activity and by trivializing artistic activity, which, forced to survive as a profitable activity, is prevented from playing its avant-garde role.

The Left's proposal: the 'civil societarian' approach

On the part of the Left, the way out of the crisis is expressed in terms of the proposal to enhance 'civil society', that is, to strengthen the various networks which are autonomous from state control (unions, churches, civic movements, co-operatives, neighbourhoods, schools of thought, etc.). This tendency originated in the ex-Second World, where, as a reaction to the Third International's ideology, a series of anti-bureaucratic movements flourished in the past decade – from Polish Solidarity to movements for a 'communism with a human face'. Later, thanks to the theoretical work of modern social democrats of the Habermas School,[60] this new tendency spread to the First World and today exerts considerable influence among social democrats, eco-socialists and others. As the civil societarian approach constitutes, in fact, the entire basis of the present Left's problematic and of the approaches under the new rubric of the so-called 'radical' democracy, I think it would be fruitful to examine this approach in some detail.

The perhaps clearest argument for the 'civil societarian' approach is given by Michael Walzer.[61] Although the Habermasian description of this approach looks more 'sophisticated' than the one given by Walzer, in fact, much of the sophistication of the former arises out of the obscure language and terminology used by Habermas who (like Althusser before him) knows well that for many 'intellectuals', especially in the non-Anglo-Saxon tradition, the 'seriousness' of an argument is related to the effort needed to understand it! I would therefore fully agree with Noam Chomsky who, referring to post-modernism, called this type of theorizing 'pseudo-scientific posturing'.[62]

Walzer, starting from a definition of civil society as 'the space of uncoerced human association and also the set of rational networks – formed for the sake of family, faith, interest and ideology – that fills this space',[63] asks what sorts of institution we should work for if our objective is the good life. To give an answer to this question Walzer refers to four principal ideologies.

The first, 'the republican ideology', holds that the preferred setting for the good life is 'the political community, the democratic state, within which we can be citizens'.[64] The author, after confusing non-statist democracy based on *demos* with present forms of statist democracy, dismisses this theory on the grounds that 'Politics rarely engages the full attention of the citizens who are supposed to be its chief protagonists. They have too many other things to worry about. Above all they have to earn a living.'[65] Thus, Walzer, while he is right in criticizing republicans like Arendt who put economic activity out of the public realm, the realm of freedom, is absolutely wrong in his conclusions. Instead of calling for an inclusive non-statist democracy of powerful citizens, which would imply democracy in all realms, the political, the economic and the social, he expresses his preference for an 'inclusive civil society'[66] of powerless citizens – members of networks, who leave the privileged in present society to enjoy undisturbed their privileges!

According to Walzer, the second ideology – 'the socialist ideology' – involves a turning away from republican politics and focuses instead on economic activity. The preferred (by socialists) setting, he argues, is the co-operative economy whereas politics would wither away within a non-political state characterized by regulation without conflict, 'the adminis-tration of things'. Here, again, the author, by exploiting the partial character of the socialist vision, in exactly the same way as he did with the republican vision, prepares the ground to sow the seed of an 'inclusive' civil society.

Walzer then moves to the third ideology, 'the capitalist ideology', where the preferred setting for the good life is considered to be the marketplace. The emphasis here is on consumer choice and, as in the socialist economy, only a minimal state (and by implication, minimal politics) is required. The main objection Walzer has against this ideology is that 'Autonomy in the marketplace provides no support for social solidarity. Despite the successes of capitalist production, the good life of consumer choice is not universally available.'[67]

Following this sort of argument, it is not surprising that civil societarians endorse fully the market economy and the state, as Walzer makes clear:

> The market, when it is entangled in the network of associations, when the forms of ownership are pluralised, is without doubt the economic formation most consistent with the civil society argument. This same argument also serves to legitimate a kind of state, liberal and pluralist more than republican (not so radically dependent upon the virtue of its citizens). Indeed, a state of this sort is necessary if associations are to flourish.[68]

Finally, in the fourth ideology, 'the nationalist ideology', the preferred (by nationalists) setting is the nation where we are bound to each other by ties of blood and history. In this setting the good life is more a matter of identity than activity, faith not works. This ideology is put by Walzer 'in the same bag' as the other three and dismissed for the same reason: 'All these answers are wrong-headed because of their singularity. They miss the complexity of human society, the inevitable conflicts of commitment and loyalty'.[69] So, in the context of the pseudo-plural society advanced by civil-societarians the important arena is located 'in the associational networks of civil society, in unions, parties, movements, interest groups and so on [where] these same people make many smaller decisions and shape to some degree the more distant determinations of state and economy'.[70] Of course, the bigger decisions, which affect the lives of the same people in a much more significant way than the smaller ones, are left to the political and economic elites who, presumably, know better!

So, the civil societarians' way out of the multidimensional crisis seems to be radically different from the one proposed by the Right. Instead of further marketization, they argue for limits (i.e. social controls) to be imposed on markets and the state by the civil society networks. Thus, Walzer, recognizing that 'the market makes for inequality' and that the main problem with inequality is that 'it commonly translates into domination and radical deprivation' concludes that 'were the market to be set firmly within civil society, politically constrained, open to communal as well as private initiatives, limits might be fixed on its unequal outcomes'.[71] Furthermore, instead of privatizations he proposes a kind of 'market pluralism' which he describes as follows: 'Civil society encompasses or can encompass a variety of market agents: family businesses, publicly owned or municipal companies, worker communes, consumer cooperatives, non-profit organisations of many different sorts.'[72] Finally, acknowledging the fact that 'civil society, left to itself, generates unequal power relationships which only state power can challenge' he concludes that 'only a democratic state can create a democratic civil society; only a democratic civil society can sustain a democratic state'.[73]

So, it is obvious that the civil societarian approach involves a high degree of statism. Furthermore, in effect, it assumes a closed market economy. In fact, there are very few versions of the civil societarian approach that explicitly assume the present degree of internationalization of the market economy. Such an internationalist version of the civil societarian approach (apart from David Held's 'cosmopolitan model of democracy', to be considered later), is the very recent study by Hirst and Thompson[74] which attempts to minimize the significance of internationalization. However, as we saw earlier, the only limits on the internationalized market economy that this approach views as feasible are various 'regulatory controls' which, of course, have very little in common with the sweeping social controls that social societarians have in mind when they discuss, abstracting from the present internationalized market economy, the limits that civil society networks should impose on markets (drastic reduction of inequalities, massive creation of jobs, etc.).

It is therefore clear that the civil societarians, who castigate radical socialists and supporters of the democratic project as utopians, are in fact much less realistic than them when they suggest that the clock could be moved back to the period of statism, that is, to a period when the market economy was characterized by a significantly smaller degree of internationalization than at present. So, the civil societarian approach is both utopian, in the negative sense of the word, and a-historical.

It is utopian, especially today, because, in effect, it is in tension with both the state and the internationalized market economy. As regards the tension with the state, neoliberalism has shown how easy it is for the state to undermine effectively the institutions of the civil society. Also, as regards the tension with the internationalized market economy, it is well known that there is an inverse relationship between the degree of competitiveness and the level of development of the civil society's institutions: the more developed these institutions are (e.g. trade unions) the lower the degree of international competitiveness, as the case of Sweden has shown. So, given that neither social democrats nor their fellow travellers in the

Green movement see the outcome of the inevitable tension between the civil society, on the one hand, and the state and the market economy, on the other, in terms of the replacement of the latter by the former, it is not difficult to predict that any enhancement of the civil society will have to be compatible with the process of further internationalization of the market economy and the implied role of the state. In other words, the 'enhance-ment' of civil society under today's conditions would simply mean that the ruling political and economic elites will be left undisturbed to continue dominating society, while, from time to time, they will have to try to address the demands of the civil societarians, provided, of course, that these demands are not in direct conflict with their own interests and the demands of competitive production. In this sense, the civil societarian approach could play today a crucial ideological role in the sense of 'justifying' the status quo from the Left's point of view.

Also, the civil societarian approach is fundamentally a-historical, since it ignores the structural changes which have led to the present neoliberal consensus and the internationalized market economy. In other words, it ignores the fact that the tendency to minimize social controls on the market, which today is dominant everywhere, is not simply a matter of policy: it reflects fundamental changes in the form of the market economy which implies that every attempt towards an effective social control of the market necessarily comes into conflict with the requirements, in terms of competitiveness, for the reproduction of today's growth economy.

In this sense, the trend to enhance civil society is even more utopian than the statist trend. When even the seizure of the omnipotent state machine by a social-democratic party can eventually lead to social liberalism (as in France in the 1980s), one can easily assess the chances of enhancing social controls 'from below'. Of course, the civil societarians' problem is not that they do not base their strategy on an effort to seize state power (the traditional statist tactics) but rather on a strategy of social transformation 'from below'.[75] The problem lies in the fact that their approach takes for granted the entire institutional framework of the market economy, representative democracy and the nation-state and therefore is as ineffective as that of the Right in dealing with the multidimensional crisis.

Thus, the adoption, first, of the market economy means that every attempt by autonomous institutions (for example, labour unions, eco-logical movements, etc.) at an effective control of the market – in order to achieve social, ecological and other aims – is in dire contradiction with the logic and dynamics of the internationalized economy. Inevitably, any attempt to press for similar controls will lead to the adoption of insignifi-cant half-measures, which have to be compatible with the institutional framework (see, for example, the fiasco of Rio's 'Earth' Conference).

The adoption, second, of representative democracy means that the direct democracy 'injections' proposed by the advocates of this tendency, in fact, function as inoculations against direct democracy. The fundamental precondition for the creation of an active citizen's consciousness is that the citizens themselves (and not others 'on their behalf') should effect the political process. Hence, the supposed 'democratic' proposals merely reinforce citizens' passivity, misleading them to believe that they exercise political power, when, in fact, the latter remains firmly the privilege of the few, and the many are relegated to the role of 'pressure groups' – now baptized as 'counter-powers'!

Finally, the adoption of the statist framework means that the effective existence of autonomous institutions is possible only insofar as they are compatible with the objectives of the state. From the moment this condition is not met, state power will undermine the power of autonomous institutions (see, for example, the crippling of British labour unions under Thatcherism) or even proceed to their dismantlement (see, for instance, the break-up of the Greater London Council, when it started creating problems for the Thatcherite neoliberal policies). Therefore, irrespective of whether one accepts the theory proposed today by some modern anarchists[76] that not only is the state not a class instrument but that it also has its own interests and actors, the case may be supported, both theoretically and historically, that any attempt to 'sublate' state power with autonomous institutions (as, for instance, James O'Connor[77] suggests) is doomed to failure. For example, one could show that the attempt to reinforce civil society, if successful, would lead to a decrease in the economic surplus (part of which is used to reproduce the state mechanism) and, therefore, it would necessarily incur the state's counter-attempt to undermine it. Thus, the dialectic of tension between state and autonomous institutions makes this 'sublation' impossible, since it necessarily leads either to a decorative role for the 'autonomous' institutions, or to their dissolution by the state.

In conclusion, the development of civil society institutions has no chance whatsoever either of putting an end to the concentration of power, or of transcending the present multidimensional crisis. This conclusion may be derived from the fact that the ultimate aim of civil societarians is to improve the functioning of existing institutions (state, parties, market), in order to make them more responsive to pressures from below when, in fact, the crisis is founded on the institutions themselves and not on their malfunctioning! In other words, in the present internationalized market economy, the need to minimize the socio-economic role of the state is no longer a matter of choice for those controlling production. It is a necessary condition for survival. This is particularly so for European capital that has to compete with capital blocs which operate from bases where the social-democratic tradition of statism was never strong (the USA, the Far East). But, even at the planetary level, one could seriously doubt whether it is still possible to enhance the institutions of civil society within the context of the market economy. Granted that the fundamental aims of production in a market economy are individual gain, economic efficiency and growth, any attempt to reconcile these aims with an effective 'social control' by the civil society is bound to fail since, as historic experience with the statist phase has shown, social control and market efficiency are irreconcilable objectives[78] (it is a different matter that some social controls, e.g. protectionism, may be useful to promote development at the early stages). By the same token, one could reasonably argue that the central contradiction of the market economy today is the one arising from the fact that any effective control of the ecological implications of growth is incompatible with the requirements of competitiveness, which the present phase of the marketization process imposes.

The very fact that even neoliberals talk today about the need to combine the civil society with the free market is indicative of how radical the demand to enhance the civil society is. Thus, following the extremities of Thatcherism and Reaganomics, which led to an explosion of unemployment and poverty at socially intolerable levels, neoliberals seem to adopt the supposedly 'radical' demand for the enhancement of the civil society. It is not therefore surprising that even the British Institute of Economic Affairs, a neoliberal think-tank which initiated many Thatcherite ideas, has come out in favour of 'civic capitalism' based on free market ideas with an emphasis on solidarity and mutual consideration (on the lines of friendly societies, etc.).[79]

Towards a new liberatory approach

The crucial question today is whether the protection of human life (which implies the satisfaction of, at least, all basic human needs) as well as the effective protection of the environment are compatible with the marketization process or whether, instead, the whole market system has to be put away. If we accept the case of incompatibility that I tried to support above, one may conclude that the aim to create effective self-protection mechanisms for society, through enhancing the *civil society*, is even more utopian than the previous attempt to achieve the same aim through enhancing the state. Any attempt to enhance autonomous social institutions (trade unions, municipalities, etc.) within the framework of the market economy is futile, as long as it does not seek to transcend the market economy itself. The reason is that any such attempt will be incompatible with the requirements of competitiveness (of the country, or the economic bloc, concerned).

Therefore, there is an imperative need today to develop a new liberatory approach which sees the causes of the present multidimensional crisis
in terms of the concentration of power that is implied by any non-
democratic institutional framework, either of the market economy or of
the socialist statism variety. So, what is needed to open the way for new
forms of social organization is the development of a similar mass consciousness about the failure of 'actually existing capitalism' to the one that
led to the collapse of 'actually existing socialism'. Today, there is a pressing
need to transcend both the neoliberal market economy and socialist statism
in order to put an end to economic misery, which oppresses the majority
of the world's population, and to arrest the ecological destruction which
threatens us all. Failure to create alternative democratic forms of social
organization means that, as the present crisis intensifies, the 'solutions' to
the social and ecological problems that will be given by 'actually existing
capitalism' in the future, are, inevitably, going to be increasingly authoritarian in character.

Thus, roughly 100 years after the adherents to socialist statism, which
collapsed even before the Soviet regime had the chance to celebrate its 75th
birthday, prevailed within the international socialist movement, it is becoming increasingly clear that the autonomy of the social individual can only be
achieved in the context of democracy – in other words, in the framework of
a structure and a process that, through direct citizen participation in the
decision-making and implementing process, ensures the equal distribution of
political, economic and social power among them. The next part of this book
will outline a proposal for an inclusive democracy.

Notes

1. Louis Uchitelle and N.R. Kleinfield, *International Herald Tribune* (6 March 1996).
2. L. Thurow, *Head to Head: The Coming Economic Battle Among Japan, Europe and America* (Brealy, 1992).
3. Louis Uchitelle and N.R. Kleinfield, *International Herald Tribune*.
4. Associated Press/*Eleftherotypia*, 2 April 1996.
5. International Labor Organization (ILO), *Yearbook of Labor Statistics* (Geneva: ILO 1994).
6. All the calculations in the text are based on the *World Development Report 1995*, World Bank, Tables 1 and 5.
7. Ted Trainer, *Developed to Death* (London: Green Print, 1989), p. 120.
8. According to the International Labor Organization, in 1993, 1.1 billion people lived in poverty conditions, whereas an earlier World Bank report classified one-third of the South's population as poor; *World Development Report 1990*, p. 28.
9. Cornelius Castoriadis, 'The era of generalized conformism', lecture given at Boston University on 19 September 1989 in a symposium under the general

title 'A metaphor for our times' (published in *The Broken World* (Athens: Upsilon, 1992) (in Greek), p. 25).

10. *The Guardian* (15 Oct. 1993).
11. John Gray, *The Guardian,* 20 Nov. 1995.
12. Martin Woolacott, 'The march of a martial law', The *Guardian* (20 Jan. 1996).
13. Geoff Mulgan, 'A high-stake society', *The Guardian* (30 Jan. 1996).
14. Peter Kellner, 'Jobs and homes worries haunting British voters', *The Observer* (5 May 1996).
15. Louis Uchitelle and N.R. Kleinfield, *International Herald Tribune.*
16. Will Hutton, *The State We're In* (London: Jonathan Cape, 1995), p. 108.
17. See, e.g., Thomas S. Kuhn, *The Structure of Scientific Revolutions* (Chicago: University of Chicago Press, 1970); Imre Lakatos, *Criticism and the Growth of Knowledge* (Cambridge: Cambridge University Press, 1970); Paul Feyerabend, *Against Method* (London: Verso, 1975); and Derek Phillips, *Abandoning Method* (San Fransisco and London: Jossey-Bass, 1973).
18. On the crisis in economic methodology in particular, see, e.g., Daniel Bell and Irving Kristol, *The Crisis in Economic Theory* (New York: Basic Books, 1981); Ken Kole *et al.,Why Economists Disagree* (London and New York: Longman, 1983); Homa Katouzian, *Ideology and Method in Economics* (London: Macmillan, 1980); T.W. Hutchinson, *Knowledge and Ignorance in Economics* (Oxford: Blackwell, 1977).
19. For an extensive bibliography on this subject, see Chapter 8.
20. Cornelius Castoriadis, 'The era of generalized conformism'.
21. See, for instance, Greg Easterbrook, *A Moment of the Earth* (New York: Penguin, 1995).
22. Carbon dioxide concentrations, measured in parts per million by volume (taken from ice-core samples) were at the level of about 280 for the period 1000–1750 but at the end of the millennium have reached a level of 361; Paul Brown, *The Guardian* (13 July 1996).
23. John Gribbin, 'Climate and ozone', *The Ecologist,* Vol. 21, No. 3 (May/June 1991).
24. See, for instance, *The Guardian*/Greenpeace, 'A report into the environmental forces shaping our future', *The Guardian* (2 June 1994).
25. Polly Ghazi, *The Observer* (11 April 1993).
26. *The Observer* (24 March 1996).
27. Tracey Clunies-Ross and Nicholas Hildyard, 'The politics of industrial agriculture', *The Ecologist,* Vol. 22, No. 2, March/April 1992, p. 67.
28. Tracey Clunies-Ross and Nicholas Hildyard, 'The politics of industrial agriculture', p. 67.
29. For a discussion of such matters, see, for instance, Andrew Dobson, *Green Political Thought* (London: Routledge, 1990, 1995).
30. For an example of liberal neo-classical economics being used in the analysis of environmental problems, see Michael Common, *Environmental and Resource Economics* (London: Longman, 1988).
31. See the works of Murray Bookchin: for instance, *The Ecology of Freedom* (Montreal: Black Rose, 1991); *The Philosophy of Social Ecology* (Montreal: Black Rose, 1995); *From Urbanization to Cities: Towards a New Politics of Citizenship* (London: Cassell, 1995).
32. For a useful description of eco-socialism and its differences from eco-

anarchism and other Green tendencies, see David Pepper, *Eco-Socialism: From Deep Ecology to Social Justice* (London: Routledge, 1993), and *Modern Environmentalism* (London: Routledge, 1996).

33. World Commission on Environment and Development, *Our Common Future* (United Nations, 1987).
34. World Commission on Environment and Development, *Our Common Future,* p. 87.
35. The Report, for instance, states that the aim should be 'an economy geared to growth and the elimination of world poverty'; World Commission on Environment and Development, *Our Common Future,* p. 18. Similarly, it is stated that sustainable development 'requires . . . an assurance that those poor get their fair share of the resources', p. 8.
36. The Report calls for economic growth and at the same time it takes for granted that this is compatible with the aim to 'enhance' and 'expand the environmental resource base', World Commission on Environment and Development, *Our Common Future,* pp. 1, 364.
37. World Commission on Environment and Development, *Our Common Future,* p. 51.
38. Ted Trainer, 'A rejection of the Brundtland Report', p. 74.
39. See, for instance, John M. Gowdy, 'Progress and environmental sustainability', *Environmental Ethics,* Vol. 16, No. 1 (Spring 1994).
40. Richard Douthwaite, *The Growth Illusion* (Devon: Resurgence, 1992), Ch. 15.
41. John M. Gowdy, 'Progress and environmental sustainability', p. 52.
42. E.G. Vallianatos, 'Subversive theory: ecology, gaiocentric sustainable development and the Third World', *Society and Nature,* Vol. 3, No. 1 (1995), pp. 93–116.
43. E.G. Vallianatos, 'Subversive theory', p. 108.
44. E.G. Vallianatos, 'Subversive theory', pp. 108–9.
45. For a critique of the 'neutrality of technology' thesis, see Cornelius Castoriadis, *Philosophy, Politics, Autonomy,* p. 192. See also Frances Stewart's study which shows that the way in which technological choices are made in practice is anything but 'neutral'; Frances Stewart, *Technology and Underdevelopment* (London: Macmillan, 1978), Ch. 1.
46. Ted Trainer, *Developed to Death,* p. 3.
47. Ted Trainer, *The Conserver Society* (London: Zed Books, 1995), p. 9.
48. Ted Trainer, *The Conserver Society,* p. 12.
49. Ted Trainer, *The Conserver Society,* p. 13.
50. See Ted Trainer, 'What is development?', *Society and Nature,* Vol. 3, No. 1 (1995), pp. 26–56.
51. Ted Trainer, *Developed to Death,* p. 204.
52. Ted Trainer, *The Conserver Society,* p. 220.
53. See, e.g., Henri Lepage, *Tomorrow, Capitalism, The Economics of Economic Freedom* (London: Open Court, 1982); Nick Bosanquet, *After the New Right* (London: Heinemann, 1983); Mark Hayes, *The New Right in Britain* (London: Pluto Press, 1994).
54. See Takis Fotopoulos, 'Economic restructuring and the debt problem: the Greek case', *International Review of Applied Economics,* Vol. 6, No. 1 (1992), pp. 38–64.

55. A. Atkinson *et al.*, *Income Distribution in OECD countries* (Paris: OECD, 1995), p. 47.
56. UN Development Program, *Human Development Report, 1992* (New York: Oxford University Press, 1992).
57. UN Development Program, *Human Development Report, 1996* (New York: Oxford University Press, 1996); see also Duncan Smith, *In Search of Social Justice* (London: The New Economics Foundation, 1995).
58. Edward Wolff, 'How the pie is sliced: America's growing concentration of wealth', *The American Prospect* (Summer 1995).
59. Francis Green *et al.*, 'Income inequality in corporatist and liberal economies: a comparison of trends within OECD countries', *International Review of Applied Economics,* Vol. 8, No. 3 (1994).
60. See John Ely, 'Libertarian ecology and civil society'; and Konstantinos Kavoulakos, 'The relationship of realism and utopianism: the theories of democracy of Habermas and Castoriadis', *Society and Nature,* Vol. 2, No. 3 (1994).
61. Michael Walzer, 'The civil society argument' in *Dimensions of Radical Democracy,* Chantal Mouffe (ed.) (London: Verso, 1992, 1995), pp. 89–107.
62. 'Now Derrida, Lacan, Lyotard, Kristeva, etc. . . . write things that I also don't understand . . . no one who says they do understand can explain it to me and I haven't a clue as to how to proceed to overcome my failures', Noam Chomsky 'On "theory" and "post-modern cults" ', *Upstream Issues* (1996).
63. Michael Walzer, 'The civil society argument', p. 89.
64. Michael Walzer, 'The civil society argument', p. 91.
65. Michael Walzer, 'The civil society argument', p. 92.
66. Michael Walzer, 'The civil society argument', p. 105.
67. Michael Walzer, 'The civil society argument', p. 95.
68. Michael Walzer, 'The civil society argument', p. 98.
69. Michael Walzer, 'The civil society argument', p. 97.
70. Michael Walzer, 'The civil society argument', p. 99.
71. Michael Walzer, 'The civil society argument', p. 100.
72. Michael Walzer, 'The civil society argument', p. 100.
73. Michael Walzer, 'The civil society argument', p. 104.
74. Paul Hirst and Grahame Thompson, *Globalization in Question* (Cambridge: Polity Press, 1996).
75. See, for instance, Hilary Wainwright, *Arguments for a New Left, Answering the Free Market Right* (Oxford: Blackwell, 1994), Ch. 3.
76. See April Carter, *Marx: A Radical Critique* (Brighton: Wheatsheaf, 1988), and 'Outline of an anarchist theory of history' in *For Anarchism: History, Theory and Practice,* D. Goodway (ed.) (London: Routledge, 1989), pp. 176–97.
77. James O'Connor, 'Socialism and ecology', *Society and Nature,* Vol. 1, No. 1 (1992), pp. 117–29.
78. See also M. Olson, *The Rise and Decline of Nations* (New Haven, Connecticut: Yale University Press, 1988).
79. See David G. Green, *Reinventing Civil Society* (London: IEA, 1993).

PART II

Towards a Confederal Inclusive Democracy

CHAPTER 5

Towards a New Conception of Democracy

The aim of this chapter is twofold: first, to show the incompatibility of democracy with any form of concentration of power and to examine the implication that neither representative democracy nor the market economy can be characterized as political or economic democracy respectively; and second, to develop a new conception of inclusive democracy which extends the public realm to the economic, social and ecological domains.

The first section demonstrates the incompatibility of democracy with the two versions of the growth economy (capitalist and 'socialist'). The second section delineates the relationship of the conceptions of democracy to the various conceptions of freedom. Also, the distinction between 'statist' and non-statist forms of democracy is introduced. In the third section the main conceptions of democracy are examined and contrasted. It is shown that the various conceptions of 'radical' democracy that the 'Left' is developing at the moment have little in common with the classical meaning of democracy as equal sharing of power.

In the final section, the conception of inclusive democracy is developed and its components are examined, i.e. political, economic, ecological, as well as 'democracy in the social realm'. It is stressed that the new conception takes for granted that democracy is not just a particular structure implying political and economic equality, but a process of social self-institution and a project – a theme which is examined further in Chapter 8. Finally, the various conceptions of citizenship are considered and contrasted with the conception of citizenship implied by inclusive democracy.

Democracy and the growth economy

As we saw in Chapter 2, the grow-or-die dynamics of the market economy led to the growth economy, which, in the twentieth century, took the form of either a capitalist growth economy or a 'socialist' growth economy – both types implying a high degree of concentration of economic power. However, as economic concentration is incompatible with the spreading of political power, it is no wonder that the growing concentration of economic power has been accompanied by a corresponding concentration of political power. Therefore, as all conceptions of democracy imply the dispersion of power, to the extent that both historical versions of the growth economy imply a high degree of concentration of power, they are also incompatible with democracy. But let us examine in more detail the compatibility of democracy with the two versions of the growth economy.

The compatibility of democracy with the capitalist growth economy

The incompatibility of democracy with the capitalist growth economy is based on the fact that the main elements of this type of growth economy, growth and marketization, are incompatible with democracy. As regards, first, growth, the grow-or-die dynamic of the capitalist growth economy has led not only to concentration of economic power but also to concentration of political power. In fact, concentration of political power has been the functional complement of the concentration of economic power. Thus, the concentration of political power in the hands of parliamentarians in the liberal phase has led to an even higher degree of concentration in the hands of governments and the leadership of 'mass' parties in the statist and neoliberal phases, at the expense of parliaments.[1] Furthermore, in confirmation of the historical incompatibility of democracy with capitalist growth, Robert Basso, a Harvard economist, in an article for the *Journal of Economic Growth* (1996), after surveying 100 countries between 1960 and 1990, reaches the conclusion that economic growth rates are negatively associated with greater democracy!

As regards, second, marketization, namely, the historical process that since the time of the emergence of the market economy involved the phased removal of social controls over the market, the incompatibility of this process with democracy is obvious. As we saw earlier, the minimization of social controls on the market is in the interest of, and has always been pursued by, the small minority who own and/or control the means of production. So, since in a capitalist growth economy it is those who are *not* in control of the economic process who constitute the vast majority of the population, the more oligarchic the form of political organization, the more amenable to the marketization process the economy is.

It is not therefore surprising that the present internationalized phase of marketization, which implies further concentration of economic power, has been accompanied by a parallel concentration of political power. So, although it is true that today, as we approach the new millennium, we see the end of sovereignty, as Thomas Martin points out,[2] it is not sovereignty in general that withers away but the nation-state's sovereignty, particularly its economic sovereignty. The decline of state sovereignty is directly linked to the present internationalized phase of the market economy and the consequent withering away of the nation-state. In this context, one may argue that state sovereignty is being replaced by market sovereignty on the one hand and a form of supra-national sovereignty on the other. The former means that, today, more than ever before, it is the market which defines effective human rights, not just economic rights, but even who can really exercise his or her human rights in general. The latter means that, at present, political and economic power is concentrated at the supra-national level of inter-state institutions ('Group of 7', European Commission) and international organizations (World Trade Organization, IMF, World Bank) and at the level of the emerging network of city-regional governments.[3]

The combined historical effect of growth and marketization on politics is that in the capitalist growth economy, politics is converted into state-craft,[4] with think-tanks – 'the systems analysts of the present hour' – designing policies and their implementation.[5] Furthermore, the continuous decline of the state's economic sovereignty is being accompanied by the parallel transformation of the public realm into pure administration. For instance, international central banks are being established, which, in the future, independent from political control, will take crucial decisions about the economic life of millions of citizens (see for instance the planned European central bank that will take over control of the common European currency). Hannah Arendt prophetically described this state of affairs, although she did not predict that it was the concentration of power at the top that would lead to pure administration rather than the 'withering away of the state':

> A complete victory of society will always produce some sort of 'communistic fiction', whose outstanding political characteristic is that it is indeed ruled by an 'invisible hand', namely by nobody. What we traditionally call state and government gives place here to pure administration – a state of affairs which Marx rightly predicted as the 'withering away of the state', though he was wrong in assuming that only a revolution could bring it about and even more wrong when he believed that this complete victory of society would mean the eventual emergence of the 'realm of freedom'.[6]

The compatibility of democracy with the 'socialist' growth economy

As far as the 'socialist' growth economy is concerned, its incompatibility with democracy is based on the fact that the dominant social paradigm in the defunct 'actually existing socialism' was grounded on the idea that the principal goal of human society was the maximization of production and the development of productive forces. Therefore, to the extent that the achievement of this goal implied the concentration of economic and political power in the hands of the bureaucratic party elite and planners, concentration of power was inevitable. Furthermore, the fact that the dominant social paradigm was supposed to be grounded on a 'science' (Marxism) implied the imperative need to 'prove' it, in the sense of out-producing all competitor economic systems. There was, therefore, no doubt whatsoever in the minds of the Soviet elite about what would have to be sacrificed in any possible clash between the dominant social paradigm and democracy. No wonder, therefore, that as early as 1920 Lenin was declaring that 'in the final analysis every kind of democracy, as political superstructure in general . . . serves production', reminding the romantics who wanted to go back to workers' control and industrial democracy that 'Industry is indispensable, democracy is not'.[7]

So, whereas the original Leninist project for the Soviet democracy, as expressed in *The State and Revolution,* was about the transformation of power relations, the Soviet elite, from 1920 onwards, consistently maintained the view (no doubt 'external' events have also played a significant role in this) that socialism consisted wholly in the equality of *ownership* relations and not at all in the equality of *power* relations. The incentive was obvious: to achieve the goal of maximizing production, which was identified as the main goal of socialism. As Harding points out:

> Socialism was conceived of as the maximisation of production which could only be achieved by state ownership of the means of production and the implementation of a national plan for the allocation of all resources . . . the trick was . . . to convince its adherents that the essential matters that concern society were not at all political matters that involved the power of some over others . . . but that they were, rather, matters whose optimal resolution proceeded from the correct application of objective or scientific knowledge.[8]

History, therefore, has shown in an unambiguous way that democracy is incompatible with both versions of the growth economy. The crucial question that arises here is whether it is not only the growth economy – as it developed historically – which is incompatible with democracy, but the very liberal and socialist conceptions of democracy, on which the two versions of the growth economy were founded.

Democracy, freedom and autonomy

Few words, apart perhaps from socialism, have been so widely abused during the twentieth century as the word 'democracy'. The usual way in which the meaning of democracy has been distorted, mostly by liberal academics and politicians but also by libertarian theoreticians, is by confusing the presently dominant oligarchic system of liberal 'democracy' with democracy itself. A good illustration of this distortion is offered by the following introduction to the subject in a modern textbook on democracy:

> The word democracy comes from the Greek and literally means rule by the people. It is sometimes said that democratic government originated in the city-states of ancient Greece and that democratic ideals have been handed down to us from that time. In truth, however, this is an unhelpful assertion. The Greeks gave us the word but did not provide us with a model. The assumptions and practices of the Greeks were very different from those of modern democrats.[9]

Thus, the author, having asserted that democracy is a kind of 'rule' (an error repeated by several libertarians and anarchists today), then goes on to argue that:

> if ruling is taken to mean the activity of reaching authoritative decisions that result in laws and regulations binding upon society, then it is obvious that (apart from occasional referendums) only a small minority of individuals can be rulers in modern, populous societies. So, for the definition to be operational, ruling must be taken in the much weaker sense of choosing the rulers and influencing their decisions.[10]

The author, therefore, having concluded that 'an objective and precise definition of democracy'[11] is not possible, goes on to devote the rest of the book to a discussion of the Western regimes, which he calls 'democracies'. However, as I will try to show below, the modern concept of democracy has hardly any relation to the classical Greek conception. Furthermore, the current practice of adding several qualifying adjectives to the term democracy has further confused the meaning of it and created the impression that several forms of democracy exist. Thus, liberals refer to 'modern', 'liberal', 'representative', or 'parliamentary' democracy, social democrats talk about 'social', 'economic' or 'industrial' democracy, and finally Leninists used to speak about 'soviet' democracy, and, later, 'people's' democracies to describe the countries of 'actually existing socialism'.

But, as this chapter will attempt to show, there is only one form of democracy at the political level, that is, the direct exercise of sovereignty by the people themselves, a form of societal institution which rejects any form of 'ruling' and institutionalizes the equal sharing of political power among all citizens. The hypothesis we make that there is only one form of political democracy has two important implications.

The first implication is that all other forms of so-called democracy ('representative', 'parliamentary', etc.) are merely various forms of 'oligarchy', that is, rule by the few. This implies that the only adjectives that are permissible to precede democracy are those which are used to extend its scope to take into account democracy at the economic or broader social domains. The use of such adjectives is justified by the fact that economic democracy, or democracy in the workplace and so on, was indeed unknown to Athenians for whom only political activity belonged to the public realm. Thus, as Hansen points out, 'historians agree that equality in Athens was a purely political concept that never spread to the social and economic spheres'.[12] This is why in this book, to denote the extension of the classical conception of democracy to the social, economic and ecological realms, the adjective 'inclusive' precedes the word democracy.

The second implication of our hypothesis is that the real meaning of the arguments advanced by the 'civil societarian' 'Left' in favour of 'deepening' democracy is to make the present regimes in the West, that have aptly been characterized by Castoriades as 'liberal oligarchies',[13] less oligarchic. A typical example of such a pseudo-democratic argument is given by David Beetham that 'disputes about the meaning of democracy which purport to be conceptual disagreements are really disputes about *how much* [emphasis added] democracy is either desirable or practicable ... of any existing set of political arrangements it is thus meaningful to ask how they might be made *more* democratic'.[14] Thus, the author, after bypassing the crucial issue of the concept of democracy by implicitly assuming that the difference between the classical and the liberal conception of democracy is just quantitative (see p. 185), derives the convenient conclusion that, since the present liberal democracy *is* a democracy, the only issue is how to make it more democratic! No wonder that the same author, on the basis of such flimsy premises, easily derives the pontifical judgement that 'there is no serious democratic alternative',[15] and he goes on undisturbed to discuss the question of the 'limitations' of democratization, i.e. how far democratization can proceed without threatening the present 'democratic' order itself.

But any conception of democracy crucially depends on the meaning assigned to freedom and autonomy. This implies that our starting point in examining the various conceptions of democracy should be a discussion of the meaning of freedom and autonomy – terms that, like democracy and socialism, have so much been used and abused, particularly in this century.

How to define freedom?

One useful starting point in defining freedom is the distinction that Isaiah Berlin[16] introduced between what he called the 'negative' and the 'positive' concepts of liberty/freedom (he used the terms interchangeably). The former referred to the absence of restraint, that is, the freedom for the individual to do whatever s/he wants to do ('freedom from'), whereas the latter referred to the freedom 'to do things', to engage in self-development or participate in the government of one's society ('freedom to'). One could, roughly, argue that, historically, the negative concept of freedom was adopted by liberals, individualistic anarchists and libertarians, whereas the positive concept was used by socialists and most anarchists.

Thus, the negative concept of freedom was developed by liberal philosophers like Thomas Hobbes, Jeremy Bentham, John Stuart Mill and others, whose main consideration was to establish criteria for determining the proper limits of state action. In liberal philosophy, citizens are free insofar as they are not constrained by laws and regulations. It is therefore obvious that the liberal conception of freedom presupposes the power relations implied by the existence of the state and the market, as long as they are 'within the law'. In other words, the liberals' conception of freedom presupposes the existence of the state as separate from society; in this sense, their conception of democracy is a 'statist' one.

The negative concept of freedom has been criticized on several grounds. Liberals themselves have criticized this conception as it does not imply even the very right to choose rulers in a liberal democracy,[17] which is clearly a 'freedom to' and not a 'freedom from'. But even more important is the philosophical criticism that human beings have always lived in communities bound together by social rules and regulations and that, therefore, their history is not just a history of isolated individuals coming together to form a civil society, as liberal philosophers like Hobbes and Locke assumed. In other words, human values are socially determined, and social rules and regulations to uphold them do not represent a restriction on some pre-existing freedom but part of the conditions of a satisfactory life.[18]

On the other hand, the positive concept of freedom is usually associated with self-realization through the political institution of society, which supposedly expresses the 'general will'. But then, of course, the question immediately arises: which type of societal institution could express this general will? Historically, the positive conception of freedom, not unlike the negative conception, has been associated with the 'statist' conception of democracy; the state is separated from society and is supposed to express the general will. In particular, during the period from the beginning of the twentieth century until World War II, the positive concept of freedom was fashionable among statists of all persuasions: from Nazis to Stalinists. No wonder that the collapse of statism as an ideology and political practice led to the corresponding decline of the positive concept of freedom and the present flourishing of its negative conception. However, as I shall show below, there is no intrinsic relationship between the positive concept of freedom and the 'statist' form of democracy. In fact, the opposite is true. A statist form of democracy is incompatible with any concept of freedom, positive or negative, given its fundamental incompatibility with both self-determination and (individual and collective) autonomy.

For all that, the ambivalent character of the connection between the statist form of democracy and freedom led to a situation where the positive conception of freedom in terms of the conscious control over society and nature was adopted by both the statist and the non-statist wings of the Left. Thus, on the state socialist side, Engels defined freedom as 'the control over ourselves and over external nature'.[19] Also, according to Kolakowski, for Marxists, 'freedom is the degree of power that an individual or a community is able to exercise over the conditions of their own life'.[20] On the anarchist side, Bakunin had exactly the same notion of freedom, which he defined as 'the domination over external things, based upon the respectful observance of the laws of Nature'.[21] Similarly, Emma Goldman explicitly adopts a positive concept of freedom: 'True liberty . . . is not the negative thing of being free from something . . . real freedom, true liberty is positive: it is freedom to something; it is the liberty to be, to do.'[22]

Finally, today's ideological hegemony of liberal ideas has influenced several libertarians who resort to individualistic conceptions of freedom. McKercher, for instance, defines freedom 'as the ability to choose between alternatives'.[23] However, this conception of freedom separates the individual's self-determination from that of the community's, in other words, the individual's self-determination from that of the *social* individual's. As a result, the link between the political institution of society and the social individual's self-determination is broken (no wonder that Milton Friedman's best seller was entitled *Free to Choose*[24]). In fact, even if we qualify the definition as the *equal* ability to choose, to bring in the ethics of equality and democracy (what McKercher calls 'the qualitative areas of choice'[25]), still, the definition does not explicitly posit the question of the political institution of society. But it is society's political institution which conditions in a decisive way what 'the alternatives' are and therefore the ability itself to choose. It is not therefore accidental that such a definition of freedom is amenable to being attached to the ethos of individualism, private property and capitalism. Nor is it surprising that the adoption of such a definition of freedom could easily lead to a situation where 'freedom becomes individualism, and individualism becomes the possession of property, and possession becomes democracy', so that, at the end, 'private property and capitalism become synonymous with "democracy" '.[26]

To my mind, the best way to define freedom is to express it in terms of individual and collective autonomy. Such a definition of freedom not only combines individual freedom with collective freedom, rooting firmly the freedom of the individual in the democratic organization of the community, but it also transcends both liberalism and socialist statism, individualism and collectivism.

The English translation of autonomy, as Murray Bookchin points out, is used to denote personal freedom or self-government and therefore creates 'a disjunction between the material and political that would have been alien to the Greek idea of independence'.[27] However, the original Greek meaning of the word had a definite political dimension, where personal autonomy was inseparable from collective autonomy. The term autonomy (*autonomia*) comes from the Greek word 'αυτο-νομος' (autonomos), which means (to give to) oneself one's law. On the other hand, the Greek word for freedom (*eleutheria*) had a broader meaning than autonomy, according to context. Thus, as Hansen points out, at least three different meanings are attested in the sources: in the social context, *eleutheria* contrasted freedom to slavery; in the constitutional context, it was associated both with political participation in the public realm and personal freedom in the private realm; whereas in the political context, '*eleutheria* in the sense of *autonomia* was the freedom of the polis, which is different from freedom within the polis'.[28]

So, autonomy refers to 'a new *eidos* within the overall history of being: a type of being that reflectively gives to itself the laws of its being'.[29] In other words, autonomy implies a process of explicit self-institution:

> *The* poleis – *at any rate Athens, about which our information is most complete* – *do not stop questioning their respective institutions; the* demos *goes on modifying the rules under which it lives. . . . This movement is a movement of explicit self-institution. The cardinal meaning of explicit self-institution is autonomy: we posit our own laws. . . . The community of citizens* – *the* demos – *proclaims that it is absolutely sovereign* (autonomos, autodikos, autoteles – *self-legislating, self-judging, self-governing* – *in Thucydides' words).*[30]

Therefore, an autonomous society is a society capable of explicitly self-instituting itself, in other words, capable of putting into question its already given institutions and what I will call the *dominant social paradigm,* namely, the system of beliefs, ideas and the corresponding values, which is associated with these institutions. In this sense, a tribal society which is not capable of questioning tradition, a religious society not questioning divine law, and, finally, a Marxist society which is incapable of questioning the dominant social paradigm are all examples of heteronomous societies, irrespective of the degree of political and economic equality they may have achieved.

The above definition of freedom in terms of autonomy has three very important theoretical implications. First, it implies democracy. Second, it implies the transcendence of the traditional division between individualism and collectivism, liberalism and socialist statism. Finally, it implies that freedom cannot and should not be based on any preconceptions about human nature or on any divine, social or natural 'laws' about social evolution. The first two implications will be examined below whereas the third will be considered in Chapter 8 (see p. 342).

As regards the first implication of the definition of freedom in terms of autonomy, i.e. the connection between autonomy and democracy, an autonomous society is inconceivable without autonomous individuals and vice versa. Thus, in classical Athens no citizen is autonomous unless he participates equally in power, that is, unless he takes part in the democratic process. In general, as Castoriadis observes, no society is autonomous unless it consists of autonomous individuals, because 'without the autonomy of the others there is no collective autonomy – and outside such a collectivity I cannot be effectively autonomous'.[31] It is therefore obvious that in the context of an indefinite plurality of individuals belonging to society, the very acceptance of the idea of autonomy inevitably leads to the idea of democracy.

In this sense, autonomy and freedom are equivalent terms, although this is not always clear in the Anglo-Saxon tradition, given its emphasis on individual autonomy. Furthermore, expressing freedom in terms of autonomy directly brings up the issue of whether the project for democracy should be founded on the citizen's self-reflective choice, rather than on an 'objective' ethic derived from a particular (and necessarily disputable) reading of natural and social 'evolution'. It is obvious that a definition of freedom in terms of autonomy is compatible with the former but not with the latter. It is therefore not surprising that supporters of 'objective' ethics discard any definition of freedom in terms of autonomy, supposedly because of its individualistic connotations, despite the fact that its classical meaning could in no way be associated with exclusively individualistic conceptions of freedom.[32]

Freedom, individualism and collectivism

As regards the second implication, the definition of freedom in terms of individual and collective autonomy is very useful in the attempt to transcend the duality of individualism versus collectivism. Thus, the conception of freedom in terms of autonomy makes clear that the issue is not, as some modern libertarians present it, a black and white choice between an 'individualist' tendency (human individuals can be free to create their world) and a 'collectivist' tendency (the world creates the individual).[33] The real issue is how we can transcend both these tendencies.

To my mind, this can only be achieved if we recognize the historical fact that individuals are not absolutely free to create their world, nor does the world just create the individual. As long as individuals live in a society, they are not just individuals but *social* individuals, subject to a process which socializes them into internalizing the existing institutional framework and the dominant social paradigm. In this sense, they are not just free to create their world but are conditioned by history, tradition and culture. Still, this socialization process is broken, at almost all times – as far as a minority of the population is concerned – and in exceptional historical circumstances even with respect to the majority itself. In the latter case, a process is set in motion that usually ends with a change of the institutional structure of society and of the corresponding social paradigm.

The above statement is just a historical observation, and I will not attempt to 'ground' it somewhere because any such 'grounding' will inevitably involve a closed theoretical system – as, for example, is the case with the Marxian or Freudian interpretations of the socialization process. This historical observation should be complemented by another one, which transcends both idealism and materialism. Namely, it is neither ideological factors alone nor just material factors that determine social change at any moment in time. Sometimes, the former may have been more influential than the latter, and vice versa, but usually, as Murray Bookchin[34] stresses, it is the interaction between the two that is decisive. However, any generalizations aimed at deriving a philosophy of history, like the ones attempted by Marxists and idealists, are just not possible.

Societies therefore are not just 'collections of individuals' but consist of social individuals who are both free to create their world, that is, a new set of institutions and a corresponding social paradigm, and are created by the world, in the sense that they have to break with the dominant social paradigm in order to be able to recreate the world.

If we adopt the conception of freedom as individual and collective autonomy, then neither liberal individualism nor collectivism, particularly in the form of socialist statism, is compatible with freedom. Liberal individualism is incompatible with freedom because it implies a negative conception of freedom, a form of 'democracy' in which the ultimate unit of society is only the individual and an idea of citizenship in which the citizen is simply a passive bearer of certain rights (mainly political) and individual freedoms. Also, socialist statism is incompatible with freedom because, although it implies a positive conception of freedom, the separation of state from society (which is supposed to continue throughout the transitional period up to the communist stage) implies an idea of citizenship in which the citizen is still a passive bearer of rights (albeit political rights are complemented by full social and economic rights).

It is therefore essential that a new liberatory project should be based on:

- a conception of freedom in terms of individual and collective autonomy; and
- a conception of democracy in which the central unit of political life is the individual as well as the community. This way, the liberatory project will acquire a universal character which is now missing from the purely Euro-centric model of liberal 'democracy' that has been exported all over the world. Thus, as Bhikhu Parekh[35] points out, in several parts of the world they still define the individual in communal terms and do not regard the atomic liberal individual as the basic unit of society. Also, there are several multi-communal societies which comprise several cohesive communities trying to preserve their traditional way of life. Clearly, the liberal model of democracy is incompatible with all these societies ('as they understand it, liberalism breaks up the community');[36] in fact, even the classical democracy model needs drastic amendment to be compatible with the multi-communal societies.

In this context, recent libertarian attempts to 'reconcile' individualism and liberalism, on the one hand, with Left libertarianism, on the other, seem extremely precarious. This applies, for instance, to L. Susan Brown's attempt to distinguish between what she calls *existential individualism* (individualism that stresses freedom as a desirable end in itself) and *instrumental individualism* (individualism that sees freedom merely as a means to achieve egocentric competitive interests), which she assigns to anarchism and liberalism respectively.[37]

But, as Castoriadis points out, 'the idea of autonomy as an end in itself would lead to a purely formal "Kantian" conception. We wish autonomy both for itself and in order to be able *to do*.'[38] One may, therefore, argue that, in fact, there is only one type of individualism, instrumentalist individualism, which sees individual autonomy as a means to achieve egocentric competitive interests. Similarly, there is only one type of collectivism, instrumentalist collectivism, which, in the form of statist socialism, sees collective autonomy as a means to achieve Progress in the sense of the development of productive forces.

So, the real point at issue is whether we wish autonomy and freedom in order to further our egocentric interests, which emanate basically from property rights, or whether, instead, we wish autonomy and freedom in order to further our self-development, which is impossible without the self-development of everybody else in society. In the first instance, we refer to liberal individualism (what Brown calls instrumental individualism), which is consistent with a negative conception of freedom and an exclusively individualistic conception of autonomy. In the second instance, ruling out socialist statism for the reasons I mentioned above, we refer to individual autonomy seen as inseparable from collective autonomy. To my mind, Brown's definition of individualism is perfectly compatible with liberal individualism and incompatible with individual and collective autonomy. In this sense, her treatment of anarchism and liberalism confuses the fundamental differences between the two, particularly with respect to their diametrically opposite conceptions of freedom and autonomy.

Democracy, sovereignty and the state

The concentration of power is incompatible not only with freedom in the sense of autonomy but even with freedom in the negative sense of 'freedom from'.[39] It is not therefore accidental that today, when the market economy and liberal democracy lead to an increasing concentration of economic and political power respectively,[40] neo-liberals and 'libertarians' of the Right try to dissociate conceptually power from freedom.[41] However, the oligarchic character of the present regimes does not just arise from the fact that real power is in the hands of a political elite, as supporters of the theory of elitism suggest, or, alternatively, in the hands of an economic class for whom politicians act directly or indirectly as agents, as instrumentalist versions of Marxism imply. The oligarchic character of the present 'democracies', which, in fact, negates any conception of freedom, is the direct outcome of the fact that the present institutional framework separates society from the economy and society from the state.

Although the market economy was formed about two centuries ago, when, within the process of marketization of the economy, most social controls over the market were abolished, the separation process had begun earlier, in sixteenth-century Europe. At the political level, the emergence of the nation-state, at about the same time and place, initiated a parallel process of concentrating political power, initially in the form of highly centralized monarchies and later in the form of liberal 'democracies'. From then on, as Bookchin points out, 'the word "state" came to mean a professional civil authority with the powers to govern a "body politic" '.[42]

It was also during the same sixteenth century that the idea of representation entered the political lexicon, although the sovereignty of Parliament was not established until the seventeenth century. In the same way that the king had once 'represented' society as a whole, it was now the turn of Parliament to play this role, although sovereignty itself was still supposed to belong to the people as a whole. However, the doctrine that prevailed in Europe since the French Revolution was not just that the French people were sovereign and that their views were represented in the National Assembly, but that the French nation was sovereign and the National Assembly embodied the will of the nation. As it was observed:

> this was a turning point in continental European ideas since, before this, the political representative had been viewed in the continent as a delegate. According to the new theory promulgated by the French revolutionaries . . . the elected representative is viewed as an independent maker of national laws and policies, not as an agent for his constituents or for sectional interests.[43]

In fact, one may say that the form of liberal 'democracy' that has dominated the West in the last two centuries is not even a representative 'democracy' but a representative *government*, that is a government of the people *by* their representatives. Thus, as Bhikhu Parekh points out:

> Representatives were to be elected by the people, but once elected they were to remain free to manage public affairs as they saw fit. This highly effective way of insulating the government against the full impact of universal franchise lies at the heart of liberal democracy. Strictly speaking liberal democracy is not representative democracy but representative government.[44]

The European conception of sovereignty was completely alien to Athenians, since the separation of sovereignty from its exercise was unknown to them. All powers were exercised directly by the citizens themselves, or by delegates who were appointed by lot and for a short period of time. In fact, as Aristotle points out, the election by voting was considered oligarchic and was not allowed but in exceptional circumstances (usually in cases where special knowledge was required), and only appointment by lot was considered democratic.[45]

Therefore, the type of 'democracy' that has been established since the sixteenth century in Europe has had very little in common with the Athenian democracy. The former presupposes the separation of the state from society and the exercise of sovereignty by a separate body of representatives, whereas the latter is based on the principle that sovereignty is exercised directly by the free citizens themselves. Athens, therefore, may hardly be characterized as a state in the normal sense of the word. As Thomas Martin[46] rightly points out, '[d]ecentralized, self-governing communities like ancient Athens or medieval Lübeck were not "city-states" . . . Without centralized authority there is no sovereign; without a sovereign there is no state.' Bookchin and Castoriadis, also, agree on the non-statist character of Athens.[47]

So, despite the fact that Greek philosophers did speak about sovereignty in the polis,[48] a fact that some could take as implying the existence of a state, I think that in the case of the Athenian polis we cannot properly speak of sovereignty and the state. Instead, I would argue that Athens was a mix of non-statist and statist democracy. It was non-statist as regards the citizen body, which was 'ruled' by nobody and whose members shared power equally among themselves, and statist as regards those not qualifying as full citizens (women, slaves, immigrants), over whom the demos wielded power.

But let us examine in more detail the historical conceptions of democracy, starting with the classical Athenian conception.

Conceptions of democracy

The Athenian conception of democracy
Although it is, of course, true that power relations and structures did not disappear in the *Polis* (not only at the economic level, where inequities were obvious, but even at the political level, where the hierarchical structure of society was clear with the exclusion of women, immigrants and slaves from the proceedings of the *ecclesia*), still, the Athenian democracy was the first historical example of the identification of the sovereign with those exercising sovereignty. As Hannah Arendt points out:

> [T]he whole concept of rule and being ruled, of government and power in the sense in which we understand them, as well as the regulated order attending them, was felt to be prepolitical and to belong to the private rather than the public sphere . . . equality therefore far from being connected with justice, as in modern times, was the very essence of freedom: to be free meant to be free from the inequality present in rulership and to move to a sphere where neither rule nor being ruled existed.[49]

So, it is obvious that libertarian definitions of politics as 'the *rule* of one, many, a few, or all over all' and of democracy as 'the *rule* of all over all'[50] are incompatible with the classical conceptions of both politics and democracy. It is, however, characteristic of the distortion involved that when libertarians attack democracy as a kind of 'rule' they usually confuse direct democracy with statist democracy. This is not surprising, in view of the fact that it is obviously impossible to talk about a 'rule' in a form of social organization where nobody is forced to be bound by laws and institutions, in the formation of which s/he does not, directly, take part.[51]

Therefore, the Greeks, having realized that 'there always is and there always will be an *explicit power,* that is, unless a society were to succeed in transforming its subjects into automata that had completely internalized the instituted order',[52] concluded that 'no citizen should be subjected to power (μή ἀρχεσθαι) and if this was not possible that power should be shared equally among citizens'.[53]

Perhaps a useful way to examine the evolution of democracy in Athens would be to relate it to a parallel effort to diminish the socio-economic differences among the citizens, which can be considered as a step towards economic democracy. I would argue that this limited form of economic democracy played a significant role in enhancing the democratic institutions. However, it was exactly the limited nature of economic democracy which, in combination with the overall partial character of democracy, eventually led to its collapse. In other words, as I will try to show here, the decline of the Athenian democracy was not due, as is usually asserted by critics of democracy, to the innate weaknesses of direct democracy, but to its failure to become an inclusive democracy and in particular to the fact that the political equality which the Athenian democracy had established for its citizens was, in the last instance, founded on economic inequality. In fact, the importance of economic inequities with respect to the stability of democracy was recognized even at the time of the classical Athenian democracy. According to Aristotle, for instance, 'some hold that property . . . is always the pivot of revolutionary movements . . . the common people are driven to rebellion by inequality in the distribution of property'.[54]

Although a fuller discussion of economic democracy will have to wait until the next chapter, a preliminary definition may be given here to elucidate the Athenian conception of democracy. If we define political democracy as the authority of the people (*demos*) in the political sphere – a fact that implies political equality – then economic democracy could be correspondingly defined as the authority of *demos* in the economic sphere – a fact that implies economic equality. And, of course, we are talking about the *demos* and not the state, because the existence of a state means the separation of the citizen body from the political and economic process. Economic democracy therefore relates to every social system that institutionalizes the integration of society and the economy. This means that, ultimately, the *demos* controls the economic process, within an institutional framework of *demotic* ownership of the means of production. In a more narrow sense, economic democracy relates also to every social system that institutionalizes the minimization of socio-economic differences, particularly those arising out of the unequal distribution of private property and the consequent unequal distribution of income and wealth.

It is obvious that economic democracy refers both to the mode of production and distribution of the social product and wealth. Let us therefore see how production and distribution were organized in classical Athens.

As regards, first, the mode of production, although the slaves made up more than half of the population of Athens, many of them either worked as independent craftsmen paying rent to their masters, or worked side by side with the free farmers in the fields. Slavery, therefore, played a decisive role in the production of economic surplus only as regards the production that was under the control of the state (e.g. the mines at Laurion) and the big landowners. The basis of the ancient Greek city, as Marx stresses, was the small independent production of farmers and craftsmen, and not slavery:

> The pre-condition for the continued existence of the community is the maintenance of equality among its free self-sustaining peasants, and their individual labour as the condition of the continued existence of their property.[55]

As regards the mode of distribution of the social product in ancient Athens, it is generally acknowledged[56] that it had played a decisive role in the appropriation of the economic surplus. That is the reason why this system is usually defined as 'appropriation by right of citizenship'. In other words, the mechanisms through which the surplus (that usually took the form of spoils, and tribute income from subservient states, but also income from taxes imposed on the citizens themselves) was extracted and distributed were not economic, but basically political. The implication is that the struggle between social groups took also a political form, mainly as a conflict between the supporters of oligarchy (oligarchs) and the supporters of democracy (democrats). The oligarchs, who were flanked by the big landowners and rich merchants/craftsmen, as well as by the aristocrats, were always in favour of limiting political rights (the right to vote and the right to be elected), but also limiting public expenditure, which, in the last instance, harmed more their own classes who were mainly responsible for financing them. On the other hand, the democrats,[57] who were made up predominantly of the lower income strata (although their leaders did not, as a rule, belong to these strata), demanded the broadening of political rights, the increase of expenditure for public works, the payment of salaries with regard to the exercise of civic rights, etc.

Hence, the citizens' ability to partake of the state's profits and revenue played a critical role in the distribution of economic surplus and therefore the content of economic democracy itself (narrow sense). That is, the more citizens were able to partake in the distributed economic surplus, the greater the degree of economic democracy. And in fact there were several ways in which citizens were taking part in the distribution of city money: either in the form of compensation (*misthos*) for the exercise of their civic rights (attending the Assembly, taking part in the People's Court as juror, etc.), or in the form of 'social security' in case they were disabled with no means of support,[58] or, finally, in the form of payment for their services with respect to public works. Furthermore, as I will try to show, the process for completing political democracy among free citizens was accompanied by a parallel process of the broadening of economic democracy. The differentiating characteristic of the Athenian democracy at its peak period, in relation to any other system in the ancient world and since then, until today, was a collective conscious effort for the continuous broadening and deepening of political democracy and, to a point, of economic democracy. From this angle, the importance today of the Athenian experience is not only that it shows the possibility, under certain preconditions, for the organizing and functioning of present-day society on the basis of the principles of direct democracy, which are the only ones that may secure real democracy; its importance lies also in the fact that it illustrates the incompatibility of political democracy and economic oligarchy.

We could distinguish the following periods in the evolution of Athenian political democracy in relation to the evolution of economic democracy: first, the period prior to Solon; second, the period from Solon to the reforms of Cleisthenes; third, the period from Cleisthenes to Pericles; fourth, the period from Pericles till the end of the Peloponnesian War; and finally, the period of decline of the Athenian democracy.

The period prior to Solon's archonship (594 BC) was characterized by a significant concentration of economic and political power. The land belonged to a few big landowners while the poor farmers who cultivated it, called the '*Hectemoroi*', were obliged to pay as rent one-sixth of their produce. The relationship of the *Hectemoroi* was not simply the result of economic pressures and debts, but expressed a traditional social status of inferiority which came into existence during the Greek 'dark ages' (1100–800 BC), when the weak and the poor offered their services to the powerful in return for their protection. In particular, all those *Hectemoroi* who could not pay their rent or, in general, all debtors who were not in a position to pay their loans, lost, both they and their children, their very freedom. Political power was still weak and real power rested with a few influential families who controlled economic and military power. The few political offices (nine *archons*, the Council of the Areopagos, etc.) belonged, according to one theory, to a hereditary ruling class, the noblemen, while, according to another theory, some property criterion had already been introduced prior to Solon. What is not, however, in dispute is that the right to be elected to the higher offices was monopolized during that period by the upper social and economic strata.

This condition of political and economic oligarchy, combined with important economic changes in production and trade (intensification of cultivation of land, expansion of exports, etc.), led to hard competition between rich and poor, to which Solon was already referring in his poems at the beginning of the sixth century. Solon's reforms, in particular the *Seisachtheia* (the shaking off of burdens) that had preceded the reforms of Cleisthenes, created the economic foundations for *Isonomia* (equality in law) and direct democracy. It should be noted here that the *Seisachtheia* was not simply a law abolishing debts, as is usually asserted. An alternative explanation, based on the fact that Solon in his *iamboi* (poems) does not refer to debts, is that the *Seisachtheia* abolished the relationship of the economic dependence of the *Hectemoroi,* who then probably acquired full rights of ownership of the land that they were cultivating. Equally important steps in the limitation of economic power of the oligarchy were the introduction of an extremely progressive income tax to cover emergency needs (on top of the usual indirect taxes) and the shifting of the burden of the expenses for the public duties (*litourgies*), as well as of a great part of military expenses, on to the higher classes.[59]

These very important steps towards economic democracy were accompanied by corresponding political reforms. The Assembly of the People (*ecclesia*), in which all citizens participated irrespective of income, acquired the right to elect the leaders (*archons*) and the deputies (we are not dealing here with the disputed historical fact as to whether Solon founded the Council of 400 Deputies – *Boule*, as mentioned by Aristotle),[60] as well as the right to scrutinize the *archons,* a previously exclusive right of the Council of the Areopagos.[61] However, the higher offices of the city remained in the hands of the elite since it is doubtful as to whether more than one-fifteenth of the citizens[62] belonged to the *pentakosiomedimnoi* (five hundred bushel producers) and the noblemen, from whom the nine *archons* were elected. Even the very right to vote was not universal, since only those who belonged to some family group (*genos*) had this right and many Athenians at that time did not belong to a *genos.*

After the fall of the Peisistratides' Tyranny (510 BC), which is viewed today as the outcome of local rather than class conflicts, and the democrats' takeover under Cleisthenes, just three years after the expulsion of the tyrants, the domination of the aristocrats was abolished in favour of a new form of constitution, 'democracy' (507 BC). The main institutional changes introduced were the following:

- The differentiation of the citizens on the basis of the class criterion of property size was abolished and was replaced by the criterion of the place of residence.
- The right to vote was universalized and part of the judicial authority was transferred to the people in the form of jury courts.
- The Council of Five Hundred was introduced, with important preliminary jurisdiction which could influence the decisions of the *ecclesia*. The particular democratic significance of this institution relates to the way its members were elected. The election of its members by lot and for only one year were necessary safety valves that prevented the monopolizing of the office of deputy by professional politicians.
- Finally, the banning of leaders by vote (*ostracism*) was adopted. This was another safety valve in the democratic process since, according to Aristotle, the aim of the new institution was to give the people the power to neutralize 'those who were dominating or exerting undue influence by virtue of their wealth or some other political strength'.[63]

Yet, the Athenian democracy was not completed with Cleisthenes. It took another 20 to 30 years before election by lot was first introduced for the *archons* (with the exception of the office of general which required specialized knowledge and experience) – 487 BC – and for the property criterion which excluded the lower strata from higher offices to be abolished after the battle of Plataia in 479 BC. Finally, almost another 20 years had to pass for the Areopagos (whose members still belonged to the two richer classes) to be deprived of its privileges, which were transferred to the Assembly of the People, the Council of the Five Hundred, and the jury courts (462 BC).[64] By the end of this process, every adult male Athenian citizen had the right to attend the *ecclesia* and if he was over 30 years he had the further right to be a magistrate (*archon*) or a legislator (*nomothetes*) or a juror (*dikastes*).[65]

The completion of Athenian democracy was associated with the era of Pericles (461–429 BC) when both political and economic democracy reached their peak. Political democracy came to its climax because it was then that the process was completed which made the '*polis*' autonomous (it set its own laws), *self-judging* (jury courts decided on every dispute) and *independent* (the Assembly of the People made all important decisions) – the three elements which, according to Thucydides, characterize a city as free. Economic democracy also peaked at this time, because it was then that compensation for the exercise of civic rights was established (judicial salary for jury duty, assembly salary for participation in the *ecclesia,* salary for deputies, soldiers, etc.). As a result of these payments 'no citizen was prevented by poverty from exercising his political rights'.[66] At the same time, a huge programme for public works was started which not only created the architectural masterpieces of Athens but also strengthened significantly the income of the lower classes. It is therefore not accidental that the greatest achievements of the ancient Greek civilization were accomplished during the Periclean era.

This deepening of economic democracy, however, was not only the outcome of the decisions of the Assembly of the People or the prompting of Pericles. An external factor, the Persian Wars, played a decisive role. The Persian Wars had a double economic effect. First, as Paparregopoulos mentions, given that the privileged position of the higher classes depended basically on land income which, because of the repeated destruction of Attica, had almost disappeared, the effect was that 'the poor became on this point similar to the wealthy, and with equality of services combined with the (albeit temporary) equality of properties, it was very natural to bring about, during these critical years, the equality of rights'.[67] Second, the formation of the Delian League and the consequent financial contributions of the allies gave the Athenian public treasury the financial ability to undertake the expenses for the upkeep of over 20,000 citizens, in the form of compensation for political and military service rendered.[68]

We should particularly stress here the importance of compensating citizens for exercising their civic rights. The establishment of any democratic institution in the political sphere is self-cancelling when a large number of its citizens are not in an objective economic position to spend the necessary time required for an effective participation in the democratic procedures. This is because time has always been a huge source of social power. In the democratic Athens of Cleisthenes, in theory, everybody could be elected to the highest offices, while in reality, the lower strata were excluded. As Paparregopoulos notes, not even the method of election by lot helped these strata because:

> a great number of the poorer people were not drawn, being absent in naval and commercial enterprises, and because the most important state offices, in particular the military ones, were given, now as before, by ordination to the most able, who naturally were not usually the poorer people. Nor did [the poor] regularly attend the Assembly of the People and the courts of the heliasts because they could not abandon, for this purpose, their income-earning jobs.[69]

And of course it should not be forgotten that despite the significance of participating in the Assembly of the People, the fact that the *ecclesia* assembled only 40 times a year meant that the office of, for example, a councillor in the Council of 500 carried significant weight in the decision-making process (although as Hansen points out, all the evidence points to the fact that 'policy at Athens really was made by the Assembly rather than by the Council (in the pre-Assembly stage)').[70]

As regards the importance of free time for the functioning of democracy, slavery played a double role with respect to the reproduction of democracy. It did play a positive role because (as Marxists assume) it contributed significantly, though not decisively, to the creation of the economic surplus that was necessary for the survival of society in general. Furthermore, slavery, as well as the patriarchal relations in the household, played a crucial role in allowing the male Athenians the time needed for the exercise of their civic rights. However, slavery played also a very significant negative role with respect to the reproduction of democracy. As slave-ownership depended on the distribution of income and wealth, the rich, who owned many more slaves than the poor, had much more time at their disposal to exercise their civic rights. One therefore may argue that the net effect of slavery on the reproduction of democracy was clearly negative – a fact that was recognized by Pericles who introduced the system of compensation for public servants, exactly as a necessary counter-balancing factor to the unequal distribution of free time.

In fact, the entire conflict between Pericles and Cimon (his conservative political rival) had as its basis the preconditions for political democracy. Cimon supported similar positions to the ones declared by the supporters of today's liberal 'democracy'. Thus, for Cimon, the legislating of democratic procedures was sufficient and it was up to each citizen to use them appropriately, through his abilities and work. On the contrary, Pericles discerned the merely formal character of political rights when they are not accompanied by social and economic rights. With the aim therefore of diminishing the economic inequality among citizens, a precondition for political equality, Pericles introduced the system of compensations. This, however, necessitated an even greater limitation of citizenship (it was for this reason that foreigners, in addition to women and slaves, were also excluded from citizenship), and the expansion of tax revenues, through what we now call the broadening of the tax base. The establishment of the Athenian hegemony over other Greek cities played exactly this role.

However, the foundations of this democracy were not solid, as the economic factors that supported Pericles' political democracy disappeared quickly. Thus:

- the relative economic equality, brought about by the Persian Wars, was completely temporary. The expansion of trade that had followed the

Persian Wars led to concentration of economic power and greater inequality in the distribution of income and wealth. As Paparregopoulos stresses:

> the compensations by the public treasury were more or less sufficient to feed the destitute, yet these people remained always destitute, whereas the richest of the Athenians during these years increased their wealth significantly; so, a very great inequality of wealth resulted, because of which the poorer, on many occasions, became the blind instruments of the wealthier.[71]

- the imposition of unequal political and economic relations by the hegemonic Athens on her allies finally led to the Peloponnesian War (431–404 BC)[72] and the end of the Athenian hegemony, with obvious consequences on the public treasury. With the end of the war and the collapse of the Athenian hegemony, the basic financial source of the economic democracy also dried up. Public revenue was no longer enough, *without significant cuts in military spending,* to finance the two main types of expenditure used by Pericles to support the income of the poorer strata, namely, what we would today call Keynesian public works and the payment of salaries, etc. The inevitable consequence was the further weakening of the military strength of the city (the increasing use of mercenaries contributed significantly to this process) that finally brought about the end of democracy itself, after the Athenians were defeated by Philip, Alexander the Great's father, in the battle of Chaeronea (338 BC – although democracy was not formally abolished until 332 BC). It is also noteworthy that Athens' decline was not checked by the second Athenian naval hegemony, following the battle of Mantineia (362 BC), despite (or, perhaps, because of) its more democratic character in relation to the first hegemony.

So, amidst increasing economic inequality domestically and growing inability to impose any more external taxes to finance its internal democracy, the material conditions on which economic democracy was based were phased quickly away. At this stage, only the conversion of the partial Athenian democracy into an inclusive one would have saved it; in other words, the introduction of a complete political democracy that would include all the city residents (free citizens, women, slaves) and a real economic democracy that would have abolished economic inequalities.

Such a democracy would not have depended for its financial support on a surplus created through inequality (domestic and external) as before, but on an expanded domestic surplus. One might speculate that the very elimination of economic inequalities in general and of slavery in particular should have had a significant effect in expanding the domestic surplus. In general, one may expect that productivity of slaves, who constituted more than half the labour force, would have vastly improved had they been offered full citizenship rights. Furthermore, slavery had an alienating effect not just on slaves but also on their masters, with corresponding adverse effects on their productivity. Thus, historians agree that in the late stages of the Athenian democracy economic inequality and slavery had become the material bases for the conversion of productive Athenian citizens into parasitical 'civil servants'.[73] So, whereas the intended function of public compensation was to decrease inequality in the distribution of free time (a basic symptom of economic inequality), it finally ended up undermining productive activity itself: financially weaker citizens were converted into public employees who were paid from the surplus produced by the subordinate cities and the slaves. A similar positive effect on the domestic surplus would have been created by the full integration of women into the citizen body.

The final failure, therefore, of Athenian democracy was not due, as is usually asserted by its critics, to the innate contradictions of democracy itself but, on the contrary, to the fact that the Athenian democracy never matured to become an inclusive democracy. This cannot be adequately explained by simply referring to the immature 'objective' conditions, the low development of productive forces and so on – important as these may be – because the same objective conditions prevailed at that time in many other places all over the Mediterranean, not only the rest of Greece, but democracy flourished mainly in Athens. Conversely, the much lower development of productive forces did not prevent higher forms of economic democracy (narrow sense) than in Athens to develop among aboriginal American communities where economic resources were available to everyone in the community for use, and 'things were available to individuals and families of a community because they were needed, not because they were owned or created by the labour of a possessor'.[74]

The liberal conception of democracy

The liberal conception of democracy is based on the negative conception of freedom and a corresponding conception of human rights. From these definitions and a world view which sees human nature as atomistic and human beings as rational agents whose existence and interests are onto-logically prior to society follow a number of principles about the constitution of society, i.e. political egalitarianism, freedom of citizens – as competitors – to realize their capabilities at the economic level and separation of the private realm of freedom from the public realm.

It is therefore clear that the above liberal principles about the constitution of society imply a form of democracy where the state is separate from the economy and the market. In fact, liberal philosophers not only took for granted the separation of the state apparatus from society but saw democracy as a way of bridging the gap between state and society. The bridging role was supposed to be played by representative 'democracy', a system whereby the plurality of political parties would provide an adequate forum for competing interests and systems of values. No wonder therefore that none of the founders of classical liberalism was an advocate of democracy, in the sense of direct democracy, let alone inclusive democracy. In fact, the opposite was the case. For instance, the American Founding Fathers Madison and Jefferson were sceptical of democracy, precisely because of its Greek connotation of direct rule. This is why they preferred to call the American system republican, because 'the term was thought to be more appropriate to the balanced constitution that had been adopted in 1787 than the term democratic, with its connotations of lower-class dominance'.[75]

However, in representative democracy, as Hannah Arendt stressed, the age-old distinction between ruler and ruled asserts itself again: 'Once more, the people are not admitted to the public realm, once more the business of government becomes the privilege of the few ... the result is that the people must either sink into lethargy, the forerunner of death to the public liberty, or preserve the spirit of resistance to whatever government they have elected, since the only power they retain is the "reserve power of revolution".'[76]

In this light, one may be led to a different understanding of the motives behind the liberal adoption of representative 'democracy'. Thus, instead of considering representative democracy as a bridge between state and society we may see it as a form of statist democracy, whose main aim is the exclusion of the vast majority of the population from political power. As John Dunn stresses:

> It is important to recognize that the modern state was constructed, painstakingly and purposefully, above all by Jean Bodin and Thomas Hobbes, for the express purpose of denying that any given population, any people, had either the capacity or the right to act together for themselves, either independently of, or against their sovereign. The central point of the concept was to deny the very possibility that any demos (let alone one on the demographic scale of a European territorial monarchy) could be a genuine political agent, could act at all, let alone act with sufficiently continuous identity and practical coherence for it to be able to rule itself . . . the idea of the modern state was invented precisely to repudiate the possible coherence of democratic claims to rule, or even take genuinely political action . . . representative democracy is democracy made safe for the modern state.[77]

It is not therefore surprising that Adam Smith, the father of economic liberalism, took pains to stress that the main task of government was the defence of the rich against the poor – a task that, as John Dunn points out, is 'necessarily less dependably performed where it is the poor who choose who is to govern, let alone where the poor themselves, as in Athens, in large measure simply *are* the government'.[78]

In conclusion, the liberal conception of democracy, which, when implemented, inevitably leads to the concentration of political power in the hands of a political elite and the situation of political oligarchy and inequality, is also compatible with the concentration of economic power in the hands of an economic elite and the state of economic oligarchy and inequality that the market economy creates. Furthermore, both political and economic oligarchy are perfectly compatible with the liberal conception of freedom.

The Marxist–Leninist conception of democracy

The starting point in the socialist conception of democracy is a critique of the liberal conception of democracy. The critique is based on the fact that the liberal conception takes for granted the separation of the political from the economic realm and therefore, in effect, protects and legitimizes the huge inequalities to which the market economy inevitably leads. In other words, the liberal democracy, even if it is supposed to secure an equal distribution of political power (which as we saw above it certainly does not) it still bypasses the crucial issue of distribution of economic power. The question therefore arises of economic democracy, i.e. of an institutional arrangement which would secure, for every citizen, an equal say in economic decision-making.

The answer traditionally given to this question by socialists can be classified, broadly speaking, in terms of the social-democratic and the Marxist–Leninist conceptions of democracy. The social-democratic conception is essentially a version of the liberal conception. In other words, social democracy consists of a 'liberal democracy' element, in the sense of a statist and representative form of democracy based on a market economy, and an 'economic democracy' element, in the sense of a strong welfare state and the state commitment to implement full employment policies. However, as we saw in Chapter 2, the social-democratic conception of democracy has been abandoned by social-democratic parties all over the world which have dropped the 'economic democracy' element of their conception of democracy. As a result, the social-democratic conception of democracy is by now virtually indistinguishable from the liberal one, in the context of what I call the present 'neoliberal consensus'.

Therefore, setting aside the traditional social-democratic conception (modern versions of 'radical' democracy will be discussed in the next section) let us examine the Marxist–Leninist conception which is still relevant to the remnants of the Marxist Left. My argument is that, appearances to the contrary notwithstanding, this conception is clearly a statist conception of democracy. In this conception, democracy is not differentiated from the state for the entire historical period which separates capitalism from communism, i.e. for the entire period that is called the 'realm of necessity', when scarcity leads to class antagonisms which make inevitable class dictatorships of one kind or another. In this view, socialism will simply replace the dictatorship of one class, the bourgeoisie, by that of another, the proletariat. Thus, for Marx:

> Between capitalist and communist society lies the period of the revolutionary transformation of the one into another. Corresponding to this is also a political transition period in which the state can be nothing but the revolutionary dictatorship of the proletariat.[79]

Also, according to Lenin, 'Democracy is also a state and consequently democracy will also disappear when the state disappears. Revolution alone can "abolish" the bourgeois state. The state in general, i.e. the most complete democracy can only "wither away".'[80] And he continues that the state (and democracy) will wither away only when:

> people have become so accustomed to observing the fundamental rules of social intercourse and when their labour becomes so productive that they will voluntarily work according to their ability . . . there will then be no need for society to regulate the quantity of products to be received by each; each will take freely according to his needs[81] . . . from the moment all members of society, or even only the vast majority have learned to administer the state themselves . . . the need for government of any kind begins to disappear altogether . . . for when all have learned to administer and actually do independently administer social production, independently keep accounts and exercise control over the idlers, etc . . . the necessity of observing the simple fundamental rules of human intercourse will very soon become a habit.[82]

It is therefore obvious that in this world view, a non-statist conception of democracy is inconceivable, both at the transitional stage leading to communism and at the higher phase of communist society: in the former, because the realm of necessity makes necessary a statist form of democracy where political and economic power is not shared among all citizens but only among members of the proletariat; in the latter, because when we reach the realm of freedom, no form of democracy at all is necessary, since no significant decisions will have to be made! Thus, at the economic level, scarcity and the division of labour will by then have disappeared, and therefore there will be no need for any significant economic decisions to be taken about the allocation of resources. Also, at the political level, the administration of things will have replaced the administration of people, and therefore there will be no need for any significant political decisions to be taken either.

However, the Marxist abolition of scarcity depends on an objective definition of 'needs', which is neither feasible, nor – from the democratic point of view – desirable. It is not feasible because, even if basic needs may be assumed finite and independent of time and place, the same cannot be said about their satisfiers (i.e. the form or the means by which these needs are satisfied), let alone non-basic needs. It is not desirable because, in a democratic society, an essential element of freedom is choice as regards the ways in which needs are formed and satisfied. As Bookchin who, in contrast to Marx, adopts a subjective definition of needs and post-scarcity, points out:

> [I]n a truly free society needs would be formed by consciousness and by choice, not simply by environment and tool-kits . . . the problems of needs and scarcity, in short, must be seen as a problem of selectivity – of choice . . . freedom from scarcity, or post-scarcity presupposes that individuals have the material possibility of choosing what they need – not only a sufficiency of available goods from which to choose but a transformation of work, both qualitatively and quantitatively.[83]

So, the communist stage of post-scarcity is in fact a mythical state of affairs – if needs and scarcity are defined objectively – and reference to it could simply be used (and has been used) to justify the indefinite maintenance of state power and power relations and structures in general. It is therefore obvious that, within the problematic of the democracy project, the link between post-scarcity and freedom should be broken. The abolition of scarcity and, consequently, of the division of labour is neither a necessary nor a sufficient condition for democracy. Therefore, the ascent of man from the kingdom of necessity to the kingdom of freedom should be de-linked from the economic process. Still, from Aristotle, through Locke and Marx, to Arendt, the distinction between the 'realm of necessity' (where nature belongs) and the 'realm of freedom' always has been considered to be fundamental. However, although this distinction may be useful as a *conceptual tool* in classifying human activities, there is no reason why the two realms must be seen as mutually exclusive in social reality. Historically, there have been several occasions when various degrees of freedom survived under conditions that could be characterized as belonging to the 'realm of necessity'. Furthermore, once we cease treating the two realms as mutually exclusive, there is no justification for any attempt to dominate Nature – an important element of Marxist growth ideology – in order to enter the realm of freedom.

In conclusion, there are no material preconditions of freedom. The entrance to the realm of freedom does not depend on any 'objective' factors, like the arrival of the mythical state of affairs of material abundance. The level of development of productive forces that is required so that material abundance for the entire population on earth can be achieved makes it at least doubtful that such a stage could ever be achieved without serious repercussions to the environment – unless, of course, 'material abundance' is defined democratically (and not 'objectively') in a way which is consistent with ecological balance. By the same token, the entrance to the realm of freedom does not depend on a massive change of consciousness through the adoption of some form of spiritualistic dogma, as some deep ecologists and other spiritualistic movements propose. Therefore, neither capitalism and socialism, on the 'objective' side, nor the adoption of some kind of spiritualistic dogma, on the 'subjective' side, constitute historical preconditions to enter the realm of freedom.

The conceptions of 'radical' democracy

In the last ten years or so, and particularly after the collapse of 'actually existing socialism', several versions of what is usually termed 'radical' democracy have flourished among state socialists (post-Marxists, neo-Marxists, ex-Marxists *et al.*). The common characteristic of all these approaches to 'radical' democracy is that they all take for granted the present institutional framework, as defined by the market economy and liberal democracy, and suggest various combinations of the market with forms of social ownership of the means of production, as well as the 'democratization' of the state.

Thus, the present ideological hegemony of liberalism has led to a situation where many 'socialists' identify socialism with an extension of (liberal representative) democracy rather than with the emancipation of the working class[84] and concentrate their efforts in theorizing, in several ways, that socialism is the fulfilment of liberalism rather than its negation. A typical example of this trend is Norberto Bobbio, who, adopting the negative definition of freedom as 'freedom from', characterizes liberal democracy as 'the only possible form of an effective democracy' capable of protecting the citizens from state encroachment.[85] In the process, Bobbio attacks what he calls the 'fetish' of direct democracy on the usual grounds of scale (ignoring the proposals of confederalists) and the experience of the student movement (ignoring the fact that democracy is not just a procedure but a form of social organization). In essence, therefore, what Bobbio, as well as Miliband[86] and other writers in the same ideological

TOWARDS AN INCLUSIVE DEMOCRACY

space promote, is a form of economic democracy to complement liberal democracy. In so doing, in effect, they try to take over the social-democratic space, which was abandoned by social democrats, after the latter moved to the right and joined the neoliberal consensus.

At the same time, the Habermasian school promotes lately a 'procedur-alist' model of democracy, as a third way between the liberal model and 'a communitarian interpretation of the republican model'. Thus, Habermas, differentiating his model of democracy from what he calls the 'state-centred understanding of politics' that, according to him, both the liberal and the republican models of democracy represent, stresses that, according to discourse theory, the success of deliberative politics depends 'not on a collectively acting citizenry but on the institutionalization of the corres-ponding procedures and conditions of communication'. His model con-sists of a 'decentred society', that is, a 'democracy' which is based on a civil society that 'provides the social basis of autonomous public spheres that remain as distinct from the economic system as from the administra-tion'.[87]

However, the Habermasian view of democracy not only converts democracy into a set of procedures instead of a regime, as Castoriadis[88] rightly points out, but it is also utterly irrelevant to the present trends of the market economy and the bureaucratization of today's 'politics'. Thus, Habermas ignores the fact that the present internationalized market econ-omy can easily marginalize any groups that are 'autonomous' from the market public spheres (co-ops etc.) – unless their creation is part of a comprehensive political programme aiming at a new form of society. Equally ignored by him is the fact that, even at the political level, the possibility of public spheres autonomous from the state is effectively undermined by the marketization process (deregulation of markets, etc.), which enhances not the 'civil society' but, instead, the elites in effective control of the means of production (see, for instance, the present withering away of the trade union movement, the decline of local authorities' power, etc.).

Similar arguments can be advanced against the various versions of 'red-green' democracy proposed by the Marxist ecological left. One could mention here the views expressed by James O'Connor, who talks about 'sublating' local and central, spontaneity and planning, exclusive and inclusive cultural identities, industrial and social labour, etc.;[89] or, alterna-tively, John Dryzek, who stresses the need for 'democratization at all possible levels: in the autonomous public spheres, such as those constituted by new social movements, at the boundaries of the state, where legitimacy is sought through discursive exercises, and even within the state, e.g. in the form of impact assessment'.[90]

Others talk about a *process* of democracy rather than a set of procedures. Thus, Chantal Mouffe's version of 'radical' democracy is differentiated from that of the Habermasians by postulating that a final realization of democracy is impossible, as a result of 'the unresolvable tension between the principles of equality and liberty'.[91] The author sees 'radical' democracy as the only alternative today and explicitly states that 'Such a perspective does not imply the rejection of liberal democracy and its replacement by a completely new political form of society, as the traditional idea of revolution entailed, but a radicalization of the modern democratic tradition.'[92] Furthermore, to the possible objection that a strategy of democratization of the state is severely constrained by the market economy Mouffe's answer is that 'political and economic liberalism need to be distinguished and then separated from each other'.[93] Mouffe's view of 'radical' democracy can perhaps be best summarized in the following excerpt:

> *The distinction between private (individual liberty)/public (*respublica*) is maintained as well as the distinction individual/citizen, but they do not correspond to discrete separate spheres . . . those two identities exist in a permanent tension that can never be reconciled. But this is precisely the tension between liberty and equality that characterizes modern democracy. It is the very life of such a regime and any attempt to bring about a perfect harmony, to realize a 'true' democracy can only lead to its destruction. This is why a project of radical and plural democracy recognizes the impossibility of the complete realization of democracy and the final achievement of the political community. Its aim is to use the symbolic resources of the liberal democratic tradition to struggle for the deepening of the democratic revolution knowing that it is a never ending process.*[94]

It is obvious that Mouffe's 'radical' democracy is another attempt to reconcile the autonomy of the individual with liberalism. Thus, Mouffe, not unlike L. Susan Brown (who, as we saw earlier, separates existential from instrumental liberalism) separates political from economic liberalism. But the fact that political and economic liberalism have always been inseparable is not a historical accident. The marketization of the economy, i.e. the lifting of social controls on the market in the last two centuries, has always been based on the ideal of a 'free' (from state controls and restrictions) individual. So, Mouffe's version of 'radical' democracy is grounded on a negative conception of freedom and an individualistic conception of autonomy, which is assumed separate from collective autonomy. Furthermore, the author, by mixing up the fact that democracy is indeed a process (in the sense that divisions among citizens will always exist and will continue necessitating a deepening of any institutionalized democracy) with the meaning of democracy itself, ends up by defining radical democracy in terms of 'extending and deepening' the present 'liberal oligarchy' (which is christened democracy) rather than in terms of the institutional preconditions of democracy. Finally, the author, starting from the premise that the identities of citizen and individual can never be reconciled, since they correspond to the tension between liberty and equality, derives the conclusion that the project for democracy will never be completed. So, the fact that this tension is the inevitable outcome of the unequal distribution of political, economic and social power is ignored. Consequently, there is no scope in this problematic for an alternative definition of an inclusive democracy that could create the necessary (but not the sufficient) conditions for eliminating the tension between equality and liberty.

A more radical version of democracy is David Miller's 'deliberative democracy'[95] which, as far as its economic aspects are concerned, is a form of market socialism,[96] i.e. a combination of social ownership of the means of production with a market economy. As the author describes the model 'the key idea is that the market mechanism is retained as a means of providing most goods and services, while the ownership of capital is socialized'.[97] This model at the micro-economic level assumes that all decisions about what and how to produce are taken by productive enterprises which take the form of workers' co-operatives (a truly radical characteristic with respect to the other forms of 'radical' democracy) and which compete for custom in the market. At the macro-economic level, apart from the socialization of capital, it is assumed that a sort of distributive policy is in place which ensures that every citizen has adequate means to satisfy his/her basic needs.[98] Finally, democracy at the workplace is secured since each enterprise is democratically controlled by those who work for it who also decide how to distribute the co-op's income.

It is obvious that this model of market socialism is as a-historical as the civil societarian approach since it presupposes a degree of statism which is no longer possible in the present internationalized market economy, as I tried to show in the first two chapters. Christopher Pierson is therefore right when in criticizing this model and similar models of market socialism he points out that:

> We must, I think, assume that any form of market society which is to be consistent with the aspirations of the market socialists will require a strong and interventionist state, indeed a state whose interventions would almost certainly be more extensive than those that we find in existing welfare states . . . there is an irony here. The market socialist model is very much one for 'socialism in one nation-state'. Yet, interest in market socialism was largely

fuelled by the seeming impossibility of pursuing a national-based socialist or social democratic strategy (largely because of the disabling effect of international markets).[99]

However, apart from this criticism of feasibility, one may hardly characterize the form of political and economic organization proposed by this model as democracy. At most, it proposes a form of workplace democracy. Thus, the form of democracy suggested is not a political democracy since it is based on representative democracy. Also, the democracy proposed cannot be characterized as economic democracy since it assumes that the allocation of productive resources will be determined not by citizens' assemblies but by competing co-ops. It is therefore clear that in such a model citizens will have no extra say in the process of allocation of resources, apart from that they will acquire those of them that are co-op members. But, this is bound to be a partial and fragmented say, referring only to the activity of the enterprise to which each citizen belongs and with all that this arrangement may imply in terms of unemployment and job security – unless, again, this is avoided through extensive state intervention in a closed economy. In a nutshell, the model of deliberative democracy (as well as similar models of market socialism) suffers from the basic drawback of much of current 'socialist' thought, i.e. that it assumes that it is only *capitalist* markets which are incompatible with democracy and not the entire system of the market economy, as we have defined it in this book.

Another version of 'radical' democracy, which criticizes models of market socialism like the above model of deliberative democracy for the fact that they concentrate on enterprises at the exclusion of other important parts of the civil society, is the model of 'associational' or 'associative' democracy.[100] However, associational democracy does not aim at a radical transformation of society as market socialism does. Its aim is much more modest: to act 'as a supplement to and a healthy competitor for the currently dominant forms of social organization: representative mass democracy, bureaucratic state welfare and the big corporation'.[101] But, despite the fact that associational democracy takes for granted the entire present institutional framework and expresses no intention to replace it, it does not hesitate to present itself as 'a third way' between the market economy and statist socialism![102]

As Hirst stresses, associationalism differs from some versions of the civil societarian approach because it treats the self-governing voluntary bodies not as 'secondary associations' but as the primary means of organizing social life in a society where the state 'becomes a secondary (if vitally necessary) public power that ensures peace between associations, protects the rights of individuals and provides the mechanisms of public finance whereby a substantial part of the activities of associations are funded'.[103] Thus, associational democracy, acknowledging the importance of concentration of economic power with respect to the concentration of social power, proposes a high degree of decentralization. In fact, associationalism is supposed to provide a rationale for the decentralization of administration and a practical means of accomplishing it. The objective therefore is 'to restore the scope of civil society by converting both companies and state welfare service agencies into self-governing associations. This will be a long haul and in the interim the most realistic policies are those which boost the co-operative economy and the voluntary sector in welfare'.[104]

However, the meaning assigned to 'co-operative economy' by associational democracy is not workers' co-ops which, together with guild socialism, are dismissed as both undesirable and obsolete in a world of international competition.[105] What is suggested instead is strengthening the small and medium sized firms by providing them with a supportive regional and local institutional context and regulating the economy by regional or local collaborative and public institutions. At the same time, associational democracy proposes the replacement of the present 'shareholders' economy' with a 'stakeholders' one. Thus, the governance of enterprises is proposed to be assigned to representatives of a tripartite relationship of stakeholders (workers, capitalists and local community) rather than to representatives of shareholders as at present — an arrangement that will help in making firms accountable to its members and society at large.

To the obvious questions of *who* is going to initiate these reforms and *why*, the answer given by this model is twofold. As regards 'who', it is suggested that 'private initiatives must go hand-in-hand with – indeed may depend on – public reforms. Legal and institutional changes would be necessary to facilitate the rapid growth of associational governance.'[106] It is therefore obvious that the state is given, again, a much more important economic role than the one that it is allowed to play at present within the framework of the internationalized market economy.

As regards 'why', there is a 'moral' and an 'economic' answer. The moral answer is that 'human welfare and liberty are both best served when as many of the affairs of society as possible are managed by voluntary and democratically self-governing associations'.[107] The economic answer is that 'those societies that have fared best have managed to balance co-operation and competition' (Germany, Japan) whereas the countries that adopt the Anglo-Saxon model (UK, USA) 'have failed to develop or sustain these quasi-collectivist and corporatist forms of social solidarity'.[108] All this, at the very moment when the 'Rhineland' model is now in a state of decline, exactly because of the characteristics admired by associational-ists, i.e. the more extensive social controls on the markets that it involves, make it less competitive than the Anglo-Saxon model!

Another version of 'radical' democracy, which might also be taken as an attempt to internationalize the hopelessly 'closed' civil societarian approach we examined earlier, is what is called the 'cosmopolitan model of democracy' proposed by David Held.[109] Thus, the author, after explicitly adopting the separation of society from the economy and the state, in other words, the system of the market economy and liberal democracy, proposes a process of 'double democratization': the interdependent transformation of both state and civil society. As I have already discussed the feasibility and desirability of the content of 'double democratization' when I examined the civil societarian approach, I will restrict the discussion here to the 'cosmopolitan' aspects of the model and in particular to the issue of whether this conception of democracy is more realistic than the usual versions of the civil societarian approach.

The basic premise of the 'cosmopolitan model' is that in today's internationalized market economy democracy has to become a 'trans-national affair'. This implies that a number of institutional requirements have to be met so that the possibility of democracy can be linked to an expanding framework of democratic institutions and agencies. Such re-quirements mentioned by Held are: the creation of regional parliaments (an enhanced European Parliament is the model), the institution of general referenda cutting across nation-states, the opening of international governmental organizations to public scrutiny, the entrenchment of a cluster of rights (political, economic, social) and a re-formed UN which 'would seek unreservedly to place principles of democratic representation above those of superpower politics',[110] The author proposes also various methods which may be used to restrict 'the activities of powerful transna-tional interest groups to pursue their interests unchecked'[111] and the model is completed with the usual array of privately and co-operatively owned enterprises so that 'the *modus operandi* of the production, distribution and the exploitation of resources must be compatible with the democratic process and a common framework of action'.[112]

As becomes obvious from the above listing of the institutional require-ments of the 'cosmopolitan model', some of them are 'painless' for the ruling political and economic elites and may emerge anyway as a result of the present development of economic blocs (regional parliaments, regional referenda, greater openness). Other arrangements fall into the area of science fiction (who is going to force the superpowers to abdicate their privileges in a re-formed UN?) Finally, between these two extremes there

is a grey area of proposed arrangements (controls on activities of multinationals, entrenchment of a cluster of economic and social rights) whose
feasibility depends on the content assigned to them – which is left vague by
the author. If the content given to these arrangements comes in conflict
with the requirements of the internationalized market economy (e.g. the
entrenchment of each citizen's right to a job and of a corresponding firm
commitment by governments, or the adoption of strict restrictions on
multinationals' activities on the basis of ecological criteria) then we move
again to the area of science fiction and everything said above could be
repeated here. If, on the other hand, the content given to these arrangements does not affect the logic and the dynamic of the internationalized
market economy, i.e. if they are painless to the ruling elites, then they are
feasible but have little to do with the aspirations of the civil societarians to
impose effective social controls on the markets.

The conception of an inclusive democracy

A fruitful way, perhaps, to begin the discussion on a new conception of
democracy may be to distinguish between the two main societal realms,
the public and the private, to which we may add an 'ecological realm',
defined as the sphere of the relations between the natural and the social
worlds. The public realm in this book, contrary to the practice of many
supporters of the republican or democratic project (Arendt, Castoriadis,
Bookchin et al.), includes not just the political realm, but also the
economic realm as well as a 'social' realm; in other words, any area of
human activity where decisions can be taken collectively and democratically. The political realm is defined as the sphere of political decision-
taking, the area where political power is exercised. The economic realm is
defined as the sphere of economic decision-taking, the area where economic power is exercised with respect to the broad economic choices that
any *scarcity society* has to make. Finally, the social realm is defined as the
sphere of decision-taking in the workplace, the education place and any
other economic or cultural institution which is a constituent element of a
democratic society.

To my mind, the extension of the traditional public realm to include the
economic, ecological and 'social' realms is an indispensable element of an
inclusive democracy. We may therefore distinguish between four main
types of democracy that constitute the fundamental elements of an inclusive democracy: political, economic, ecological and 'democracy in the
social realm'. Political, economic and democracy in the social realm may
be defined, briefly, as the institutional framework that aims at the equal
distribution of political, economic and social power respectively; in other
words, as the system which aims at the effective elimination of the

domination of human being over human being. Correspondingly, we may define ecological democracy as the institutional framework that aims at the elimination of any human attempt to dominate the natural world; in other words, as the system which aims to reintegrate humans and nature.

Political democracy

We may distinguish various forms of political power-sharing in history, which, schematically, may be classified as either democratic or oligarchic. In the former, political power is shared equally among all those with full citizen rights (typical example is the Athenian *ecclesia*), whereas in the latter political power is concentrated, in various degrees, in the hands of miscellaneous elites.

In the political realm there can only be one form of democracy, what we may call *political* or *direct democracy,* where political power is shared equally among all citizens. So, political democracy is founded on the equal sharing of political power among all citizens, the self-instituting of society. This means that the following conditions have to be satisfied for a society to be characterized as a political democracy:

1. That democracy is grounded on the conscious *choice* of its citizens for individual and collective autonomy and not on any divine or mystical dogmas and preconceptions, or any closed theoretical systems involving social/natural 'laws', or tendencies determining social change.
2. That there are no institutionalized political *processes* of an oligarchic nature. This implies that all political decisions (including those relating to the formation and execution of laws) are taken by the citizen body collectively and without representation.
3. That there are no institutionalized political *structures* embodying unequal power relations. This means, for instance, that where delegation of authority takes place to segments of the citizen body, in order to carry out specific duties (e.g. to serve as members of popular courts, or of regional and confederal councils, etc.), the delegation is assigned, on principle, by lot, on a rotation basis, and it is always recallable by the citizen body. Furthermore, as regards delegates to regional and confederal bodies, the mandates should be specific. This is an effective step towards the abolition of hierarchical relations, since such relations today are based, to a significant extent, on the myth of the 'experts' who are supposed to be able to control everything, from nature to society. However, apart from the fact that the knowledge of the so-called experts is doubtful (at least as far as social, economic and political phenomena is concerned), in a democratic society, political decisions are not left to the experts but to the users, the citizen body.

This principle was consistently applied by the Athenians for whom 'all citizens were to take part, if they wished, in running the state, but all were to be amateurs ... professionalism and democracy were regarded as, at bottom, contradictory'.[113]

4.   That all residents of a particular geographical area (which today – for reasons I will explain in the next chapter – can only take the form of a geographical community), beyond a certain age of maturity (to be defined by the citizen body itself) and irrespective of gender, race, ethnic or cultural identity, are members of the citizen body and are directly involved in the decision-taking process.

The above conditions are obviously not met by parliamentary 'democracy' (as it functions in the West), soviet 'democracy' (as it functioned in the East) or the various fundamentalist or semi-military regimes in the South. All these regimes are therefore forms of political oligarchy, where political power is concentrated in the hands of various elites (professional politicians, party bureaucrats, priests, military and so on). Similarly, in the past, various forms of oligarchies dominated the political domain, when emperors, kings and their courts, with or without the co-operation of knights, priests and others, concentrated political power in their hands.

On the other hand, several attempts were made in the past to institutionalize various forms of direct democracy, especially during revolutionary periods (for example, the Parisian sections of the early 1790s, the Spanish assemblies in the civil war, etc.). However, most of these attempts were short-lived and usually did not involve the institutionalization of democracy as a new form of political *regime* that replaces, and not just complements, the state. In other cases, democratic arrangements were introduced as a set of procedures for local decision-making. Perhaps the only real parallel to the Athenian democracy, as Hansen notes, were four Swiss cantons and four half cantons which were governed by assemblies of the people (*Landsgemeinden*) and, in their day, were sovereign states.[114]

So, the only historical example of an *institutionalized* direct democracy where, for almost two centuries (508/7 BC to 322/1 BC), the state was subsumed in the democratic form of social organization, was the Athenian democracy. Of course, the Athenian democracy, as we saw above, was a partial political democracy. But, what characterized the Athenian democracy as partial was not the political institutions themselves but the very narrow definition of full citizenship adopted by the Athenians – a definition which excluded large sections of the population (women, slaves, immigrants) who, in fact, constituted the vast majority of the people living in Athens.

Furthermore, I refer to 'institutionalized' direct democracy in order to make clear the distinction between democratic *institutions* and democratic *practice*. The latter, as critics of democracy have pointed out, could sometimes be characterized as *de facto* 'oligarchic', in the sense that the decision-taking process was often effectively controlled by a strong leader (e.g. Pericles), or a small number of demagogues. However, this could hardly be taken as a serious criticism of the democratic institutions themselves. In fact, as it was argued above, it was precisely the partial character of the Athenian political democracy which, combined with the prevailing significant disparities in the distribution of economic power, not only created serious contradictions in the democratic process but also, at the end, by weakening the economic base on which this process was built, led to the collapse of the democratic institutions themselves.

It is therefore clear that the institutionalization of direct democracy is only the necessary condition for the establishment of democracy. As Castoriadis puts it: 'The existence of a public space (i.e. of a political domain which belongs to all) is not just a matter of legal provisions guaranteeing rights of free speech, etc. Such conditions are but conditions for a public space to exist'.[115] Citizens in Athens, for instance, before and after deliberating in the assemblies, talked to each other in the *agora* about politics.[116] Similarly, a crucial role in the education of citizens is played by *paedeia*. *Paedeia* is not just education but character development and a well-rounded education in knowledge and skills, i.e. the education of the individual as citizen, which can only 'give valuable, substantive content to the "public space"'.[117] As Hansen points out on the crucial role of *paedeia*:

> [T]o the Greek way of thinking, it was the political institutions that shaped the 'democratic man' and the 'democratic life', not vice versa: the institutions of the polis educated and moulded the lives of the citizens, and to have the best life you must have the best institutions and a system of education conforming with the institutions.[118]

Economic democracy

Historically, in contrast to the institutionalization of political democracy, there has never been a corresponding example of an institutionalized economic democracy. Most economic decisions, in historical societies, until the rise of the market economy, were taken at the micro-level, namely, at the individual production unit, although society used to exercise in various ways its power on markets, where part of economic activity had to go through, as we saw in Chapter 1. In most of these societies economic power was unequally shared, in accordance with the established patterns of unequal distribution of income and wealth. But, even when the degree of inequality in the distribution of income and wealth was low, this was not necessarily associated with economic democracy in the sense of collective decision-taking about the allocation of economic resources.

Similarly, even when direct democracy was introduced in the political realm, this was not necessarily associated with economic democracy. Thus, in classical Athens the question of economic power was never a public issue. The reason was, of course, that the accumulation of capital was not a structural characteristic of the Athenian democracy and consequently part of the dominant social paradigm. Therefore, questions about the way economic resources were to be allocated did not belong to the public realm (Aristotle was explicit about it)[119] except to the extent that they referred to the setting of social controls to regulate the limited market, or to the financing of 'public' spending. No wonder that, as Hansen points out, 'the Athenians of the classical period had a complicated network of political institutions but, as far as we can tell from the sources, no parallel economic organizations'.[120]

It was only when the market economy appeared, two centuries ago, that the question arose of how important economic decisions should be taken (how, what and for whom to produce) and the corresponding issue of sharing economic power emerged. It is equally clear that the forms of economic organization that have prevailed since the emergence of the market economy, that is, capitalism and socialist statism, were just versions of economic oligarchy, where economic power was concentrated in the hands of capitalist and bureaucratic elites.

Thus, in the type of society that emerged since the rise of the market economy, there was a definite shift of the economy from the private realm into what Hannah Arendt called the 'social realm', where the nation-state also belongs. It is this shift that today makes hollow any talk about democracy which does not also refer to the question of economic power; to talk about the equal sharing of political power, without conditioning it on the equal sharing of economic power, is at best meaningless and at worse deceptive. It is not therefore accidental that the present decline of representative democracy has led many liberals, social democrats and others to pay lip service to direct democracy, without referring to its necessary complement: economic democracy.

From this point of view, I think that statements which, for instance, describe the USA as 'an unusually free country' (as Noam Chomsky seemed to suggest in a recent interview with an Athens daily[121]) are wrong. I think that such an assessment would only stand if we could separate political freedom and equality from economic freedom and equality. But, taking into account Chomsky's political work,[122] I think that he would not agree with such a separation of the two freedoms. Therefore, even if one agrees that a significant degree of political freedom may have been secured in the USA at the legislative level (though, of course, one may have serious reservations about how the relevant legislation is implemented with respect to minorities, etc.), still, the very high degree of economic inequality and poverty that characterize this country with respect to its level of economic development would definitely not classify it as 'an unusually free country'.

So, on the basis of the preliminary definition of economic democracy given earlier in this chapter we may say that the following conditions have to be satisfied for a society to be characterized as an economic democracy:

- That there are no institutionalized economic *processes* of an oligarchic nature. This means that all 'macro' economic decisions, namely, decisions concerning the running of the economy as a whole (overall level of production, consumption and investment, amounts of work and leisure implied, technologies to be used, etc.) are taken by the citizen body collectively and without representation, although 'micro' economic decisions at the workplace or the household levels are taken by the individual production or consumption unit.
- That there are no institutionalized economic *structures* embodying unequal economic power relations. This implies that the means of production and distribution are collectively owned and directly controlled by the *demos*, the citizen body. Any inequality of income is therefore the result of additional voluntary work at the individual level. Such additional work, beyond that required by any capable member of society for the satisfaction of basic needs, allows only for additional *consumption*, as no individual accumulation of capital is possible and any wealth accumulated, as a result of additional work, is not inherited.

Democracy in the social realm

The satisfaction of the above conditions for political and economic democracy would represent the reconquering of the political and economic realms by the public realm, that is, the reconquering of a true social individuality, the creation of the conditions of freedom and self-determination, both at the political and the economic levels. However, political and economic power are not the only forms of power and therefore political and economic democracy do not, by themselves, secure an inclusive democracy. In other words, an inclusive democracy is inconceivable unless it extends to the broader social realm to embrace the workplace, the household, the educational institution and indeed any economic or cultural institution which constitutes an element of this realm.

Historically, various forms of democracy in the social realm were introduced, particularly during this century, usually in periods of revolutionary activity. However, these forms of democracy not only were short-lived but seldom extended beyond the workplace (e.g. Hungarian workers' councils[123] in 1956) and the education institution (e.g. Paris student assemblies in 1968).

A crucial issue that arises with respect to democracy in the social realm refers to relations in the household. Women's social and economic status has been enhanced this century, as a result of the expanding labour needs of the growth economy on the one hand and the activity of women's movements on the other. Still, gender relations at the household level are mostly hierarchical, especially in the South where most of the world population lives. However, although the household shares with the public realm a fundamental common characteristic, inequality and power relations, the household has always been classified in the private realm. Therefore, the problem that arises here is how the 'democratization' of the household may be achieved.

One possible solution is the dissolution of the household/public realm divide. Thus, some feminist writers, particularly of the eco-feminist variety, glorify the *oikos* and its values as a substitute for the *polis* and its politics, something that, as Janet Biehl observes, 'can easily be read as an attempt to dissolve the political into the domestic, the civil into the familial, the public into the private'.[124] Similarly, some green thinkers attempt to reduce the public realm into an extended household model of a small-scale, co-operative community.[125] At the other end, some Marxist feminists[126] attempt to remove the public/private dualism by dissolving all private space into a singular public, a socialized or fraternal state sphere. However, as Val Plumwood points out, the feminists who argue for the elimination of household privacy are today a minority although most feminists stress the way in which the concept of household privacy has been misused to put beyond challenge the subordination of women.[127]

Another possible solution is, taking for granted that the household belongs to the private realm, to define its meaning in terms of the freedom of all its members. As Val Plumwood points out:

> *When feminists speak of democratizing the household they do not of course mean that it should be stripped of its private status and become open to the 'tyranny of the majority', state regulation or regulation by general voting in a single universal, public sphere: they mean that household relationships themselves should take on the characteristics of democratic relationships, and*

that the household should take a form which is consistent with the freedom of all its members.[128]

To my mind, the issue is not the dissolution of the private/public realm divide. The real issue is how, maintaining and enhancing the autonomy of the two realms, such institutional arrangements are adopted that introduce democracy in the household and the social realm in general (workplace, educational establishment etc.) and at the same time enhance the institutional arrangements of political and economic democracy. In fact, as was argued above, an effective democracy is inconceivable unless free time is equally distributed among all citizens, and this condition can never be satisfied as long as the present hierarchical conditions in the household, the workplace and elsewhere continue. Furthermore, democracy in the social realm, particularly in the household, is impossible, unless such institutional arrangements are introduced which recognize the character of the household as a needs-satisfier and integrate the care and services provided within its framework into the general scheme of needs satisfaction.

Ecological democracy

The final question that arises with respect to the conception of an inclusive democracy refers to the issue of how we may envisage an environmentally friendly institutional framework that would not serve as the basis of a Nature-dominating ideology. Some critics of inclusive democracy misconceive the issue as if it was about the guarantees that an inclusive democracy might offer in ensuring a better relationship of society to Nature than the alternative systems of the market economy, or socialist statism. A well-known eco-socialist, for instance, asserted very recently that 'the "required" ecological consensus among ecotopia's inhabitants might not be ensured merely by establishing an Athenian democracy where all are educated and rational'.[129] This is a clear misconception of what democracy is about because, if we see democracy as a process of social self-institution where there is no divinely or 'objectively' defined code of human conduct, such guarantees are by definition ruled out. Therefore, the replacement of the market economy by a new institutional framework of inclusive democracy constitutes only the *necessary condition* for a harmonious relation between the natural and social worlds. The sufficient condition refers to the citizens' level of ecological consciousness. For all that, the radical change in the dominant social paradigm that will follow the institution of an inclusive democracy, combined with the decisive role that *paedeia* will play in an environmentally friendly institutional framework, could reasonably be expected to lead to a radical change in the human attitude towards Nature.

In other words, a democratic ecological problematic cannot go beyond the institutional preconditions that offer the best hope for a better human relationship to Nature. However, there are strong grounds to believe that the relationship between an inclusive democracy and Nature would be much more harmonious than could ever be achieved in a market economy, or one based on socialist statism. The factors supporting this view refer to all three elements of an inclusive democracy: political, economic and social.

At the political level, there are grounds for believing that the creation of a public space will by itself have a very significant effect in reducing the appeal of materialism. This is because the public space will provide a new meaning of life to fill the existential void that the present consumer society creates. The realization of what it means to be human could reasonably be expected to throw us back toward Nature. Thus, as Kerry H. Whiteside points out referring to the work of Hannah Arendt:

> Political participation is not just a means to advance a Green agenda. Nor is it simply a potentially fulfilling activity that would remain available in a world less given to material consumption. A community that takes pride in collective deliberation fosters a way of life that limits the appeal of labour and work . . . a world in which labour is seen as only one part of a meaningful life will find consumption less tempting.[130]

Also, at the economic level, it is not accidental that, historically, the process of destroying the environment *en masse* has coincided with the process of marketization of the economy. In other words, the emergence of the market economy and of the consequent growth economy had crucial repercussions on the society–Nature relationship and led to the rise of the growth ideology as the dominant social paradigm. Thus, an 'instrumentalist' view of Nature became dominant, in which Nature was seen as an instrument for growth, within a process of endless concentration of power. If we assume that only a confederal society could secure an inclusive democracy today, it would be reasonable to assume further that once the market economy is replaced by a democratically run confederal economy, the grow-or-die dynamics of the former will be replaced by the new social dynamic of the latter: a dynamic aiming at the satisfaction of the community needs and not at growth *per se*. If the satisfaction of community needs does not depend, as at present, on the continuous expansion of production to cover the 'needs' that the market creates, and if the link between society and economy is restored, then there is no reason why the present instrumentalist view of Nature will continue conditioning human behaviour.

Finally, democracy in the broader social realm could also be reasonably expected to be environmentally friendly. The phasing out of patriarchal relations in the household and hierarchical relations in general should create a new ethos of non-domination which would engulf both First and Second Nature. In other words, the creation of democratic conditions in the social realm should be a decisive step in the creation of the sufficient conditions for a harmonious nature–society relationship.

But, apart from the above political and economic factors, an ecological factor is involved here, which strongly supports the belief in a harmonious democracy–Nature relationship: the 'localist' character of a confederal society might also be expected to enhance its environmentaly friendly character. Thus, as Martin Khor of the Third World Network argues, 'Local control, while not necessarily sufficient for environmental protection, is necessary, whereas, under state control, the environment necessarily suffers.'[131] The necessity of local control becomes obvious if we take into account the fact that the environment itself, as Elinor Ostrom puts it, is local:

Small scale communities are more likely to have the formal conditions required for successful and enduring collective management of the commons. Among these are the visibility of the commons resources and behaviour toward them, feedback on the effect of regulations, widespread understanding and acceptance of the rules and their rationales, the values expressed in these rules (equitable treatment of all and protection of the environment) and the backing of values by socialization, standards and strict enforcement.[132]

Furthermore, it is reasonable to assume – and the evidence about the remarkable success of local communities in safeguarding their environments is overwhelming[133] – that when people rely directly on their natural surroundings for their livelihood, they will develop an intimate knowledge of those surroundings, which will necessarily affect positively their behaviour towards them. However, the precondition for local control of the environment to be successful is that the community depends on its natural surroundings for its long-term livelihood and that it therefore has a direct interest in protecting it – another reason why an ecological society is impossible without economic democracy.

In conclusion, the present-day ecological crisis is basically susceptible to two solutions: one solution presupposes radical decentralization. Thus, the economic effectiveness of the renewable forms of energy (solar, wind, etc.) depends crucially on the organization of social and economic life in smaller units. This solution, however, has already been marginalized by the internationalized market economy, precisely because it is not compatible with today's concentration of economic political and social power. This is also why alternative solutions are being advanced which are supposed to concentrate many advantages of renewable energy, but without necessitating any radical changes in the market/growth economy. For example, the programme for the 'International Thermonuclear Reactor' is being advertised as producing clean, safe and unlimited energy. What is usually not mentioned is that for this new form of energy to be commercially viable, it should be produced from vast stations providing massive centralized power. As a researcher aptly stresses, 'Size is vital to fusion because efficiency requires building big'.[134]

A new conception of citizenship

After this discussion of the fundamental components of an inclusive democracy, we are now in a position to summarize the conditions necessary for democracy and their implications for a new conception of citizenship. Democracy is incompatible with any form of a closed system of ideas or dogmas at the ideological level and with any concentration of power at the institutional level. So, democracy is founded on a self-reflective choice (not inspired by any religious beliefs or dogmas) and on institutional arrangements which secure the equal sharing of political, economic and social power. But, as was stated above, these are just necessary conditions for democracy. The sufficient condition so that democracy will not degenerate into some kind of 'demago-cracy', where the *demos* is manipulated by a new breed of professional politicians, is crucially determined by the citizens' level of democratic consciousness which, in turn, is conditioned by *paedeia*.

Historically, the above conditions for democracy have never been satisfied fully. We already saw why the Athenian democracy was only a partial democracy. Similarly, the 'people's democracies' that collapsed a few years ago did not satisfy any of the above conditions, although they represented a better spreading of economic power (in terms of income and wealth) than liberal 'democracies'. Finally, today's liberal 'democracies', also, do not satisfy the above conditions, although they represent a better spreading of political power than socialist 'democracies'. However, an argument can be put forward that today's advanced liberal 'democracies', like classical democracy, may satisfy the ideological condition in the sense that they are not rooted on any divine and mystical dogmas, or 'laws' about social change.

In conclusion, the above conditions for democracy imply a new conception of citizenship: economic, political, social and cultural. Thus, *political citizenship* involves new political structures and the return to the classical conception of politics (direct democracy). *Economic citizenship* involves new economic structures of demotic ownership and control of economic resources (economic democracy). *Social citizenship* involves self-management structures at the workplace, democracy in the household and new welfare structures where all basic needs (to be democratically determined) are covered by community resources, whether they are satisfied in the household or at the community level. Finally, *cultural citizenship* involves new democratic structures of dissemination and control of information and culture (mass media, art, etc.), which allow every member of the community to take part in the process and at the same time develop his/her intellectual and cultural potential.

Although this sense of citizenship implies a sense of community, which, defined geographically, is the fundamental unit of political, economic and social life, still, it is assumed that it interlocks with various other communities (cultural, professional, ideological, etc.). Therefore, the community and citizenship arrangements do not rule out cultural differences or other differences based on gender, age, ethnicity and so on but simply provide the public space where such differences can be expressed; furthermore, these arrangements institutionalize various safety valves that aim to rule out the marginalization of such differences by the majority. What therefore unites people in a political community is not some set of common values, imposed on the community by a nationalist ideology, a religious dogma, a mystical belief, or an 'objective' interpretation of natural or social 'evolution', but the democratic institutions and practices, which have been set up by citizens themselves.

It is obvious that the above new conception of citizenship has very little in common with the liberal and socialist definitions of citizenship which are linked to the liberal and socialist conceptions of human rights respectively. Thus, for the liberals, the citizen is simply the individual bearer of certain freedoms and political rights recognized by law which, supposedly, secure equal distribution of political power. Also, for the socialists, the citizen is the bearer not only of political rights and freedoms but, also, of some social and economic rights, whereas for Marxists the citizenship is realized with the collective ownership of the means of production.

Finally, the definition of citizenship here is not related to the current social-democratic discourse on the subject, which, in effect, focuses on the institutional conditions for the creation of an internationalized market economy 'with a human face'. The proposal for instance for a redefinition of citizenship within the framework of a 'stakeholder capitalism'[135] belongs to this category. This proposal involves an 'active' citizenship, where citizens have 'stakes' in companies, the market economy and society in general and managers have to take into account these stakes in the running of the businesses and social institutions they are in charge of.

The conception of citizenship adopted here, which could be called a *democratic* conception, is based on our definition of inclusive democracy and presupposes a 'participatory' conception of active citizenship, like the one implied by the work of Hannah Arendt.[136] In this conception, 'Political activity is not a means to an end, but an end in itself; one does not engage in political action simply to promote one's welfare but to realize the principles intrinsic to political life, such as freedom, equality, justice, solidarity, courage and excellence'.[137] It is therefore obvious that this conception of citizenship is qualitatively different from the liberal and social-democratic conceptions which adopt an 'instrumentalist' view of citizenship, i.e. a view which implies that citizenship entitles citizens to certain rights that they can exercise as means to the end of individual welfare.

To conclude, this chapter, I think that today, more than ever in the past, the choice we have to make is clear and can be described as 'democracy or barbarism'. Democracy, however, does not mean the various oligarchic regimes that call themselves democratic. It also does not mean an anachronistic return to the classical conception of democracy. Democracy can only mean a synthesis of the two major historical traditions, namely, the democratic and the socialist with the radical Green, feminist and libertarian traditions.

Notes

1. See Konstantinos Kavoulakos, 'The relationship of realism and utopianism in the theories of democracy of Jürgen Habermas and Cornelius Castoriadis', *Society and Nature,* Vol. 2, No. 3 (1994), pp. 69–98.
2. Thomas Martin, 'The end of sovereignty', *Democracy and Nature* (formerly *Society and Nature*), Vol. 3, No. 2 (1996).
3. As it was recently observed: 'For the first time, instead of being primarily part of national economy, cities now form part of a world system, sometimes with closer connections to each other than to the countries of which they form part', Sir Richard Rogers' Reith Lecture – quoted in *The Observer* (19 Feb. 1995).
4. See Murray Bookchin, *From Urbanization to Cities* (London: Cassell, 1995), Ch. 6; and Cornelius Castoriadis, *Philosophy, Politics, Autonomy* (Oxford: Oxford University Press, 1991), Ch. 7.
5. See Charlotte Raven, *The Observer* (30 July 1995).
6. Hannah Arendt, *The Human Condition* (Chicago: The University of Chicago Press, 1958), p. 45.
7. Quoted by Neil Harding, 'The Marxist-Leninist detour' in *Democracy, the Unfinished Journey, 508 BC to AD 1993,* John Dunn (ed.) (Oxford: Oxford University Press, 1992), p. 173.
8. Neil Harding, 'The Marxist–Leninist detour', p. 178.
9. Anthony H. Birch, *The Concepts and Theories of Modern Democracy* (London: Routledge, 1993), p. 45.
10. Anthony H. Birch, *The Concepts and Theories of Modern Democracy*, p. 48.
11. Anthony H. Birch, *The Concepts and Theories of Modern Democracy*, p. 48.

12. Mogens Herman Hansen, *The Athenian Democracy in the Age of Demosthenes* (Oxford: Blackwell, 1991), p. 81.
13. Cornelius Castoriadis, *Philosophy, Politics, Autonomy*, p. 221. See also, for an incisive analysis of the nature of the Athenian democracy, Castoriadis's *The Ancient Greek Democracy and its Significance for us Today* (Athens: Upsilon, 1986) (in Greek).
14. David Beetham, 'Liberal democracy and the limits of democratization' in *Prospects for Democracy,* David Held (ed.) (Cambridge: Polity Press, 1993), p. 55.
15. David Beetham, 'Liberal democracy and the limits of democratization', p. 58.
16. Isaiah Berlin, 'Two concepts of liberty' in Isaiah Berlin, *Four Essays on Liberty* (Oxford: Oxford University Press, 1969).
17. Anthony H. Birch, *The Concepts and Theories of Modern Democracy*, p. 101.
18. Anthony H. Birch, *The Concepts and Theories of Modern Democracy*, pp. 102–3.
19. Friedrich Engels, *Anti-Dühring* (London: Lawrence & Wishart, 1969), p. 137.
20. Leszek Kolakowski, *Main Currents of Marxism,* Vol. 1 (Oxford: Oxford University Press, 1981), p. 387.
21. G.P. Maximoff (ed.), *The Political Philosophy of Bakunin* (New York: The Free Press, 1953), p. 265.
22. Alix Kates Shulman (ed.), *Red Emma Speaks* (New York: Vintage Books, 1972), p. 98.
23. William McKercher, 'Liberalism as democracy: authority over freedom', *Democracy and Nature* (formerly *Society and Nature*) Vol. 3, No. 2 (1996).
24. Milton & Rose Friedman, *Free to Choose* (Harmondsworth: Penguin, 1980).
25. William McKercher, 'Liberalism as democracy: authority over freedom'.
26. William McKercher, 'Liberalism as democracy: authority over freedom'.
27. Murray Bookchin, *From Urbanization to Cities*, p. 68. See also his article 'Communalism: the democratic dimension of anarchism', *Democracy and Nature* (formerly *Society and Nature*) Vol. 3, No. 2 (1996).
28. Mogens Herman Hansen, *The Athenian Democracy in the Age of Demosthenes,* p. 75.
29. Cornelius Castoriadis, *Philosophy, Politics, Autonomy*, p. 164.
30. Cornelius Castoriadis, *Philosophy, Politics, Autonomy*, pp. 105–6.
31. Cornelius Castoriadis, *Philosophy, Politics, Autonomy*, p. 76.
32. Murray Bookchin, 'Communalism: the democratic dimension of anarchism', *Democracy and Nature,* Vol. 3, No. 2 (1996), pp. 2–4.
33. L. Susan Brown, *The Politics of Individualism* (Montreal: Black Rose Books, 1993), p. 11.
34. Murray Bookchin, *The Philosophy of Social Ecology* (Montreal: Black Rose Books, 1995), p. 151.
35. Bhikhu Parekh, 'The cultural particularity of liberal democracy' in *Prospects for Democracy,* David Held (ed.), pp. 168–70.
36. Bhikhu Parekh, 'The cultural particularity of liberal democracy', p. 172.
37. L. Susan Brown, *The Politics of Individualism*, p. 3.
38. Cornelius Castoriadis, *Philosophy, Politics, Autonomy*, p. 121.
39. For the logical contradictions of Right-wing libertarianism, see Alan

Haworth, *Anti-Libertarianism: Markets, Philosophy and Myth* (London: Routledge, 1994).

40. See Konstantinos Kavoulakos, 'The relationship of realism and utopianism in the theories of democracy of Jürgen Habermas and Cornelius Castoriadis', as regards political concentration, and Takis Fotopoulos, 'The end of socialist statism', as regards economic concentration, *Society and Nature*, Vol. 2, No. 3 (1994), pp. 69–97 and 11–68, respectively.

41. Alan Haworth, *Anti-Libertarianism*, pp. 37–40.

42. Murray Bookchin, *From Urbanization to Cities*, p. 43. As Bookchin points out 'until recent times, professional systems of governance and violence coexisted with richly articulated community forms at the base of society . . . which were largely beyond the reach of centralised state authorities'. *Ibid.*

43. Anthony H. Birch, *The Concepts and Theories of Modern Democracy*, p. 58.

44. Bhikhu Parekh, 'The cultural particularity of liberal democracy', p. 165.

45. According to Aristotle, ' . . . I say that the appointment by lot is commonly held to be characteristic of democracy, whereas the process of election for that purpose is looked upon as oligarchic'; Aristotle, *Politics*, Book IV, 1294b, John Warrington (ed.) (London: Heron Books, 1934).

46. Thomas Martin, 'The end of sovereignty'.

47. For Bookchin, 'the "state", as we know it in modern times, could hardly be said to exist among the Greeks' (*From Urbanization to Cities*, p. 43), whereas for Castoriadis, 'the Polis is not a "state" since in its explicit power – the positing of nomos (legislation), dike (jurisdiction) and telos (government) – belongs to the whole body of citizens' (*Philosophy, Politics, Autonomy*, p. 157).

48. Aristotle was clear on this when he discussed the various types of regimes: 'next we ask: what should be the sovereign in polis? The people? The rich? The better sort of man? The one best man? Or a tyrant?' Aristotle, *Politics*, Book III, 1281a. He then goes on to define democracy as the case where the free citizens are sovereign; Aristotle, *Politics*, Book IV, 1290b.

49. Hannah Arendt, *The Human Condition*, pp. 32–3.

50. William McKercher, 'Liberalism as democracy'.

51. April Carter seems to agree with the conclusion that direct democracy does not involve a form of 'rule': 'The only authority that can exist in a direct democracy is the collective "authority" vested in the body politic . . . it is doubtful if authority can be created by a group of equals who reach decisions by a process of mutual persuasion'; April Carter, *Authority and Democracy* (London: Routledge, 1979), p. 380. She further states, 'commitment to direct democracy or anarchy in the socio-political sphere is incompatible with political authority'; p. 69.

52. Cornelius Castoriadis, *Philosophy, Politics, Autonomy*, p. 156.

53. 'Εντευθεν δ' ελήλυθε το μή άρχεσθαι, μάλιστα μεν υπο μηδενός, ει δε μή, κατα μέρος. Και συμβάλλεται ταύτη προς την ελευθερ ίαν την κατα το ίσον' Aristotle, *Politics*, Book VI, 1317b.

54. Aristotle, *Politics*, Book II, 1266b, 1267a.

55. K. Marx, *Pre-capitalist Economic Formations* (London: Lawrence and Wishart, 1964), pp. 72–3.

56. See, for instance, Hindess and Hirst, *Pre-Capitalist Modes of Production* (London: Routledge & Kegan Paul, 1975), p. 82.

57. The distinction between democrats and oligarchs, on the basis of the criterion used in the text, is consistent with the definition of democracy

given by Aristotle as the case where government is in the hands of the
majority of the poor and free citizens, and of oligarchy as the case in which
government is in the hands of the minority of the rich and aristocrats
(Aristotle, *Politics*, 1290b, 20).

58. Mogens Herman Hansen, *The Athenian Democracy in the Age of Demosthenes,*
p. 98.
59. K. Paparregopoulos, *History of the Greek Nation*, N. Bees (ed.) (Athens:
Seferlis, 1955), Vol. A1, p. 218 (in Greek). See also Mogens Herman Hansen,
The Athenian Democracy in the Age of Demosthenes, pp. 108–15.
60. Aristotle, *The Athenian Constitution*, Ch. viii, 4.
61. K. Paparregopoulos, *History of the Greek Nation*, Vol. A1, p. 217.
62. A. Prokopiou, *Athens* (London: Elek Books, 1964), p. 97.
63. Aristotle, *Politics*, 1284a, 20.
64. A. Prokopiou, *Athens*, p. 148. See also Mogens Herman Hansen, *The
Athenian Democracy in the Age of Demosthenes*, p. 37.
65. Mogens Herman Hansen, *The Athenian Democracy in the Age of Demosthenes,*
p. 97.
66. Mogens Herman Hansen, *The Athenian Democracy in the Age of Demosthenes,*
p. 317.
67. K. Paparregopoulos, *History of the Greek Nation*, Vol. A2, p. 118.
68. Aristotle, *The Athenian Constitution*, Ch. xxiv, 3. See also Mogens Herman
Hansen, *The Athenian Democracy in the Age of Demosthenes*, p. 319.
69. K. Paparregopoulos, *History of the Greek Nation*, Vol. A2, p. 118.
70. Mogens Herman Hansen, *The Athenian Democracy in the Age of Demosthenes,*
p. 140.
71. K. Paparregopoulos, *History of the Greek Nation*, Vol. A2, p. 146.
72. K. Paparregopoulos, *History of the Greek Nation*, Vol. A2, pp. 258–9.
73. K. Paparregopoulos, *History of the Greek Nation*, Vol. A2, p. 146.
74. Murray Bookchin, *Remaking Society* (Montreal: Black Rose Books, 1989),
p. 50.
75. Anthony Birch, *The Concepts and Theories of Modern Democracy*, p. 50.
76. Hannah Arendt, *On Revolution* (London: Penguin, 1990), pp. 237–8.
77. John Dunn, 'Conclusion' in *Democracy, the Unfinished Journey, 508 BC to AD
1993*, pp. 247–8.
78. John Dunn, 'Conclusion' in *Democracy, the Unfinished Journey, 508 BC to AD
1993*, p. 251.
79. Karl Marx, *Critique of the Gotha Programme* (Moscow: Progress Publishers,
1937), p. 25.
80. V.I. Lenin, *The State and Revolution* (Moscow: Foreign Languages Publishing
House, 1917), pp. 31–2.
81. V.I. Lenin, *The State and Revolution*, p. 165.
82. V.I. Lenin, *The State and Revolution*, pp. 174–5.
83. Murray Bookchin, *The Ecology of Freedom: The Emergence and Dissolution of
Hierarchy* (Montreal: Black Rose Books, 1991), p. 69.
84. For an analysis of these trends, see Andrew Gamble, 'Class politics and radical
democracy', *New Left Review*, No. 164 (July-Aug. 1987), p. 115.
85. See Perry Anderson, 'The affinities of Norberto Bobbio', *New Left Review*,
No. 170 (July-Aug. 1988), p. 21.
86. Ralph Miliband, 'Fukuyama and the socialist alternative', *New Left Review*,
No. 193 (May-June 1992).

87. Jürgen Habermas, 'Three normative models of democracy', *Constellations*, Vol. 1, No. 1 (1994), pp. 1–10.

88. Cornelius Castoriadis, 'La démocratie comme procédure et comme régime' in *La Montée de l'insignificance, Les Carrefours du Labyrinthe IV* (Paris: Seuil, 1996), pp. 221–41 (reprinted in *Democracy and Nature* (Greek edition), No. 1 (1996)).

89. James O'Connor, 'Democracy and ecology', *Capitalism, Nature, Socialism*, Vol. 4, No. 4 (Dec. 1993).

90. John Dryzek, 'Ecology and discursive democracy', *Capitalism, Nature, Socialism*, Vol. 3, No. 2 (June 1992), p. 37.

91. Chantal Mouffe, 'Democratic politics today' in *Dimensions of Radical Democracy*, Chantal Mouffe (ed.) (London: Verso, 1992, 1995), p. 13.

92. Chantal Mouffe, 'Democratic politics today' in *Dimensions of Radical Democracy*, p. 1.

93. Chantal Mouffe, 'Democratic politics today' in *Dimensions of Radical Democracy*, p. 2.

94. Chantal Mouffe, 'Democratic citizenship and the political community' in *Dimensions of Radical Democracy*, p. 238.

95. David Miller, 'Deliberative democracy and social choice' in *Prospects for Democracy*, David Held (ed.) (Cambridge: Polity Press, 1993), pp. 74–92.

96. David Miller, *Market, State and Community: Theoretical Foundations of Market Socialism* (Oxford: Clarendon Press, 1989).

97. David Miller, *Market, State and Community*, p. 10.

98. David Miller, *Market, State and Community*, pp. 148–9.

99. Christopher Pierson, 'Democracy, markets and capital: are there necessary economic limits to democracy?' in *Prospects for Democracy*, David Held (ed.), pp. 193–4.

100. Paul Hirst, 'Associational democracy' in *Prospects for Democracy*, pp. 112–35. See also Paul Hirst, *Associative Democracy: New Forms of Economic and Social Governance* (Amherst: University of Massachusetts Press, 1994).

101. Paul Hirst, 'Associational democracy', p. 131.

102. Paul Hirst, 'Associational democracy', p. 128.

103. Paul Hirst, 'Associational democracy', p. 117.

104. Paul Hirst, 'Associational democracy', p. 125.

105. Paul Hirst, 'Associational democracy', p. 127.

106. Paul Hirst, 'Associational democracy', p. 130.

107. Paul Hirst, 'Associational democracy', p. 112.

108. Paul Hirst, 'Associational democracy', p. 113.

109. David Held, 'Democracy: from city-states to a cosmopolitan order?' in *Prospects for Democracy*, pp. 13–52. See also, Held's latest book *Democracy and the Global Order*, (Cambridge: Polity Press, 1995), where the proposal for a cosmopolitan model of democracy is further expanded. In this book, the author, starting from a liberal definition of autonomy in terms of equal rights (p. 147), which has no connection whatsoever with the classical notion of autonomy and the notion developed in the present book, ends up with a list of proposals, similar to the ones I outlined in the text which, within the context of the logic and dynamic of the internationalized market economy that the author takes for granted, amount to little more than wishful thinking.

110. David Held, 'Democracy: from city-states to a cosmopolitan order?' in *Prospects for Democracy*, pp. 40–1.

111. David Held, 'Democracy: from city-states to a cosmopolitan order?' in *Prospects for Democracy,* p. 42.
112. David Held, 'Democracy: from city-states to a cosmopolitan order?' in *Prospects for Democracy,* p. 43.
113. Mogens Herman Hanson, *The Athenian Democracy in the Age of Demosthenes,* p. 308.
114. Mogens Herman Hanson, *The Athenian Democracy in the Age of Demosthenes,* p. 2.
115. Cornelius Castoriadis, *Philosophy, Politics, Autonomy,* p. 113.
116. Mogens Herman Hansen, *The Athenian Democracy in the Age of Demosthenes,* p. 311.
117. Cornelius Castoriadis, *Philosophy, Politics, Autonomy,* p. 113.
118. Mogens Herman Hansen, *The Athenian Democracy in the Age of Demosthenes,* p. 320.
119. Aristotle, *Politics,* Book 1.
120. Mogens Herman Hansen, *The Athenian Democracy in the Age of Demosthenes,* p. 63.
121. *Eleftherotypia* (31 July 1995).
122. See e.g., Noam Chomsky, *The Prosperous Few and the Restless Many* (Berkeley, California: Odonian Press, 1993), pp. 18–20.
123. Andy Anderson, *Hungary 56* (London: Solidarity, 1964).
124. Janet Biehl, *Rethinking Ecofeminist Politics* (Boston: South End Press, 1991), p. 140.
125. Ted Trainer, *Abandon Affluence!* (London: Zed Books, 1985).
126. Pat Brewer, *Feminism and Socialism: Putting the Pieces Together* (Sydney: New Course, 1992).
127. Val Plumwood, 'Feminism, privacy and radical democracy', *Anarchist Studies,* Vol. 3, No. 2 (Autumn 1995), p. 107.
128. Val Plumwood, 'Feminism, privacy and radical democracy', p. 111.
129. David Pepper, *Modern Environmentalism* (London: Routledge, 1996), p. 324.
130. Kerry H. Whiteside, 'Hannah Arendt and ecological politics', *Environmental Ethics,* Vol. 16, No. 4 (Winter 1994), p. 355.
131. M. Khor, presentation at World Rainforest Movement (1 March 1992), New York, quoted in *The Ecologist,* Vol. 22, No. 4 (July-Aug. 1992).
132. E. Ostrom, 'The rudiments of a revised theory of the origins, survival and performance of institutions for collective action', *Working Paper 32* (Indiana University, Workshop in Political Theory and Political Analysis, Bloomington, 1985).
133. For evidence, see *The Ecologist,* Vol. 22, No. 4 (July-Aug. 1992).
134. J. Vidal, *The Guardian* (16 Nov. 1991).
135. See Will Hutton, *The State We're In* (London: Jonathan Cape, 1995), Ch. 12.
136. Maurizio Passerin d'Entreves, 'Hannah Arendt and the idea of citizenship' in *Dimensions of Radical Democracy,* pp. 145–68.
137. Maurizio Passerin d'Entreves, 'Hannah Arendt and the idea of citizenship', p. 154.

CHAPTER 6

A Confederal Inclusive Democracy

The aim of this chapter is to explore the conditions under which an inclusive democracy, the elements of which were described in the last chapter, could work under today's conditions. Even though it is up to the citizens' assemblies of the future to design the form an inclusive democracy will take, I think that it is important to demonstrate that such a form of society is not only necessary, as I tried to show in the first part of the book, but feasible as well. This is particularly important today when the self-styled 'Left' has abandoned any vision of a society that is not based on the market economy and liberal 'democracy', which they take for granted, and dismiss any alternative visions as 'utopian' (in the negative sense of the word). It is therefore necessary to show – as I tried to do in the first part of the book – that it is in fact the Left's vision of 'radical' democracy which, in taking for granted the present internationalized market economy, may be characterized as utterly unrealistic. But I think it is equally important to attempt to outline how an alternative society based on an inclusive democracy might try to sort out the basic socio-economic problems that any society has to deal with, under conditions of scarce resources and not in an imagined state of post-scarcity. Such an attempt may not only help supporters of the democratic project form a more concrete idea of the society they wish to see, but also assist them in addressing the 'utopianism' criticisms raised against them.

In the first part of the chapter the relationship of democracy to community is examined, in an attempt to show why an inclusive democracy, under today's conditions, can only be a confederation of communities, in which the communities are the basic units of political, social and economic life.

In the second part, the conditions for a confederal economic democracy are specified and the two traditional methods of allocating resources (market and central planning), as well as the proposal for a type of participatory planning, are discussed.

In the final part, a model of economic democracy is outlined, based on a new kind of democratic planning which is combined with an artificial 'market'. The explicit aim of this model is to meet the basic needs of all citizens in the confederation, as well as those of the non-basic needs that citizens in each community decide to meet, within an institutional framework of a scarcity society which is moneyless, marketless and stateless.

Democracy and community

Today, few doubt, and research has conclusively shown, that participation should infuse any model of social change; in other words, that social change needs to be at least initiated at the local level. The proposal for a stakeholder market economy is just another expression of the current discourse that aims at enhancing 'participation'. The real issue therefore is not whether the participatory model of social change is desirable or not, but whether any real participation is feasible within the present institutional framework. This is a framework which is defined at the political level by liberal forms of democracy, and at the economic level by the internationalized market economy and its institutions (TNCs, IMF, World Bank, etc.) – a framework which, today, tends to develop into a series of networks of city regions within federated structures of political power. In short, the real issue is decentralization versus remaking society.

In this context, it is interesting to note that today many of the proposals either to decentralize or to remake society are centred at the community level. Thus, on the one hand, there are proposals to decentralize society, in the sense of empowering communities at the expense of the centre[1] and, on the other, there are radical proposals to remake society on the basis of a new community-based social system.[2] This is not of course a surprising development, as it just represents the inevitable consequence of the collapse of socialist statism and the failure of 'actually existing capitalism'. At the same time, the void created by the present decline of statism, particularly in Western Europe, has not been filled by a process that empowers communities. The decay, therefore, of communities and community values, which was enhanced by the current acceleration of the marketization process, combined with the drastic rise of unemployment and the decline of the welfare state following the collapse of the social-democratic consensus, could go a long way to explain the attempt to revive the community in the current discourse.

The meaning of community

A new consciousness is emerging today among radical movements in the North and the various community movements in the South – a consciousness which ascribes the basic cause of the failure of both the market economy and socialism to the concentration of power. It is therefore becoming increasingly understood that collective and individual autonomy can only be achieved in the context of a radical dispersion of power.

However, the creation of an inclusive democracy is today possible only at the level of the confederated communities. It is at the community level that the *demos* might revive. It is also at the level of the confederated communities that the conditions that would make a confederal economic democracy possible could be fulfilled (see p. 237); finally, it is, again, at the same level of confederated communities that the preconditions for an ecological democracy can be met.

Despite the revival of interest in the community, the concept of the community is still a notoriously disputed – some even say anachronistic – concept. The issue, therefore, is how we may develop a concept of the community as the fundamental social, political and economic unit on which an inclusive democracy could be founded; in other words, a concept in which the community is seen as the foundation of a third social system beyond socialist statism and the neoliberal market economy.

A useful starting point in this effort might be David Clark's definition of community in terms of what he calls *'ecumenicity'* (defined as a sense of solidarity that enables people to feel themselves part of and not hostile towards wider society) and *autonomy* (defined as a sense of significance that enables people to feel they have a role to play in the social scene, a role that is determined by rules that members of the community choose themselves and feel free to modify).[3]

But, to my mind, the ecumenicity and autonomy elements constitute only the *necessary conditions* defining community relations. I think that community members cannot have a real sense of solidarity, and especially a real sense of significance, unless a third element is present, which defines the institutional framework of a community – what I would call the *democracy element*. The democracy element, which rules out the concentration of political and economic power, is in fact the *sufficient* condition for any true community. Historically, this has always been the case. Thus, as Michael Taylor[4] has shown, drawing on the experience of stateless primitive societies, peasant communities and 'intentional' (utopian) communities, a community requires rough economic equality, as well as relations between its members that involve reciprocity (mutual aid, co-operation, sharing) and that are *direct* (i.e. not mediated by representatives, leaders, etc.) and many-sided.[5]

So, taking into account all three of these elements (ecumenicity, autonomy, democracy) and adding the confederal element, which is necessary to avoid the trap of localism, we may end up with a definition of community like the one recently put forward by Bookchin as 'a municipal association of people reinforced by its own economic power, its own institutionalization of the grass roots, and the confederal support of nearby communities organized into a territorial network on a local and regional scale'.[6] I think that starting from a definition of community, like the above, we may outline a model of a confederal inclusive democracy.

Communitarianism: the false 'third' way

The concept of community, however, is not used only by supporters of a radical project to remake society. 'Community' has become fashionable again, although of course the usual definitions given to the term differ widely from the conception given in the previous section. Thus, religious 'Communitarianism', with its notion of 'community' that is irrelevant to the political organization of society, competes with a kind of cultural Communitarianism, where the revival of the 'community' explicitly aims at the restoration of old community values (solidarity, mutual aid, etc.) or the creation of new common values. To the left of these tendencies a more radical community economic development movement has developed lately which, however, by not challenging directly the present institutional framework, has already been marginalized. But let us explore first the cultural Communitarianism (from now on 'communitarianism') which has particularly flourished in the USA since the late 1980s.

Communitarians concentrate their efforts on cultural factors and declare themselves in favour of enhancing traditional hierarchical structures like the family and creating new ones. Thus, some argue for compulsory community service for teenagers, others back curfews on them, increased police powers to search for drugs and guns in urban areas and so on.[7] However, the real objective of communitarians is to mobilize citizens, first, in an effort to alleviate the effects of the social decay that the neoliberal consensus involves (crime explosion, drug abuse, moral irresponsibility, etc.) and, second, to recover some of the welfare services which are presently effectively undermined by the demise of the welfare state.

Therefore, communitarianism is, in effect, a middle-class movement against the social *symptoms* of the neoliberal consensus and the internationalization of the market economy. So, it is not accidental that, today, parts of the old social-democratic movement, like, for instance, the British Labour Party, turn to various forms of 'Communitarianism' and preach the empowerment of communities as counterbalancing forces to the market and the supranational federal forms of statism which are presently under formation. Communitarians, by working to recover some of the welfare services abandoned by the state, offer the opportunity of creating an image of a 'neoliberal consensus with a human face' at no extra cost to the state budget!

It is obvious that communitarians want to have their cake and eat it, since, in effect, they wish to enjoy the privileges which the market economy and its internationalization allows them to enjoy, without paying the price of living in a society of tremendous inequality in the distribution of income and wealth. It is not, therefore, surprising that the socio-economic framework is ruled out of the communitarian problematic, and Etzioni, the guru of Communitarianism, gives an unequivocal answer when asked about socio-economic rights and the communitarian economic agenda. 'The short answer is,' he says, 'there is none.'[8] Still, Etzioni has no qualms in presenting his Communitarianism as a 'third' way between liberalism and socialism![9]

This position is, of course, consistent with the fact that any real revival of communities is impossible within the framework of today's internationalized market economy where the economic life of every community, that is, the jobs, incomes and welfare of every member of the community, is utterly dependent on economic forces, which no community can control any more. Global free trade and movement of capital means that no community can be economically viable, since the level of economic viability has now moved to the new city regions and the multinational networks. No wonder that the communitarian argument is full of contradictions, particularly when the declared ultimate aim is a social fabric 'designed to facilitate fraternity' while at the same time the price mechanism is cheered enthusiastically:

> Democratic Communitarianism supports multiple sources of economic initiative as a matter of principle. It offers 'two cheers for the price mechanism' . . . the social principle is to permeate right through to the inner workings of a decentralized, primarily market-based economic system . . . Economic Communitarianism . . . means developing a social fabric in and around the economic system which would, at the very least, make such interactions as are bound to exist between economic units and government and society more open, constitutional and accountable. At best, such a fabric would be designed to facilitate fraternity, inter-institutional associateship and democratic participation whilst also nurturing a balanced, sustained form of economic development.[10]

It is therefore obvious that Communitarianism could play a significant role with respect to the present phase of marketization, as it is perfectly compatible with a shift of the power centre away from the decaying nation-state, without challenging in any way the market economy and its internationalization. From this viewpoint, it is not accidental that Communitarianism is supported not only by social democrats but also by pure neoliberals in the USA and in Europe.

Similar arguments could be put forward against the type of a more radical Communitarianism presently expanding, particularly in North America and Britain, in the form of what is usually called Community Economic Development (CED). This involves a strategy of gradual removal of land, labour and capital from the market economy (through the establishment of Community Land Trusts, community financial institutions, community enterprises, etc.) with the double aim of creating a community culture and making private firms and the state socially responsible. However, CED, although useful with respect, in particular, to its first objective, cannot seriously challenge the present concentration of political and economic power, as supporters of this movement themselves admit:

> New forms of economic activity and institutions created in the community will never be adequate, within an economy dominated by private enterprise, to generate enough jobs and wealth at a local level to compensate for the consequences of economic centralization outside of the community. . . . Since communities do not control in any direct way economic resources, partnerships with both government agencies and representatives of business have been accepted as inevitable by CED activists in order to secure both recognition and resources. These are tricky relationships because of the inequality of power.[11]

It is therefore obvious that only a truly radical economic and political restructuring at the community level can create again the conditions for the revival of communities, in fact, for the transcendence of both the market economy and statism as well as the corresponding forms of statist democracy. CED, by not aiming at establishing a political and economic power base at the community level, could easily end up as just another hopeless attempt at radical decentralization. Within the existing institutional framework, radical decentralization is neither feasible nor desirable. It is not feasible because, in the context of the present internationalized market economy, any attempt to create real counterbalancing centres of power would inevitably fail, unless these centres of power are compatible with the logic and dynamic of competitiveness. It is not desirable because the problem of democracy today is not just how to force the present centres of political and economic power to delegate some of their power to local centres – a move that would simply reproduce at the local level the present concentration of power at the centre. The problem is how we can create new forms of social organization that do not presuppose centres of power at all, but require, instead, the equal sharing of power among all citizens, that is, true democratic forms of organization and a return to the classical meaning of politics. Let us therefore examine the form that a confederal inclusive democracy might take.

A confederal inclusive democracy

The political institutional framework of a confederal democracy has already been outlined in the work of Murray Bookchin and others,[12] and there is no need therefore to describe it in detail here. Briefly, the basic unit of decision-making in a confederal democracy is the community assembly, which delegates power to community courts, community militias, etc. Still, a lot of important decisions have to be taken at the regional or confederal level by delegates from the community assemblies. Murray Bookchin's description of the role of the regional and confederal councils is very clear:

> What then is confederalism? It is above all a network of administrative councils whose members or delegates are elected from popular face-to-face democratic assemblies in the various villages, towns and even neighbourhoods of large cities. The members of these confederal councils are strictly mandated, recallable, and responsible to the assemblies that choose them for the purpose of co-ordinating and administering the policies formulated by the assemblies themselves. Their function is thus a purely administrative and practical one, not a policy-making one like the function of representatives in republican systems of government.[13]

The first issue that arises with respect to a confederal democracy is whether, given the size of modern societies, direct democracy is feasible today. A related issue is how the regional and confederal councils can be prevented from developing into new power structures that will start 'representing' community assemblies. As regards the question of feasibility in general, as Mogens Herman Hansen points out, summarizing the results of recent research on the topic, 'modern technology has made a return to direct democracy quite feasible – whether desirable or not is another matter'.[14] Also, as regards the related issue of how the degeneration of confederal councils into new power structures may be avoided, modern technology may, again, play a significant role. An electronic network could connect the community assemblies at the regional or confederal level, forming a huge 'assembly's assembly'. This way, the confining of the members of the regional or confederal councils to purely administrative duties of co-ordination and execution of the policies adopted by community assemblies is made even easier.[15] Furthermore, at the institutional level, various safety valves may be introduced into the system that will secure the effective functioning of democracy. However, in the last instance, it is *paedeia* that may effectively condition democratic practice.

Another common objection against the democratic decision-taking process is that it may easily lead to the 'tyranny of the majority', where various minorities – defined by cultural, racial, or even political, criteria – are simply oppressed by majorities. Thus, some libertarians declare that 'the majority has no more right to dictate to the minority, even a minority of one, than the minority to the majority'.[16] Others stress that 'democratic rule is still a rule . . . it still inherently involves the repression of the wills of some people'.[17]

I think that there are two issues here that have to be examined separately. First, the question whether democracy is still a 'rule', and second, how minorities, even of one, may be protected. As regards the first issue, it is obvious that those assuming, erroneously as we have seen in Chapter 5, that democracy involves a form of 'rule', confuse non-statist democracy with statist forms of it. The fact, which is simply ignored by libertarians adopting this sort of objection against democracy, is that in a non-statist conception of democracy there is no conflict between democracy and freedom of the social individual, *since all social individuals equally share power* and may take part in the decision-taking process. Furthermore, as Bookchin points out, the alternative proposed by them, consensus, is 'the individualistic alternative to democracy'[18] – an alternative which, in fact, assumes away individual diversity that supposedly is oppressed by democracy!

As regards the second issue, it is true that there is a problem of how minorities, 'even of one', are protected against majorities and, in particular, how certain fundamental individual freedoms are safeguarded against democratically taken decisions by the majority. The historical answer given to this question by supporters of statist democracy has taken the form of 'human rights'.

Thus, it was the liberal conception of human rights that was developed first by liberal philosophers of the seventeenth and eighteenth centuries (John Locke, Montesquieu, Voltaire, Rousseau) and the associated English, French and American revolutions. Liberal individualism and the economic doctrine of *laissez-faire* constitute the pillars on which these rights are based. Furthermore, in consistency with the liberal conception of freedom, which is defined negatively as the absence of constraints on human activity, these rights are, also, defined in a negative way as 'freedom from', their explicit objective being to limit state power.

Then, it was the turn of the 'second generation' of human rights (social and economic rights), which originated in the socialist tradition, namely the socialist thinkers and the mass movements and revolts of the nineteenth and twentieth centuries. The starting point here was the realization that the liberal conception involved a complete abstraction of individual freedoms from their socio-economic base, i.e. it ignored the power conferred by economic status. 'Equal right', according to Marx, 'is still a bourgeois right', in the sense that it presupposes inequality. 'It is therefore a right of inequality, in its content, like every right.'[19] In consistency with the socialist conception of freedom, which is defined positively, the socio-economic rights in this category are, also, defined positively; their aim is social equality, mainly in the form of an equitable participation in the production and distribution of the social product, achieved through state intervention. These rights are therefore 'collective' in the sense that they belong more to communities or whole societies rather than to individuals (right to work, paid leave, social security, education, etc.).

Both the liberal and the socialist conceptions involve a view which sees political and socio-economic rights as somehow separate from each other, a view that, as a Green activist put it, is a by-product of a conception that sees social existence as being truncated into separate – political and economic – spheres and which is incapable of perceiving that 'notions such as group, feelings, relationships, sense, nature, culture – all that is un-definable, unquantifiable, sensual, but yet innately human' – could only be realized within a holistic view of human rights.[20]

However, a more fundamental characteristic that both the liberal and socialist conceptions of rights share is that they presuppose a statist form of democracy. Human rights are mostly rights against the state; it is only in forms of social organization where political and economic power is concentrated in the hands of elites that many 'rights' are invested with any meaning, whereas in a non-statist type of democracy, which by definition involves the equal sharing of power, these rights become meaningless. This is, for instance, the view adopted by Karl Hess when he states that 'Rights are power, the power of someone or some group over someone else ... rights are derived from institutions of power.'[21]

In principle, therefore, the issue of human rights should not arise at all in the case of a non-statist democracy as we defined it. Still, even in an inclusive democracy, the question remains of how best to protect the freedom of the single individual from the collective decisions of the assemblies. Classical anarchists like Proudhon and Kropotkin, as well as modern ones like Karl Hess, look to contracts in the form of voluntary agreements to regulate affairs between people in a non-statist society. However, to my mind, the issue of protecting individual freedoms against majority decisions cannot just be left to voluntary agreements, which could be easily broken. This is a very important issue that should be decided democratically like all other important issues. If a consensus requirement in establishing (or in annulling) such freedoms may be impractical or even morally wrong, this should not mean that such an important issue just could be left to be decided by the simple majority of a local or regional assembly. This is therefore perhaps an area where decisions have to be taken by confederal assemblies with the requirement of exceptional quorum and majorities.

However, democracy requires a significant degree of cultural homogeneity for it to be tolerable. Cultural divisions may create resentment against majority rule or intolerance with respect to the rights of minorities. Therefore, despite the above safeguards, there may still be problems of oppression of racial or ethnic minorities by majorities. One possible solution to such problems may be the one suggested by Howard Hawkins in connection with the US experience:

> *A municipalist approach, starting from the existing geographical segregation of people of color by white racism, can advance a program of confederations of self-governing communities. These self-governing confederations could develop a measure of mutual aid and self-reliance that could insulate them somewhat from an intransigent white racist majority . . . At the least, by entering into the larger society with an independent power base, radicalized communities of color would confront white communities with a choice between continuing racism or developing a new relationship of mutual respect and equality.*[22]

So, wherever minorities are geographically segregated the above solution may safeguard their position. But, in case such geographical segregation is non-existent, perhaps, different institutional arrangements should be introduced, creating separate minority assemblies within the confederation, or perhaps giving minorities a veto 'block' vote.

Of course, institutional arrangements create only the preconditions for freedom. In the last instance, individual and collective autonomy depends on the internalization of democratic values by each citizen. Therefore, *paedeia* plays, again, a crucial role in this connection. It is *paedeia*, together with the high level of civic consciousness that participation in a democratic society is expected to create, which will decisively help in the establishment of a new moral code determining human behaviour in a democratic society. I suppose it will not be difficult to show that the moral values which are consistent with individual and collective autonomy and living in a community-based society are those that are based on co-operation, mutual aid and solidarity. The adoption of such moral values will therefore be a conscious choice by autonomous individuals living in a community, as a result of the fundamental choice for autonomy, and not as the outcome of some divine, natural or social 'laws', or tendencies.

Criticisms raised against the confederal democracy

It is precisely because the confederal democracy offers, perhaps, the only realistic way out of the multidimensional crisis, and, at the same time, represents a form of social organization that meets the institutional conditions for individual and social autonomy, that it is today under attack from statists of every persuasion and, paradoxically (prima facie), by some libertarians as well. As regards the former, it is not surprising that *civil societarians,* like André Gorz, are today attacking the community-based society. However, what is surprising is that one of the main arguments he uses against this type of society is that it will necessarily be in opposition to individual autonomy, presumably because it will represent another *system*, whereas the objective should be to abolish everything that makes society a system.[23] In the process, however, Gorz makes clear that he takes for granted the system of market economy and the state, insisting that 'The socialist aim should not be to eliminate the system or the sphere of heteronomy, but to restrict it where it cannot be dispensed with.'[24]

A common objection raised against a community-based democracy is that the 'complexity' and the size of today's societies make such a society a utopian dream. Thus, André Gorz, again, argues that a community-based society is impossible because it implies the 'radical elimination' of industrial techniques, of specialized functions and of the division of labour:

> *It is obvious and generally accepted that a complex society cannot exist without commodity relations and markets. The total elimination of commodity relations would presuppose the abolition of the social division of labour and specialization and the return to autarchic communities or to a kibbutz type of society. . . . The state should undertake defence and the general interest, including the existence of a market system.*[25]

However, a confederal democracy presupposes nothing of the sort. Not only is modern technology perfectly compatible with such a society, as Murray Bookchin has shown,[26] but also the talk about a return to autarchic communities or to a kibbutz-type of society represents a total misconception of the proposals concerning the economic organization of such a society. As I will attempt to show in the next section, a confederal democracy could function on the basis of a mix of democratic planning and an artificial 'market', involving the use of personal vouchers issued to each citizen. A system like the proposed one neither rules out specialization and the division of labour, nor depends on a system of autarchic communities – a system which, today, is not feasible anyway. What the proposed system *does* rule out is the market economy and the state, institutions that the 'radical' thought of thinkers like André Gorz cannot do without!

Still, all this is conveniently ignored by Gorz, in his effort to support the development of a post-industrial society, in which capitalism would transcend itself[27] (a transcending which, the author insists, must not be confused with the abolition of capital[28]) through the self-organization of individuals into 'countervailing powers'.[29] Thus, Gorz, obviously totally blind to the historical dynamics and the logic of the market economy, which have led to the present neoliberal internationalized economy and the minimization of social controls on the markets, describes as utopian the proposal for a community-based society, whereas at the same time he advocates the creation of a 'European eco-social space ... in which commercial competition and commodity rationality can be subjected to restrictive rules'![30]

Finally, John Clark, an ex-social ecologist, recently[31] attacked community-based democracy in order to promote an alternative individualistic and spiritualist view – one that, in effect, involves no conception of democracy at all. In what he calls the 'eco-communitarian' approach John Clark seems to dissolve uniquely human communities in a hazy, often metaphorical 'Earth community', reminiscent of the pantheistic ideas advanced by the Catholic deep-ecology priest, Thomas Berry.[32]

The first step Clark takes in attacking any objective goal of democracy is to efface the very subject of a democratic life, namely the citizen, who, as Murray Bookchin observes, 'embodies the classical ideal of philia, autonomy, rationality and, above all, civic commitment'.[33] Clark erodes the very concept of the citizen by converting it into a purely subjective, indeed idealistic, being – a 'citizen' of an ecosystem, of a bio-region, in fact of the 'Earth' itself! In addition, as if this etherealization of citizenship were not enough, Clark has no difficulty with invoking an asocial, apolitical and basically abstract 'person', so characteristic of the personalistic age in which we live today. In his view the concept of citizenship is limited and implicitly preserves the idea of a particularistic interest, as citizens will be guided by the interests and needs of their own communities against those of other communities.

However, although it is true that the citizenry in a specific community may hold views that differ from those in other communities (indeed, even within the same community itself), still, the exact aim of a confederal democracy is to provide an institutional framework for the democratic resolution of such differences. Clark's endeavour to resolve the problem of differences between or within communities treads the well-worn path of a largely mystical idealism. Presumably, everything will be resolved, in Clark's view, if we create a virtually metaphorical condition called 'Earth citizenship' that will somehow solidarize us with each other and with all forms of life. Or, as Clark puts it: 'We need a spiritual revolution more than a political platform and a regenerated community more than a political movement.'[34] Clearly, Clark totally ignores the institutional conditions, in terms of the equal sharing of political and economic power among all citizens and the resulting abolition of hierarchical domination and class exploitation, which, however, are vital in fostering the very 'spiritual revolution' and 'regenerated community' he calls for. It is obvious that a spiritual revolution, by itself, will never lead to a radical transformation of society.

The next step in Clark's attack against the goal of democracy is to denigrate the idea of the popular assembly, which is a crucial democratic institution. Thus, the 'affinity group', the familial group and some sort of community living are simplistically counterpoised to and even privileged over popular assemblies, which, supposedly, may very well lead to failure, unless the appropriate 'cultural and psychological preconditions' have been developed. In fact, he specifically refers to cases where 'power to the popular assemblies' could easily lead to harsh anti-immigrant regulations, capital punishment and, who knows, torture and similar practices.

But, as regards, first, the 'affinity group', which today is appropriated by many New Agers and is even promoted as a useful organizational form for 'forward-looking' corporations, it should be noted that it was created by the Iberian Anarchist Federation (FAI) as an organizational unit, often for 'action' purposes such as 'expropriations, and not as an institution for a future anarchist society'.[35] Second, Clark's conclusions can be applied just as easily to his own 'cultural and psychological preconditions', which, in many respects, have unsettling affinities with current eco-fascist notions that subordinate the individual to a chthonic 'Mother Earth', and 'bio-regional' beliefs in the redeeming virtues of the soil. Third, it is obvious that Clark does not seem to realize that problems like the explosion of crime, poverty, and illegal immigration have their objective roots in present-day inequities in the distribution of economic and political power and that therefore once these inequities are abolished in an inclusive democracy the corresponding problems are expected to be phased out.

It therefore seems that the main reason why John Clark de-emphasizes – if not completely dismisses – popular assemblies is that he has no conception of democracy as a constellation of institutions (i.e. the structures and processes which, at the institutional level, secure the equal sharing of power), as well as of values. Hence, forms of collective decision-making are simply irrelevant in Clark's treatment of democracy – to the extent that he deals with them at all. Indeed, democracy, in Clark's view, essentially becomes a system of values, a mere state of mind, where, as he puts it, every action in every sphere of life is a kind of legislating.

But, not only does John Clark's eco-communitarian view lack any conception of political democracy; it is, also, woefully lacking in any conception of economic democracy. Thus, Clark allows not only for privately owned enterprises (small partnerships, individual producers, etc.), but even a market economy! Still, this does not prevent him from envisaging an economy where a co-operative sector would dominate the private sector – all this under conditions of a market economy which inevitably (as we have seen in Chapter 2) must lead, in the course of competition, to the concentration of capital and formation of modern corporate conglomerates. It is clear that not only does Clark lack any knowledge of the dynamics of a market economy, but he also ignores the past two centuries of economic concentration in which co-operative and similar experiments were marginalized or simply swept into the dustbin of history.

The bio-regionalist approach adopted by eco-communitarians like Clark has no relation to democracy and is easily compatible with any type of socio-economic system, even an eco-fascist one of the 'Green Adolf' variety. Ecological values, divested of a democratic context, can easily be used to undermine any serious attempt to offer a liberatory alternative to the present society, or be twisted freely into forms that lend themselves to very authoritarian ends. The establishment of various co-operative endeavours may be useful for cultural and experimental ends, but taken by themselves, they are grossly inadequate for transforming society, as history, and even recent efforts such as the increasingly hierarchical Mondragon experiment, have shown (see Chapter 7). More often than not, such endeavours, at most, simply provide the system of the market economy with the facade of a benign and presumably humane image, if they do not degenerate into crassly capitalistic enterprises in their own right.

The preconditions of economic democracy

This section examines the preconditions of economic democracy in an attempt to outline the economic model on which an inclusive democracy may be founded. The dominant characteristic of this model, which differentiates it from similar models of centralized or decentralized planning, is that, although it does not depend on the prior abolition of scarcity, it does secure the satisfaction of basic needs, without sacrificing freedom of choice, in a stateless, moneyless and marketless economy.

Clearly, the type of economic democracy proposed here does not assume what Arendt calls the 'communistic fiction' that there is one interest in society as a whole. Such an assumption (which implies that the 'invisible hand' in a market economy – or, alternatively, the planning process in a state socialist economy – would satisfy the general interest) abstracts from the essential fact that social activity is the result of the intentions of numerous individuals.[36] What I propose, instead, is explicitly to assume the diversity of individuals (which, in turn, implies that consensus is impossible) and to institutionalize this diversity through the adoption of a combination of democratic planning procedures on the one hand and voucher schemes within an artificial 'market' on the other. The aim is to secure an allocation of resources that ensures both freedom of individual choice and the satisfaction of the basic needs of all citizens.

Also, the proposed economic democracy assumes away the mythical stage of free communism and addresses the issue of how, within the context of a *scarcity society*, i.e. a society where resources are still scarce with respect to needs, a method of resource allocation might be found which ensures that the above aim is achievable. From this viewpoint, it is not accidental that some modern libertarians who support the 'politics of individualism' find it necessary, in order to attack democracy, to resort, on the one hand, to the myth of free communism and, on the other, to the distortion that democracy involves a kind of 'rule' in the form of majority rule. The intention is clear: the former makes economic democracy superfluous, whereas the latter makes direct democracy undesirable. L. Susan Brown, for instance, starting from the anarcho-communist slogan 'from each according to ability, to each according to need', agrees with Goldman that 'It is up to individuals to decide, voluntarily, how best to live and work together. It is not something imposed on them from above, or dictated by the majority but rather individuals themselves freely and voluntarily create and recreate the social and economic forms of organization that they desire.'[37] However, as it will be shown below, economic democracy and freedom of choice are not as incompatible as this statement seems to imply.

Economic democracy defined

The usual definitions given to economic democracy by liberals, socialists and Green economists can be shown to be either inadequate or *particular* or both, and sometimes they tend to emphasize only one of the two main aspects of economic power: ownership and control.

Neoliberals, for instance, identify economic democracy with 'popular capitalism', which, however, can secure neither democratic ownership nor control. Thus, as the Thatcherite experiment of popular capitalism has shown, a wider spreading in the ownership of shares does not imply a smaller concentration of ownership and economic power. Furthermore, the spreading of shares is not, by itself, related to a higher degree of democratic control since the crucial economic decisions are still taken by managers and technocrats on the basis of profit-making considerations.

The practice of socialist statism tended to identify economic democracy with the narrow sense we defined in the previous chapter, namely, as a system that institutionalizes the minimization of socio-economic differences which, according to Marxist theory, were due, 'in the last instance', to the unequal distribution of private property. This implied that the state should be involved in either a process of redistributing income through taxation and the welfare system (social democracy) or in a process of abolition of private ownership of the means of production (actually existing socialism). However, as private ownership of the means of production is only one aspect of economic power, the attempt to minimize the effects of its unequal distribution on income, or even the abolition of private ownership of the means of production, could not secure, by itself, the elimination of economic power relations. So, the outcome was that the economic power of the *capitalist elite controlling the private sector* in capitalist economic 'democracy' was simply replaced by the economic power of the *party elite controlling the state sector* in socialist economic 'democracy'.

Today, after the collapse of 'actually existing socialism', most self-styled 'socialists' have abandoned any vision for a marketless, stateless, non-capitalist society and identify economic democracy with the enhancement of 'civil society' within the context of what they call a 'radical' democracy. Furthermore, they do not propose any dialectical tension between the nation-state and civil society. The enhancement of the latter has nothing to do anymore with the process of withering away of the former, but it solely aims to counterbalance or just check the state's power, within a market economy system. In other words, the vision of a socialist planned economy, to emerge after a transition period, has simply been abandoned by most 'socialists' today.[38]

Finally, some Green economists identify economic democracy with various forms of 'employee ownership' and 'workplace democracy'.[39] However, even when such forms of economic organization presuppose democratic control/ownership, control is narrowly defined to cover only workers and employees and not society at large. Combined with the fact that in this type of economic democracy it is still the market that ultimately determines what is to be produced and how, this could imply that what is involved is not a fundamental change in the nature of a competitive system. In other words, despite the anti-growth rhetoric of mainstream Green economists, as long as they take for granted the system of the market economy and its 'grow-or-die' dynamic, they indirectly adopt the growth economy itself. Such proposals, therefore, do not imply the abolition of economic power but simply its further decentralization, while, at the same time, they cannot secure (similarly to the liberal and socialist versions of economic democracy) the pursuit of the general interest. It is therefore obvious that we need a definition of economic democracy which involves the abolition of economic power itself.

A perhaps useful way to define economic democracy, in a way that implies the abolition of economic power relations, would be to start with the definition of direct democracy. We may simply define direct (or political) democracy as the form of political organization which, through direct citizen participation in the political decision-taking and decision-implementing process, secures an equal distribution of political power among citizens. This definition of democracy explicitly involves the negation of political power, and it implies the authority of the people in the political sphere. Correspondingly, we might define economic democracy as an economic *structure* and a *process* which, through direct citizen participation in the economic decision-taking and decision-implementing process, secures an equal distribution of economic power among citizens. As with the case of direct democracy, economic democracy today is only feasible at the level of the confederated communities. In other words, it involves the *demotic* ownership of the economy (i.e. the means of production belong to each *demos*), something radically different from both the two main forms of concentration of economic power (capitalist and 'socialist' growth economy), as well as from the various types of collectivist capitalism, either of the 'workers' control' type, or of the milder versions that social democrats of the post-Keynesian variety suggest.[40]

Thus, demotic ownership of the economy provides the economic *structure* for democratic ownership, whereas direct citizen participation in economic decisions provides the framework for a comprehensively democratic control *process* of the economy. The community, therefore, becomes the authentic unit of economic life, since economic democracy is not feasible today unless both the ownership and control of productive resources are organized at the level of the confederated communities. In fact, the community concept itself implies the negation of economic power.[41] So, unlike the other definitions of economic democracy, the definition given here involves the explicit negation of economic power and implies the authority of the people in the economic sphere. In this sense, economic democracy is the counterpart, as well as the foundation, of direct democracy.

However, given today's high degree of concentration of economic power and international interdependence, it is difficult even to imagine a radically different form of society based on economic democracy. Is such a society feasible today? What should be the system of allocation of resources that would be compatible with economic democracy? The magnitude of the questions asked obviously implies the need for significant collective research work. Here, we can only make some tentative proposals about the general guidelines that could be used in such an undertaking. Of course, theory can only explore possibilities, and it is up to social 'praxis' to give concrete content to the new form of social organization. In what follows an attempt is made to put forward a new vision of economic democracy, as well as some concrete proposals about how such a democratic model of the economy could function. In this double sense, the approach proposed here represents an original community-oriented model of the economy.

We may identify three preconditions that must be satisfied for economic democracy to be feasible:

(a) community self-reliance;
(b) *demotic* ownership of productive resources; and
(c) confederal allocation of resources.

The preconditions of economic democracy: community self-reliance

Self-reliance is meant here in terms of autonomy, rather than in terms of self-sufficiency, which, under today's conditions, is neither feasible nor desirable. A useful definition of self-reliance is the one given by the 1974 Cocoyoc Declaration of non-aligned countries as 'reliance primarily on one's own resources, human and natural, and the capacity of autonomous goal-setting and decision-making'.[42] Thus, although self-reliance implies maximal utilization of local resources and sources of energy, it should not be confused with autarchy and should always be seen within the context of confederalism. As the direct democratic control of the economy and society is only possible today at the level of the confederated communities, it is obvious that community self-reliance is a necessary condition for political and economic autonomy.

However, it is not only the demand for autonomy that necessitates self-reliance, so that control over one's own affairs can be restored. Self-reliance also becomes necessary by the fact that the historical trend away from self-reliance has had important adverse implications at the macro-economic, the cultural, the environmental and the social levels.

At the macro-economic level, millions of people all over the world have been condemned by the market forces (that ultimately control their fate once they have moved away from self-reliance) to unemployment, poverty and even starvation. Today, local economies depend on outside centres for the organization of production and work, for covering their needs in goods and services, even for the provision of social services (education, health, etc.). For example, to attract investors, very expensive incentives are used which usually overlook the ecological implications, while the investments themselves do not maximize local employment and create a significant outflow of local income. The latest GATT agreement, for instance, which since January 1995 converted GATT into the World Trade Organization, would make self-reliance in agriculture almost impossible, destroying in the process the livelihood of millions of farmers all over the world and transforming agriculture into an even more chemical-intensive process controlled by big agro-business. On the contrary, local self-reliance implies maximal utilization of local resources and sources of energy, a process that leads to a corresponding maximization of local employment and, through the 'multiplier effects', of local income.

Also, at the cultural level, the shift away from self-reliance has led to the dismantling of the social ties and values that unite communities, or even whole cultures. The *market values* of competitiveness and individualism have replaced the *community values* of solidarity and co-operation, transforming human beings into passive citizens and consumers.

At the environmental level, the trend away from self-reliance has led to the irrationality of a system that has to rely, for its everyday functioning, on the transport of goods and people over huge distances, with all the implications for the environment that this massive movement implies.[43] It should therefore be stressed that self-reliance is a necessary condition (though, of course, not a sufficient one as well) for the creation of an ecologically sustainable world order. This is so because self-reliant communities constitute today the only way to reverse the process of overproduction and overconsumption that is the main effect of the 'growth economy' as well as the main cause of the ecological threat.

Finally, the trend away from self-reliance has also been associated with significant socio-economic costs that have been particularly emphasized lately by Green economists.[44] Thus, de-skilling, vulnerability and economic dependence are the respective costs of the division of labour, specialization and free trade. In other words, the trend away from self-reliance implies a radical shift away from individual and social autonomy. So, the pre-'market economy' hierarchical social structures, which were, mainly, based on non-economic factors, were simply replaced in the market economy by new hierarchical structures built on economic foundations. It is therefore necessary for these economic foundations to be eliminated so that domination of human by human can be abolished.

Economic democracy is therefore impossible without a radical decentralization of economic power so that self-reliance becomes feasible. However, a radical decentralization implies, in fact, that the type of development which historically has identified Progress with economic growth and efficiency has to be abandoned. The trend away from local economic self-reliance was, in fact, an inevitable by-product of the rise of the market economy. In other words, the features associated with this trend (division of labour, specialization, exploitation of comparative advantage through free trade) followed inevitably from the expansionary nature of the system of the market economy and its grow-or-die dynamic. Similarly, the Marxist adoption of the capitalist idea of Progress led to the 'socialist' growth economy, where the huge concentration of economic power in the hands of the bureaucrats controlling central planning destroyed any chance for self-reliance.

Today, a form of decentralization is taking place within the internationalized market economy, a decentralization which is facilitated by technological changes. Stages within the production process (for some products, even the production process itself) that used to take place in advanced capitalist countries have been moving to the periphery and semi-periphery (Mexico, Korea, Taiwan, Mediterranean Europe, Thailand, Malaysia, China, Eastern Europe). Multinational corporations now have the technological capability to shift parts of productive activity from the centre to the periphery in order to minimize production costs (including environmental costs). But the decentralization that takes place within this process is physical, not economic, since economic power remains at the metropolitan centres. The very dynamics of the neoliberal phase, which is a process of liberating markets from the 'constraints' imposed by the state in the statist phase of marketization, lead to further concentration of economic power at the metropolitan centres, as was shown in the first part of this book. I will therefore call this process *dependent decentralization* because it does not lead to the creation of self-reliant communities but is instead an integral part of today's process of concentration of economic power in the metropolitan centres and of some parallel decentralization of production on a global scale.[45] Therefore, this process implies a reproduction of the hierarchical division of labour and the dominance/dependence relations.

A clear example of dependent decentralization is the 'principle of subsidiarity' that is being presently introduced in the European Union to calm the fears of the European peoples, who see even their present minimal capability for self-determination being usurped. This principle, which requires decisions to be taken at the lowest possible level, refers mainly to the decentralization of political decisions, whereas the main economic decisions are left to be taken at the centre, by the political and technocratic elite, through the institutions of the Economic and Monetary Union that are being established. Therefore, the European Union's decentralization not only does not reduce the dependence of its periphery on the centre but in fact enhances it. The metropolitan areas determine the quantity and content of development of the peripheral areas not only at the micro-economic but also at the macro-economic level: at the micro level, because it is from the metropolitan areas that the multinational capital, needed for the development of the periphery, originates; and at the macro level, because the economically stronger areas are able, through the European Union institutions, to impose directly their will on the weaker ones.

Opposed to this type of decentralization is a *self-reliant decentralization* which can only be founded on the horizontal interdependence of economically self-reliant communities. The economic relations between the confederated communities should therefore be structured in a way to enhance mutual self-reliance, in the context of collective support, rather than domination and dependency, as today. This could only be achieved within the framework of a confederal democratic planning process. Self-reliance within this framework should imply that the basic needs, democratically defined, should, as far as possible, be covered at the community level, although the level of satisfaction of these needs should be same across the confederation (see p. 255). Therefore, exchanges between communities in a confederation are both necessary and desirable, given that self-reliance can never lead to the satisfaction of all needs. The real issue is who controls such exchanges: is it the community itself, as for instance happened in the free medieval cities,[46] or the 'market', namely, those who because of their economic power are in a position to control the market, i.e. the economic elite.

An important question that has to be asked with respect to self-reliance is the size of the economic unit (i.e. the size of the community), which, on the one hand, makes self-reliance viable and, on the other, is compatible with direct and economic democracy. As regards economic viability, no general a priori answer can be given, in view of the significance of such factors as the access to raw materials, climate, geography and others. However, it is indicative that, at the beginning of the 1990s, 70 per cent of the countries with less than 100,000 in population belonged to the group of countries classified by the World Bank as 'high-income' or 'upper-middle income'.[47] It illustrates the fact that economic viability is not determined exclusively or even decisively by size, provided, of course, that it exceeds a certain minimum (say, 30,000) that would allow the local satisfaction of many, if not most, basic needs.

It is therefore compatibility with direct and economic democracy, that is, the feasibility of decision-taking in face-to-face assemblies, that should be the basic determinant of the size of the self-reliant community. On these grounds, the municipality (the *demos*) emerges as the most appropriate economic unit that could constitute the nucleus of an inclusive democracy. However, given the huge size of many modern cities, this implies that many of them will have to be broken up for this purpose. Still, this does not require their immediate *physical* decentralization, which is obviously a long-term project, but only their institutional decentralization, which could be introduced immediately.

The preconditions of economic democracy: demotic ownership of productive resources

The question of ownership refers to who owns and controls the productive resources and should not be confused with the issue of allocation of resources, which refers to the mechanism through which the basic questions of *what, how* and *for whom* to produce are answered. The two modern forms of ownership of productive resources are the capitalist and the socialist ones, whereas the two main forms of allocation of resources are the market and the planning mechanisms. Historical experience has provided us with all sorts of combinations between systems of ownership/control and allocation of resources, from state-owned firms within a market economy system to capitalist firms within a planned economy.

By the same token, the question of ownership should not be confused with the question of control. I do not just refer to the usual argument about the divorce of ownership from control in today's giant stock companies, where shareholders are the owners but actual control is exercised by managers and technocrats. In fact, the famous 'divorce' is in this case meaningless since shareholders and managers/technocrats in a sense – the most important one from our viewpoint – share common motives: to make profits and to reproduce the hierarchy relations that exclude most of the employees from effective decision-taking. I also refer here to the case where a firm may be owned by its employees and still be managed and effectively controlled by technocrats, managers and others (e.g. the Mondragon[48] type of workers' co-op). In that case, potentially, there may be a real divorce of interest between those who own the firm (workers) and those who control it (managers, etc.) since, even if profitability is a common aim, hierarchy may not be. This conflict of interest is illustrated by the fact that, as even supporters of workers' co-ops admit, 'many co-operatives have indeed suffered from mismanagement, primarily due to a lack of discipline with respect to shopfloor workers ignoring management orders'.[49]

The capitalist system of ownership implies private ownership of productive resources and is usually associated with a market system of allocating them among various uses. Private ownership of productive

245

resources irrespective of whether it is combined with a market system or not, implies control to serve *particular* interests (of shareholders, managers or workers) rather than the general interest. Furthermore, when private ownership of productive resources is combined with a market allocation of resources, (the system of the market economy) it implies inequality, concentration of political/economic power, unemployment and maldevelopment or 'inappropriate'[50] development. The grow-or-die dynamic that inevitably develops in such a system leads to systematic efforts to conquer nature and, consequently, to ecological damage. Therefore, this system is clearly incompatible with an inclusive democracy.

On the other hand, the socialist system of ownership implies a 'social ownership' of the means of production, which can exist within either the market or the planning system. This historically has taken two main forms:

(a)   nationalized enterprises; and
(b)   collectivized self-managed enterprises.

In *nationalized enterprises,* a real divorce between ownership and control is introduced: whereas formal ownership belongs to society at large, effective control of production is left to either technocratic elites (in a market economy system) or to bureaucratic elites (in a planned system) which take all important economic decisions. That implies that in this form of organization, the pursuit of particular interests is achieved not through ownership but through control. This is true whether such enterprises function within a market economy system (in which case they usually do not differ from normal capitalist firms, regarding the real objectives pursued) or within a 'socialist' planned system (in which case they are controlled by the party elite, through its control of the state apparatus, within the context of a bureaucratic top-down control). It is therefore obvious that nationalized enterprises are incompatible with economic democracy.

In *collectivized self-managed enterprises,* the ownership belongs, wholly or partially, to the workers/employees of the enterprise. Historically, we meet self-managed enterprises both within a market economy system (e.g. the Mondragon co-ops) and within a 'socialist' planned economy (e.g. the Yugoslav self-managed enterprises). The main problem with such self-managed enterprises is that the more independent of each other and of society at large they are, the more they tend to satisfy the *particular* interest of their employees, as against the general interest of citizens in the community. Also, to survive in a competitive world, they usually have to use the same production methods as capitalist firms (methods which may be alienating, damaging to the environment, labour saving, etc.). Furthermore, collectivized self-managed enterprises tend to compete with each other for productive resources (natural, labour, etc.) in a way very similar to the competition among capitalist firms. Finally, such forms of self-management cannot secure the autonomy of the worker as citizen. Thus, although some forms of it, supported by syndicalists and parts of the Green movement, may promote democratic procedures within the enterprise (what we defined as 'democracy in the social realm'), they do nothing to promote democracy in general, for the community as a whole. So, these forms of self-management, as Bookchin observes, usually represent 'exploitative production with the complicity of the workers'[51] since they cannot guarantee freedom from the tyranny of the factory and rationalized labour. Therefore, collectivized self-managed enterprises are, also, incompatible with an inclusive democracy in general and an economic democracy in particular.

It is therefore obvious that economic democracy requires another type of social ownership which secures a democratic ownership *and* control of productive resources and that the only form of ownership which can guarantee it is *demotic* (community) ownership. This type of ownership leads to the politicization of the economy, the real synthesis of economy and polity – a synthesis, which can only be achieved within the institutional framework of an inclusive democracy. This framework, by definition, excludes any divorce of ownership from control and secures the pursuit of the general interest. This is so because, as shown below, economic decision-making is carried out by the entire community, through the citizens' assemblies, where people take the fundamental macro-economic decisions which affect all the community, *as citizens,* rather than as vocationally oriented groups (workers, technicians, engineers, farmers, etc.). At the same time, people at the workplace, apart from participating in the community decisions about the overall planning targets, would also participate *as workers* (in the above broad sense of vocationally oriented groups) in their respective workplace assemblies, in a process of modifying/implementing the Democratic Plan and in running their own workplace.

Thus, the democratic planning process would be a process of continuous information feedback from community assemblies to workplace assemblies and back again. Finally, the running of the *demotic* enterprise could be supervised by a kind of supervisory board appointed by the workplace assembly. This supervisory board should include personnel with specialist knowledge and its members would be constantly recallable by the workplace assembly, apart from being indirectly controlled by the citizens' assemblies. Thus, workplace assemblies would function both as institutions of 'democracy in the social realm' and as fundamental components of economic democracy, given their role in the process of democratic planning. As such, workplace assemblies, together with community assemblies, constitute the core of the inclusive democracy.

The preconditions of economic democracy: confederal allocation of resources

Although self-reliance implies that many decisions can be taken at the community level, still a lot remains to be resolved at the regional/national/ supra-national level. To mention just a few of the problems that cannot be solved at the community level:

- problems generated by the unequal distribution of energy supplies, natural resources and the consequent unequal distribution of income between the confederated communities;
- problems generated by exchanges of goods and services between individual citizens of different communities or between the confederated communities themselves;
- problems generated by the supra-local character of the environmental implications of production and consumption;
- problems of transportation/communication;
- problems generated by the free mobility of labour between communities; and
- problems of technology transfer.

Apart, however, from the problems of co-ordination, there is the problem of the mechanism that would secure a fair and efficient allocation of resources both within the community and between communities. The problem is particularly crucial today as it has become obvious that both mechanisms that were developed historically to deal with this problem, that is, the market mechanism and central planning, have failed miserably.

The market mechanism

The market is an automatic mechanism within which Adam Smith's *invisible hand* allocates resources in a supposedly rational way. As liberal economists hypothesize, the free combination of individual rational decisions leads to a socially rational allocation. It is further hypothesized that the market mechanism is the most economical *information* system which provides the correct *incentives* that can secure an efficient decentralization of resources. The implication of all these hypotheses is that the market mechanism is the best system to guarantee a rational allocation of resources, without compromising the autonomy of each individual.

However, all these hypotheses are valid only under certain very strict assumptions. As a result, the properties of the market that supposedly result in a rational allocation are usually lost once the mythical state of *equilibrium* is disturbed. Today, even one of the pioneers of general equilibrium theory, the Nobel-prize winner Kenneth Arrow, admits defeat in his efforts to develop a theory showing the capability of a market economy to reach general equilibrium and, after discussing various insoluble technical problems of the theory, he emphasizes that 'the best-known falsification is the recurrent and now chronic existence of mass unemployment, which is a straightforward contradiction of equilibrium'.[52] In other words, as Will Hutton notes: 'The major tenet of free market economics – that unregulated markets will of their own accord find unimprovable results for all participants – is now proved to be nonsense.'[53] And of course, liberal economists, like Keynes, have shown, long ago, that the market is a crisis-laden system which cannot secure full utilization of resources and especially of labour. Finally, the inherent tendency of the market economy to lead to concentration of economic power and inequality that was examined earlier shows that *maldevelopment* is the by-product of a crisis-laden system where only money-backed wants are covered, which do not necessarily coincide with basic human needs. Therefore, orthodox economists who take for granted the market economy and its supposed 'superiority', in fact, rationalize the inequality, poverty and misery of millions of people all over the world for the benefit of the privileged minorities to which they themselves belong.

The freedom of choice that the market economy system supposedly secures, in reality, means 'rationing by the wallet'. In fact, citizens in a market economy system are not free to choose either as consumers or as producers: as consumers, because their choice is constrained by their income/wealth; as producers, because the 'decisions' about what and how to produce are taken for them by the market. Furthermore, producers are crucially constrained by their purchasing power, as their access to productive resources and, therefore, their productivity depends on their financial ability. If, for example, an Indian farmer has a much lower productivity than an English or American farmer, this is due to the respective access to fertilizers, machines, etc.,[54] as well as to educational and technological differentials, which are also related to income differentials. However, economic development became a function of the financial ability of producers very recently, that is, when productive resources became available exclusively through the market. As market relations penetrated all sectors of human activity and local self-reliance was destroyed all over the world, any access to productive resources became a matter of purchasing power. No wonder that today one-fifth of the world population uses up four-fifths of the world's annual resource output.[55]

In a market economy system, therefore, the basic economic decisions that a society has to take (i.e. *what, how* and *for whom* to produce) are crucially conditioned by the purchasing power of those income groups that can back their demands with money. A continuous bidding is going on for goods, services, resources, and those with the biggest purchasing power are the winners. Thus, the market economy system, contrary to liberal mythology, is the worst system for allocating resources when purchasing power is unequally distributed. Under conditions of inequality, which is of course an inevitable outcome of the dynamic of the market economy, the fundamental contradiction regarding the market satisfaction of human needs becomes obvious: namely, the contradiction between the *potential* satisfaction of the basic *needs* of the whole population versus the *actual* satisfaction of the money-backed *wants* of part of it. No wonder that orthodox economists make the convenient assumption of a 'given distribution of income' when they try to show that the best allocation of resources is the one achieved through the market economy system! Thus, the famous analysis of Pareto optimality, which shows the potential of the market mechanism to secure an optimal allocation of resources, is based on acceptance of the prevailing income distribution.[56]

In today's neoliberal phase of the marketization process, inequality is growing rapidly both at the country level, between the North and the South, as well as within them, at the personal level, as we saw in the first part of this book. Given, therefore, the 'bidding mechanism' of the market described above, the system increasingly caters to the needs of the 'new' North. So, it is through inequality that maldevelopment is produced and reproduced. Furthermore, inequality is a basic cause for the enthusiastic adoption of the eco-destructive growth objective by the elites all over the world, since the aim of trickle-down economics is, exactly, to maintain the social cohesion of a very unequal society through expanding, rather than re-dividing, the 'pie'.

The central planning mechanism
In contrast to the automatic character of the market, planning is a consciously controlled mechanism of allocating resources. There are many varieties of planning both in theory and in historical experience. Excluding the case of *indicative planning,* that is, planning within a market economy system (e.g. post-war French planning) which is basically a form of macro-economic management in a mixed economy, planning can be either *centralized* or *decentralized*. An extreme form of centralized planning was the Stalinist model where the Planning Bureau (in other words, the

bureaucrats/technocrats of the Soviet elite) determined the level of output, its mix, the methods of production to be used, distribution, etc., and passed on the orders from top to bottom. Centralized planning not only leads to irrationalities (which had eventually led to its collapse) and is not effective in covering needs; it is also highly undemocratic. Still, as we saw in the first part, centralized planning has achieved security of employment and a better distribution of income (although not a better distribution of power) than for other countries at a similar level of development.

After the failure of centralized planning became clear, Marxist economists like Ernest Mandel[57] proposed a form of 'democratically centralized planning' which, in a transitional phase, combines workers' self-management and the state, until the latter eventually – in classical Marxist fashion – withers away. However, this form of planning still suffers from the problem that it ignores the dialectic of statism. In other words, it ignores the fact that the bureaucrats who control the state apparatus cannot be prevented, within such an institutional framework, from institutionalizing, formally or informally, significant privileges for themselves, creating such powerful interests that will eventually corrode the organs of self-management, rather than the other way round.

Marxists today attempt to dissociate socialism (in the sense of social ownership of the means of production) from planning and suggest various forms of a 'social market' or a 'socialist market economy', as we saw in Chapter 2. In fact, some of them, like the editors of the French Marxist journal *Actuel Marx*, go further and find a direct connection between the adoption of central planning in Eastern Europe, which, according to them, became 'inevitable' once the market was abolished, and the totalitarian character of these regimes. For them, 'the socialist project is not about the abolition of commodity relations but about the elimination of class relations'.[58] This way, modern Marxists, by suggesting a synthesis of the market economy, and all that it implies, with 'social' control of the means of production (which in the framework of the market will serve even more than in a centrally planned economy the partial interest), end up with proposals which constitute a synthesis of the worst elements of the market economy and 'socialism'!

Participatory planning and freedom of choice

A democratic planning mechanism, therefore, has to be decentralized. One obvious way to decentralize planning is through some kind of 'synthesis' of the market and planning. This is the type of approach suggested by civil societarians. Thus, for a supporter of this approach who is engaged in a search for 'new forms of democracy', the real question about economic democracy is whether 'there are mechanisms of economic co-ordination and regulation which allow an element of competition between self-managed enterprises, and which at the same time promote social and environmental goals arising from society-wide democratic processes in economic affairs'.[59] However, what the author means by 'democratic processes' has nothing to do with political and economic democracy, as defined in this book. All that is meant, as becomes clear from the book's eulogizing of the 'new economic networks' (trade union committees, health and safety projects, initiatives for socially responsible fair trade, lesbian and gay movements, etc.), is 'socializing the market through mechanisms embedded in independent democratic associations sharing practical knowledge, rather than the state'.[60]

The logic behind this proposal is that any *scarcity society* faces a problem of democratizing knowledge and particularly economic knowledge, what economists usually call the 'information flow' problem. Hayek, Mises and other economists of the Right have argued for long against the possibility of a planned socialist economy on the grounds that because of the nature of economic knowledge no administrative system can have all the information needed for efficient economic decision-taking. As Hayek put it: 'The economic problem of society is thus not merely a problem of how to allocate "given" resources … it is a problem of the utilization of knowledge which is not given to anyone in its totality'.[61] He concludes that only an unregulated market, through a price mechanism providing correct signals of scarcities and desires, could efficiently produce the required information. In fact, it is this supposed efficiency of the free market that made the market, according to Hayek, a 'spontaneous' product of civilization.

In view of what was said in the first part of this book, there is obviously no need to deal here with the historical distortions of Hayek[62] about the 'spontaneous' development of markets, nor with the ridiculous assumption that it is state regulations and social controls that 'distort' prices and not the built-in trend in any market economy for concentration of economic power, which then invites social controls to check it. If, as I attempted to show, both central planning and the market economy inevitably lead to concentration of power, then neither the former nor the latter can produce the sort of information flows and incentives which are necessary for the best functioning of any economic system. It is therefore only through genuine democratic processes, like the ones involved in an inclusive democracy, that these problems may be solved effectively.

Still, socialist statists of the 'civil society' tendency, acknowledging this problem of knowledge, end up with proposals to create independent from the state democratic organizations and to 'socialize' the market 'through a public process of price formation in which social and environmental considerations would be central'.[63] In other words, disregarding all history to date, they still suggest the 'socialization' of the market economy! However, as it will be shown below, it is possible to devise a truly democratic process of economic decision-taking, namely, a system that may combine an inclusive democracy and planning on the one hand and freedom of choice on the other. But such a system has to assume away what 'civil societarians' take for granted: a market economy and a 'statist' democracy.

As regards the proposals of the libertarian socialist Left, there are two main models of decentralized planning which attempt a synthesis of democracy and planning: worker-oriented models and community-oriented models. As far as the worker-oriented models are concerned, it can be argued that they cannot provide a meaningful alternative vision of society for today's conditions: first, because such models usually express only a *particular* interest, that of those in the workplace, rather than the general interest of citizens in a community; and second, because the relevance of such worker-oriented models (like that of Castoriadis's[64] model for workers' councils which represents perhaps the most elaborate version) is very limited in today's conditions of post-industrial society. This is why community-oriented models offer, perhaps, the best framework for integrating workers' control and community control, the particular and the general interest, individual and social autonomy.

However, there is a recent proposal for 'participatory' planning which, although it is not based on a community-oriented model, can reasonably claim that it expresses the general rather than the particular interest. Thus, Michael Albert and Robin Hahnel[65] put forward an elaborate model of participatory planning in which the allocation of resources is effected through two types of councils: workers' councils and consumers' councils. These councils, working at various levels (from neighbourhood up to the national level) determine production and consumption respectively, through an elaborate planning process which starts with every citizen formulating individual work and consumption plans which are then aggregated and adjusted by means of a series of 'iterations'.

Nonetheless, although participatory planning does represent a significant improvement on the usual type of socialist planning proposals and it does secure a high degree of decentralization, serious reservations may be raised about its feasibility as well as its desirability. As regards its feasibility first, the problem that arises here concerns also any kind of democratic planning which is not market-based. Any such planning has to involve an arbitrary and ineffective way of finding out what future needs will be (the information-flow problem) – a problem particularly crucial for non-basic needs. The notion suggested by supporters of planning, including Albert and Hahnel, that people's needs can be discovered very easily 'just by asking them what they want', in fact, as was pointed out by Paul Auerbach *et al.*, 'flies in the face of decades of evidence both from East European planners and from marketing experience in the West'.[66] Even more important are the reservations about the desirability of such a model. Not only does it involve a highly bureaucratic structure that was aptly characterized as 'participatory bureaucracy' and which, together with the multiplicity of proposed controls to limit people's entitlement to consume, 'would lay the ground for the perpetuation or reappearance of the state',[67] but, to my mind, it also involves a serious restriction of individual autonomy in general and freedom of choice in particular.

This becomes obvious, for instance, from the principles that according to Albert and Hahnel should guide consumption decision-making. Prominent among the three principles mentioned is that 'decisions about what individuals wish to consume will be subject to *collective criticism* [authors' emphasis] by fellow council members with specific guarantees for preserving individual freedoms and privacy'.[68] Although the proviso about 'guarantees' is an obvious attempt by the authors to disperse any impression of Maoist totalitarianism given by this principle, still, the meaning of the principle is sufficiently clear. To my mind, the reason for this creeping totalitarianism is the fact that the model does not make any distinction between basic needs that obviously have to be met in full and non-basic needs which in a democratic society have to be left to the citizen's freedom of choice. The result of not drawing this important distinction is that the authors end up with a system where each citizen's consumption, production and workload has, ultimately, to conform to the 'average' ('If a person did request more than the average, she might be questioned, and if her answers were unconvincing, she would be asked to moderate her request'[69]).

Coming now to the community-oriented models, the main recent proposal for a community-based society is the one offered by confederal municipalism. However, the proposals for confederal municipalism do not offer a mechanism for allocating resources which, within the institutional framework of a stateless, moneyless and marketless economy and *under conditions of scarcity*, will secure both the satisfaction of the basic needs of all citizens and freedom of choice. Confederal municipalist proposals usually seem to imply a post-scarcity society in which an allocation mechanism is superfluous. Thus, Murray Bookchin points out that:

> *a confederal ecological society would be a sharing one, one based on the pleasure that is felt in distributing among communities according to their*

needs, not one in which 'cooperative' capitalist communities mire themselves in the quid pro quo of exchange relationships.[70]

Alternatively, some supporters of confederal municipalism seem to presuppose a 'scarcity society' and support an allocation mechanism based on democratic planning. Thus, Howard Hawkins argues that:

While self-management of the day-to-day operations by the workers of each workplace should be affirmed, the basic economic policies concerning needs, distribution, allocation of surplus, technology, scale and ecology should be determined by all citizens. In short, workers' control should be placed within the broader context of, and ultimately accountable to, community control.[71]

However, such a model, although it may secure a synthesis of democracy and planning, does not necessarily ensure freedom of choice. In fact, all models of democratic planning (either of the worker-oriented or community-oriented variety) which do not allow for some sort of synthesis of the market and planning mechanisms do not provide a system for an effective exercise of freedom of choice. The issue therefore is how we can achieve a synthesis of democratic planning and freedom of choice, *without resorting to a real market,* which would inevitably lead to all the problems linked with a market allocation of resources. In the next section, a model which combines the advantages of the market (in the form of an artificial 'market') with those of planning is outlined.

Outline of a model of economic democracy

The proposed system here aims at satisfying the double aim of: (a) meeting the basic needs of all citizens – which requires that basic macro-economic decisions have to be taken democratically; and (b) securing freedom of choice – which requires the individual to take important decisions affecting his/her own life (what work to do, what to consume, etc.).

Both the macro-economic decisions and the individual citizen's decisions are envisaged as being implemented through a combination of democratic planning and an artificial 'market'. But, while in the 'macro' decisions the emphasis would be on planning, the opposite would be true as regards the individual decisions, where the emphasis would be on the artificial 'market'.

So, the system consists of two basic elements:

- A 'market' element that involves the creation of an artificial 'market', which secures a real freedom of choice, without incurring the adverse effects associated with real markets.
- A planning element that involves the creation of a feedback process of

democratic planning between workplace assemblies, community assemblies and the confederal assembly.

The cornerstone of the proposed model, which also constitutes its basic feature differentiating it from socialist planning models, is that it explicitly presupposes a stateless, moneyless and marketless economy, which precludes the institutionalization of privileges for some sections of society and private accumulation of wealth, without having to rely on a mythical post-scarcity state of abundance. In a nutshell, the allocation of economic resources is made, first, on the basis of the citizens' collective decisions, as expressed through the community and confederal plans, and, second, on the basis of the citizens' individual decisions, as expressed through a voucher system.

The main assumptions on which the model is based are as follows:

- the community assembly is the ultimate *policy-making* decision body in each self-reliant community;
- communities are co-ordinated through regional and confederal *administrative* councils of mandated, recallable and rotating delegates (regional assemblies/confederal assembly);
- productive resources belong to each community (*demos*) and are leased to the employees of each production unit for a long-term contract; and
- the aim of production is not growth but the satisfaction of the basic needs of the community and those non-basic needs for which members of the community express a desire and are willing to work extra for.

The general criterion for the allocation of resources is not efficiency, as defined currently in narrow techno-economic terms. Efficiency should be redefined to mean effectiveness in satisfying human needs and not just money-backed wants. However, this raises further questions relating to the meaning of needs, the existence of any hierarchy of needs and, finally, the question of how real freedom of choice can be secured in the process of needs-satisfaction.

As far as the meaning of needs is concerned, it is important to draw a clear distinction between, on the one hand, basic and non-basic needs and, on the other, between needs and satisfiers,[72] i.e. the form or the means by which these needs are satisfied. Both these distinctions are significant in clarifying the meaning of freedom of choice in an inclusive democracy.

As regards, first, the distinction between basic and non-basic needs, it is clear that the rhetoric about freedom of choice in the West is empty. Within the framework of the market economy, only a small portion of the earth's population can satisfy whatever real or imaginary 'needs' they have, drawing on scarce resources and damaging ecosystems, whereas the vast majority of people on the planet cannot even cover their basic needs. But freedom of choice is meaningless, unless basic needs have already been met. However, what constitutes a 'basic' need and how best it can be met cannot be defined in an 'objective' way. So, from the democratic viewpoint advanced in this book, there is no need to be involved in the debates between universalist and relativist approaches to needs.[73] In the framework of an inclusive democracy, what is a need, a basic need or otherwise, can only be determined by the citizens themselves democratically. Therefore, the distinction between basic and non-basic needs is introduced here because each sector is assumed to function on a different principle. The 'basic needs' sector functions on the basis of the communist principle 'from each according to his/her ability, to each according to his/her needs'. On the other hand, the 'non-basic needs' sector is assumed to function on the basis of an artificial 'market' that balances demand and supply, in a way that secures the sovereignty of both consumers and producers.

Second, as regards the distinction between needs and satisfiers, this distinction is adopted here not because of the usual argument that it allows us to assume that basic needs are finite, few and classifiable, being in fact the same in all cultures and all historical periods. Although it may be true that what changes over time and place is not the needs themselves but the satisfiers, from our viewpoint, the distinction is useful for clarifying the meaning of freedom of choice. Today, there is, usually, more than one way of producing a good or service that satisfies a human need, even a basic one (types of clothing, etc.). So, freedom of choice should apply to both basic and non-basic needs. In fact, in an inclusive democracy, a priority decision that citizens' assemblies will have to take regularly concerns the quantity and quality of satisfiers that satisfy basic needs. However, what the best satisfier to meet each particular need is should be determined individually by each citizen exercising his/her freedom of choice.

But, how can we create effective information flows about individual needs? The idea explored here involves the combination of a democratic planning process with a system of vouchers that could be used for the satisfaction of basic and non-basic needs. Thus, we could imagine the creation of a system in which there are two main types of vouchers: Basic Vouchers (BVs) and Non-Basic Vouchers (NBVs), all of them issued on a personal basis, so that they cannot be used, like money, as a general medium of exchange and store of wealth.

Meeting the basic needs of all citizens in the confederation
Basic vouchers are used for the satisfaction of basic needs. These vouchers, which are personal and issued on behalf of the confederation, entitle each citizen to a given level of satisfaction for each particular type of need that

has been characterized as 'basic', but do not specify the particular type of satisfier, so that choice could be secured. To ensure consistency as regards basic needs satisfaction throughout the confederation, the definition of what constitutes a basic need, as well as the level at which it has to be satisfied, should be determined by the confederal assembly, on the basis of the decisions of the community assemblies and the available resources in the confederation.

The overall number of BVs that are issued is determined on the basis of criteria which satisfy both demand and supply conditions, at the confederal level. Thus, as regards demand, planners could estimate its size and mix, on the basis of the size of the population of the confederation, the size of the 'basic needs' entitlement for each citizen and the 'revealed preferences' of consumers as regards satisfiers, as expressed by the number of vouchers used in the past for each type of satisfier. As regards supply, planners could estimate, on the basis of technological averages, the production level, the mix, and the resources needed, including the amount of work that each citizen has to do. Thus every member of the confederation, if s/he is able to work, will have to work a 'basic' number of hours per week, in a line of activity of his/her choice, to produce the resources needed for the satisfaction of the basic needs of the confederation.

Draft plans could then be drawn on the basis of these estimates, and the confederal assembly could select, on the basis of the decisions of the community assemblies and workplace assemblies, the plan to be implemented and the implied amount of resources needed for its implementation. Each citizen is then issued a number of BVs according to the special 'category of need' to which s/he belongs. Thus, the confederal assembly would determine a list of categories of basic needs for each section of the population using multiple criteria, including sex, age, special needs, etc. Then, in cases where this 'objective' allocation of BVs has to be amended to take into account personal circumstances, the community assemblies could make appropriate adjustments.

As regards caring for the needs of the elderly, children and disabled, those unable to work are entitled to BVs, in exactly the same way as every other citizen in the confederation. In fact, one might say that the BVs scheme will represent the most comprehensive 'social security' system that has ever existed, as it will cover *all* basic needs of those unable to work, according to the definition of basic needs given by the confederal assembly. It is also up to the same assembly to decide whether, on top of these BVs, NBVs will be allocated to those unable to work. As far as the supply of caring services is concerned, if caring is classified as a basic need, as, of course, it should be, then every member of the community should be involved in the provision of such services (and would be entitled to BVs)

– a significant step in the direction of establishing democracy in the household.

Meeting the non-basic needs of all citizens in the community

Non-basic vouchers are used for the satisfaction of non-basic needs (non-essential consumption) as well as for the satisfaction of basic needs beyond the level prescribed by the confederal assembly. NBVs, like BVs, are also personal but are issued on behalf of each community, rather than on behalf of the confederation. Work by citizens over and above the 'basic' number of hours is *voluntary* and entitles them to NBVs, which can be used towards the satisfaction of non-essential needs. However, while with basic needs there should be no discrepancies in the degree of their satisfaction, so that the basic needs of all citizens in the confederation are met equally (as they should be in an economic democracy), there are no corresponding compelling reasons for an equal satisfaction of non-basic needs across the confederation. In fact, community covering of non-basic needs is just an extension of the individual citizen's freedom of choice. Therefore, if in a particular community people wish to put more or less work in for the production of non-basic goods and services, they should be free to do so.

However, the system should be organized in such a way that differences among communities as regards non-essential consumption should reflect only differences in the amount of work involved and not differences in the area's natural endowments. A basic guiding principle should be that the benefits from the natural endowments of the confederation as a whole, irrespective of their geographical location, should be distributed equally among all communities and regions. This principle should apply to both basic and non-basic needs satisfaction so that no regional inequities may be created, other than those due to the amount of work involved.

With technical progress, one could expect that the satisfaction of non-essential needs will become increasingly important in the future – a fact confirmed by statistical studies on consumption patterns in the West that show a verifiable trend of basic-needs saturation.[74] Correspondingly, remuneration will take more and more the form of NBVs. There is, therefore, a double economic problem with respect to NBVs. First, we need a fair measure to remunerate non-basic work and, second, we need a measure of valuing non-basic goods/services that will secure a balance between their supply and demand at the community level. The classical solution of expressing the value of goods and services in terms of man hours (proposed by Proudhon and Marx among others), apart from the fact that it creates all sorts of problems about equivalence of various types of work, the 'conversion' of tools/equipment used into man hours, etc., is also fundamentally incompatible with a libertarian society[75] and, as I will discuss below, with a system of allocation based on freedom of choice.

I would therefore propose that to avoid these problems and, at the same time, to achieve a balance of demand and supply that satisfies fairness criteria, we should introduce a kind of 'rationing values' in order to value non-basic goods/services. The market mechanism, as is well known, represents *rationing by price,* something that, as we have seen, represents the most unfair way of rationing scarce resources, as, in effect, it means rationing by the wallet. What I propose is a reversal of the process, so that *price by rationing* takes place, that is, prices, instead of being the cause of rationing – as in the market system – become the *effect* of it. Therefore, whereas in the market system prices basically reflect scarcities relative to a skewed income and wealth pattern, and they function as rationing devices to match the former with the latter, in the proposed system prices reflect scarcities relative to citizens' desires, and they function as guides for a democratic allocation of resources. Thus, to calculate the 'rationing value' (and consequently the price, expressed in terms of a number of non-basic vouchers) of a particular good/service, planners could divide the total of NBVs that were used over a period of time (say, a year) to 'buy' a specific good or service over the total output of that particular good/service in the same time period. If, for instance, the confederal assembly has ruled that a mobile phone is not a basic good then the 'price' of a mobile can be found by dividing the number of NBVs used over the past 12 months for the 'purchase' of mobiles (say 100,000) over the total number of mobiles produced in the same period (say 1000) giving us a 'price' per mobile of 100 NBVs.

The problem that might arise in this system is that there may be a mismatch between demand and supply of particular non-basic goods and services. Thus, to continue with the example of mobiles, the producers of mobiles and of their components may wish to offer only a limited number of hours over their 'basic' number of hours of work. In fact, the problem may arise even if *some* of them are unwilling to offer extra work, given that their activity, along with many other activities in today's societies, are done in the form of team work. In that case, the proposed adjustment mechanism of artificial 'prices' will be set in motion. The 'price' of mobiles, expressed in NBVs, will rise pushing the demand for mobiles down and the rate of remuneration (see next section) up, attracting more work in this activity. Of course, labour constitutes only part of the resources used and the overall availability of other resources has to be determined at regular intervals by the community assembly.

This way, production reflects real demand, and communities do not have to suffer all the irrationalities of the market economy or of the socialist central planning systems I mentioned above. The artificial 'markets' proposed here offer, therefore, the framework needed so that planning can start from *actual* demand and supply conditions (reflecting real preferences of consumers and producers) and not from abstract notions formed by bureaucrats and technocrats about *what the society's needs* are. Also, this system offers the opportunity to avoid both the despotism of the market that 'rationing by the wallet' implies, as well as the despotism of planning that *imposes* a specific rationing (even if this if is done through majority vote in the community assembly).

It is obvious that the system proposed has nothing to do with a money economy or the labour theory of value. Both are explicitly ruled out in this scheme: the former, because money, or anything used as an impersonal means of exchange, cannot be stopped from being used as a means of storing wealth; the latter, because (apart from the problems mentioned above) it cannot secure freedom of choice. The reason is that even if the labour theory of value can give a (partial) indication of availability of resources, it certainly cannot be used as a means to express consumers' preferences. The inability of East European central planning to express consumers' preferences and the resulting shortages that characterized the system were not irrelevant to the fact that it was based on a system of pricing influenced by the labour theory of value.[76] Therefore, the labour theory of value cannot serve as the basis for an allocative system that aims at both meeting needs and, at the same time, securing consumer sovereignty and freedom of choice. Instead, the model proposed here introduces a system of rationing, which is based on the revealed consumers' preferences on the one hand and resource availability on the other.

However, a well-known eco-socialist had no difficulty very recently in comparing an earlier version of the above proposals[77] to the labour theory of value, in order to conclude that 'Fotopoulos suggests a system of work vouchers (really a form of money based on the labour theory of value) . . . this is not a new idea, having been postulated by Skinner (1948) and tried in the American "Walden II" community in the 1970s'.[78] As is clear from this statement, the critic is unaware of the fact that a money model is not compatible with a system of vouchers in which, as I had stressed in my article, 'all [of the vouchers are] issued on a personal basis, so that they cannot be used, like money, as a general medium of exchange and store of wealth'.[79] Furthermore, for any careful reader of the proposed system it is obvious that it has nothing to do with the simplistic description of a utopian community and the primitive scheme of labour credits described by Skinner[80] – a scheme which does not provide for any freedom of choice, the division of needs into basic and non–basic ones, etc. Finally, only a gross misunderstanding of my proposal for economic democracy could make anybody find similarities between it and the hierarchical scheme of Walden II, extolled by Skinner, who has rightly been described by Noam Chomsky as 'a trailblazer of totalitarian thinking and lauded for his advocacy of a tightly managed social environment'.[81]

Allocation of work

The proposed system of allocation of work reflects the basic distinction we have drawn above between basic and non-basic needs.

Allocation of work in the basic needs sector

As it was pointed out above, covering basic needs is a confederal rather than a community responsibility. Therefore, allocation of resources for this purpose is determined by the confederal assembly. So, in the case that a community's resources are inadequate to cover the basic needs of all citizens, the extra resources needed should be provided by the confederal assembly. A significant by-product of this arrangement would be a redistribution of income between communities rich in resources and poor communities.

Once the confederal assembly has adopted a plan about the level of basic needs satisfaction and the overall allocation of resources, the community assembly determines the sorts of work tasks which are implied by the plan, so that all basic needs of the community are met. As regards the specification of work tasks, we may adopt the proposal that Albert and Hahnel make about 'job complexes'. So, wherever possible, specific jobs are replaced by job complexes which are described as follows by the authors:

> *A better option (than the capitalist and the co-ordinator approach) is to combine tasks into job complexes, each of which has a* mix of responsibilities *guaranteeing workers roughly comparable circumstances. Everyone does a unique bundle of things that add up to an equitable assignment. Instead of secretaries answering phones* and *taking dictation, some workers answer phones* and *do calculations while others take dictation* and *design products.*[82]

In principle, therefore, the choice of activity will be an individual one. However, as the satisfaction of basic needs cannot be left either to the mercy of the artificial 'market' for BVs, or just to the benevolence of each citizen, a certain amount of rotation of work may have to be introduced in case individual choices about working activities to cover basic needs are not adequate to secure all necessary work.

Rotation of work is suggested here as an exceptional means to balance demand and supply of work and not as an obligatory rule imposed on all citizens, as suggested by Albert and Hahnel. I think that the creation of comparably empowering lives, which is secured by taking part in community and workplace assemblies, in combination with work in job complexes, does not need, as a rule, a system of job rotation which may create more resentment than benefit to the community. Hierarchical structures at work and in society in general will be abolished only if citizens have equal power at workplace and community assemblies rather than if they are just rotated between jobs. As the authors themselves admit, rotation may not have the desired effect of balancing inequalities between plants ('hierarchies of power will not be undone by temporary shuffling').[83] It is clear that in order to decide what constitutes a hierarchical structure some subtle distinctions have to be made on the various types of authority, like the ones discussed by April Carter.[84] The possibility of rotating work is neither an element of a non-hierarchical structure, nor, necessarily, an element of job equality.

Allocation of work in the non-basic needs sector

As regards non-basic needs, I would propose the creation of another 'artificial' market which, however, in contrast to the capitalist labour market, would not allocate work on the basis of profit considerations, as in market economies, or, alternatively, on the basis of the instructions of the central planners, as in 'actually existing socialism'. Instead, work would be allocated on the basis of the preferences of citizens as producers and as consumers. Thus, citizens, *as producers,* would select the work they wish to do and their desires would be reflected in the 'index of desirability' I describe below, which would partially determine their rate of remuneration. Also, citizens, *as consumers,* through their use of NBVs, would influence directly the 'prices' of non-basic goods and services and indirectly the allocation of labour resources in each line of activity, through the effect of 'prices' on the rate of remuneration.

Therefore, the rate of remuneration for non-basic work, namely, the rate which determines the number of non-basic vouchers a citizen receives for such work, would express the preferences of citizens both as producers and consumers. As regards their preferences as producers, it is obvious that given the inequality of the various types of work, equality of renumeration will in fact mean unequal work satisfaction. As, however, the selection of any objective standard (e.g. in terms of usefulness, effects on health, calories spent, etc.) will inevitably involve a degree of subjective bias, the only rational solution may be to use a kind of 'inter-subjective' measure, like the one suggested by Baldelli,[85] that is, to use a 'criterion of desirability' for each kind of activity.

But desirability cannot be simply assessed, as Baldelli suggests, by the number of individuals declaring their willingness to undertake each kind of work. Given the present state of technology, even if we assume that in a future society most of today's hyper-specialization will disappear, still, many jobs will require specialized knowledge or training. Therefore, a complex 'index of desirability' should be constructed with the use of multiple rankings of the various types of work, based on the 'revealed' preferences of citizens in choosing the various types of basic and non-basic activity. The remuneration for each type of work could then be determined as an inverse function of its index of desirability (i.e. the higher the index, that is the more desirable a type of work, the lower its rate of remuneration). Thus, the index will provide us with 'weights' which we can use to estimate the value of each hour's work in the allocation of non-basic vouchers.

However, the index of desirability cannot be the sole determinant of the rate of remuneration. The wishes of citizens as consumers, as expressed by the 'prices' of non-basic goods and services, should also be taken into account. This would also have the important effect of linking the set of 'prices' for goods and services with that of remuneration for the various types of work so that the allocation of work in the non-basic sector may be effected in a way that secures balance between demand and supply. We could therefore imagine that half the rate of remuneration in the production of non-basic goods and services is determined by the index of desirability and the rest is determined by the 'prices' of goods and services.

Of course, given that labour is only part of total resources needed for the production of non-basic goods and services and that the non-basics sector is the responsibility of each community, in practice, problems of scarcity of various – other than labour – resources may be created. However, I think that such problems could be sorted out through a system of exchanges between communities similar to the one described below.

An important issue, raised by a penetrating examination of an earlier version of the above proposals,[86] refers to the specialist nature of some of the services needed for covering basic needs (doctors, teachers etc.) and the problems that their remuneration creates. Is it fair that 'a highly trained healer would get only basic vouchers (BVs) to satisfy the basic needs of the community, while an artist would get non-basic vouchers (NBVs) for a few hours extra put in painting'?[87]

To answer this question, let's see how the proposed system is supposed to work in some more detail:

- First, the confederal assembly decides which needs are basic and which are not and presumably most (but not all) health and education services would be classified as 'basic'.
- Next, the same assembly selects a particular plan to be implemented that would secure a balance between confederal demand and supply, as regards the satisfaction of basic needs. The plan would specify the number of hours of work and other resources needed in each type of activity, so that the basic needs of all citizens in the confederation would be covered.
- Finally, citizens would choose individually the line of basic activity in which they wished to be involved.

It is obvious that for the types of activity which do not involve special training or knowledge there should be no problem of work allocation and remuneration. However, for lines of activity that require special training or knowledge, a question of remuneration arises, given that most, if not all, of the work involved is 'basic'. How then might the 'doctor vs. artist paradox' be resolved? I think a solution to this sort of problem could be found in terms of specifying the part of the total *basic* work that does not involve any specialized training or knowledge and the part which does (planners could easily estimate the relevant parts). Then, as regards non-specialized work, all the work might be considered as 'basic' and entitle citizens to BVs only. The number of hours that each citizen would have to work on this type of activity would be determined according to the requirements of the plan adopted by the confederal assembly. However, as regards specialized work, people engaged in activities requiring specialized training or knowledge could be entitled to NBVs, for each hour of 'basic' work done. Thus, a doctor, on top of his/her BVs, may receive a number of NBVs (determined on the basis of the index of desirability) for each hour of 'basic' work done. This way, the 'doctor/artist paradox' will not arise because a doctor will automatically get, apart from the BVs, a number of NBVs, whereas an artist – if his work is not considered by the assembly to be satisfying a basic need – will receive only BVs and as many NBVs as the number of hours s/he is prepared to work as an artist. On the other hand, if the confederal assembly considers the work of an artist as covering a basic need, then s/he will be entitled to NBVs, the number of which however will be determined by the index of desirability. Of course, the proposed solution involves a certain built-in bias in favour of specialized lines of activity but, given that in a complex society most activities do involve various degrees of specialized training and knowledge, I do not think this creates a serious problem – as long as the index of desirability accurately reflects the community's preferences regarding the various types of work.

Production targets and technology

All workplaces, producing either basic or non-basic goods and services, would be under the direct control of workplace assemblies which determine conditions of work and work assignments, on the basis of citizens' preferences. As regards production targets in particular we have to distinguish between the various types of production.

Basic goods and services

The overall production targets for the confederation would be determined by the confederal assembly, in the procedure described above. The specific production levels and mix for each workplace would be determined by workplace assemblies, on the basis of the targets set by the confederal plan and the citizens' preferences, as expressed by the use of vouchers for each type of product. Thus, production units could claim a share of the community resources that would be available (according to the confederal plan) for their type of production, which would be proportional to the vouchers offered to them by the citizens as consumers.

Non-basic goods and services

Producers of non-basic goods and services would adjust at regular intervals their production levels and mix to the number of vouchers they received (i.e. to demand), provided, of course, that resources were available for their type of activity. This implies that, apart from the confederal plan, there should be community plans addressing the allocation of resources in the non-basics sector; their main aim would be to give an indication of availability of resources to workplace assemblies so that they could determine their own production plans in an informed way that would avoid serious imbalances between supply and demand, as well as ecological imbalances. So, community planners, on the basis of past demand for particular types of non-basic goods, the projections for the future, the aim to achieve ecological balance as well as a balance between supply and demand, could make recommendations to the community assembly about possible targets with respect to available resources, so that the assembly could take an informed decision on a broad allocation of productive resources between various sectors. However, the actual allocation between production units would be on the basis of the demand for their products (shown by the NBVs offered to each unit for its product) and would take place directly between production units, and not through a central bureaucratic mechanism.

Intermediate goods

Producers of intermediate goods (equipment, etc.), which are needed for the production of basic and non-basic goods, would produce a product mix determined 'by order'. Thus, production units of final goods would place orders with producers of intermediate goods on the basis of the demand for their own products and the targets of the plan. So, the confederal and community plans should also include targets about intermediate goods as well as decisions about the crucial question of resource allocation through time (i.e. resources to be devoted for community investment).

Technology

Finally, an important issue that arises with respect to production refers to the question of whether a new economic system based on economic democracy presupposes the discarding of present technology. As was pointed out earlier, technology is directly related to the social organization in general and the organization of production in particular. It is therefore obvious that the change in the aims of the economic system, that the introduction of economic democracy implies, will be embodied in the technologies that will be adopted by the community and workplace. Of course, this does not exclude the possibility that the new technologies might contain parts of the existing technology, provided that they are compatible with the primary aims of a community-based inclusive democracy.

In a dynamic economic democracy, investment in technological innovations, as well as in research and development in general, should constitute a main part of the deliberations of the confederated community assemblies. The advice of workplace assemblies, as well as that of consumers' associations, would obviously play a crucial role in the decision-taking process.

Distribution of income

The effect of the proposed system on the distribution of income will be that a certain amount of inequality will inevitably follow the division between basic and non-basic work. But, this inequality will be quantitatively and qualitatively different from today's inequality: quantitatively, because it will be minimal in scale, in comparison to today's huge inequities; qualitatively, because it will be related to voluntary work alone and not, as today, to accumulated or inherited wealth. Furthermore, it will not be institutionalized, either directly or indirectly, since extra income and wealth – due to extra work – will not be linked to extra economic or political power and will not be passed to inheritors, but to the community.

The introduction of a minimal degree of inequality, as described above, does not negate in any way economic democracy, which has a broader meaning that refers to equal sharing of economic power and not just to equal sharing of income. From this viewpoint, Castoriadis's[88] proposal for economic democracy suffers from a series of drawbacks arising from the fact that it assumes a money economy, as well as a real market which is combined with some sort of democratic planning. Money is still used as an impersonal means of exchange and a unit of value, although it is supposedly deprived of its function as a store of wealth, as a result of the fact that the means of production are collectively owned. However, although collective ownership of means of production does stop money from being used as capital, nothing – save the use of authoritarian means – can stop people using it as a means of storing wealth, creating serious inequalities in the distribution of wealth. Furthermore, the proposed system is based on a crucial institutional arrangement, what the author describes as 'non-differentiation of salaries, wages and incomes'.[89] But such an arrangement not only is impractical and makes this system utopian in the negative sense of the word, but it is also undesirable. As I pointed out above, some diversity in remuneration as regards non-basic production is necessary to compensate for the unequal work satisfaction created by widely diverse types of work.

Exchanges between communities

Self-reliance implies not only an economic but also a physical decentralization of production into smaller units, as well as a vertical integration of stages of production that modern production (geared to the global market) has destroyed. Therefore, the pursuit of self-reliance by each community will help significantly in balancing demand and supply. Still, as self-reliance does not mean self-sufficiency, despite the decentralization, a significant amount of resources will have to be 'imported' from other communities in the confederation. Also, a surplus of various types of resources will inevitably be created that may be available for 'export' to the other communities.

These 'exchanges' refer to both basic and non-basic production. As regards the exchanges in basic goods and services, these would be taken care of by the confederal plan. Although most basic needs would be met at the community level, the resources needed for the satisfaction of basic needs would come both from the local community and from other communities. Also, the satisfaction of basic needs involving more than one community (e.g. transport, communications, energy) would be

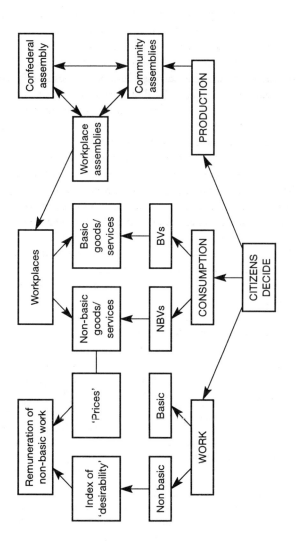

Figure 1: How economic democracy works

co-ordinated through the confederal plan. So, as regards BVs there can be no problem with respect to their exchangeability between communities.

But, as regards exchanges of non-basic goods, a problem of exchange-ability of NBVs arises. This is because the satisfaction of non-basic needs is not part of the confederal plan and the resources needed for these needs are basically domestic. Furthermore, the valuation of non-basic goods and services will differ from community to community, depending on avail-able resources. Therefore, regional or confederal assemblies should deter-mine a system of exchanging goods/services, on the basis of criteria that will take into account the geographical disparity of non-human resources. Finally, as regards exchanges of goods and services with other confedera-tions (or countries still characterized by a market economy system), these might be regulated on the basis of bilateral or multilateral agreements.

To conclude, the above discussion should have made it clear that the double aim of meeting basic needs and securing freedom of choice presupposes a synthesis of collective and individual decision-making, like the one proposed here in terms of a combination of democratic planning and vouchers. In fact, even if we were ever to reach the mythical stage when resources are not scarce, questions of choice will continue arising with respect to satisfiers, ecological compatibility, etc. From this point of view, the anarcho-communist reference to a usufruct and gift economy, to the extent that it presupposes 'objective' material abundance, also belongs to the mythology of a communist paradise. This is an additional reason why the system proposed here offers a realistic model of how we may enter the realm of freedom now, rather than in a mythical post-scarcity society.

Notes

1. See, among others, Jonathan Boswell, *Community and the Economy, The Theory of Public Co-operation* (London: Routledge, 1990); Dick Atkinson, *The Common Sense of Community* (London: Demos, 1994); Amitai Etzioni, *The Spirit of Community* (New York: Simon & Schuster, 1994).
2. See Murray Bookchin, *Remaking Society* (Montreal: Black Rose Books, 1990). See also Takis Fotopoulos, 'The crisis of the growth economy, the withering away of the nation-state and the community-based society' in *Education, Culture and Modernization*, Peter Alheit et al. (eds) (Roskilde, Denmark: Roskilde University Centre, 1995).
3. David Clark, 'The concept of community education' in *Community Education*, Garth Allen et al. (eds.) (Milton Keynes: Open University Press, 1987), pp. 58–60.
4. Michael Taylor, *Community, Anarchy, and Liberty* (Cambridge: Cambridge University Press, 1982), pp. 26–32.
5. Michael Taylor also shows conclusively why the liberal arguments of the 'anarcho-capitalist school' (F. Hayek, R. Nozick and others), which claim that no equality would survive for long without state interference, are

logically and historically invalid and that, in fact, community is a necessary condition for the maintenance of an approximate equality; Michael Taylor, *Community, Anarchy, and Liberty,* pp. 95–104.

6. Murray Bookchin, *From Urbanization to Cities, Toward a New Politics of Citizenship* (London: Cassell, 1995), p. 222.

7. Paul Anderson and Kevin Davey, 'Communitarianism', *New Statesman & Society* (3 March 1995).

8. Amitai Etzioni, 'Common Values', *New Statesman & Society* (12 May 1995).

9. See his interview in the Athens daily *Eleftherotypia* (29 May 1995).

10. Jonathan Boswell, *Community and the Economy, The Theory of Public Co-operation,* pp. 189–90.

11. Eric Shragge, 'The politics of community economic development' in *Community Economic Development* (Montreal: Black Rose Books, 1993), pp. 9–10. See also Dick Atkinson, *The Common Sense of Community,* on the topic of Community Economic Development in the United Kingdom.

12. See particularly Bookchin, *From Urbanization to Cities* and *Remaking Society.* See also *Society and Nature,* Vol. 1, No. 3 (1993) and in particular the articles by Murray Bookchin, 'The meaning of confederalism', pp. 41–54; Howard Hawkins, 'Community control, workers' control and the cooperative commonwealth', pp. 55–85; and Takis Fotopoulos, 'The economic foundations of an ecological society', pp. 1–40.

13. Murray Bookchin, 'The meaning of confederalism', *Society and Nature,* Vol. 1, No. 3 (1993).

14. Mogens Herman Hansen, *The Athenian Democracy in the Age of Demosthenes* (Oxford: Blackwell, 1991), p. 1. The references quoted by Hansen on the feasibility of direct democracy today include: F.C. Arterton, *Teledemocracy* (Washington, DC, 1987), I. McLean, *Democracy and New Technology* (Cambridge, 1989).

15. See Takis Fotopoulos, 'Direct democracy and electronic "democracy" ', for a critique of a recent pilot scheme on electronic democracy, financed by the European Union, which in fact aims at the modernization of the existing oligarchic system of decision-taking; *Eleftherotypia,* 25 Feb. 1995.

16. Peter Marshall, *Demanding the Impossible,* p. 22.

17. L. Susan Brown, *The Politics of Individualism* (Montreal: Black Rose Books, 1993), p. 53.

18. Murray Bookchin, 'The democratic dimension of anarchism', *Democracy and Nature,* Vol. 3, No. 2 (1996).

19. Karl Marx, *Critique of the Gotha Programme* (Moscow: Progress Publishers, 1966), p. 16.

20. V. Ramaswamy, 'A new human rights consciousness', *IFDA Dossier 80* (Jan.–March 1991), p. 9.

21. Karl Hess, 'Rights and reality' in *Renewing the Earth: The Promise of Social Ecology,* John Clark (ed.) (London: Green Print, 1990), pp. 130–3.

22. Howard Hawkins, 'Community control, workers' control and the cooperative commonwealth', *Society and Nature,* Vol. 1, No. 3 (1993) p. 75.

23. See André Gorz, *Capitalism, Socialism, Ecology* (London: Verso, 1994), p. 3.

24. Finn Bowring, 'André Gorz: ecology, system and lifeworld', *Capitalism, Nature, Socialism,* No. 24 (Dec. 1995).

25. André Gorz, 'A gauche c'est par où?', *Lettre Internationale,* Summer 1990.

26. See Bookchin's essay 'Towards a liberatory technology' in *Post-Scarcity Anarchism* (London: Wildwood House, 1974).
27. André Gorz, *Capitalism, Socialism, Ecology*, p. 7.
28. André Gorz, *Capitalism, Socialism, Ecology*, p. x.
29. As Gorz proposes, quoting Rainer Land; *Capitalism, Socialism, Ecology*, p. 11.
30. André Gorz, *Capitalism, Socialism, Ecology*, p. 12.
31. John Clark, 'The politics of social ecology: beyond the limits of the city'. Unpublished paper presented at the International Social Ecology Conference, Dunoon, Scotland (14–19 Aug. 1995). As the author will not allow any quoting from his paper on the grounds that it is a draft copy, this critique of eco-communitarianism will not be accompanied with quotes from the author's paper.
32. See John Clark's review of *Deep Ecology for the 21st Century*, George Sessions (ed.) in *Trumpeter*, Vol. 12, No. 2 (Spring 1995), p. 98. See also Thomas Berry, *The Dream of the Earth* (San Francisco: Sierra Club, 1988).
33. Murray Bookchin, *The Rise of Urbanization and the Decline of Citizenship* (San Francisco: Sierra Club Books, 1987), p. 55.
34. John Clark, 'The spirit of hope', *Delta Greens Quarterly*, No. 39 (Summer 1995), p. 2.
35. See Vernon Richards, *Lessons of the Spanish Revolution* (London: Freedom Press, 1972), p. 146.
36. Hannah Arendt, *The Human Condition* (Chicago: The University of Chicago Press, 1958), p. 44.
37. L. Susan Brown, *The Politics of Individualism*, pp. 127–8.
38. See, e.g., the article by Robin Blackburn, editor of the once radical *New Left Review*, that now advocates a 'socialized market'!; R. Blackburn, 'Fin de siècle: socialism after the crash', *New Left Review* (Jan./Feb. 1991), pp. 5–68.
39. See, for instance, M.A. Lutz and K. Lux, *Humanistic Economics* (New York: Bootstrap, 1988), Ch. 12; C. George Benello *et al.*, *Building Sustainable Communities* (New York: Bootstrap, 1989), Chs 18–20.
40. See, e.g., the work of G. Hodgson, *The Democratic Economy* (Gretna, LA: Pelican, 1984), *Economics and Institutions* (Cambridge: Cambridge University Press, 1988), and *Rethinking Economics* (Cheltenham: Edward Elgar, 1992).
41. Michael Taylor, *Community, Anarchy, and Liberty*, pp. 26–32.
42. Quoted in Paul Ekins, *Trade for Mutual Self-Reliance* (London: TOES Publication), 1989, p. 13.
43. See, e.g. Paul Ekins, *Trade for Mutual Self-Reliance*, p. 9.
44. For an examination of this topic from a Green economics perspective, see, e.g., Paul Ekins, *Local Economic Self-Reliance* (London: TOES Publication, 1988).
45. See Takis Fotopoulos, *Dependent Development: The Case of Greece* (Athens: Exantas Press, 1985 and 1987), Ch. A.
46. Pëtr Kropotkin, *Mutual Aid* (Boston: Extending Horizons, 1914), pp. 181–6.
47. In 1990–91, 27 out of 45 countries with less than 500,000 population and 9 out of 13 with less than 100,000 belonged to the 'high-income' category; *Britannica World Data*, 1992. Of course, the fact should be taken into account that size may play a less significant role with respect to the economic viability

of an export-led small economy than for that of a self-sufficient one but then, again, the technology used by the two types of economies may be radically different.

48. M.A. Lutz and K. Lux, *Humanistic Economics,* Ch. 12.
49. M.A. Lutz and K. Lux, *Humanistic Economics,* p. 258.
50. See for a definition of appropriate/inappropriate development, Ted Trainer, 'What is development?', *Society and Nature,* Vol. 3, No. 1 (1995).
51. Murray Bookchin, 'Municipalization: community ownership of the economy', *Green Perspectives* (Feb. 1986).
52. Kenneth J. Arrow, 'Problems mount in application of free market economic theory', *The Guardian* (4 Jan. 1994).
53. Will Hutton, *The State We're In* (London: Jonathan Cape, 1995), p. 237.
54. 'The Americans use more fertilizers for their gardens and tennis lawns than the Indians for all uses', *New York Times* (14 June 1979).
55. Ted Trainer, *Developed to Death* (London: Green Print, 1989), p. 118.
56. As two economists put it in a classical book of orthodox economics (James M. Henderson and Richard Quandt, *Microeconomic Theory, a Mathematical Approach* (New York: McGraw-Hill, 1958)): 'The analysis of Pareto optimality accepts the prevailing income distribution' (p. 208), and 'It is in this sense that perfect competition represents a welfare optimum. It does not guarantee that the second order conditions are fulfilled; nor does it ensure that the distribution of income (or of utility) is optimal in any sense' (p. 222).
57. Ernest Mandel, 'In defence of socialist planning', *New Left Review* (Sept./Oct. 1986), pp. 5–39.
58. Interview with Jacques Bide, editor of *Actuel Marx*, in *Le Monde* (reprinted in *Eleftherotypia*, 26 Nov. 1995).
59. Hilary Wainwright, *Arguments for a New Left* (Oxford: Blackwell, 1994), pp. 147–8.
60. Hilary Wainwright, *Arguments for a New Left,* p. 148.
61. F. Hayek, *Individualism and Economic Order* (London: Routledge & Kegan Paul, 1945/1949), pp. 77–8.
62. For an effective critique of Hayek and the 'libertarian' Right, see Alan Haworth, *Anti-Libertarianism, Markets, Philosophy and Myth* (London: Routledge, 1994).
63. Hilary Wainwright, *Arguments for a New Left,* p. 170.
64. Cornelius Castoriadis, *Workers' Councils and the Economics of a Self-Managed Society* (Philadelphia: Wooden Shoe, 1984), originally published in *Socialisme ou Barbarie*, 'Sur le contenu du Socialisme', *Socialisme ou Barbarie*, No. 22 (July-Sept. 1957) and first published in English as a Solidarity pamphlet *Workers' Councils and the Economics of a Self-Managed Society* (London: Solidarity, 1972).
65. Michael Albert and Robin Hahnel, *Looking Forward: Participatory Economics for the Twenty-First Century* (Boston: South End Press, 1991).
66. Paul Auerbach *et al.,* 'The transition from actually existing capitalism', *New Left Review* No. 170 (July/August 1988), p. 78.
67. John Crump, 'Markets, money and social change', *Anarchist Studies,* Vol. 3, No. 1 (Spring 1995), pp. 72–3.
68. Michael Albert and Robin Hahnel, *Looking Forward,* p. 48.
69. Michael Albert and Robin Hahnel, *Looking Forward,* p. 49.

70. Murray Bookchin, *Urbanization Without Cities* (Montreal: Black Rose Press, 1992), p. 298.
71. Howard Hawkins, 'Community control, workers' control and the cooperative commonwealth', *Society and Nature*, Vol. 1, No. 3 (1993), p. 60.
72. Manfred Max-Neef, 'Human-scale economics: the challenges ahead' in *The Living Economy*, Paul Ekins (ed.) (New York: Routledge & Kegan Paul, 1986), pp. 45–54, and 'Development and human needs' in *Real Life Economics: Understanding Wealth Creation*, Paul Ekins and M. Max-Neef (eds) (London: Routledge, 1992), pp. 197–213.
73. See Len Doyal and Ian Gough, *A Theory of Human Need* (London: Macmillan, 1991).
74. Ernest Mandel, 'In defence of socialist planning', pp. 14–15.
75. See, for a powerful critique of the classical solution, Pëtr Kropotkin, *The Conquest of Bread* (New York: Penguin, 1972), Ch. 13.
76. See Heinz Kohler, *Welfare and Planning* (New York: Wiley & Sons, 1966), pp. 129–36. See also Morris Bornstein, 'The Soviet centrally planned economy' in *Comparative Economic Systems*, Morris Bornstein (Homewood, Illinois: Richard Irwin, 1985).
77. Takis Fotopoulos, 'The economic foundations of an ecological society', *Society and Nature*, Vol. 1, No. 3 (1993).
78. David Pepper, *Modern Environmentalism* (London: Routledge, 1996), p. 321.
79. Takis Fotopoulos, 'The economic foundations of an ecological society', p. 32.
80. B.F. Skinner, *Walden II* (New York: Macmillan, 1976), Ch. 8.
81. Noam Chomsky, *The Chomsky Reader,* James Peck (ed.) (London: Serpent's Tail, 1987), p. 158.
82. Michael Albert and Robin Hahnel, *Looking Forward*, p. 20.
83. Michael Albert and Robin Hahnel, *Looking Forward*, p. 19.
84. April Carter, *Authority and Democracy* (London: Routledge, 1979), Ch. 2.
85. Giovanni Baldelli, *Social Anarchism* (New York: Penguin, 1972), pp. 144–5.
86. Takis Fotopoulos, 'The economic foundations of an ecological society'.
87. Steve Millett in personal communication with the author.
88. Cornelius Castoriadis, 'An interview', *Radical Philosophy*, Vol. 56 (Autumn 1990), pp. 35–43. Some of the ideas expressed in this interview and particularly that of wage equality repeat earlier ideas expressed in *Workers' Councils and the Economics of a Self-Managed Society.*
89. Cornelius Castoriadis, 'An interview', p. 66.

CHAPTER 7

From 'Here' to 'There'

The immediate problem facing the proponents of an inclusive democracy today is the design of a transitional strategy that would lead to a state where the democratic project becomes the dominant social paradigm. In this chapter, a proposal is made for a political and economic strategy that will create the institutional framework for an inclusive democracy. This strategy involves a new kind of politics and the parallel gradual shifting of economic resources (labour, capital, land) away from the market economy.

In the first part of the chapter, two radical strategies for social change are assessed: the lifestyle strategy and a variation of it, which attempts a synthesis of deep ecology and the civil societarian approach. Then, a transitional strategy towards a confederal democracy is proposed which involves direct participation in the political and social arena in a way that does not create incompatibility between the end of an inclusive democracy and the means to achieve it. In the next section, a new type of political organization is proposed, which, again, aims at meeting the means–ends compatibility criterion. Finally, in the last section, a comprehensive programme for social transformation is proposed.

In the second part of the chapter, an economic strategy for the transition to economic democracy is explored. Based on the discussion in the previous chapter, this section is structured around the transitional steps required in order to create the preconditions for economic democracy. Thus, the discussion of the steps that may be taken to enhance self-reliance is followed by proposals about the transition to a 'demotic' economy and to a confederal allocation of resources.

The point that is particularly stressed in this chapter is that all the proposed strategies for political and economic change and the transitional projects involved are useless unless they are part of a comprehensive programme for social transformation that explicitly aims at replacing the market economy and statist democracy by an inclusive democracy.

A new kind of politics

Old politics are doomed, as the accelerating internationalization of the market economy is met by the continuous decline of representative 'democracy'. The impotency of the state to control effectively the market forces, in order to tackle the fundamental problems of massive unemployment, poverty, rising concentration of income and wealth and the continuing destruction of the environment, has led to massive political apathy and cynicism, particularly among the underclass and the marginalized. As a result, all parties today compete for the vote of the '40 per cent society' which, effectively, determines the political process.

At the same time, the pipe dreams of some parts of the 'Left' for a democratization of the civil society are also doomed. The internationalization of the market economy is being inevitably followed by the internationalization of the civil society. In other words, competition imposes the least common denominator standards as far as social and ecological controls on markets are concerned. Therefore, that type of civil society is bound to prevail which is consistent with the degree of marketization that characterizes the most competitive parts of the global economy.

The cul-de-sac of lifestyle strategies

Setting aside the approaches for social change which take for granted the existing institutional framework of the market economy and liberal democracy, like the various versions of the 'civil societarian approach', the main approaches today which aim at a radical social change are a lifestyle strategy and a strategy based on confederal municipalism.

There are several versions of the *lifestyle strategy*. However, there is a common element that characterizes all these approaches. They all involve no intervention at all in the political arena and usually not even in the general social arena, in the form of participating in the collective struggles of workers, the unemployed and other social groups – other than in struggles on specific 'Green' issues, like animal rights campaigns, etc.

Thus, there is first the approach usually adopted by the supporters of deep ecology, as well as by those libertarians attempting to develop a new hybrid between deep and social ecology, like Peter Marshall's[1] 'libertarian ecology' in Britain, or John Clark's 'eco-communitarianism' in the USA. This approach involves no direct interference in the political and social arenas but a process which, starting from the individual, and working through affinity groups, aims at setting an example of sound and preferable lifestyles at the individual and social level: Community Economic Development projects, 'free zones' and alternative institutions (free schools, self-managed factories, housing associations, Local Employment and Trading Systems (LETS), communes, self-managed farms and so on).

However, such an approach, which has been criticized as individualistic in nature,[2] is, by itself, utterly ineffective in bringing about any radical social change. Although helpful in creating an alternative culture among small sections of the population and, at the same time, morale-boosting for activists who wish to see an immediate change in their lives, this approach does not have any chance of success – in the context of today's huge concentration of power – in building the democratic majority needed for radical social change. The projects suggested by this strategy may too easily be marginalized, or absorbed into the existing power structure (as has happened many times in the past) whereas their effect on the socialization process is minimal – if not nil. Furthermore, lifestyle strategies, by concentrating on single issues (animal rights campaigns, etc.), which are not part of a comprehensive political programme for social transformation, provide a golden opportunity to the ruling elites to use their traditional divide and rule tactics. For instance, the British government prefers to rely on private security firms (and only in the last resort on the police), recruiting people from the underclass, to deal with Green protests. The result is that the repressive nature of the state is hidden and Green activists are reduced to fighting battles with the unemployed and the marginalized disguised as 'security guards'![3]

An alternative lifestyle approach, which seems, prima facie, to be critical of lifestyle strategies, but, in effect, is also based on individual rather than political activity, is the one suggested by Ted Trainer.[4] This approach is based on the supposition that if enough people are educated and persuaded to change *individually* their lifestyle then 'capitalism will shrivel and die':

> If increasing numbers of people move to the slow lane where they can live satisfactorily without consuming much then capitalism is doomed. It fears nothing so much as declining sales. No corporation will ever sell me fashionable clothes or a sports car. If we make it convenient and attractive for more and more people to move to conserver ways, capitalism will shrivel and die.[5]

However, radical social change can never be achieved outside the main political and social arena. The elimination of the present power structures and relations can neither be achieved 'by setting an example' nor through education and persuasion. A power base is needed to destroy power. But the only way that an approach aiming at a power base would be consistent with the aims of the democratic project is, to my mind, through the development of a comprehensive programme for the radical transformation of local political and economic structures.

The *strategy of confederal municipalism* offers a radical alternative to the lifestyle strategies and is perfectly compatible with the democratic project. This approach aims 'to transform and democratize city governments, to root them in popular assemblies, to knit them along confederal lines, to appropriate a regional economy along confederal and municipal lines'.[6] In other words, the goal is to develop 'a public sphere – and in the Athenian meaning of the term, a *politics* – that grows in tension and ultimately in a decisive conflict with the state'.[7]

Although some of the steps proposed by the lifestyle strategy are not incompatible with the logic of confederal municipalism (for example, co-ops, local currencies, etc.), still, there is a crucial difference between the two strategies. As Murray Bookchin aptly pointed out:

> *Specific proposals for decentralization, small-scale communities, local auton-omy, mutual aid and communalism . . . are not intrinsically ecological or emancipatory. Such an outcome depends ultimately on the social and philosophical context in which we place such programmes.*[8]

To my mind, the basic difference between the two approaches as regards their 'context' refers to the role of the individual with respect to social change. In lifestyle strategies, social change is seen to start from the lifestyle of the individual, and to proceed through bypassing the state and the market economy, rather than through contesting and attempting to replace them with new social institutions. On the other hand, the con-federal municipalism strategy emphasizes the role of the *social* individual, that is, of the individual who takes part in political struggles at the local level and social struggles in general, with the aim to effect social change, not 'through setting an example', but through creating a confederation of municipalities which will be in tension with the nation-state, until the latter is replaced by the former.[9] So, this strategy not only avoids the social marginalization to which the lifestyle strategy inevitably leads (as the almost insignificant social impact of movements inspired by this strategy has shown in the last 25 years) but it also escapes the trap of being 'so skewed towards the idea of the reforms of the individual's values and lifestyle, as the primary political route to radical social change, that it ends up seeming positively antipathetic to the notion of the collective'[10] – the New Age movement being a clear indication of this trap.

Industrialism and the transition to an ecological 'democracy'

A recent attempt to define 'ecological democracy' in terms of a community-based society and confederations has created the impression that it may be related to the project for an inclusive democracy and confederal municipalism. This impression is utterly false. As I will try to show in this section, this approach has nothing to do with either democracy or confederal municipalism. In essence, it represents a cross between, on the one hand, deep ecology and the lifestyle approach and, on the other, the civil societarian approach we considered earlier.

The close affinity of this approach to deep ecology becomes obvious by the fact that it prefers to describe the present socio-economic system as 'industrialism' rather than as a market economy or capitalism. Industrialism, for Roy Morrison, 'is not simply' capitalism. Instead, industrialism is defined as 'a system for maximizing production and consumption, but it is also something more: industrialism is a civilization'.[11] Further on, we are informed that industrialism is characterized everywhere 'by two central imperatives: to maximize production and consumption, and to maximize profit and/or power ... hierarchy, progress and technique, linked to form the steel triangle of industrialism'.[12]

The above definition makes immediately clear that the author is not in effect talking about the institutional framework of the market economy and the consequent growth economy but about a 'civilization'; in other words a cultural phenomenon rather than a socio-economic system and its ideology. No wonder that Morrison sees maximization of production and consumption, as well as maximization of profit, as two central imperatives characterizing industrial civilization and not as imperatives implied by the dynamics of the market economy and capitalist property relations respectively. Furthermore, by confusing the growth economy with growth ideology, he puts in the same bag of 'industrialism' market economies as well as the defunct regimes of 'actually existing socialism', although power structures in the latter had taken very different forms from those in the former. His description of hierarchy confirms the suspicion that the author is not talking about a socio-economic system but about what he calls 'a basic organizing principle of our civilization'.[13] Thus, hierarchy is described as 'the basic industrial ordering principle. Industrial hierarchies rest not on caste or class, but on success in fulfilling industrial imperatives'.[14] So, the fact that industrial hierarchies, which control the means of production, pursue basically the same objectives as the elites owning the means of production is ignored by the author who seems to adopt the myth (presently almost defunct) of the divorce of ownership from control in industry.

Still, this problematic is not original at all. It seems that deep ecologists are presently reaching the logical conclusions of their approach, which has always emphasized in its interpretation of the ecological crisis the importance of value systems, rather than of institutions, and of science and technology, rather than of the market system. It is not therefore surprising that they now assume away the market economy itself. Thus, as Janet Biehl points out in a review of a recent book on the Industrial Revolution: 'Kirkpatrick Sale explicitly defines industrialism as "the ethos encapsulating the values and technologies of Western civilization". This subjectivization of "industrialism" as an "ethos" precludes a capitalistic component in Sale's industrialism.'[15]

It is clear that deep ecologists and Morrison, using a simplistic 'historical' analysis, which cannot distinguish between basic concepts like capitalist property relations, the market economy and the growth economy on the one hand, and the growth ideology on the other, end up by mixing everything up under the rubric of 'industrialism', which is supposed to be the cause of all our ills! Therefore the fact that, as I tried to show earlier, the Industrial Revolution happened in a society where the means of production were under private ownership and control is simply ignored by this approach. Equally ignored is the fact that the defunct regimes of 'actually existing socialism', in fact, had the option of not adopting a growth economy but simply did not pursue it. Not because they aimed at becoming industrial societies and therefore had to adopt the comprehensive system of social relations shaped by industrial reality, as Morrison seems to argue; not even because of the 'objective' factors which obviously necessitated a certain amount of economic development to meet the needs of their peoples. Although these factors did play a role, the main reason they did so was a 'subjective' factor, that is, the fact that the identification of Progress with economic growth was an essential part of their ideology (see Chapter 2).

Also, the affinity of this approach to civil societarianism and the fact that Morrison, like civil societarians, has no real understanding of democracy as a different form of society, becomes obvious by the meaning he attaches to political and economic democracy, as well as the transition to it. Thus, the ecological civilization is, according to Morrison, 'predicated upon the ability of civil society to create a wide range of voluntary social forms that allow democratic choices to creatively limit and transform industrialism'.[16] Like civil societarians, Morrison takes for granted the institutional framework defined by the market economy and 'statist' democracy. This is why, as he stresses in describing the transition to an ecological democracy, 'Civil society and its creations are not contesting for power, but working for community and freedom ... their goal is not to seize or abolish state power, or to substitute planning for market mechanisms, but to transform both state and market.'[17] It is therefore obvious that this approach, utterly ignorant of the dynamics of the market economy and statism, assumes that a new ecological democracy could somehow emerge out of the present institutional framework, not through contesting it but through bypassing it!

In this context, it is not surprising that the economic democracy is not defined in terms of a marketless, moneyless and stateless society. As Morrison puts it: 'An ecological or "green" economy involves community-based, voluntary market exchange, combined with decentralized, democratic political mediation and planning that flows from the grassroots.' And to dispel any doubts about the meaning of this economic democracy he describes Mondragon in Spain, Seikatsu in Japan and Co-op Atlantic in Canada as representing 'ecological democracy in action'.[18]

Similarly, the fact that the author does not have any real understanding of what democracy means is made abundantly clear when he seems unable to see the qualitative difference between the classical meaning of democracy and what passes as 'democracy' today: 'Democracy's record ranges from the very imperfect Athenian system of 2,500 years ago to the still quite imperfect US democracy . . . and to the dozens of fragile new systems across the world that may represent democracy's new beginning. These new beginnings come with the assertion of civil society as a creative venue for change, as with Solidarity in Poland.'[19]

In consistency with this approach's notion of 'democracy', the transition to ecological democracy will not be achieved through a programme that contests the present institutional framework, but, instead, through 'a program for the devolution of power to be advanced from below, from the arena of civil society'.[20] This would mean a community empowerment strategy involving community associations, organizations, institutions and community enterprises, which, without any power base, will be followed, like magic, by the withering away of the state and the market economy! In this context, it is interesting to see how even the concept of confederation is distorted by this approach. Thus, confederation does not mean any more the integration of community-based democracies into a new form of social organization to replace the state and the market economy. Instead, we learn that:

> an ecological democracy is organized on the basis of confederation, the third broad theme in society's transformation. Confederation is not simply a matter of formal relationships between governments. It embraces a limited degree of sovereignty and association. . . . Confederation is the broad mix of social connections that form the dynamic matrix of an ecological society, involving groups on all levels and of all sorts. For example, confederations with children will include relations between schools, parent groups, hospitals, day-care centres and co-operative economic groups. Confederation means multiple alliances.[21]

It is therefore obvious that neither the transitional strategy described by this approach nor the meaning assigned by it to democracy itself are relevant to the project for an inclusive democracy.

A strategy for the transition to a confederal inclusive democracy

To my mind, the only realistic approach in creating a new society beyond the market economy and the nation-state, as well as the presently emerging new international statist forms of organization, is a political strategy that comprises the gradual involvement of increasing numbers of people in a new kind of politics and the parallel shifting of economic resources (labour, capital, land) away from the market economy. The aim of such a transitional strategy should be to create changes in the institutional framework and value systems that, after a period of tension between the new institutions and the state, would, at some stage, replace the market economy, statist democracy, as well as the social paradigm 'justifying' them, with an inclusive democracy and a new democratic paradigm respectively.

It is clear that the transitional stage contains features which would not be in the ultimate society. Many of the features, for instance, that constitute a transitional economic democracy will obviously not be components of future society. The inclusive democracy, as I described it in the previous two chapters, is a stateless, moneyless, marketless society. On the other hand, the transitional strategy, taking for granted the statist 'democracy' and the market economy, aims to create alternative institutions and values that will lead to the phasing out of present hierarchical institutions and values. In this context, the criticisms raised by a well-known eco-socialist against an earlier version[22] of the proposals in this chapter are obviously out of place. Thus, David Pepper, mixing up the economic features of a transitional strategy towards economic democracy with the proposal for economic democracy itself, concludes that 'Fotopoulos clearly advances a money economy: indeed all these components also feature in "mainstream" green capitalistic economics'.[23]

So, the question that arises here is what sort of strategy can ensure the transition to an inclusive democracy – in particular, what sort of action and political organization can be part of the democratic project. In this problematic we have to deal with questions about the significance of struggles and activities which are related to every component of the inclusive democracy: the economic, political, social and ecological. A general guiding principle in selecting an appropriate transitional strategy is consistency between means and ends. It should be clear that a strategy aiming at an inclusive democracy cannot be achieved through the use of oligarchic political practices, or individualistic activities.

Thus, as regards, first, the significance of collective action in the form of class conflicts between the victims of the internationalized market economy and the ruling elites, I think there should be no hesitation in supporting all those struggles which can assist in making clear the repressive nature of statist democracy and the market economy. However, the systemic nature of the causes of such conflicts should be stressed and this task can obviously not be left to the bureaucratic leaderships of trade unions and other traditional organizations. This is the task of workplace assemblies that could confederate and take part in such struggles, as part of a broader democratic movement which is based on communities and their confederal structures.

Next comes the question of the significance of grassroots action in the form of education or, alternatively, direct action and activities like Community Economic Development projects, self-managed factories, housing associations, LETS schemes, communes, self-managed farms and so on. It is obvious that such activities cannot lead, by themselves, to radical social change. On the other hand, the same activities are necessary and desirable parts of a comprehensive political strategy, where contesting local elections represents the culmination of grassroots action. This is because contesting local elections does provide the most effective means to massively publicize a programme for an inclusive democracy, *as well as the opportunity to initiate its immediate implementation on a significant social scale.*

In other words, contesting local elections is not just an educational exercise but also an expression of the belief that it is only at the local level, the community level, that direct and economic democracy can be founded today. Therefore participation in local elections is also a strategy to gain power, in order to dismantle it immediately, by substituting the decision-taking role of the assemblies for that of the local authorities, the day after the election was won. Contesting local elections gives the chance to start changing society *from below,* which is the only democratic strategy, as against the statist approaches which aim to change society *from above.* It is because the community is the fundamental social and economic unit of a future democratic society that we have to start from there to change society, whereas statists, in consistency with their statist view of democracy, believe they have to start from the top, the state, in order to 'democratize' it.

Statists therefore are perfectly consistent with their aims when they take part in national elections, federal elections or Euro-elections, whereas supporters of an inclusive democracy would be utterly inconsistent with their declared aims in doing so. In brief, the fundamental difference between local elections on the one hand and parliamentary elections on the other (national or Euro-elections) is that whereas contesting the former is compatible with the aim of an inclusive democracy and is also amenable to lead, by itself, to the dismantling of power structures, contesting parliamentary elections is neither of the two. From this viewpoint, the distinction that Howard Hawkins[24] makes between running for national elections (just to educate) and running for local elections (to educate and win in order to implement the confederal municipalist programme) introduces a double inconsistency: first, an inconsistency between the end of an ecological democracy and the means to achieve it, which, at least, could result in confusion about the real nature of the movement; second, an inconsistency between the true nature of running for a statist office, which is a process that incorporates the logic of a different social system ('I am running in order to use my office and solve your problems') and the educational nature assigned to it by Hawkins ('I am running not to hold office'), an inconsistency which could easily marginalize the candidates as irrelevant to the election process.

The immediate objective should therefore be the creation, from below, of 'popular bases of political and economic power', that is, the establishment of local public realms of direct and economic democracy which, at some stage, will confederate in order to create the conditions for the establishment of a new society. To my mind, this approach offers the most realistic strategy today to tackle here and now the fundamental social, economic and ecological problems we face and at the same time to dismantle the existing power structures. A political programme based on the commitment to create institutions of an inclusive democracy will eventually capture the imagination of the majority of the population, which now suffers from the effects of the political and economic concentration of power:

- through their exclusion from today's 'public' realm, which is monopolized by the professional politicians;
- through their deprivation of the possibility of controlling the way their needs are satisfied, which is now left to the market forces; and
- through the everyday worsening of the quality of life because of the inevitable deterioration of the environment, which the market dynamics impose.

Once the institutions of inclusive democracy begin to be installed, and people, for the first time in their lives, start obtaining real power to determine their own fate, then the gradual erosion of the dominant social paradigm and of the present institutional framework will be set in motion. A new popular power base will be created. Town by town, city by city, region by region will be taken away from the effective control of the market economy and the nation-state, their political and economic structures being replaced by the confederations of democratically run communities. A dual power in tension with the state will be created. Of course, at some stage, the ruling elites and their supporters (who will surely object to the idea of their privileges being gradually eroded) after they have exhausted subtler means of control (mass media, economic violence, etc.), may be tempted to use physical violence to protect their privileges, as they have always done in the past. But, by then, an alternative social paradigm will have become hegemonic and the break in the socialization process – the precondition for a change in the *instituted* society – will have occurred. The legitimacy of today's 'democracy' will have been lost. At that stage, the majority of the people will be prepared to counter state violence in order to defend the new political and economic structures. Once citizens have tasted a real democracy, no amount of physical or economic violence will be enough to 'persuade' them to return to pseudo-democratic forms of organization.

A new type of political organization

The implementation of a strategy like the one outlined above requires a new type of political organization which will mirror the desired structure of society. This would not be the usual political party, but a form of 'democracy in action', which would undertake various collective forms of intervention at:

- the political level (creation of 'shadow' political institutions based on direct democracy, neighbourhood assemblies, etc.);
- the economic level (establishment of community units at the level of production and distribution which are collectively owned and controlled);
- the social level (democracy in the workplace, the household, etc.); and
- the cultural level (creation of community-controlled art and media activities).

However, all these forms of intervention should be part of a comprehensive programme for social transformation aiming at the eventual change of each municipality won in the local elections into an inclusive democracy (see next section). The new political organization could, for instance, take the form of a confederation of autonomous groups (at regional, national, continental and world levels) aiming at the democratic transformation of their respective communities. The members of this organization are not committed to any closed philosophical system but only to the project for an inclusive democracy based on a confederation of communities. The activists in this movement function not as 'party cadres' but as a catalyst for the setting up of the new institutions. Their commitment is to the democratic institutions themselves and not to the political organization, or, as Murray Bookchin puts it, to 'the *social* forms, not the *political* forms'.[25]

The establishment of democracy is bound to be a long process involving a huge popular movement. As Castoriadis points out, the setting up of democracy can only come about

> *from an immense movement of the population of the world and it can only be conceived of as extending over an entire historical period. For such a movement – which goes far beyond everything habitually thought of as 'political movement' – will not come about unless it also challenges all institutional significations, the norms and values which dominate the present system . . . as a profound psychical and anthropological transformation, with the parallel creation of new forms of living and new significations in all domains.*[26]

It is therefore necessary that the new political organization be founded on the broadest political base possible. To my mind, this means a broad spectrum of radical movements, involving radical ecologists, supporters of the autonomy project, libertarian socialists, radical feminists, libertarian leftists and every other current that adopts the democratic project.

Given the broad perspective of the project for an inclusive democracy, the new movement should appeal to almost all sections of society, apart from the overclass and the ruling elites. Thus the economic democracy component of the project should primarily appeal to the main victims of the internationalized market economy, the '60 per cent disadvantaged majority' which, as we saw above, includes the underclass and the marginalized, i.e. the unemployed, blue collar workers, low-waged white collar workers, part-timers, occasional workers, farmers who are phased out because of the expansion of agribusiness, as well as the prospective members of the professional middle classes, the students, who also see their dreams for job security disappearing fast in the 'flexible' labour markets being built. It should also appeal to a significant part of the '40 per cent' society which, unable to join the 'overclass', lives under conditions of constant insecurity.

But, apart from the class problems which an economic democracy promises to solve, there are also the transclass problems of gender, age, ethnic and hierarchical oppression[27] as well as the major ecological problem. An inclusive democracy, and in particular its components of direct democracy, democracy in the social realm and ecological democracy, should appeal not just to the victims of the market economy system but also to all those alienated by the present statecraft which passes as 'politics'; workers who are alienated by the hierarchical structures at the workplace; women who are alienated by the hierarchical structures both at home and the workplace; ethnic or racial minorities who are alienated by a discriminatory 'statist' democracy, and so on. Finally, the ecological democracy component of the project should appeal to every section of society which is concerned about the destruction of the natural world in general and the accelerating deterioration in the quality of life in particular.

The development of a new, broad radical democratic movement today would represent the synthesis, as well as the transcendence, of the major social movements for change in this century. I think the only realistic way out of the present multidimensional crisis is the creation of such a radical movement, which, without any ideological preconceptions, apart from its commitment to an inclusive democracy, will fight to stop the continuing – and lately accelerating – destruction of human life and natural resources and for the establishment of the realm of freedom here and now.

A comprehensive programme for social transformation

An explicit part of a comprehensive programme for social change should be the elaboration of the overall objective to create a different form of social organization, based on an inclusive democracy. In other words, the programme should make absolutely clear that the ultimate objective of the various projects included in it is the replacement of the present oligarchic structure with an inclusive democracy. This implies that such a programme should be fought for not just as a kind of new politics but as the political structure itself leading to an inclusive democracy. This is why, as it was stressed above, the community level is the only political level at which supporters of such a programme should develop their political activity. Once a new political structure has been created in a number of communities, then the growing change in the balance of power against statism and the market economy will create the preconditions for a change in the economic structure as well.

Thus, the economic programme for a transition to an inclusive democracy, starting from demands that mobilize people around their immediate concerns, should have the following basic aims:

(a) to develop an alternative consciousness to the present one, as regards methods of solving the economic and ecological problems in a democratic way. It should therefore connect today's economic and ecological crisis to the present socio-economic system and the need to replace it with an inclusive democracy based on confederated self-reliant communities; and

(b) to make proposals on how to start building the economic institutions themselves that would lead to an inclusive democracy. It should therefore propose measures that could lead both to greater economic self-reliance and to democratic procedures in taking decisions affecting the economic life of the people in the community.

As regards (a), that is, the aim of creating an alternative consciousness, the programme should show clearly that problems like unemployment, poverty and work alienation as well as poor quality of life, pollution and environmental destruction are all connected to an economic system based on the concentration of political and economic power in the hands of elites that represent a very small proportion of the population. The relationship of each of the main institutions of society to these problems should be particularly stressed. Thus, it should be shown that:

- the market allocation of resources leads to maldevelopment, unemployment and poverty;
- the private ownership of productive resources does not allow any economic democracy to flourish but instead leads to economic and political oligarchy, the alienation of the vast majority of people with respect to their jobs, as well as the perpetuation of inequality; and
- the hierarchical organization of society, both at the 'macro' level (state) and the 'micro' level (hierarchical relations at work, family, school, etc.) is incompatible with democracy in the social realm, autonomy and freedom.

As regards (b), that is, the aim of building alternative economic institutions leading to economic democracy, the programme should make clear why the taking over by a radical democratic movement of several municipalities could create the conditions for:

- the drastic increase of the community's economic self-reliance;
- the setting up of a *demotic* economic sector, i.e. a sector owned by the demos; and
- the creation of a democratic mechanism to make economic decisions affecting the demotic sector of the community, as well as decisions affecting the life of the community as a whole (local production, local spending, local taxes, etc.).

Thus, a comprehensive programme for social change should make clear that citizens, for the first time in their lives, will have a real power in determining the economic affairs, albeit partially at the beginning, of their own community. All this, in contrast to today's state of affairs when citizens supposedly have the power, every four years or so, to change the party in government and its tax policies but, in effect, they are given neither any real choice nor any way of imposing their will on professional politicians. This becomes obvious, for instance, if one looks at the economic programmes of national parties which are expressed in such broad and vague terms that they do not commit politicians to anything concrete. Furthermore, as regards the spending of money collected by taxation, or borrowing, it is clear that people have no power at all to decide its allocation among different uses.

The transition to economic democracy

But, let us examine the steps that may be taken in the transitional period, so that we can move towards meeting the preconditions for economic democracy. These preconditions were identified in the previous chapters as community self-reliance, demotic ownership of productive resources, and confederal allocation of resources.

Self-reliance in the transitional period

The question that arises here is how can we create the conditions for self-reliance today; that is, how can we help the transition from 'here' to 'there', from dependent to self-reliant communities? There is significant literature on local economic self-reliance[28] which can provide valuable clues for the steps to be taken in a transitional phase towards an inclusive democracy. Furthermore, lately, more and more local communities, which suffer the consequences of dependent decentralization, are beginning to encourage local self-reliance through local initiatives, to meet local needs with local resources.[29] However, all this literature, as well as the corresponding local efforts, aim to enhance self-reliance, taking for granted the market economy and the liberal democracy. On the other hand, a movement for an inclusive democracy has to develop a transitional strategy for a radical decentralization of power to the municipalities with the explicit aim of *replacing* the present political and economic institutional framework. The following proposals may be taken as a contribution to this effort.

The basic preconditions for the increase in local economic self-reliance refer to the creation of local economic power, in the form of:

- financial power;
- tax power; and, above all,
- power to determine production.

As regards financial power, the establishment of a community bank network is necessary in this process. However, the establishment of such a network presupposes that the movement for an inclusive democracy has contested local elections and already taken over a number of municipalities. Still, even before this happens, there are a number of steps that can be taken in this direction, even at the level of single municipalities. Such steps are:

- *Demotic credit unions* (i.e. financial co-ops, supported by the *demos*) could be set up to provide loans to their members for their personal and investment needs. One could also imagine the extension of the role of credit unions, so that the savings of members are used for local development and social investment, in other words, for investment in local people to enable them to build up viable employment. This way, demotic credit unions could become the basis on which a community bank network could be built at a later stage.
- A *demotic currency* (i.e. a currency controlled by the *demos*) could play a crucial role in enhancing local economic self-reliance. This is because a local currency makes possible the control of economic activity by the community and, at the same time, could be used as a means for enhancing the income of the community members. The demotic currency does not replace the national currency but complements it. As a first step, present LETS[30] schemes could be muncipalized. Later on, a *demotic credit card scheme* may be created with the aim of covering the basic needs of all citizens. Thus, citizens may be issued with free demotic 'credit cards' in which the credit limit would be determined by income and wealth (i.e. the higher the citizen's level of income and wealth the lower the credit limit). These credit cards could be used for the purchase of locally produced goods and services. Such a scheme could therefore play a useful role in the transition to a voucher system that would replace all currencies in an inclusive democracy.

As regards taxing power, the transitional programme for an inclusive democracy should involve steps for the shift of taxing power from the national to the local level, as a basic step in creating conditions of economic self-reliance. Then, a new *demotic tax system* (i.e. a tax system controlled by the *demos*) could be introduced that could attempt to meet, as far as possible within the constraints of a market economy that would still exist in the transitional period, the basic principles of an inclusive democracy. Thus, a certain shift in the tax load should take place, away from taxing income and towards taxing wealth, the occupation of land, the use of energy and resources, as well as activities creating environmental and social costs for the community. The main goals of a demotic tax system should be:

- the financing of a programme for the municipalization of the local productive resources, which would provide employment opportunities for all citizens in the community;

- the financing of a programme for social spending that would cover the basic needs of all citizens, in the form of a basic income (its size depending on the citizen's income and wealth) guaranteed for every citizen, irrespective of ability to work;
- the financing of institutional arrangements that would make democracy in the household effective;
- the financing of programmes for the replacement of traditional energy sources with local energy resources, especially natural energy (solar, wind, etc.) which would minimize both the dependence of local economies on outside centres, as well as the energy-related implications on the environment; and
- the parallel economic penalization of the anti-ecological activities of branches and subsidiaries of large corporations based in the community.

So, the combined effect of the above measures will be to redistribute economic power within the community, in the sense of greater equality in the distribution of income and wealth. This, combined with the introduction of the democratic planning procedures (see p. 298), should provide significant ground for the transition towards full economic democracy.

As regards the all-important power to determine production, comprehensive programmes should be designed that would contain concrete proposals on the changes required in the economic structure of each municipality, so that the objectives of an inclusive democracy may be achieved. A transitional strategy towards greater self-reliance would involve people in the community producing more for themselves and one another, as well as substituting locally produced goods and services for goods produced outside the community. Financial incentives may be provided to local shopkeepers in order to induce them to stock locally produced goods and to citizens to buy them. This, in turn, would encourage local producers (farmers, craftsmen, etc.) to produce for and sell at the local market, breaking the chains of big manufacturers and distributors.

However, the creation of *demotic enterprises* (i.e. enterprises owned by the *demos*) in production or distribution would only have a political significance, in this transitional stage towards an inclusive democracy, if and only if they constitute part of a comprehensive political programme towards radical social transformation. As Murray Bookchin put it in connection with his Confederal Municipalism programme:

> *Removed from a libertarian municipalist context and political movement focused on achieving revolutionary municipalist goals as a dual power against*

corporations and the state, food coops are little more than benign enterprises
that capitalism and the state can easily tolerate with no fear of challenge.[31]

It should be noted that the revival of local economy, in the context of wider national and supranational entities, could play a decisive role, not only in founding economic democracy but also in restructuring the economically weaker regions. Only the lessening of the degree of dependence of these regions on the metropolitan centres would allow the creation of a new production and consumption model, compatible with the economic potential of each region. For example, for a country like Greece, the revival of local economies constitutes today the only way out from the chronic economic crisis created by the historical failure of both statism and private initiative to create a modern productive structure that would be in a position to meet the country's basic needs without a large part of the population, especially of the youth, being condemned to unemployment and emigration.[32]

Finally, a transitional strategy towards greater self-reliance should involve the creation of a *demotic welfare system,* i.e. a welfare system controlled by the *demos.* The shift to municipalities of important social services (education, health, housing, etc.) is particularly important today when the welfare state is in ruins and is being gradually replaced by safety nets for the very poor and the parallel enhancement of private provision with respect to basic needs. The use of local productive resources in these services should be maximized, both in order to provide local employment and create local income and, also, to drastically reduce outside dependence. However, a comprehensive demotic welfare system that involves the provision of social services at higher levels (tertiary education, big hospitals, etc.) could only be established with the co-operation of several municipalities and could be the basis for a confederal welfare system. A demotic welfare system will not only be less prone to bureaucratization but will also provide a much more effective mechanism than the state welfare system, as a result of its smaller size and its easier management by citizens with full knowledge of the local problems. Furthermore, as the municipalization of social services will be part of a programme to enhance individual and social autonomy, the effect will not be the creation of a new dependency culture.

The transition to a 'demotic' economy
The creation of a demotic economic sector is a crucial step in the transition to an inclusive democracy, not only because of its importance with respect to economic democracy but also because the establishment of self-managed productive units constitutes the foundation for workplace de-

mocracy. A demotic sector would involve new collective forms of owner-ship that would ensure control of production, not only by those working in the production units, but also by the *demos*. The productive units could belong to the *demos* and be managed by the workers working in those units, while their technical management (marketing, planning, etc.) could be entrusted to specialized personnel. However, the overall control of demotic enterprises should belong to the community assemblies which would supervise their production, employment and environmental policies. For instance, as a step in the transition to an economic democracy, community assemblies could decide to reduce drastically the wage differ-entials of people employed in demotic enterprises.

Hence, the new forms of organization of production and collective ownership would not only create the preconditions for economic democ-racy, but also enhance the 'general social interest'. This is in contrast to the partial interest that inevitably is being pursued by the social classes and groups of the hierarchically organized social systems. Therefore, the answer to the economic failure of socialist enterprises is not the neoliberal (with social-democratic connivance) privatization of them but their mu-nicipalization. The establishment of a series of demotic enterprises that belong to and are controlled by the *demos* (through the community assemblies) in collaboration with the people working in them (through the workplace assemblies) would create local employment opportunities and expand local income under conditions that secure:

- economic democracy in the sense of democratic participation in the running of these enterprises;
- workplace democracy with no institutionalized hierarchical structures;
- security of employment; and
- ecological balance.

The two significant questions that arise with respect to the municipali-zation of the economy in the transitional period are, first, how to establish such demotic enterprises and, second, how to run them until they become parts of a full economic democracy.

As regards the question of establishing demotic enterprises, this could be achieved by a combination of methods. Some may be used even before supporters of an inclusive democracy programme take over a municipality. *Community Land Trusts,* for instance, are a useful way of raising finances for the purchase of land to be held collectively, by using the value of the land itself as security. Such trusts have already been used in several places in connection with community development.[33]

Other measures can only be taken up effectively after the successful contestation of local elections. Thus, an important step in the establishment of a demotic economic sector is the creation of a *network of demotic bank co-operatives*, similar, for example, to the very successful Basque network of the *Caja Laboral Popular* in Spain,[34] which supports the Mondragon co-ops. In Spain, this network is not owned by the municipalities and was set up by the people involved in the creation of the co-op movement – a procedure which raises serious objections as regards the desirability of such a scheme but also as regards its feasibility outside the strongly nationalist Basque community of Mondragon. A more feasible and desirable way may be for the municipalities which are controlled by supporters of inclusive democracy to establish a municipality-owned and controlled bank network. Thus, each municipality could have its own demotic bank that could be integrated into a regional and later a confederal network. Such a network could be used:

- to absorb local savings that would be attracted to the network by the fact that savers would be able to control the character of its investment activities. This control would be exercised by the community assemblies, in collaboration with the bank employees' assemblies, to ensure that savings will be channelled to projects aiming at local development, maximization of local employment, limitation of the environmental effects of production, etc.;
- to finance investments in modern production units which have as their goal the local creation of social wealth and the consequent lessening of the local economy's dependence on outside centres. So, the proceeds of local taxation would be used not just for the financing of infrastructure projects and local social services but also for the financing – through the network of demotic banks – of investment in new (or the purchase of old) production units to be included in the demotic sector of the economy. Most of the initial capital to establish the demotic enterprises would therefore have to come from the community savings which, through the demotic bank network, would be lent to groups of citizens who wished to establish community co-ops; and
- to offer other specialized services that would allow the establishment and running of these demotic enterprises by any interested social group in the community, which would not necessarily possess the required specialized knowledge (e.g. workers of bankrupt companies, unemployed, low-waged people, etc.). In any case, decentralization of information today is widely spread. For example, in Emilia-Romana, Italy, a whole network has been developed with centres which offer specialized services to the small enterprises (from marketing to industrial research, etc.), while in Japan, with the Kohsetsushi system, each city has

its own centre of research and applied technology for small enterprise.[35]

The *demotic bank* could undertake research on the type of production units to be established in the local community. It is obvious that private initiative could not undertake either the co-ordination of investment programmes or the research work for the sectors in which the new units should be developed, since this work demands a general knowledge of economic data and needs. The fragmentary character of private investment is, anyway, the basic cause of the uneven character of capitalist development. The research, therefore, on the particular units towards which local investments should be directed as well as on their geographical distribution (that is the potential of local economies to undertake their materialization) could be undertaken, in a first phase, by the research centres of the network of demotic banks and, in a later stage, by the confederation of communities. The criteria, however, to be used in this research programme should not be the narrow technocratic economic criteria based on efficiency, but alternative criteria which would aim at the maximization of local employment and of local (and consequently of confederal) economic self-reliance and productivity, as well as at the minimization of the effects on the environment. So, a kind of social investment appraisal and social accounting has to be introduced to evaluate particular investment proposals, to monitor them and generally to evaluate social wealth creation. That means that new economic indicators have to be used, on the basis of the ones already being developed,[36] in place of today's measures of welfare. Finally, the demotic bank should provide specialized services on planning the production layout, designing the factory, manpower training, accounting systems, etc.

As regards the question of how these demotic enterprises should be run in the transitional period, I think that forms of self-management, like the Yugoslav type of co-op and the Employee Stock Ownership Plan (ESOP) – the former bending towards state socialism and the latter towards the market economy – should be excluded. In the Yugoslav system of self-management, all capital investment was owned by the state rather than by the enterprise itself. Workers, therefore, had no incentive at all to invest in the capital base of the plant and, as a result, productivity suffered a lot. On the other hand, in ESOP schemes, we have an indirect worker-ownership system, based on an employee pension plan, rather than a workplace democracy. Voting, for instance, is based on stock held by employees and not on the democratic one-person-one-vote formula. The whole system therefore results in a perfect capitalist stock company, and the only difference from other companies is that this scheme turns workers into share-owning capitalists.

The demotic enterprises should neither recreate the bureaucratic structure of socialist co-ops nor should they be indistinguishable from capitalist firms. Thus, apart from ownership (which belongs to the *demos* rather than to capitalists or the state), the whole structure and functioning of the enterprises should be different from both capitalist and state socialist firms. There should therefore be as much decentralization as possible, both to avoid their bureaucratization and to secure as much autonomy as possible for the people working in them, within the constraints set by the community objectives.

Thus, decentralization of decision-making, within the framework of community-owned but independently run co-ops, is perhaps the best solution. In other words, the community assembly could determine social and ecological targets that the demotic enterprise would have to achieve (e.g. the proportion of revenue set aside for the achievement of the community's social and ecological goals, ecological standards to be maintained, security of employment, etc.), whereas the enterprise itself could be run like, for example, a Mondragon co-op – with some significant adjustments that would make its structures democratic. One possible way to achieve this high degree of decentralization in decision-making would be, for instance, for the community assemblies to lease the demotic enterprises to employees' collectives.

As regards the management structure in particular, the problem is usually set in terms of a conflict between managerial efficiency and employee democracy. In the Mondragon type of co-op, the emphasis is on efficiency rather than on democracy, with a limited role played by the General Assembly, which elects only one-third of the members of a Supervisory Board that, in turn, elects the managers. The managers effectively run the enterprise. The General Assembly of workers meets no more than once or twice per year. In a modified version, the General Assembly could elect half the members of the Supervisory Board, to express the employees' interest, whereas the other half could be elected by the Community Assembly, to express the general interest of the community. The members of the Supervisory Board should be people with specific knowledge of the type of production activity involved (to be able effectively to supervise the managers) and should be recallable by the respective assemblies. The Supervisory Board would in turn elect and supervise the managerial staff, which would consist of people with specialized knowledge on the line of activity involved. Their authority would therefore originate in their knowledge, which implies that no hierarchical power, other than the influence derived from their knowledge, would be tolerable against the rank and file. Finally, the workplace assembly, which should meet much more frequently than the Mondragon General Assembly, would determine which decisions would be taken by itself and which ones would be delegated to the Supervisory Board and the managers so that efficiency and democracy could be in balance.

However, it should not be forgotten that this type of demotic enterprise is useful only for a transitional period, until the economy is fully municipalized. This is so because it suffers from a serious drawback: despite the suggested amendments to satisfy the general interest, the very fact that, in a market economy system, these units would be under steady competitive pressure by capitalist firms means that the particular interest of the employees would tend to transcend the general interest of the community. That is why a community spirit is an important precondition for the creation and social functioning of these co-ops; members therefore of demotic enterprises should be bearers of such a community spirit. Another important problem with respect to demotic enterprises is that they may not be able to survive competition, especially from capitalist firms enjoying large economies of scale and significant productivity differentials. I think, however, that this problem will lose a significant part of its importance in a self-reliant economy, where demotic enterprises direct their production activity mainly to the local market. This is particularly so if we take into account that the social responsibility and satisfaction that self-reliance and democratic control enhance are guarantees of product quality. Furthermore, one could expect that the new political and economic institutions would create a new consciousness which will make citizens more resistant to pure financial incentives.

Finally, an important condition that would differentiate demotic enterprises from the Mondragon-type of co-ops and turn them into truly transitional production units in the move to an inclusive democracy is that they should produce exclusively for the local market, with the use of local resources. If instead, they start producing for the broad market outside the community, as for instance the Mondragon co-ops are doing at the moment, then a process would be initiated that would end with their absorption into the market economy, even if formally they were still called co-ops. Thus, in the Mondragon case, as even an enthusiastic supporter of them observes, the competitive pressures created by Spain's integration into the EU have led to 'strengthening the integration of co-op groups to make them more competitive with transnational competitors, expanding the highly successful retail co-op system beyond the Basque region in joint ventures with other co-ops and with non-profits that may not allow workers to become members immediately, increasing the maximum wage differential within co-ops to attract skilled technicians and managers'[37] etc.

It is therefore obvious that for demotic enterprises to be successful they should be part of a comprehensive programme to municipalize the economy – in other words, a programme whose constituent elements are self-reliance, demotic ownership and community allocation of resources. The aim of this process is to gradually shift more and more human and non-human resources away from the market economy into the new 'demotic' economy that would form the basis of an inclusive democracy. At the end of this process, the demotic enterprises would control the community's economy and would be integrated into the confederation of communities, which could then buy or expropriate privately owned big enterprises.

The transition to a confederal allocation of resources

The fundamental problem of the strategy leading to a confederal allocation of resources is how to create such institutional arrangements for economic democracy that are compatible with an institutional framework that is still a market economy. As the confederal allocation of resources was described in the previous chapter, the system involves two basic mechanisms for the allocation of resources: (a) a democratic planning mechanism for most of the macro-economic decisions; and (b) a voucher system for most of the micro-economic decisions. The voucher system, in effect, creates conditions of freedom of choice, by replacing the real market with an artificial one. It is obvious that the voucher system cannot be introduced until a full economic democracy in the form of a confederation of communities has been introduced, although steps in this direction could be taken earlier, as we saw above. However, a democratic planning system could be introduced even in the transitional period although, obviously, its decision-making scope would be seriously constrained by the market economy. Still, it could play a useful role in educating people in economic democracy and at the same time in creating the preconditions for individual and social autonomy.

But, for any democratic mechanism to be significant and to attract citizens in the decision-taking process, it is presupposed that the decisions themselves are important. The case of classical Athens shows that, as long as this condition is met, it is perfectly feasible to attract thousands of people to exercise their civic rights. Thus, as Hansen observes, 'The level of political activity exhibited by the citizens of Athens is unparalleled in world history, in terms of numbers, frequency and level of participation . . . an Assembly meeting was normally attended by 6000 citizens (out of 30,000 male citizens over eighteen), on a normal court day some 2000 citizens were selected by lot and besides the 500 members of the Council there were 700 other magistrates.'[38] It is therefore crucial that during the transition to an inclusive democracy the *demos* should be empowered with significant powers that would convert it into a coherent system of local taxation, spending and finance. Then, community assemblies (or neighbourhood assemblies, in big cities, confederated into community assemblies) could be empowered to make decisions affecting the economic life of the community, which would be implemented by the Town Council or other relevant body, after it has been converted into a body of recallable delegates.

Thus, the shift of tax power to the municipalities, which should be a basic demand of a democratic movement, would allow community assemblies to determine the amount of taxes and the way in which taxes would be charged on income, wealth, land and energy use, as well as on consumption. Community assemblies could, at annual intervals, meet and discuss various proposals about the level of taxation for the year to come, in relation to the way the money collected by the municipality should be spent. This way, community assemblies would start taking over the fiscal powers of the state, as far as their communities are concerned, although in the transitional period, until the confederation of communities replaces the state, they would also be subject to the state fiscal powers.

Similar measures can be taken as regards the present state powers with respect to the allocation of financial resources. The introduction of a demotic banking system, in combination with demotic currencies, will give significant power to community assemblies to determine the allocation of financial resources in the implementation of the community's objectives (creating new enterprises, meeting ecological targets, etc.)

Finally, assemblies would have significant powers in determining the allocation of resources in the municipalized sector of the community, namely, the demotic enterprises and the demotic welfare system. As a first step, community assemblies could introduce a voucher scheme with respect to social services. At a later stage, when a significant number of communities have joined the confederation of inclusive democracies, community assemblies could expand the voucher system to cover *basic* needs of all citizens, at the beginning, in parallel with the market economy – until the latter is phased out.

In concluding this chapter, nobody should have any illusions that the implementation of a transitional strategy to economic democracy will not receive a hard time from the elites controlling the state machine and the market economy. However, as long as the level of consciousness of a majority in the population has been raised to adopt the principles included in a programme for an inclusive democracy – and the majority of the population has every interest in supporting such a programme today – I think that the above proposals are perfectly feasible, although of course there may be significant local variations from country to country and from area to area, depending on local conditions. Without underestimating the difficulties involved in the context of today's all-powerful methods of brain control and economic violence which, in fact, might prove more effective methods than pure state violence in suppressing a movement for an inclusive democracy, I think that the proposed strategy is a realistic strategy on the way to a new society.

Notes

1. Peter Marshall, *Nature's Web, an Exploration of Ecological Thinking* (London: Simon & Schuster, 1992).
2. See, for instance, David Pepper, *Eco-Socialism: From Deep Ecology to Social Justice* (London: Routledge, 1993), p. 199.
3. For a graphic description of the recruitment of private guards from the underclass to 'deal' with the Green activists protesting against the partial destruction of a forest so that the Newbury bypass could be constructed in Britain, see John Vidal, *The Guardian* (25 Jan. 1996).
4. See Ted Trainer, *The Conserver Society: Alternatives for Sustainability* (London: Zed Press, 1995).
5. Ted Trainer, *The Conserver Society*, p. 220.
6. Murray Bookchin, 'Libertarian municipalism: an overview', *Society and Nature*, Vol. 1, No. 1 (1992) p. 102.
7. Murray Bookchin, 'Communalism: the democratic dimension of anarchism', *Democracy and Nature* (formerly *Society and Nature*), Vol. 3, No. 2 (1996).
8. Murray Bookchin and Dave Foreman, *Defending the Earth, A Debate Between Murray Bookchin and Dave Foreman* (Montreal: Black Rose Books, 1991), pp. 61–2.
9. Murray Bookchin, 'Libertarian municipalism: an overview', p. 102.
10. David Pepper, *Eco-Socialism*, p. 200.
11. Roy Morrison, *Ecological Democracy* (Boston: South End Press, 1995), p. 25.
12. Roy Morrison, *Ecological Democracy*, pp. 8–9.
13. Roy Morrison, *Ecological Democracy*, p. 25.
14. Roy Morrison, *Ecological Democracy*, p. 9.
15. See Janet Biehl's book review of Kirkpatrick Sale, *Rebels Against the Future: The Luddites and Their War on the Industrial Revolution, Lessons for the Computer Age* (Reading, MA: Addison-Wesley, 1995) in *Green Perspectives*, No. 36 (Feb. 1996), p. 8.
16. Roy Morrison, *Ecological Democracy*, p. 12.
17. Roy Morrison, *Ecological Democracy*, pp. 138–40.
18. Roy Morrison, *Ecological Democracy*, pp. 14–15.
19. Roy Morrison, *Ecological Democracy*, p. 22.
20. Roy Morrison, *Ecological Democracy*, p. 144.
21. Roy Morrison, *Ecological Democracy*, p. 161.

22. Takis Fotopoulos, 'The economic foundations of an ecological society', *Society and Nature*, Vol. 1, No. 3 (1993).
23. David Pepper, *Modern Environmentalism* (London: Routledge, 1996), p. 321.
24. Howard Hawkins, *The Greens Bulletin* (April 1992), pp. 27–30.
25. Murray Bookchin, *Post-Scarcity Anarchism* (London: Wildwood House, 1971), p. 217.
26. Cornelius Castoriadis, *Philosophy, Politics, Autonomy* (Oxford: Oxford University Press, 1991), p. 204.
27. See Murray Bookchin, 'The ghost of anarcho-syndicalism', *Anarchist Studies*, Vol. 1, No. 1 (Spring 1993).
28. I would mention, indicatively, the significant works on the subject by James Robertson; see, e.g., his article 'Economics of local recovery' in *Society and Nature*, Vol. 1, No. 1 (1992), and his book *Future Wealth* (London: Cassell, 1989), Ch. 5. See also Paul Ekins, *Trade for Mutual Self-Reliance,* (London: TOES Publication, 1989), *Local Economic Self-Reliance* (London: TOES Publication, 1988); Johan Galtung's contribution in *The Living Economy,* Paul Ekins (ed.) (New York: Routledge & Kegan Paul, 1986), pp. 97–109; and C. George Benello *et al., Building Sustainable Communities* (New York: Bootstrap, 1989), Chs 18–20.
29. See, for instance, the Homegrown Economy Project in the city of Saint Paul, Minnesota, mentioned by James Robertson, which uses a number of comprehensive criteria to enhance the local economy in the process of founding new enterprises and supporting old ones (J. Robertson, *Future Wealth* (London: Cassell, 1989), p. 43) and similar experiments in Bologne, Bremen, etc., which I have mentioned elsewhere, for example, *Eleftherotypia* (22 Sept. 1990).
30. See for a description of the LETS system, Ross V.G. Dobson, *Bringing the Economy Home from the Market* (Montreal: Black Rose, 1993).
31. Murray Bookchin, 'Comments on the international social ecology network gathering and the "deep social ecology" of John Clark', *Democracy and Nature* Vol. 3, No. 3 (1996).
32. Takis Fotopoulos, *Dependent Development: The Case of Greece* (Athens: Exantas Press, 1985 and 1987).
33. For instance, in Australian aboriginal communities, but also in the UK where a self-planned, self-built settlement was developed in Shropshire. For further developments on the Community Land Trusts, see C. George Benello *et al., Building Sustainable Communities,* Part 1.
34. See M.A. Lutz and K. Lux, *Humanistic Economics* (New York: Bootstrap, 1988), pp. 263–8.
35. See Will Hutton, *The Guardian* (1 June 1992).
36. See, e.g., V. Anderson's *Alternative Economic Indicators* (New York: Routledge & Kegan Paul, 1991).
37. Roy Morrison, *Ecological Democracy*, p. 154.
38. Mogens Herman Hansen, *The Athenian Democracy in the Age of Demosthenes* (Oxford: Blackwell, 1991), p. 313.

PART III

Towards a Democractic Rationalism

CHAPTER 8

How Do We Justify the Project for an Inclusive Democracy?

In this chapter, the foundations of 'objectivity' in both its positivist and dialectical versions will be examined, and the feasibility, as well as the desirability, of grounding the project for an inclusive democracy on an 'objective' theoretical system will be questioned. The question that arises here is whether there is in fact a genuine dilemma in attempting to justify the democratic project, a dilemma that forces us to choose between either a modernist 'objectivist' approach or a post-modernist subjectivist approach.

The choice of the former implies that, following the *modernist* tradition, in order to justify the need for an inclusive democracy, we have to rely on *objective* theories and methods, i.e. on procedures that are valid, irrespective of our expectations, wishes, attitudes and ideas. The implicit argument in favour of such an approach is that such theories and methods reflect in fact 'objective processes' at work in society or the natural world. However, as I will try to show in this chapter, the choice of an 'objectivist' method to justify the need for an inclusive democracy is both problematic and undesirable. It is problematic because few still believe today, after the decisive introduction in twentieth-century science of the uncertainty principle and chaos theory, that it is still possible to derive any 'objective' laws or 'tendencies' of social change. If cause and effect can be uncertain even in physics, the most exact of sciences, and the reference to necessary and universal laws is disputed even with respect to the natural world, it is obvious that postulating objective laws or tendencies that can be applied to society is absurd. It is *undesirable* because, as the case of the socialist project has shown, there is a definite link between the 'scientification' of that project in the hands of Marxists–Leninists and the consequent bureau-cratization of socialist politics and the totalitarian transformation of social organization.

But, if modernist objectivism seems problematical and undesirable, this does not mean that post-modernist subjectivism is less problematical, as it

305

may easily lead to general relativism and irrationalism, if not to complete abandonment of radical politics. Thus, adopting the post-modern 'generalized conformism',[1] in effect, implies the abandonment of any idea of a liberatory project under the (miserable) pretext of letting 'polyphony' flourish and under the (right) banner that 'politics, rightly understood, is firmly *subjective*'.[2]

My aim in this chapter is to attempt to show that the above dilemma is, in fact, a false one. Today, it is possible to define a liberatory project for an inclusive democracy without recourse to controversial objective grounds or to post-modern neo-conservatism. If we define freedom and the liberatory project in terms of the demand for social and individual autonomy,[3] as we did in Chapter 5, we do so because we responsibly choose autonomy, as well as its expression in democracy, and we explicitly rule out the possibility of establishing any 'objective' laws, processes or tendencies which, inevitably, or 'rationally', lead to the fulfilment of the autonomy project. However, once we have chosen, broadly, the content of the liberatory project, some definite implications follow regarding our interpretation and assessment of social reality. In other words, the very definition of a liberatory project conditions the 'way of seeing' and criticizing social reality.

In the first part of this chapter, the claim of objectivity of the 'orthodox' epistemological tradition (empiricism/positivism and rationalism) is questioned, at least as far as the interpretation of social reality is concerned. The decisive influence of power relations in the interpretation of social phenomena is reflected in the much lower degree of intersubjectivity that characterizes social versus natural sciences. Next, the objectivity claim of the alternative tradition, dialectics, is considered with respect to two major applications in the interpretation of social reality, dialectical materialism and dialectical naturalism, and it is concluded that it is neither feasible nor desirable to derive a general theory of social 'evolution' on the basis of an 'objective' interpretation of social or natural history. Finally, in the last section it is argued that the liberatory project for an inclusive democracy can only be based on a democratic rationalism which transcends 'scientism' and irrationalism as well as general relativism.

The myth of objectivity: orthodox 'objectivity'
The first question arising in any attempt to 'objectivize' an interpretation of social reality refers to the methodology used in this process. The term 'methodology' is taken here in the broad sense of the philosophy of science – as an investigation of the concepts, theories, assumptions and criteria of assessing them. The concerns with methodology have, of course, a long history in the debates between orthodox social scientists on the one hand

and Marxist theorists on the other, and it has recently reappeared, explicitly or implicitly, in the debates within the Green movement. Thus, it can be shown that significant disagreements between various streams in the Green movement are due to methodological differences with respect to the way 'reality' is seen. Such differences sometimes make even the very communication between the Green currents extremely difficult, if not impossible (see, e.g., the debate between social ecologists and deep ecologists). It is therefore of crucial importance to clarify the methodological issues involved in the current debates.

Any attempt to objectivize the interpretation of social reality either takes the existing socio-economic order for granted, implicitly aiming at the justification of its reproduction (as 'orthodox' social 'scientists' do) or discards it, explicitly aiming at drastic social transformation (as radical theorists do). For reasons that I will develop later in this chapter, it can be shown that the concepts of objectivity developed within the two main traditions in the philosophy of science, the empiricist/positivist tradition and the dialectical one, have an intrinsic relationship to the above aims of social analysis. The conception of objectivity developed by empiricists/positivists (orthodox 'objectivity') is most amenable to a kind of 'objective' interpretation of social reality that takes the existing social-economic system for granted, and, vice versa, the conception of objectivity developed by dialectical philosophers (dialectical 'objectivity') is most suited to an effort to justify a radical transformation of society.

An immediate question which arises here is whether dialectics can be seen as a 'method'. Dialectical philosophers like Murray Bookchin disagree with the conception of dialectics as a method on the grounds that 'it distorts the very meaning of dialectic to speak of it as a "method" [since] it is an ongoing protest against the myth of "methodology": notably that "techniques" for thinking out a process can be separated from the process itself'.[4]

However, even if we see the dialectical approach principally as an ontological logic, this does not negate the fact that this approach, in assessing the truth value of theories, does use a set of concepts, categories and criteria which are very different from those used by positivists and that, in this sense, it is *also* a method. Furthermore, the very fact that, even today, contemporary dialecticians in very different traditions (e.g. Marxism and social ecology) use the dialectical approach to elucidate the same realm of reality (social evolution) and in the process derive very different conclusions at the interpretational and ethical levels is a clear indication that dialectics is being used *and* as a method.

Coming now to the orthodox epistemological tradition, the main streams in this tradition are rationalism and empiricism/positivism with its later versions of falsificationism and 'scientific research programmes'. A brief outline of these currents in the orthodox tradition may be useful in understanding the methodological differences among various schools of social thought in their endeavour to interpret social reality.

Rationalism versus empiricism/positivism

Rationalism mainly flourished in continental Europe (Descartes, Spinoza, Leibniz, Wolff *et al.*), whereas empiricism (Bacon, Hume, Berkeley), with its descendants of positivism (classical and logical) and falsificationism, has always been dominant in Britain and the USA. Rationalists as well as empiricists share a common pursuit of certainty in knowledge, that is, of truths that are certain because they are necessary. It is for this reason that in both traditions it is possible to speak of proof. Still, rationalists and empiricists differed between themselves, both as regards the source of truth and as regards the procedure to be employed in grounding knowledge on these truths. Rationalists find the source of truth in 'reason', whereas empiricists/positivists find it in sense-data, the 'facts'.

These differences, in turn, reflect different theories of truth. Thus, rationalism reflects a coherence theory of truth,[5] according to which the criterion of truth is coherence with other propositions or judgements, something consistent with the deductive method of analysis. The foundation for this criterion of truth is the belief in the impossibility of developing a 'neutral' language, that is, a language not dependent on a particular theoretical system or conception of reality. Therefore, as there is no neutral way of comparing reality with out judgements, all that we can do is to compare one set of judgements with others. Knowledge, in other words, is conceptually mediated, and objectivity can only be established within a particular conceptual framework. This has two important implications. First, the incommensurability of rival theories, as well as their inferences, is the consequence of different assumptions/axioms used. Second, that any selection among such theories is based eventually on non-scientific criteria.

So, there is no objective way of demonstrating the superiority of one theoretical system (in explaining reality) over another when both systems are internally consistent and coherent. If, for instance, both the Marxist and the neo-classical theories of value can be shown to be internally consistent and coherent, then there is no 'objective' way to demonstrate the superiority of one over the other. For rationalists, therefore, knowledge of the world inevitably involves a priori truths, namely, truths which are not inductive generalizations from experience, but are virtually innate and, therefore, in no need of empirical confirmation. By pure reasoning, rationalists argue, we can arrive at substantial knowledge about the nature of the world, through the use of concepts and propositions, where the connection between subject and predicate is necessary. The rationalists' ideal was 'a deductive system of truths, analogous to a mathematical system, but at the same time capable of increasing our factual information ... a system of deducible truths [that] can be considered as the self-unfolding of the reason itself'.[6]

It was in reaction to rationalism's a priori and subjective character of knowledge that the alternative tradition of empiricism developed. Empiricism reflects a completely different theory of truth, a correspondence theory, according to which the criterion of truth is correspondence with fact, although, as modern versions of the theory have shown, it is certainly not always the case that every statement can be correlated with a fact.[7] Experience therefore becomes the necessary basis for all our knowledge, and as factual knowledge is based on perception, we cannot obtain factual knowledge by a priori reasoning. All a priori propositions are analytic ones (where the concept of the predicate is contained in the concept of the subject) true by definition, so that their denial involves a contradiction. As such, they do not claim knowledge of the world, they are not truths about matters of fact. On the other hand, all synthetic propositions (where the predicate is not contained in the subject) are a posteriori; i.e. the connection between subject and predicate is not and cannot be necessary.

Still, not all synthetic propositions are a posteriori. Some are a priori, independent of experience. Thus, as Kant first emphasized, concepts like that of causality (the truth that every event has a cause) are necessary truths and yet afford information about the world, in some sense quite independent of experience. More important, perception is not just an unconscious process. As, for instance, Kuhn[8] points out, perception itself, though unconscious, is conditioned by the nature and amount of prior experience and education. There are therefore no 'brute facts': all facts are theory-laden, and perception is always concept-dependent. But, as any meaningful talk about knowledge founded on sense-data presupposes that language is neutral, the lack of such a language implies that the empiricist position is untenable, since sense-data are not independent of our knowledge of the world.

However, in spite of the attacks by rationalists, Kantians/neo-Kantians, Marxists, relativists and others, empiricism, in its various forms, has become the dominant epistemology among orthodox social scientists – a process that was helped enormously by the success of natural sciences and the corresponding rise of scientism. It was, in particular, during the emergence of what could be called the 'scientific-industrial complex' that

Comte's philosophy of (classical) positivism – the next step in the evolution of empiricism – began dominating social sciences. Comtean positivism introduced the well-known fact/value dichotomy, a dichotomy to be used widely by orthodox social scientists in their effort to develop a neutral, 'value-free' science of the economy, or society in general. Still, the introduction of the fact/value dichotomy, far from creating the conditions for a 'value-free' science of society, not only helped enormously in creating the myth of scientific 'objectivity' but, also, as Murray Bookchin observes, denied speculative philosophy the right to reason from the 'what is' to the 'what-should-be', i.e. its right to become a valid account of reality in its 'truth'.[9]

Orthodox social scientists were helped enormously in their effort to develop a 'science' of the economy and society by two parallel developments: first, the advent of logical positivism and, second, significant advances in the theory of testing hypotheses in the 1930s and 1940s that made possible the application of empirical testing procedures in the study of social phenomena, i.e. phenomena that, by nature, are not subject to experiment. In fact, logical positivism, which became dominant in the orthodox philosophy of science at about the same time that the developments in statistics were taking place, explicitly asserted the doctrine of *methodological monism*, that is, that all sciences, natural or social, could and should use the same method.

Logical positivism, initially expressed by a group of philosophers – subsequently known as the Vienna Circle – which included M. Schlick, R. Carnap and others, claimed to produce a synthesis between the two epistemological traditions, that is, between the deductive and a priori rationalism on the one hand, and the inductive and a posteriori empiricism on the other. Still, logical positivism is more firmly founded in the emperical tradition, as is obvious from the fact that its main theses are well within the empiricist tradition. This applies, in particular, to the thesis that a theory must be verifiable to be scientific, namely, that it must not contain metaphysical statements and value judgements. It also applies to the thesis that the primary source of knowledge is considered to be (once more) observation, or sense-experience; reason is merely mediating as a logical check on the coherence between hypotheses and their implications.

However, although logical positivism, by insisting on verifiable truths, definitely represented an improvement and, at the same time, a retreat, with respect to the extreme empiricist position of a belief in proven truths, it still suffered from serious weaknesses. I would mention here just three of the criticisms raised against it. Thus, first, the Carnapian proposition, that although scientific theories are equally unprovable, still, they have different degrees of probability relative to available evidence, was shown by Karl

Popper to be untenable on the grounds that under very general conditions, all theories, whatever the evidence, can be shown to be not only equally unprovable, but, also, equally improbable.[10] Second, as there is no specification whatsoever of the number of tests a theory has to pass in order to be verified, the question arises as to how we know that the regularity established today will also be valid tomorrow. Finally, as Katouzian points out, the two most important criteria of logical positivism (verifiability/ verification) are normative (as they have not been verified themselves) and normative statements, according to the principles of logical positivism, are simply tautologies. Logical positivism, therefore, far from providing an objective methodology, became an ideology 'inhibiting the growth of knowledge and serving the interest of the status quo'.[11]

Falsificationism and scientific research programmes (SRP)

The weaknesses of logical positivism led to another version of empiricism, falsificationism, which represents a further retreat from the original empiricist position. The demarcation criterion of what is scientific now changes from verifiability/verification to falsifiability/falsification. It is therefore explicitly recognized that theories are equally unprovable/ improbable, but, still, they may not be equally disprovable: a finite number of observations can disprove a theory, so that empirical counter-evidence becomes the one and only arbiter in assessing a theory. However, even this further retreat from empiricism did not produce a tenable thesis. Sophisticated falsificationists (like Karl Popper in his later writings, Lakatos and others) rejected this form of 'dogmatic falsificationism', as they called it, on the basis that it rested on false assumptions and a too narrow demarcation criterion between scientific and non-scientific.

The false assumptions were, first, that we can distinguish between theoretical and factual propositions. Such an assumption, however, is based on the belief that non-theory-laden facts do exist. Second, that propositions satisfying the criterion of being factual are true – an assumption implying that factual propositions can be proved from an experiment. But as Lakatos[12] emphasizes: 'We cannot prove theories and we cannot disprove them either; the demarcation criterion between the soft, unproven "theories" and the hard proven "empirical basis" is non-existent: all propositions of science are theoretical and incurably fallible.' Finally, the falsificationist demarcation criterion is so narrow that it would leave out of science the most admired scientific theories, which can easily be shown to be neither provable nor disprovable. Thus, as Lakatos pointedly noticed, acceptance of the falsificationist criterion would mean that all probabilistic theories, together with Newton's, Maxwell's and Einstein's theories, would have to be rejected as unscientific, since no finite number of observations could ever disprove them.[13]

The next development in the empiricist/positivist tradition was the Lakatosian approach of Scientific Research Programmes (SRP), which were defined as sets, first, of hard-core hypotheses or propositions that are not subject to the falsification process and, second, of less fundamental auxiliary hypotheses forming a 'protective belt' around this core, which are the proper object of testing and amendment. Lakatos, starting from the position that scientific theories are not only equally unprovable/ improbable but also equally undisprovable, attempted to provide some scientific standards (a demarcation criterion) which, though founded again on some sort of empirical basis, still, would not be subject to the inflexibility characterizing 'dogmatic' or 'naive' falsificationism. Thus, he changed the demarcation criterion so that the empirical basis was no longer required to prevent the disproval of a theory, but just to make possible its rejection. A theory may therefore be falsified and still remain true. Also, a non-falsifiable theory can now become falsifiable by specify- ing certain rejection rules in advance. That would allow probabilistic theories back into the scientific fold, provided the scientist specifies the rejection rules that would render the statistical evidence found inconsistent with the theory. Finally, whereas for the 'naive' falsificationist any theory which can be interpreted as experimentally falsifiable is acceptable/ scientific, for Lakatos, a theory, or, better, an SRP, is acceptable/scientific if it has corroborated excess empirical content over its rival, that is, if it leads to the discovery of novel facts.

Lakatos therefore claimed that he had solved the problem of objective criteria that so much bothered the orthodox philosophy of science. An SRP, including its untestable hard core, could be rejected, 'objectively', using normal testing procedures. However, as Feyerabend[14] points out, the standards that Lakatos offered are, in fact, vacuous because they neither specify any time limit over which the 'excess' empirical content of an SRP should be verified, nor could they possibly do so, if return to naive falsificationism was to be avoided. That is why, Feyerabend concludes, Lakatos seems to retain these (supposedly permanent) standards, 'a verbal ornament, a memorial to happier times when it was still thought possible to run a complex and often catastrophic business like science by following a few simple and "rational" rules'.[15]

Objectivity versus intersubjectivity
It is clear that orthodox philosophers of science have failed to provide criteria either of 'proven' truth (the truth of rationalists and classical empiricists) or of 'provable/verifiable' truth (the logical positivists' truth)

or even of truth based on permanent falsificationist standards (the Lakatosian truth). Therefore, as 'the requirements [for objectivity] were gradually weakened until they disappeared into thin air',[16] the 'Kuhnian revolution' brought the power relation into orthodox epistemology through the adoption of the relativistic position of 'truth by consensus'. What is 'scientific' or 'objectively true' becomes a function of the degree of intersubjectivity, that is, of the degree of consensus achieved among the theorists in a particular discipline. Objectivity, of course, implies intersubjectivity, but the opposite is not true. Intersubjectivity simply means:

> a common framework against the background of which people can communicate [so that] . . . what counts as fact depends on how we have come to see the world and upon the conceptual structure that is presupposed in our seeing it in this way.[17]

All this brings us to the concept of 'scientific paradigm' that was developed by Thomas Kuhn. The concept of paradigm has been used (and abused) extensively in its 30-year history. Part, at least, of the blame for the abuse can be attributed to the father of the concept himself since, as Masterman[18] observes, the term is used in Kuhn's book in at least 22 different ways! In its broadest sense, which is the most useful one for the purposes of our discussion, paradigm refers to the 'entire constellation of beliefs, values, techniques and so on shared by the members of a given community'.[19] Although Kuhn in his later writings,[20] under pressure from Popperians, Lakatos *et al.*, seems to be retreating in his definition of the scope of the paradigm concept and ends up with a narrower concept, rather similar to the Lakatosian SRP, I believe it is the broad sense that is the most original one. Anyway, this is the version that, as Blaug[21] observes, is predominantly retained by most readers of his book. In this broad sense, the paradigm includes not only a theory, or even a set of theories, but also a world view, a way of seeing the object of study, which in turn is conditioned by the overall world view of scientists, i.e. the set of shared beliefs about the individual's relationship to the natural world and to other humans in society. Further, the concept contains a set of admissible problems to be solved, as well as the methods to achieve legitimate problem-solutions. A paradigm, in this sense, is a tradition.[22] For example, the eco-Marxist paradigm differs from the liberal-environmentalist one, not just because each uses a different theory to explain the ecological problems (and therefore suggests different solutions), but also because each uses different methods (concepts, assumptions, criteria of assessing theories) – all these differences based, in the last instance, on different world views.

It is therefore obvious that the paradigm concept, in its broad sense, is

313

much broader than the Lakatosian SRP. This has very important implications with respect to the issue of objectivity criteria. As the very criteria for assessing the paradigm-based normal scientific activity (the Lakatosian protective belt) are part of the paradigm, any 'objective' comparison of paradigms is impossible. Thus, as Kuhn puts it:

> The choice between competing paradigms cannot be determined merely by the evaluative procedures characteristic of normal science, for these depend in part upon a particular paradigm and that paradigm is at issue.[23]

This means that any incommensurability between paradigms, as a result of differences about the list of admissible problems – due to different world views – or about the methods to solve these problems and the criteria to use in choosing between these methods, is an absolute one. People sharing different paradigms 'live in different worlds', see different things or things in a different relation to one another and can only shift from one paradigm to another in a *gestalt*-switch that converts them from adherents of one way of seeing things to another. This is inevitable as soon as we accept that there are no objective criteria which are not paradigm-dependent for choosing among paradigms. Therefore, scientists (or theorists in general), by adopting a paradigm, in fact adopt a 'package deal' consisting of theories, facts that fit them, a world view *and* criteria to assess them. Thus, the paradigm notion implies the non-existence of objectivity: there are neither tradition-independent truths (a material notion of objectivity), nor tradition-independent *ways of finding* truths (a formal notion of objectivity).[24]

In this paradigmatic view of science, the scientific 'maturity' of a discipline and the amount of 'truths' produced by the respective scientific community depend on the degree of intersubjectivity achieved among its practitioners over a specific time period. The fact, therefore, that, historically, there is a crucial difference in the degree and type of intersubjectivity that has been achieved among social and natural scientists is very important with respect to the 'status' of their respective disciplines. Furthermore, there is a very significant difference in the degree of success the two types of science have historically enjoyed in explaining their object of study, that is, social and natural phenomena, respectively. But these differences do not arise out of 'exogenous' factors; they arise from the object of study itself – a fact that has important implications for the question of whether the liberatory project can be objectivized.

To illustrate these differences, let us take the example of economics, which is considered to be the hardest 'science'[25] among social sciences, mainly because of its greater ability to quantify the relations it studies. For more than 100 years after the publication of *Das Capital,* two economics paradigms, based on radically different world views and traditions, divided the economics profession: the Marxist versus the 'orthodox' paradigm. I make this division on the assumption that, despite the significant differences between the various schools of thought (especially those in the orthodox camp, i.e. neo-classicals, Ricardians, Keynesians, monetarists, etc.), still, there is a fundamental common characteristic in the respective groups of theories: all orthodox theories take the market economy system for granted, whereas all Marxist theories see capitalism as a historical phase in the evolution of human society. Out of this fundamental difference arise all other differences between orthodox and Marxist theories with respect to concepts and methods to be used in the analysis of economic phenomena.

One could possibly argue that the criteria that economic theorists used in choosing between the two main paradigms were not mainly scientific. In fact, it was social factors, that is, factors directly linked with their own object of study (economy/society), that played a crucial role in this choice. Thus, the institutional framework, within which economists functioned in connection with their own social position and career ambitions, as well as the way they perceive themselves in society, conditioned their social, political and moral preconceptions. In other words, social factors, like the ones mentioned, conditioned their world view, on the basis of which their paradigm choice was made. As regards the institutional framework in particular, it is not accidental that before the collapse of 'existing socialism', the dominant (i.e., the one most widely accepted) paradigm in the Western and Eastern scientific communities used to be the orthodox and the Marxist ones, respectively. After the collapse of these regimes, there was a massive conversion of economists all over the world to the orthodox paradigm. However, as the collapse itself has nothing to do with the Marxist paradigm's analysis of the market economy, it is clear that the present worldwide domination of the orthodox paradigm is unconnected to any scientific criteria which supposedly demonstrate its superiority over the competing Marxist paradigm, and it simply reflects the incommensurability between the two paradigms and the lack of any scientific criteria to choose objectively between them.

It is therefore obvious that the object of study plays a much more important role in social than in natural sciences, with respect to determining the choice of a paradigm. This is due to the fact that the social theorist's world view cannot possibly be separated from his object of study – society. Furthermore, given the social divisions characterizing a hierarchical (or heteronomous) society, there is an inevitable division among social theorists, particularly with respect to the fundamental question of whether they should take for granted the existing social system in their theoretical work.

The fact that no similar inevitable division could arise among natural scientists, combined with the possibility of experiment that is available in the natural sciences, could go a long way towards explaining the much higher degree of intersubjectivity that natural sciences have traditionally enjoyed over social sciences in interpreting their object of study. Finally, the above facts could easily explain why natural sciences are characterized as more mature than social sciences. It is obvious that this is related to the higher degree of intersubjectivity that can *actually* be achieved at a given time and place among natural scientists compared to the relatively lower degree of intersubjectivity that can *potentially* be achieved among social scientists.

The myth of objectivity: dialectical 'objectivity'

As is obvious from the above discussion, the orthodox philosophy of science has been unable to solve what has been called the 'problem of method', that is, the problem of establishing objective criteria in assessing theories. Still, for those adopting the dialectical method of analysis, the problem is non-existent, since, for them, 'techniques' for thinking out a process cannot be separated from the process itself. A useful way of introducing the dialectical approach would perhaps be to start with Kant's contribution that exerted significant influence on it.

Although the Kantian system was intended to supersede both continental rationalism and British empiricism, history did not vindicate this intention. Nevertheless, Kantianism can be considered as a synthesis (in the Hegelian sense) of the other two traditions, that is, as an original system subsuming both of them. In the Kantian system, knowledge is seen as founded not just on pure reason, nor simply on sense-data, but on both. Thus, the truth of propositions can only be assessed with reference to the categories we use, which are methodical rules of an entirely a priori nature, that is, independent of experience. The categories, therefore, are the conditions of knowledge; although by themselves they give no knowledge of objects, they serve to make empirical knowledge possible. Things cannot be known except through the medium of categories which, created by the mind, assume the function of synthesizing the sense-data.

The importance, however, of Kant in the alternative philosophy of science is that, for the first time, a philosopher attains in his system of knowledge one of the most important dialectical oppositions: between empiricism and totality, between form and content, a theme that was later expanded by Hegel and Marx. This is achieved, according to Goldmann,[26] through the development of the idea of totality. Thus, we may distinguish three philosophical traditions with respect to their world views about the fundamental category of human existence:

- First, the individualist/atomist tradition (Descartes, Leibniz, Locke, Hume, Vienna Circle *et al.*), where the world view adopted sees the *individual* as the principal category of human existence. Society, according to this view, is a set of interactions among autonomous individuals.
- Second, the holistic tradition (Schelling, Bergson, Heidegger *et al.*), where the world view adopted sees the *whole* as the fundamental category of human existence. The part here exists only as a necessary means for the existence of the whole, and the autonomous individual becomes the exception within the system (the leader, the hero, etc.).
- Finally, the tradition which uses as its principal category the concept of *totality* in its two main forms of the universe and the human community. The totality differs from the whole of the holistic world view because the former is a contradictory whole. Thus, as Goldmann puts it:

The parts [of the totality] presuppose for their possibility their union in the whole; the autonomy of the parts and the reality of the whole are not only reconciled but constitute reciprocal conditions; in place therefore of the partial and one-sided solutions of the individual or the collective, there appears the only total solution, that of the person and the human community.[27]

The concept of totality is a fundamental category of the dialectical method because, according to dialectical philosophers, it not only allows us to see a number of important contradictions in knowledge and social reality, but it may also be used to resolve the contradictions between theory and practice, the individual and the community. Thus, using the concept of totality in its two main forms, we may see the following dialectical contradictions:

- The contradiction between the parts and the whole in knowledge: the parts can only be seen through the whole which envelops them, whereas the whole can only be seen through factual knowledge of the parts.
- The contradiction between individuals and society: individuals can only be seen through society, whereas society can only be seen through knowledge of individuals. The motor of change is contradiction between parts whose tension transforms the totality itself. Society, therefore, cannot be seen as a set of interactions among autonomous individuals. In fact, it is exactly because empiricists/positivists deny the existence of any totality (theoretical or practical) and concentrate instead on atomic propositions that they cannot unite the whole with the individual. Thus, by assuming that knowledge is constructed by factual connections, they rule out a theoretical totality. Also, by adopting the fact/value dichotomy which implies that 'what is' – the positive element

– has always to be distinguished from 'what should be' – the normative element – they exclude a practical totality.

• The dialectical contradiction between the real given and the possible: a contradiction arising out of the conception of reality as a goal, something to be achieved by action. As such, totality unites theory and practice, the individual and the community. This is in contrast not only to empiricism/positivism but, also, to rationalism, which is equally dualistic and creates an artificial division between subject and object, theory and practice.

The dialectical conception of objectivity

However, the contradiction between the real given and the possible does not just refer to the conception of reality as a goal. In fact, if we use a broader understanding of this particular contradiction, we may see clearly the fundamental differences between the orthodox and the dialectical conceptions of 'objectivity'. As dialectical philosophers argue, the contradiction between the real given and the possible adds two important dimensions in the way we see reality: the historical and the ethical dimension.

Thus, unlike positivism, which, lacking any historical dimension, focuses on appearances, the dialectical approach, seeing the potentiality as historical possibility, may examine the hidden causes of empirical phenomena, the essence behind the appearances. Furthermore, the dialectical approach can be used to derive an 'objective' ethics. Thus, whereas for empiricists reality is 'what is', for dialecticians reality is 'what should be', given the potentialities latent in development. So, 'what is' should always be assessed in terms of what it could potentially become. This implies that while reality for empiricists is factual and structural, for dialectical philosophers it is processual. The very meaning of a 'fact' is therefore very different in the dialectical method, since it consists not just of a set of immutable boundaries but, instead, of a set of fluid boundaries *and* its mode of becoming; in other words, it includes the past, the present and its future.

Therefore, the concept of objectivity in dialectics takes on a very different meaning from the traditional notion of objectivity in empiricism/positivism. What is 'objectively true' is not what corresponds to facts/what can be verified or, alternatively, what cannot be falsified/rejected, on the basis of an appeal to sense-data, which, anyway, can only give information about 'what is'. Instead, what is 'objectively true' in dialectics is, as Bookchin puts it, 'the very process of becoming – including what a phenomenon has been, what it is and what, given the logic of its potentialities, it will be, if its potentialities are actualized'.[28] In this sense, the dialectical 'real' is even more 'real' than the empiricist one; it expresses the logical implications of the potential – it is the realization of the potential, the rational. As a consequence of the fundamental differences between the orthodox and the dialectical conceptions of objectivity, the criteria of assessing the truth value of the theories derived from the use of the respective methods are, also, very different. Thus, as Bookchin stresses: 'The kind of verification that validates or invalidates the soundness of dialectical reasoning, in turn, must be *developmental*, not relatively static or for that matter "fluctuating" kinds of phenomena.'[29]

The dialectical method's historical and ethical dimensions introduce a high degree of compatibility between it and radical analyses proposing an alternative form of social organization. The dialectical approach, by distinguishing between the real 'given' and what 'should be', offers itself as an 'objective' justification of a liberatory project, both from the historical and the ethical points of view. It is not surprising therefore that the dialectical approach has been used by radical philosophers, from Marx to Bookchin, to justify 'objectively' the need for an alternative society, a socialist or an ecological society, respectively. By the same token, the orthodox philosophy of science provides a concept of objectivity that can be used in an 'objective' justification of the status quo. Thus, empiricism/positivism, especially when used in the analysis of social phenomena, may offer an 'objective' justification of 'what is', simply by draining social development off its historical or moral content.

Needless to add that the incommensurability between the orthodox and the dialectical conceptions of objectivity implies a corresponding incommensurability between the orthodox paradigms in social sciences and the ones based on the dialectical method. As Murray Bookchin puts it: 'For analytical logic, the premises of dialectical logic are nonsense; for dialectical logic, the premises of analytical logic ossify facticity into hardened, immutable logical "atoms"'.[30]

However, the dialectical approach is also unable to solve the problem of 'objectivity', as the following discussion will attempt to show. Mainly, this is because for reality to be assimilated by dialectical thought, the condition is that it should be dialectical in form and evolution and therefore rational. This means that a dialectic has to *postulate* the rationality of the world and of history at the very moment when this rationality is a theoretical, as well as a practical, problem.[31] As Castoriadis puts it:

The operative postulate that there is a total and 'rational' (and therefore 'meaningful') order in the world, along with the necessary implication that there is an order of human affairs linked to the order of the world – what one could call unitary ontology – has plagued political philosophy from Plato, through liberalism and Marxism. The postulate conceals the fundamental fact that human history is creation – without which there would be no genuine question of judging and choosing, either 'objectively' or 'subjectively'.[32]

In fact, the dialectical approach suffers no less than the orthodox approach from what Hindess and Hirst[33] call the 'epistemological fallacy', that is, the construction of an a priori core of concepts, *assuming* their own conditions of validity. This is, of course, a position which easily brings to mind the Kuhnian position that a paradigm contains its own criteria of validity. But, let us examine first the Marxist version of dialectical objectivity, which shows clearly the problems of dialectical 'objectivity'.

Marxist 'objectivity' and dialectics

The Marxist conception of objectivity is, of course, different from the one used by orthodox philosophers of science as it is qualified by a 'social' element, namely, that concepts and theories are conditioned by social (class) interests, and a 'historical' element, in other words, that concepts and theories are, also, conditioned by time. Still, these qualifications do not aim to deny the supposed 'objective' and 'scientific' character of Marxist analysis.

Thus, Marx, on the basis of changes in the 'economic sphere' (i.e. the sphere that was mainly responsible for the transformation of society at a specific place and time – Europe in the transition to capitalism), attempted to provide a universal interpretation of all human history and render the socialist transformation of society historically necessary. Marx had no doubts about the 'scientific' character of his economic laws, which he viewed as 'iron' laws yielding inevitable results, or about the 'objective' character of his conception, which he paralleled to a natural history process:

> *It is a question of these laws themselves, of these tendencies working with iron necessity towards inevitable results ... My standpoint, from which the evolution of the economic formation of society is viewed as a process of natural history ...*[34]

As regards Lenin, he was even more explicit:

> *[M]aterialism provided an* absolutely objective criterion *[my emphasis] by singling out the 'relations of production' as the structure of society ... creating the possibility of a strictly scientific approach to historical and social problems.*[35]

The Marxist claim for 'objectivity', inevitably, led to methodological debates among Marxists, which were very similar to the ones that have taken place in the orthodox camp between positivists and rationalists/neo-

Kantians. The debates concerned what has been called 'the problem of knowledge', that is, the problem of the criteria by which a body of knowledge can be assessed and, in particular, whether and how a theory's correspondence to reality can be judged and demonstrated.

I would classify the variety of Marxist tendencies with respect to the problem of knowledge as follows.

First, there is what I would call the 'philosophical tendency', a tendency within which Practice is given priority over Theory. It is the tendency which is inspired by what Castoriadis[36] identifies as the revolutionary element in Marx, that is, the element declaring the end of philosophy as a closed system, which is expressed in the famous Eleventh Thesis of Marx on Feuerbach: 'The philosophers have only interpreted the world in various ways, the point however is to change it.'[37] Within the context of this tendency, no problem of knowledge arises. But then, as we shall see below, the belief in a Marxist science based on objective truths also becomes untenable, given the implicit or explicit relativism that characterizes this tendency.

Second, there is what I would call the 'scientistic' tendency, where a reversal of emphasis takes place, that is, the theoretical or scientific element is given priority. This is the element that eventually dominated Marx's work and Marxism thereafter, and it is what Castoriadis calls the traditional element in Marxism. In fact, for an important school of modern Marxism, that is, Althusser's structuralist Marxism, an *epistemological break* (a leap from a pre-scientific to a scientific world view) should describe Marx's shift from his early philosophical/humanist writings to his late (post-1845) scientific ones.[38] It is due to this 'scientific' element that Marxism ends up as just another theory, another closed system to explain the essence of society, and, in this sense, it faces exactly the same problem as other scientific theories do about the guarantee of truth. The common feature of all the currents belonging to this tendency is that they explicitly adopt the desirability and feasibility of a neutral 'scientific' explanation of external (social) reality.

Starting with the *philosophical tendency,* I will have to clarify, first, that what I call the 'philosophical tendency' does not have much to do with dialectical materialism, the view of *Marxism-as-philosophy.* Philosophy in dialectical materialism is in fact a science, or, better, *the* science of history and society, and as such belongs to the scientistic tendency we shall consider next. McLennan, for example, is clear about it: 'The role of philosophy, not as metaphysics but as generalizations from science and its concepts, takes on a "scientific" aspect that stands or falls not with ideology, but with science itself.'[39] Such a view, however, of Marxism-as-philosophy also suffers (for the reasons mentioned above) from the 'epistemological fallacy' that Hindess and Hirst emphasize.

An alternative to the Marxism-as-philosophy view, more relevant to the philosophical tendency, is the *Marxism-as-method* view. Lukacs, for instance, argues that even if research disproved all Marxist theses *in toto* this should not worry orthodox Marxists because 'orthodoxy refers exclusively to method'.[40] This view, however, can be criticized on several grounds. First, as McLennan points out,[41] the idea that Marxism is no more than a methodological tool is not only strange, but also as philosophical as the Marxism-as-philosophy view. Second, as Castoriadis emphasizes,[42] method and content are inseparable, the one creating the other, and Marxist categories are themselves historical. A similar position was also taken by Karl Korsh, who argued that Marxism, like all theories, has historical conditions of existence, to which it alone is relevant.[43]

The view commonly supported by the writers in the philosophical tendency (Karl Korsh, George Lukacs (with some qualifications), Peter Binns, Derek Sayer, Phillip Corridan and others) is that the starting point in knowledge is neither pure self-awareness, as in rationalism, nor sense-data, as in empiricism. The former creates an artificial duality between subject and object, theory and reality, while the latter not only is dualistic but also identifies essence with appearances. Instead, the starting point in knowledge is considered to be human beings' active contact with society and the natural world. Science, therefore, is the unity of Theory and Practice, which not only interprets reality but also becomes part of the force changing it, a part of praxis, that is, the conscious determinate shaping of history. Thus, scientific laws are not predictive – not even in a probabilistic sense, as Lukacs[44] points out; instead, they only constitute a framework within which theoretically informed and therefore effective social practice is possible.

The fact that social practice is the source, the test and the aim of knowledge is, of course, a commonplace among Marxists. The real issue, therefore, is whether practice should be seen as the *creator of truth* and knowledge or, alternatively, as a *criterion of verifiability* of knowledge. For the philosophical tendency, practice creates knowledge within the context of an empirically open-ended system. As Peter Binns puts it: 'Objective truths are not uncovered so much as created; it is in the act of creating them that they become revealed.'[45] Therefore, the only criterion of validity here is life, action, struggle.[46] On the other hand, for the scientistic tendency, knowledge constitutes in effect a closed theoretical system, and practice functions as a criterion of its verifiability. It is therefore obvious that no problem of criteria and of scientificity could arise within the philosophical tendency, as such a problem presupposes a distinction made between subject and object, between theory and reality, a distinction explicitly denied by this tendency. By the same token, one can explain the ultimate cause of the problem of knowledge. The problem arises because in the orthodox philosophy of science the criterion of validity is external, outside the social being of those holding the ideas: it is located either somewhere in an autonomous and a-social realm of reason (rationalism) or in experience (positivism).

The price, however, to be paid in order to overcome the problem of knowledge in this way is heavy: Marxism cannot claim any longer that it has a scientific status based on objective truths, as Marxist critics of the above thesis were quick to point out. Obviously, if we accept that theory is based on practice, by which it is meant the class practice of the proletariat, we are going to end up not with a science based on objective truths, but with a *class science*. The Marxist argument that the proletariat expresses the general interest of society in abolishing class society does not make the scientific claim of Marxism any more valid because the super-iority of Marxist theory still depends on its unique ability, as potential working-class consciousness, to abolish the class system. This is why Marxist critics of the scientistic tendency, like Collier,[47] argue that the above view of Marxism transforms it into theology and that practice should be seen not as *creating* truth but as merely *ascertaining* its occurrence, a position that Kolakowski,[48] rightly, characterizes as 'Marxism of a positivistic orientation'. In this light, one may observe that it is no accident that Marx himself, as Castoriadis[49] has shown, had to abstract from the class struggle in deriving his 'laws' of motion of capitalism, because only in that way could he develop a scientific theory of socialism. The class struggle is absent in deriving his scientific laws and reappears again only at a different level of analysis, namely, in bringing down a system whose essential nature has been demonstrated by abstracting from it.

Therefore, the 'solution' to the problem of knowledge that was pro-vided by the philosophical tendency is vacuous. As orthodox social science could, also, be seen as a class science to serve the dominant class's interests, we end up with two class sciences, in other words, two incommensurable paradigms, and no possibility of developing an objective science of society. Furthermore, the view, sometimes expressed by Marxist writers,[50] that the class character of Marxian economics does not call into question its scientific validity, on the grounds that this validity depends entirely on its ability to explain reality, obviously begs the question, as there is no 'objective' way to decide which paradigm better explains reality.

However, the basic thesis of the philosophical tendency, that dialectical materialism is not only distinct from, but also a safeguard against, orthodox epistemology and, further, that method can be separated from content, is not universally accepted among Marxists,[51] and particularly not by those emphasizing the scientific nature of Marxism (scientistic tendency). The common elements shared by Marxists in this tendency are, first, that reality is independent of theory (though the reverse is not true); second, that theory is independent of its subject, and, finally, that the truth of a theory is found in its ability to 'appropriate' or reproduce reality in thought. But, as there are several ways to establish that a theory corresponds to, or adequately reflects, reality, the main division among orthodox philosophers of science (rationalists versus empiricists/positivists) is, inevitably, reproduced within the Marxist scientistic tendency.

Thus, as regards, first, the empiricist tendency within Marxism, it originated in the late writings of Engels[52] and was further developed by Plechanov, Bucharin and Lenin.[53] In modern times, this tendency has dominated Anglo-American Marxism, reflecting, one could suspect, the traditional dominance of empiricism/positivism in this part of the world. The problem of knowledge does exist in this tendency, and the solution to it is given in terms of empiricist criteria that could establish the adequacy of the theory with respect to its correspondence to reality.

So, although the exact testing procedures are not specified, it is clear that a correspondence theory of truth is involved here. Still, it should be stressed that, notwithstanding the fact that experience is the ultimate criterion of truth in both orthodox and Marxist positivism, the methodological individualism of the former is explicitly rejected by the latter. Sense-data therefore are not considered to be the starting point of knowledge; nor does reality have to be reduced to atomic components to be understood scientifically. Furthermore, the aim remains the discovery of the essence behind appearances. However, since the ultimate aim of empiricist Marxism is the raising of the socialist project from a utopian ideal to a science of the economy/society, all those elements of Marxist dialectics – principally the class struggle – that could not be built into the scientific laws of the economy have to be abstracted from and transferred to a different level of abstraction.

In my view, empiricist Marxism not only is not in a position to solve the problems orthodox empiricists/positivists face (non-existence of 'brute' facts, lack of non-vacuous standards to assess rival theories, etc.), but it also adds some extra problems due to its vagueness. For instance, how the adequacy of a theory with respect to experience should be assessed: through a verification/falsification procedure, through success in social practice or through some other criterion? Let us examine the problem with a concrete example. As is well known, the Marxist theory of value does not meet the positivist/falsificationist requirements of a scientific hypothesis. That is why some Marxists attempted to solve the problem by suggesting (on the basis of Marx's spare writings on methodology) that value, as well as 'all specifically Marxian laws and developmental constructs', should be treated as Weberian ideal-types.[54] However, as Weber points out,[55] the function of an ideal-type is always the comparison with empirical reality; therefore, the problem of the guarantee of the ideal-type's truth still remains unresolved.[56]

Furthermore, the question remains as to how the distinction between the praxis of the social subject and his awareness of that praxis can be removed; in other words, how empiricism could be reconciled with Marxist dialectics.[57] Finally, the fundamental question still remains: how can we be sure that we have discovered the essence behind appearances, especially when the essence is contradicted by phenomena?

The second major current in the scientistic tendency is the rationalist one. The starting point here is the necessity for the conceptualization of reality, prior to the possibility of science. This implies a denial of the empiricist position that beliefs/propositions about reality could be derived from a world experienced, but not yet conceptualized. The French Marxist structuralist school might be classified in this current of Marxism, although Marxist structuralists themselves might deny their classification as rationalists in the above sense. However, their affinities to rationalism are much more significant than those to any other tendency/current in Marxism.[58]

For structuralist-Marxists, the problem of knowledge is an ideological problem,[59] as ideological as all traditional epistemology. The real issue for them is not one of criteria of scientificity, but of *mechanisms* producing a knowledge effect. The criteria of knowledge are defined within the science itself, by its scientificity, its axiomatics. As Althusser puts it:

> *Theoretical Practice is indeed its own criterion and contains in itself definite protocols with which to validate the quality of its products, i.e., the criteria of the scientificity of the products of scientific practice.*[60]

In fact, Marxism, according to structural-Marxists, is not only a science but a superior science, the science of all sciences, given its ability to synthesize the various special sciences. Marxism therefore becomes the general theory of Theoretical Practice and 'the key to and judge of what counts as genuine knowledge'.[61]

However, Althusser's operation to do away with the philosophy of guarantees is also a failure. As several (Marxist) critics have pointed out, Althusserians base their theory of Theoretical Practice on a coherence theory of truth, where the criterion of truth is simply comprehensiveness and lack of contradictions with respect to the thought structure of Marxism.[62] Therefore, Althusserian Marxism can only claim superiority over other sciences (which might be equally comprehensive and non-contradictory) if one accepts a priori the world view embodied in the structuralist paradigm. As Binns points out:

> *Not only are the parameters in terms of which the world is to be examined structure-specific, but so too are the very conceptualizations of the world they are used to explain. The very incommensurability of these world-syntheses effectively prevents any demonstration of the superiority of any of them. To accord any of these the honorific description of being scientific in these circumstances, as does structuralist Marxism, seems quite gratuitously and pompously misleading.*[63]

Althusserian Marxism is, therefore, a clear example of objectivist rationalism, where, as Castoriadis puts it, 'Past history is rational ... future history is rational ... the connection between the past and the present is rational.'[64] The implication of such a view of history is that, as the same author points out: 'Marxism does not transcend the philosophy of history, it is just another philosophy of history; the rationality which Marxism supposedly induces from the facts is, in fact, imposed on them',[65] so that, in the end, 'Marxism is not any more, in its essence, but a scientific objectivism, supplemented by a rationalist philosophy.'[66] But then, as was effectively shown,[67] the creative and imaginary element in history plays a very limited role, namely one that is consistent with the Althusserian view, according to which the true subjects and real protagonists of history are not biological men but the relations of production. Men, in this context (which nobody who wishes to call himself a believer in Marxist dialectical and historical materialism can discard), are only the 'supports' (*Träger*) or bearers of the functions assigned to them by the relations of production.[68]

Finally, the latest development in Marxist epistemology is 'realist Marxism', which can be seen as an attempt at a dialectical synthesis of modern empiricism/positivism on the one hand and rationalism/Kantianism on the other. In fact, some recent Marxist work considers the realist epistemology as a way to overcome the present crisis of Marxist theory, in the sense that it avoids the pitfalls of both the dialectical approach (essentialism, teleology) and of empiricism/relativism (a-theoretical character).[69]

The object of scientific knowledge, according to realist philosophers of science, is neither atomistic events and phenomena (as in empiricism/positivism), nor models, that is, human constructs imposed on phenomena (as in rationalism/Kantianism). Instead, the object of scientific knowledge is structures and *mechanisms* that generate phenomena, which operate independently of our knowledge and experience. Science, as defined by a realist philospher, is 'the systematic attempt to express in thought the structures and ways of acting on things that exist and act independently of thought'.[70]

The realist definition of science is based on three fundamental assumptions: first, that the world is structured (so that science is possible); second, that the world is an open system (i.e. a system where no constant conjunction of events prevails) consisting of enduring and non-empirically active natural mechanisms; and third, that the ontological order is completely independent from the epistemological order. The last assumption implies that philosophical ontology (Is the world structured/ differentiated?) should not be confused with epistemological ontology (Which are the particular structures contained in the world?). The only link between the two orders can be provided by experimental activity, which can give us access to the enduring and active mechanisms that constitute the real world, through the creation of close conditions that make the confirmation/falsification of a theory possible.

Therefore, an open system cannot be adequately grasped in terms of the constant conjunction of observed phenomena (as empiricists attempt to do) because perception gives access only to *things*, not to *structures* that exist independently of us. Thus, the empiricist causal laws are only expressing tendencies of things, not conjunctions of events, and are tied up to closed systems. The inadequacy of the empiricist/positivist criteria of confirmation/falsification is due to the fact that they are based on the assumption that a closed system is the rule, rather than the artificially generated exception. Although, therefore, realists do not reject the general relativity of knowledge that Kuhn, Feyerabend and others emphasize, and according to which descriptions of the world are always theoretically determined and not just neutral reflections of it, still, they argue that, provided that we can create closed conditions, we can get access to the structures of the world. This has the important implication that a criterion of choosing among incommensurable theories is possible. Thus, as Bhaskar puts it:

> A theory T_a is preferable to theory T_b, even if in the terminology of Kuhn and Feyerabend it is incommensurable with it, if theory T_a can explain under its descriptions almost all the phenomena $p_1 \ldots p_n$ that T_b can explain under its descriptions $Bp_1 \ldots Bp_n$, plus some significant phenomena that T_b cannot explain.[71]

However, the applicability of this criterion crucially depends on the possibility of experimental activity, a fact that turns any idea of methodological monism into a fantasy; the realist safety valve to preclude relativism cannot, by definition, work with social sciences. This is so because, although society may be an open system – as realists assume – it is impossible to create artificially closed conditions in order to confirm/falsify our theories about it.

Realist philosophers of science are, of course, well aware of the problem and make a determined effort to 'solve' it, or, at least, bypass it. McLennan, for instance, argues that social theory is necessarily historical, given the constitutive role that agency and thought play with respect to its object of study. However, the procedures he suggests, so that the lack of experimental activity in social sciences does not play a decisive role in differentiating them from natural sciences, are obviously inadequate. Thus, the criteria that he mentions, in his attempt to support the 'objectivity' of social inquiry (theoretical abstraction, systematic and coherent theoretical explanations at a number of levels, explanation of concrete phenomena by causal and other sets of propositions),[72] do not provide any effective solution to the problem. For instance, two paradigmatic theories, the neoclassical and the Marxist theories of value, can perfectly satisfy all the above criteria, without – in the absence of experimental activity – providing any solution to the problem of choosing between them.

The inescapable conclusion is that the problem of choosing among incommensurable theories in the social sciences and – by implication – the problem of scientifying or objectivizing the liberatory project, have not been solved by realist philosophers either.[73]

Dialectical naturalism: an objective ethics?
However, if the project for a future society cannot be justified on the basis of a teleological conception, either a teleological view of social evolution (as Marxists attempted to do) or a teleological view of natural evolution (as some deep ecologists suggest today),[74] the question remains whether such a project may be justified on the basis of a non-teleological view of natural and social evolution, which, however, is objectively rational. This is the case of Murray Bookchin's[75] dialectical naturalism, which, although it assumes a directionality towards a democratic ecological society – a society that may never be actualized because of 'fortuitous events' – is an explicitly non-teleological conception. Thus, as Bookchin stresses:

> Dialectical naturalism does not terminate in a Hegelian Absolute at the end of a cosmic developmental path, but rather advances the vision of an ever-increasing wholeness, fullness, and richness of differentiation and subjectivity.[76]

The attempt to establish a directionality towards an ecological society depends on two crucial hypotheses:

(a) That there is a directionality in natural change, which yields a clearly discernible evolutionary development towards more complex forms of life, greater subjectivity and self-awareness, growing mutuality, i.e. a development towards an 'ever-greater differentiation or wholeness insofar as potentiality is realized in its full actuality'.[77] Thus, Bookchin, differentiating his process of 'participatory evolution' from the prevalent neo-Darwinian synthesis, sees 'a natural *tendency* toward greater complexity and subjectivity in first (biological) nature, arising from the very interactivity of matter, indeed a *nisus* toward self-consciousness.[78]

(b) That there is a graded evolutionary continuum between our first nature and our second (social and cultural nature, so that 'every social evolution is virtually an extension of natural evolution into a distinctly human realm'.[79] Although, of course, it is explicitly acknowledged that social evolution is profoundly different from organic evolution, still, social change is characterized by a process of progress, defined as 'the self-directive activity of History and Civilization towards increasing rationality, freedom'.[80] Thus, 'second nature', namely, the evolution of society, 'develops both in continuity with first nature and as its antithesis, until the two are sublated into "free nature", or "nature" rendered self-conscious, in a rational and ecological society'.[81]

Let us therefore assess in more detail these two hypotheses. As regards, first, the hypothesis about the existence of a rational process of natural evolution, Castoriadis points out that although the fact of evolution itself is incontestable, biologists have never developed a *genuine* theory of evolution, which means that the neo-Darwinian synthesis is in fact a theory of species differentiation, not of the evolution of species, and that therefore nothing in this theoretical scheme implies that differentiation occurs in the direction of increasing complexity.[82] However, one may counter-argue here that the results of recent biological research support the hypothesis of increasing complexity. Thus, modern developments in biophysics, in terms of the self-organization theory, introduce into biology a type of 'law of increasing complexity' which is consistent with dialectical naturalism.[83]

But, although the hypothesis about a rational process of natural evolution is not groundless, the hypothesis about the existence of a rational process of social evolution is, to my mind, both undesirable and untenable. It is undesirable, not only because it creates unintentional links with heteronomy, but also because it may easily lead to inadvertent affinities with intrinsically anti-democratic eco-philosophies. And it is untenable because history does not justify the existence of progress towards a free society, in the sense of a form of social organization which secures the highest degree of individual and social autonomy at the political, the economic and the social levels, what we defined in Chapter 5 as an inclusive democracy.

Thus, as regards, first, the undesirablity of the social directionality hypothesis, one may point out that the postulate according to which there is a 'rational' order in the world and a corresponding order of human affairs linked to the order of the world not only is essentially linked to heteronomy (because it conceals the fundamental fact that history is creation), but also conceals or eliminates the question of responsibility.[84] Therefore, unless we underplay the significance of the imaginary element in human history, as Marxists do, we have to conclude that it is impossible to establish any sort of social evolution towards a particular form of society:

> History does not happen to society: history is the self-deployment of society. By this affirmation, we contradict the entire spectrum of existing tenets: history as the product of the will of God; history as the result of the action of ('natural' or 'historical') laws; history as a 'subjectless process'; history as a purely random process . . . we posit history in itself as 'creation and destruction'.[85]

Furthermore, the attempt to establish a directionality in society might easily create undesirable affinities with deep ecology. Although such affinities are utterly repugnant to social ecologists, still, they are implicit in the fact that both deep ecologists and social ecologists adopt a process of evolutionary unfolding and self-realization and ground their ethics in scientific observations about the natural world, in natural 'tendencies' or directionalities. This fact could go a long way to explain the various hybridized approaches developing at the moment among John Clark, an ex-social ecologist whose anti-democratic views we considered in Chapter 5, Peter Marshall[86] and others. The inevitable outcome of such affinities is that the debate on what form of society meets the demands for autonomy and ecological balance becomes not a matter of conscious choice, but a matter of interpretation of what natural change really means with respect to society. However, as it is not possible to establish any 'authentic' interpretation about the meaning of natural change, we may easily end up not just with liberatory interpretations, like the ones offered by social ecology, but also with interpretations which are consistent with any form of heteronomy and repression, from eco-fascism to mysticism and irrationalism.

Second, as regards the untenability of the social directionality hypothesis it should be made clear that society is not 'alien' to a self-organizing Nature and that Bookchin's contribution in demolishing the nature–society dualism is of paramount importance. But, although one may have no reservations in adopting the hypothesis that self-consciousness and self-reflection have their own history in the natural world and are not *sui generis*, 'the product of a rupture with the whole of development so unprecedented and unique that it contradicts the gradedness of all phenomena',[87] still, it would be a big jump to adopt a similar hypothesis about progress towards a free society. In other words, even if one accepts the hypothesis that self-consciousness and self-reflection, in very broad terms, are part of a dialectical unfolding in Nature and do not just represent a rupture with the past, this does not imply that there is a similar dialectical unfolding towards a free society, i.e., an inclusive democracy. Such a view is incompatible with historical evidence which clearly shows that the historical attempts at a free society have always been the result of a rupture with the instituted heteronomy which has been dominant in the past, rather than a sort of processual 'product'.

The fact that societies, almost always and everywhere, have lived in a state of *instituted heteronomy* (namely a state of non-questioning of existing laws, traditions and beliefs that guarantee the concentration of political and economic power in the hands of elites), with no trace of an 'evolution' towards democratic forms of organization securing individual and social autonomy, clearly vitiates any hypothesis of a directionality towards a free society. In fact, if there is any continuity in history, it is a continuity in heteronomy interrupted by usually sudden and temporary leaps into 'autonomous' forms of organization. Thus, an autonomous form of political organization (direct democracy) has always been the rare exception and even rarer have been the cases of autonomous forms of economic and social organization (economic democracy and 'democracy in the social realm'). It is only, therefore, with respect to social change in a broad sense, which includes the accumulation of scientific and technological knowledge, as well as improvements with respect to gender relations, human rights, etc., that we may perhaps speak of some sort of progress. However, these changes in no way justify the hypothesis of a directionality towards a free society, an inclusive democracy.

Thus, as regards scientific and technological change, few would argue today, particularly after the experience of this century, that there is some sort of correlation between progress in these fields and the degree of autonomy achieved in society at the political and economic levels. Furthermore, several writers have noted the increasing vulnerability of the human species because of the worldwide reliance on the same technology and the fact that increasing technological complexity is accompanied by an increasing lack of flexibility and adaptive capacity.[88] However, if one accepts the non-neutrality of technology thesis,[89] one may counter-argue here that the homogenization of technology is not an 'independent variable' but just the inevitable outcome of the marketization of the economy.

As regards the alleged improvements in gender, race, ethnic relations, human rights in general, they hardly justify the hypothesis of directionality towards a free society, in the sense of an inclusive democracy. The improvements in social relations and structures have not been matched by a corresponding progress in political and economic relations and structures towards political and economic democracy. The widening and deepening of women's rights, minorities' rights, etc., may have improved the social position of the members of the respective communities. But, from the democratic viewpoint, this process simply has led to the expansion of the ruling political and economic elites to include representatives of these communities. Furthermore, these improvements do not imply any significant changes with respect to democracy in the workplace, the education place, etc. Even as regards the human rights record one may raise serious doubts about the progress achieved. Torture, for instance, after tapering off with the Enlightenment in Europe in the seventeenth century to the extent that it had almost disappeared, came back with a vengeance this century. According to a very recent report, torture practised by governments around the world increased dramatically this century, especially in Europe, to the extent that the twentieth century may become known as 'the torturer's century'.[90]

At the cultural level, as Polanyi[91] has persuasively shown, the establishment of the market economy implied sweeping aside traditional cultures and values. This process, as we have seen in Chapter 3, was accelerated in the twentieth century with the spreading of the market economy and the implied growth economy all over the world and the inevitable elimination of all cultures not based on the system of the market economy. As a result, today, there is an intensive process of cultural homogenization at work, which not only rules out any directionality towards more complexity, but in effect is making culture simpler, with cities becoming more and more alike, people all over the world listening to the same music, watching the same soap operas on TV, buying the same brands of consumer goods, etc.

Finally, as regards ethical progress, i.e. the evolution towards moral 'improvement' (in terms of mutuality, solidarity, etc.), it is indicative that even social democrats like Habermas and Bobbio, who have an obvious vested political interest in the idea of progress and social evolution, do admit that it is not possible to assert the existence of ethical progress, despite the acknowledged rapid technological progress of the last 100 years or so. Thus, Habermas, countering the pessimism of the Frankfurt School about progress, argues that the error in the Marxist and other optimistic theories of social evolution lies in the presumption that progress on the system's level (which attends to the material reproduction of society) would automatically entail an improvement on the level of moral-practical conscience.[92] So, one may argue that the unmistakable trend, at least in the past two to three centuries, has been for growing selfishness and growing competition, rather than for enhanced mutuality and solidarity. Similarly, it is at least doubtful whether there has been an ethical progress in terms of environmental values.[93]

But let us look in more detail at the historical appearance of the autonomy tradition and assess the case of evolution towards a free society. Following Castoriadis's[94] periodization, the autonomy project emerged in classical Athens, where, for the first time in human history, the institution of society was questioned both at the institutional and the imaginary level. This was in contrast to the state of heteronomy, which characterized all societies up to then and almost all societies since then, where 'a society, despite the fact that it is always a self-creation which creates its own institutions, still, in order to protect these institutions it imagines and legislates that they are not a human creation but an extra-social creation: a creation of God, or of the laws of Nature, History or Reason, which therefore we can not change'.[95] The autonomy project, which reached its peak in classical Athens, was eclipsed for almost 15 centuries, a period during which heteronomy was dominant.

The autonomy project reappeared again in the twelfth century AD, in the medieval free cities of Europe, but soon came into conflict with the new statist forms of heteronomy which, in the end, destroyed the attempts at local self-government and federalism.[96] In the period 1750–1950, a fierce political, social and ideological conflict developed between the two traditions. The heteronomy tradition is expressed by the spreading of the market economy and of new social forms of hierarchical organization. These forms embodied a new 'social imaginary signification' (adopted by the socialist movement): the boundless spreading of 'rational domination', which identifies progress with the development of productive forces and the idea of dominating Nature. During the same period, the autonomy project, under the influence of the Enlightenment's ideas, was radicalized at the intellectual, social and political levels (e.g. Parisian Sections of the early 1790s, collectives in the Spanish Civil War, etc.)

Finally, in the present era (1950 onwards), both traditions have entered a period of serious crisis. Thus, although the spreading of the market economy's rational domination is accelerating, the system itself is in a deep crisis, a crisis not in the Marxist sense of the capitalist relations of production hindering the further development of forces of production, but in the sense, as we have seen in previous chapters, first, of the market economy's dismal failure to create a successful growth economy in the South (where the vast majority of the earth's population lives); and second, of the growing ecological destruction that not only degrades the quality of life but threatens life itself on the planet. Paradoxically, at the same time, the autonomy tradition, after its brief explosion in the late 1960s, is also in a state of 'total eclipse', a fact illustrated by the lack of social, political and ideological conflicts.

The issue that arises therefore is whether changes in the historical forms of social organization reveal some kind of directionality towards a free society, which would represent the graded actualization of unfolding human potentialities (in the dialectical sense of the word) for freedom (as dialectical naturalism maintains), or whether, instead, they do not reveal any form of directionality, since the form society takes each time just represents social creations conditioned (but not determined) by time and space constraints, as well as by institutional and cultural factors. The former view sees history as a process of progress, the unfolding of reason, and assumes that there is an evolution going on towards autonomous or democratic forms of political, economic and social organization, a view which, to my mind, is not supported by history. The latter view sees the autonomous society as a rupture, a break in the historical continuity that the heteronomous society has historically established.

Of course, 'autonomy/heteronomy' is not an ironclad distinction. Autonomous and heteronomous forms of social organization historically interact with each other, and elements of both may coexist within the boundaries of the same society. For instance, as we have seen in Chapter 5, the Athenian democracy was a form of society that embodied strong elements of autonomy (direct democracy – as regards free citizens) and heteronomy (economic inequality, gender inequality, slavery – as regards the rest). Furthermore, in today's sophisticated heteronomous societies, there are several elements of autonomy, remnants, usually, of past conflicts between the autonomy and the heteronomy tradition. Taking, therefore, for granted the interaction between autonomy and heteronomy, in other words, explicitly assuming that the two traditions change themselves and, to some extent, each other over time, the real issues are, first, whether the two traditions are qualitatively different and, second, assuming they are, whether any evolutionary pattern may be established towards the auto-nomous form of social organization.

As regards the first question, I think few would disagree with the thesis that autonomy and heteronomy are not just quantitatively but qualitatively different. Historically, the autonomy and heteronomy traditions are ex-pressed in various forms of social organization: the former in the form of the Athenian democracy, the Swiss cantons, the French revolutionary sections, to mention just a few examples; and the latter, in the form of absolute monarchies, constitutional monarchies, parliamentary 'democracies' and state socialism. The common characteristic of autonomous forms of social organization is that they are all based on the fundamental principle of the equality in the distribution of power, whereas the opposite is true for all heteronomous forms. It is therefore obvious that the differences between the various types of heteronomous (as well as types of autonomous) forms of social organization are quantitative, whereas the differences between the autonomous and heteronomous forms themselves are qualitative. Autonomy and heteronomy are two fundamentally different traditions expressing completely different 'paradigms' about social living; they are incommensurable. The question therefore here is whether, as the famous Hegelian 'law' maintains, quantitative differences beyond a certain point are transformed into qualitative changes, or whether, instead, there is no possibility of establishing any sort of evolutionary process between the autonomy and the heteronomy traditions.

This brings us to the second question I raised above. According to dialectical naturalism, 'between [autonomy and heteronomy] is a dialectic that has to be unravelled in all its complexity, involving interrelationships as well as antagonisms',[97] whereas, according to the view presented here, despite the development *within* each tradition and the possible interaction, still, no development *between* them may be established. For instance, one may support the case that although constitutional monarchy did express a more sophisticated form of heteronomy than absolute monarchy and, by the same token, parliamentary 'democracy' does represent the most sophisticated form of oligarchy in history, still, the differences between the political regimes involved refer to the size and the composition of the ruling elites, not to the fundamental distinction itself between ruling elites and the rest of the population – a distinction that excludes the vast majority of the population from any effective political decision-taking. Similarly, the Parisian Sections of the early 1790s,[98] where women had an equal share in the distribution of political power, did express a more complete form of democracy than the Athenian assemblies. Finally, the Spanish collectives in the Civil War,[99] which contained a significant element of economic democracy, did express a more complete form of autonomy than both the Athenian and the Parisian assemblies.

Also, although it is recognized that the break with the heteronomy tradition takes place in a specific time and place and that therefore history, tradition, and culture certainly condition the form that society takes, institutional and historical factors never determine when and where this break will take place, or even the specific form the autonomous organization of society will take. An autonomous form of social organization has always been a *creation* expressing a break with past development. The rare historical cases of relatively free forms of social organization came about as a result of the fact that at certain historical moments, for reasons that only partly refer to the concrete historical circumstances, social imaginary significations expressing the autonomy project had become hegemonic and led to a rupture of the dominant social paradigm of heteronomy.[100] That such ruptures do not fit in any unfolding dialectical pattern of history, and cannot even be considered as 'reactions' to heteronomous forms of organization, becomes obvious by the fact that repeatedly in history similar, if not identical, institutional and historical circumstances led to very different forms of social organization. As a rule, they led to heteronomous forms of social organization and only very exceptionally to attempts at autonomy.

The classical Athenian democracy is a characteristic example. There is no doubt that the movement from tribal blood ties to civic ties represents a form of development. The question is whether this development is a development within the heteronomous tradition or, alternatively, one between the two traditions. I would argue that although elements of autonomous organization may be found in tribal societies (e.g. tribal assemblies), still, the movement from tribes to cities represents a development predominantly *within* the heteronomous form of social organization and only in one exceptional case (Athenian democracy) towards a new form of autonomous organization. This fact, in turn, illustrates the significance of the imaginary or creative element in history, rather than of any kind of an evolutionary pattern in political organization. As Castoriadis puts it:

> Democracy and philosophy are not the outcome of natural or spontaneous tendencies of society and history. They are themselves creations and they entail a radical break with the previously instituted state of affairs. Both are aspects of the project of autonomy . . . the Greeks [discovered] in the sixth and fifth centuries that institutions and representations belong to nomos and not to physis, that they are human creations and not 'God-given' or 'nature-given'.[101]

A view of history based on an evolutionary pattern could not explain why a similar movement from tribes to cities in many parts of the world, even in classical Greece itself, has led on the one hand to the classical Athenian democracy and on the other to a variety of oligarchic, if not despotic, forms of political organization. Of course, few would deny that specific 'objective' factors (geography, climate, etc.) may have played a significant, but never a decisive, role on each historical occasion. What is disputable is whether there has been a long-term pattern of social evolution that led to classical Athenian democracy – an experiment that, in its full democratic form, was not repeated elsewhere at the time and which re-emerged hundreds of years later.

Parliamentary 'democracy' is another example. As we have seen in Chapter 5, parliamentary democracy is not a form of political democracy; as it has developed in the West, it may better be described as a form of liberal oligarchy. Furthermore, parliamentary democracy can in no way be seen as a stage in the development of democracy. This is obvious not only from the fact that direct democracy historically preceded parliamentary 'democracy' but also because, as the experience of the past two centuries or so has shown, parliamentary democracy, if it evolves into something, evolves into a further concentration of political power in the hands of professional politicians' elites, at national or supra-national levels. Social development, in terms of political organization, is not 'cumulative', i.e. one leading from various forms of 'democracy' which reflect quantitative differences (constitutional monarchy, parliamentary democracy, etc.), towards direct democracy – which is clearly a qualitative change.

By the same token, the market economy is neither a relative (even a poor one) to economic democracy, nor does it constitute a kind of stage in the development of economic democracy. Instead, as I tried to show in Chapter 1, today's market economy represents a definite step backwards in comparison to the socially controlled economies of the medieval free cities. Furthermore, if the market economy evolves into something it evolves towards further concentration of economic power, and there is no prospect whatsoever that a market economy will ever lead, through cumulative quantitative changes, to the qualitative change of economic democracy.

Finally, the various attempts at 'democracy in the social realm', particularly workplace democracy (workers' councils, soviets), and for democracy in educational institutions have always been associated with historical 'moments' of insurrection and as soon as 'order' has been restored, either by the institutionalization of a 'revolutionary' new regime of heteronomy (e.g., the Soviet Union) or the continuation of the old one, the democratic forms have been replaced by forms of pseudo-democracy at the workplace, the university, etc.

So, it is not possible to derive any sort of evolutionary process towards a free society, what we called an inclusive democracy. The historical attempts to establish autonomous forms of political, social and economic democracy, although, of course, they did not appear *ab novo*, cannot be fitted into any grand evolutionary process. This is clearly indicated by the fact that such attempts took place in specific times and places and as a break with past development, rather than in several societies at the same stage of development and as a continuation of it. Therefore, although the ideals of freedom may have expanded over time, the last 25 years or so notwithstanding, this expansion has not been matched by a corresponding evolution towards an autonomous society, in the sense of greater participation of citizens in decision-taking. In fact, the undermining of communities, which was intensified by the emergence of the market economy 200 years ago and has been accelerated by the development of the present internationalized market economy, as well as the growing privacy and self-interest of individuals encouraged by the consumer society, are clear indications of a trend towards more heteronomous forms of society rather than the other way round. Therefore, if we accept the view that I tried to develop in Chapter 1, i.e. that the present internationalized market economy marks a new, higher phase in the marketization process, then all the signs are that we have entered a new period where the '40 per cent' societies of the North will be based on sophisticated forms of heteronomy, whereas the miserable societies of the South will rely on various forms of brutal authoritarianism.

So, one may assume that if inclusive democracy ever replaces the present heteronomous forms of political and economic organization, this will represent not the actualization of unfolding potentialities for freedom but simply the conscious choice among two social possibilities, which schematically may be described as the possibility for autonomy versus the possibility for heteronomy. In other words, to my mind, the dialectical idea of unfolding objective potentialities, i.e. of real latent possibilities which may (or may not) be actualized, is not applicable at all in the case of social change. To talk about any particular being that, in developing itself, actualizes what at first was only a latent possibility and in this way attains its own truth, we have to assume that there is a specific possibility in the first place and not a choice of different possibilities. Therefore, whereas it is true that an acorn has the potentiality to become an oak tree and a human embryo to become a fully mature and creative adult, we cannot extend the analogy to human society and assume that the potentiality of society to become free 'is equivalent'[102] to these natural potentialities. The obvious difference between the potentialities of acorns and human embryos to become oak trees and adults, respectively, and those of society to become free is that the former represent single possibilities whereas the latter is just one possibility out of two broad possibilities: for autonomy or heteronomy. In other words, if we take into account that 'the very history of the Greco-Western world can be viewed as the history of the struggle between autonomy and heteronomy',[103] it is obvious that the heteronomous forms of society which have dominated history cannot just be considered as 'fortuitous events', similar to those that may not allow an acorn to become an oak tree. So, to assume that the possibility for autonomy is an unfolding and therefore rational *potentiality* (in the dialectical sense of the word) and conversely to assume away the possibility for heteronomy as just a *capacity* for irrationality[104] may easily be seen as a deliberate objectivization of one possibility at the expense of the other, in order to conceal our choice for the autonomy tradition under the cover of dialectical 'objectivity'.

From this viewpoint, one may have serious reservations with respect to the classical Marxist and anarchist views adopting the idea of dialectical progress in history. Thus, it should not be forgotten that the adoption of the idea of progress implies also the endorsement of such conclusions as the Marxist one about the 'progressive' role of colonialism,[105] or the corresponding anarchist one that the state is a 'socially necessary evil'.[106] However, if we adopt the view that there is no unilinear or dialectical process of progress nor a corresponding evolutionary process towards forms of social organization grounded on autonomy and we assume, instead, that the historical attempts at democracy represent a break with the past, then, forms of social organization like colonialism and the state can be seen as just 'social evils', with nothing 'necessary' about them, either as regards their emergence in the past, or the form that social change has taken since, or will take in the future.

One might conclude therefore that the logic of society's development does not show that it is constituted to become autonomous, in the sense of the actualization of a latent potentiality for freedom. But, if the hypothesis of directionality in social change and of a rational historical process is untenable, then the question arises whether it is still possible to develop an 'objective' ethics which assesses forms of social organization as 'good' or 'bad' on the basis of the degree according to which they represent the actualization of the latent potentialities for freedom. The obvious criticism, which is implied by the above analysis, is that any attempt to develop an objective ethics based on the assumption of a process of social evolution is little more than an effort to mask a conscious choice among the autonomy and the heteronomy tradition, the democratic and the non-democratic society.

Therefore, although Murray Bookchin is, of course, right in insisting that in developing a democratic ethics we should adopt a non-hierarchical interpretation of nature,[107] it should not be forgotten that this is just one possible form of interpretation of Nature that we consciously have *chosen* because it is compatible with our choice for autonomy in the first place. This is obviously very different from assuming that a non-hierarchical interpretation of nature is an 'objective' one and that, as a consequence, a democratic society will be the product of a cumulative development, a rational process of realization of the potentiality for freedom. To my mind, social ecology's attempt to develop an objective ethics not only undermines its democratic credentials but also gives an easy target to statists and irrationalists of various sorts, as is indicated by the fact that most attacks against social ecology focus on its philosophy.[108]

A democratic society will simply be a social creation, which can only be grounded on our own conscious selection of those forms of social organization which are conducive to individual and social autonomy. An important side effect of this approach is that it avoids falling into the trap of grounding the free society on 'certain' truths at the very moment when most certainties, not only in social sciences but even in natural sciences, are collapsing.

However, the fact that a democratic society represents a conscious choice does not mean that this is just an arbitrary choice. This is clearly implied by the very fact that the autonomy project turns up in history again and again, particularly in periods of crisis of the heteronomous society. Furthermore, the fact that heteronomous society has been the dominant form of social organization in the past is not indicative of its intrinsic superiority over an autonomous society. Heteronomous societies have always been created and maintained by privileged elites, which aimed at the institutionalization of inequality in the distribution of power, through violence (military, economic) and/or indirect forms of control (religion, ideology, mass media).

Finally, the grounding of a free society on a conscious choice does not deprive us of an ethical criterion with which to assess the various forms of social organization. In fact, the degree to which a form of social organization secures an equal distribution of political, economic and social power is a powerful criterion with which to assess it. But this is a criterion chosen by us and not implied by some sort of evolutionary process. In other words, it is a criterion which is consistent with the view that I will develop in the next section, that the project for a democratic society can neither be grounded on scientism and objectivism nor on utopianism and irrationalism.

Beyond 'objectivism', irrationalism and relativism

The conclusions one can derive from the above analysis may be classified as follows:

(a) Paradigms about social reality on which a liberatory project can be founded may be incommensurable in the Kuhnian sense. In particular, to the extent that the formulation of such paradigms is crucially related to the question of whether the present social system should be taken for granted or not, incommensurability between them is inevitable. The incommensurability, for instance, between the orthodox and the Marxist paradigms on the mode of operation of the market economy, or between social ecology and deep ecology on the causes of the ecological crisis,[109] is an absolute one, in the sense that it implies deep differences, not just in world views, but also in the criteria/methods for assessing theories. As Feyerabend points out:

> Scientific theories ... use different (and occasionally incommensurable) concepts and evaluate events in different ways. What counts as evidence, or as an important result, or as 'sound scientific procedure' depends on attitudes and judgements that change with time, professions and occasionally even from one research group to the next.[110]

(b) In case of incommensurability, there are no objective criteria with which to choose among competing paradigms, a fact which implies that the only way to switch from one 'way of seeing things' to another is through a process of conversion rather than through a process of producing extra evidence, rational argument, etc., which are paradigm-dependent methods of establishing the 'truth' of a theory.

However, it is not only the objectivity of the liberatory project that is, at least, doubtful. The desirability of grounding it on an objective basis is also under question. The essence of democracy, as we have seen in Chapter 5, is not just its institutions but the fact that it is a constant *process* of debating and deciding institutions and traditions.[111] In this sense, one could argue that to the extent that the socialist project is 'scientified' it becomes part of the heteronomy tradition. A clear illustration of this process is the case of 'existing socialism'. It was exactly the Marxist conversion of the socialist project into an 'objective' science that contributed significantly to the establishment of new hierarchical structures, initially in the socialist movement and, later, in society at large. The basis of the new hierarchical structures was the social division created between, on the one hand, the avant-garde, that was alone in an objective position to lead the movement (because of its knowledge of the scientific truth that Marxism embodied) and, on the other, the 'masses'. Thus, it is a well-known historical fact that in the pre-revolutionary Marxist movements, as well as in the post-revolutionary governments, the justification of the concentration of power in the hands of the party elite was based on the 'fact' that they alone 'knew' how to interpret history and take appropriate action in order to accelerate the historical process towards socialism. As Marcuse pointed out, 'A straight road seems to lead from Lenin's "consciousness from without" and his notion of the centralized authoritarian party to Stalinism'.[112] This is so, not only because, according to Lenin, workers are not able, on their own, to develop a scientific theory of socialism, a task which historically has been left to the intellectuals,[113] but also because the custodians of the scientific orthodoxy, 'the party, or rather the party leadership, appears as the historical repository of the "true" interests of the proletariat and above the proletariat'.[114]

Similarly, in the case of capitalist societies, it is the mystification of the 'expert' that allows technocrats to present their 'solutions' to economic or social problems as if based on an 'objective' theory founded on 'scientific' premises. In fact, their theory is very much based on assumptions that presuppose the existing status quo of the market economy system and all that this implies in terms of inequality in the distribution of resources, income and wealth. Thus, the separation of society from the state and the economy has converted politics and the running of the economy into an 'art' and a 'science', respectively, where 'experts' (professional politicians, economists, etc.) play a crucial role in decision-taking. In contrast, a basic principle on which the Athenian democracy (where there was no separation of society from the state) was founded was that in politics there is no science but only the citizens' opinion. Thus, as Castoriadis stresses, it was the ancient Greeks who introduced the idea that

> on political affairs there is no science, in other words a systematic knowledge based on evidence, specialized training, etc., but doxa, i.e. the opinion of men, which should of course be trained as well, and which improves by experience, but which is not science.[115]

What is the foundation of freedom and democracy?

Although, as I pointed out in Chapter 5, the connection between freedom/autonomy on the one hand and democracy on the other can be taken for granted, the question still remains about the foundations of democracy, indeed freedom itself. Traditionally, most libertarians, from Godwin to Bakunin and Kropotkin, based their ethics and politics, freedom itself, on a fixed human nature governed by 'necessary and universal laws', by which – in contrast to Marxists who emphasized economic 'laws' – they usually meant natural laws. This reflected the same nineteenth-century incentive which led Marx to develop his 'scientific' economic laws, namely, the incentive to make the liberatory project look 'scientific' or, at least, 'objective'. However, this approach is not tenable any more, since it is not possible today to continue talking about objectivity, at least as far as the interpretation of social phenomena is concerned.

It is not therefore accidental that some libertarians today (Benello, Brown, Marshall *et al.*) question the traditional grounding of freedom on a fixed human nature, or on 'scientific' laws and 'objective' tendencies. However, several of those libertarians usually link this questioning with liberal individualistic assumptions about society. I think that such linking is anything but necessary. If we adopt a definition of freedom in terms of individual and collective autonomy, as we did in Chapter 5, then it is possible to avoid the trap of objectivism without succumbing to liberal individualism.

Furthermore, by defining freedom in terms of autonomy it is possible to see democracy not just as a *structure* institutionalizing the equal sharing of power, but, also, as a *process of social self-institution*, in the context of which politics constitutes an expression of both collective and individual autonomy. Thus, as an expression of collective autonomy, politics takes the form of calling into question the existing institutions and of changing them through deliberate collective action. Also, as an expression of individual autonomy, 'The polis secures more than human survival. Politics makes possible man's development as a creature capable of genuine autonomy, freedom and excellence.'[116] This is important if we take particularly into account the fact that a common error in libertarian discussions on democracy is to characterize various types of past societies, or communities, as democracies, just because they involved democratic forms of decision-taking (popular assemblies) or economic equality.

Democracy, as a process of social self-institution, implies a society which is open ideologically, namely, which is not grounded on any closed system of beliefs, dogmas or ideas. 'Democracy', as Castoriadis puts it, 'is the project of breaking the closure at the collective level.'[117] Therefore, in a democratic society, dogmas and closed systems of ideas cannot constitute parts of the dominant social paradigm, although, of course, individuals can have whatever beliefs they wish, as long as they are committed to uphold the democratic principle, namely the principle according to which society is autonomous, institutionalized as inclusive democracy.

It is indicative that even in classical Athens, 2500 years ago, a clear distinction was made between religion and democracy. As Hansen points out, 'there is no doubt that religion figured prominently in the life of a Greek *polis* just as in an Italian *città* or a German *Reichsstadt*, but in none of them did the state have its root or centre in religion'.[118] Similarly, Castoriadis stresses that all the laws approved by the *ecclesia* started with the clause 'εδοξε τη Βουλη και τω Δημω' (i.e. this is the opinion of the *Demos*), with no reference to God. This is in sharp contrast to the Judeo-Christian tradition, where, as the same author points out, the source of the laws in the Old Testament is divine: Jehovah gives the laws to Moses.[119] So, although Bookchin is right in stating that 'the city's festivals inter-mingled secular with religious themes, just as trade fairs in Mayan city-states accompanied religious fairs',[120] it is important not to forget the fact, which Hannah Arendt stressed (quoting Herodotus), that whereas in other religions God is transcendent, beyond time and life and the universe, the Greek gods are *anthropophyeis*, i.e. they have the same nature, not simply the same shape, as man.[121]

So, the democratic principle is not grounded on any divine, natural or social 'laws' or tendencies, but in our own conscious and self-reflective choice between the two main historical traditions: the tradition of heteronomy which has been historically dominant, and the tradition of autonomy. The choice of autonomy implies that the institution of society is not based on any kind of irrationalism (faith in God, mystical beliefs, etc.), as well as on 'objective truths' about social evolution grounded on social or natural 'laws'. This is so because any system of religious or mystical beliefs (as well as any closed system of ideas), by definition, excludes the questioning of some fundamental beliefs or ideas and, therefore, is incompatible with citizens setting their own laws. In fact, the principle of 'non-questioning' some fundamental beliefs is common in every religion or set of metaphysical and mystical beliefs, from Christianity to Taoism. Thus, as far as Christianity is concerned, it is rightly pointed out that 'Jesus' ethics are theologically based: they are not autonomous, i.e. derived from the needs of human individuals or society'.[122] Similarly, Taoism (adored by some anarchists today!) also explicitly condemns reasoning and argumentation ('Disputation is a proof of not seeing clearly' declares Chuang Tzu).[123]

Therefore, the fundamental element of autonomy is the creation of our own truth, something that social individuals can only achieve through direct democracy, that is, the process through which they continually question any institution, tradition or 'truth'. In a democracy, there are simply no given truths. The practice of individual and collective autonomy presupposes autonomy in thought, in other words, the constant questioning of institutions and truths. This could also explain why in classical Greece it was not just democracy that flourished, but, also, philosophy, in the sense of questioning any 'truths' given by custom, tradition or previous thought. In fact, questioning was the common root of both philosophy and democracy. While popular assemblies, as a form of decision-taking, existed both before and after the Athenian *ecclesia* (usually having their roots in tribal assemblies), still, the differentiating characteristic of the Athenian *ecclesia* is the fact that it was not grounded on religion or tradition but on citizens' *doxa* (opinion).

From this point of view, the practice of several modern libertarians of characterizing some European Christian movements or Eastern mystery religions as democratic is obviously out of place. For instance, George

Woodcock's references to 'mystery religions that emerged from the East', or to the Christian Catharist movement of the eleventh century are completely irrelevant to the democratic tradition.[124] Similarly out of place is Peter Marshall's focusing on those philosophical currents which emphasized natural law (Cynics, Stoics, etc.) and his understating of the significance of the *polis* as a form of social self-instituting and equal sharing of power among citizens.[125] No wonder that the same author, as well as many anarchists today, stress the significance of mysticist and spiritualist 'philosophical' currents of the East (Taoism, Buddhism, etc.). But these currents, as Bookchin, Castoriadis and others have stressed, have nothing to do with democracy and collective freedom, let alone philosophy, which always consisted in the questioning of any type of law (natural or man-made) rather than in interpreting the teachings of the masters. No wonder, also, that in the non-democratic societies of the East, where the spiritualist philosophies have flourished, the attachment to tradition meant that 'new ideas were often offered as the rediscovery, or the correct interpretation, of earlier lore . . . the focus was on how to perfect a given system, not how to justify any system by the pure dictates of reason'.[126]

But, if it is neither feasible nor desirable to ground the demand for democracy on 'scientific' or 'objective' 'laws' or 'tendencies' which direct social 'evolution' towards the fulfilment of objective potentialities, then this demand can only be founded on a liberatory *project*. Such a liberatory project today can only constitute a synthesis of the democratic, the socialist, the libertarian and radical Green and feminist traditions. In other words, it can only be a project an inclusive democracy, in the sense of political, economic, 'social' and ecological democracy.

Still, the fact that the project of autonomy is not objectively grounded does not mean that 'anything goes' and that it is therefore impossible to derive any definable body of principles to assess social and political changes, or to develop a set of ethical values to assess human behaviour. Reason is still necessary in a process of deriving the principles and values which are consistent with the project of autonomy and, in this sense, are rational. Therefore, the principles and values derived within such a process do not just express personal tastes and desires and in fact, they are much more 'objective' than the principles and values that are derived from disputable interpretations of natural and social evolution. The logical consistency of the former with the project of autonomy could be assessed in an indisputable way, unlike the contestable 'objectivity' of the latter.

Neither 'scientism' nor 'utopianism'

The fact that the liberatory project cannot be 'scientified' or 'objectivized' does not mean that it is just a utopia (or, in its ecological version, an ecotopia) in the negative sense of the word. A liberatory project is not a utopia if it is based on today's reality. And today's reality is summed up by an unprecedented crisis of the 'growth economy', a crisis which engulfs all societal realms (political, economic, social, cultural) as well as the Society–Nature relationship. Furthermore, a liberatory project is not a utopia, if it expresses the discontent of significant social sectors and their, explicit or implicit, contesting of existing society. Today, the main political, economic and social institutions on which the present concentration of power is founded are increasingly contested. Thus, not only are basic political institutions contested in various ways, as we have seen in Chapter 4, but also fundamental economic institutions, like private property, are challenged in a massive way. The explosion of crime against property in the last quarter of a century (in Britain, for instance, burglary has increased by 160 per cent and theft from vehicles by nearly 200 per cent since 1979),[127] despite the drastic enhancement of private and public security, is not just a cultural or temporary phenomenon. It should be seen, instead, as a long-term trend reflecting the creation of massive unemployment and the massive abuse of drugs (which are also systemic phenomena) as well as the growing discontent with the rising inequality in the distribution of income and wealth – an inequality which, within the context of the present consumer society, becomes unbearable.

The rejection of the view which sees the liberatory project as a 'scientific' project, or, alternatively, as a utopia, has very important implications, as far as political organization is concerned. First, it rules out the traditional form of hierarchical radical organization ('those who know' and therefore have an automatic right to lead, and those who do not). Second, it rules out the various lifestyle strategies which explicitly exclude direct involvement in the political process. In this context, a useful distinction could be drawn between, on the one hand, a scientific *project* and a *programme* and, on the other, between *politics* and *technique*.

As far as the programme is concerned, it is obvious that although we do need a programme, in the sense of a 'provisional and fragmentary concretization of the projects' goals',[128] we definitely do not need, for the reasons stated above, a 'scientific' project. Supporters of 'scientific' projects in politics (as well as 'eco-topians') are, in fact, against democratic politics, as we defined it in Chapter 5. The reason for this hostility is the usual inability to draw a clear distinction between politics and technique. This inability, in fact, constitutes a common characteristic of any hierarchical conception of politics, as the following crude representation of Marxist politics clearly indicates:

If for more complex items like aircraft, bridges and the like we need one or

more sciences, then to produce a new society, different from the one we suffer,
we need the most elaborate and advanced sicence of all, since it must deal with
the most complex organism with the most complex material, structures and
functions.[129]

The implicit assumption in the above extract is that as engineering, making use of the scientific laws of physics or chemistry, produces today's marvels of technology, in exactly the same way we could use the 'scientific' laws of Marxism to produce another society! Apart, therefore, from the very disputable fact we already considered about the feasibility of developing such a science of social change, Marxist or otherwise, it is obvious that this view implies a conception of politics which is utterly incompatible with individual or social autonomy.

In this context, Castoriadis's[130] distinction between *politics as a technique* and *politics as praxis* is very useful. A technique is a 'purely rational' activity which relies on exhaustive (or practically exhaustive) knowledge of its domain. As, therefore, the same author puts it, 'to demand that the revolutionary project is founded on a complete theory is in fact to equate politics with a technique'. But politics, in the word's original Greek meaning, belongs to a different domain, the domain of praxis 'which sees the development of autonomy as an end and uses autonomy as a means to this end . . . where the others are seen as autonomous beings and as the essential factors for the development of their own autonomy'.[131] So, although praxis is a conscious activity, it can only rely on a *fractional* knowledge, because there can never be an exhaustive knowledge of humans and their history, and a *provisional* knowledge, because the praxis itself leads to the continuous emergence of new knowledge. If, therefore, the aim of politics is not, as at present, the manipulation of the electorate and 'statecraft' but, instead, is the autonomous activity of autonomous individuals in managing their own affairs, then what is needed is a programme, and not a Marxist or any other 'science', with its 'iron' laws and the implied 'engineering-view' of politics.

Neither general relativism nor irrationalism

However, discarding scientism (Marxist or otherwise) should not push us to the alternative trap of general relativism and irrationalism. As regards relativism, first, we should make an important distinction between *political* and *democratic relativism* on the one hand and *philosophical relativism* on the other. It is obvious that *democratic relativism,*[132] i.e. that all traditions, theories, ideas, etc. are debated and decided upon by all citizens, is an essential element of democracy. The same applies to political relativism, i.e. that all traditions have equal rights. Still, a strong case can be made against *philosophical relativism*, i.e. that all traditions have equal truth value, in the sense of all being accepted as equally true or false. This is particularly the case when philosophical relativism contradicts democratic relativism.[133]

Thus, although one may accept the post-modernist view that history cannot be seen as a linear (Kant *et al.*) or dialectical (Hegel, Marx) process of progress that embodies reason, this does not imply that we should assign equal value to all historical forms of social organization: from classical Athens, the Swiss cantons and the Parisian sections, to the present 'democratic' regimes. This type of general relativism, which is adopted by post-modernism, simply expresses the latter's abandonment of any critique of the institutionalized social reality and a general retreat to conformism, as Castoriadis[134] rightly points out.

In other words, one cannot assign equal value to the autonomy and the heteronomy traditions, as the adoption of the latter precludes democratic relativism itself. The very possibility of instituting democratic relativism depends on the rejection of philosophical relativism: a conscious choice has therefore to be made between these two traditions and the implied conceptions of politics. It is only in this way that one may avoid the pitfalls of scientism/objectivism, without falling into the post-modernist trap of a general relativism that will assign equal value to all traditions.

But, once we have made a choice among the main traditions, in other words, once we have defined the content of the liberatory project in terms of the autonomy tradition, certain important implications follow at the ethical level, as we have seen above, as well as at the interpretational level. For instance, in interpreting the ecological crisis, its causes and the implied solutions, it is impossible to accept the peculiar pluralism that, for example, Naess[135] proposes, since the very choice of the autonomy tradition implies that only a specific set of interpretations is compatible with it. Irrespective, therefore, of whether we choose the orthodox or the dialectical method, or no method at all, our choice of the autonomy world view constrains us to see the roots of the ecological crisis in terms of the hierarchical social relations and structures which have been dominant for so long (as social ecology does) and not in terms of the relationship between an un-differentiated 'society' and nature (as environmentalists, deep ecologists and others do). For the same reason, environmentalist (liberal or social-democratic), mystical and metaphysical 'solutions' to the ecological problem should be rejected, not because they are not compatible with supposedly 'objective', social or natural, processes at work, but because they could be shown to be incompatible with social and individual autonomy, that is, incompatible with freedom itself. The problem today, therefore, is not *either* to adopt general relativism, a stand that may lead to a post-modern conformism *or*, alternatively, to adopt some kind of 'objectivism'. What is lacking today is not a new 'objective' justification of the liberatory project, but the political will to define it and take part in its realization!

Another important issue that arises once scientism/objectivism is rejected is how we can avoid the retreat to the various types of irrationalism that currently abound in the Green movement (e.g. deep ecology), the feminist movement (some versions of eco-feminism) and so on. As is well known, versions of irrationalism and spiritualism are frequently adopted widely both in the North (revival of the old religions, adoption of some spiritualist 'fruits' from the East, like Taoism, which influence several Anglo-Saxon anarchists, etc.) and in the South (Muslim fundamentalism).

In my view, the stand on relativism that was suggested above, combined with the conscious choice of the autonomy tradition, which is implied by democratic relativism, rules out all forms of irrationalism. This is so because the common characteristic that the various forms of irrationalism share is that they all lie outside the field of *logon didonai* (rendering account and reason), which, as Castoriadis puts it, 'in itself entails the recognition of the value of autonomy in the sphere of thinking'[136] that is synonymous with reason itself. In this sense, science, properly understood, is a form of *logon didonai*. From the democratic viewpoint, the essence of science lies not in its content, although of course natural sciences, by fostering a secular approach to reality, played a significant liberatory role in subverting religious and metaphysical beliefs; the essence of science lies in the constant questioning of truths, i.e. in the procedures it uses to derive its truths. Therefore, science, although from the point of view of its content (as well as its technological applications) it may enhance either autonomy or heteronomy (mainly the latter, given the usual heteronomous institution of society which conditions the development of science), from the point of view of the procedures used, it has historically been an expression of autonomy. This is because of the crucial difference regarding the procedures used by scientists in deriving scientific 'truths', versus the methods used by prophets, church fathers and gurus of various sorts to create beliefs, dogmas, mystical 'truths', etc. The very fact that the scientific procedures of finding and assessing 'truths' have so drastically changed over time is a clear indication of the autonomous nature of the scientific method. Scientific 'truths', as well as the procedures used to derive them, unlike mystical, intuitional and irrational 'truths' and procedures in general, are subject to constant questioning and critical assessment.

By the same token, the fact that autonomy is not an 'individual' affair and it is 'decisively conditioned by the institution of society'[137] implies that the project of autonomy can only be realized through the autonomous activity of the people, within a process of creating social institutions, which make autonomous thinking possible, and not through some kind of spiritual process of 'self-realization', as deep ecologists,[138] for instance, suggest. In fact, such a process of self-realization could only enhance privacy and the withdrawal from the social process that institutes society. A hierarchical society based on the domination of human over human could perfectly survive the self-transformation (usually of its middle classes) in the form of Mahayana Buddhism's enlightenment, or reborn Christianism. It is not accidental, anyway, that self-transformation of millions of Americans and West Europeans along these lines, in the past decade, was fully compatible with one of the most vicious attacks by the ruling elites that took the form of neoliberal policies (Reaganomics, Thatcherism, etc.).

Conclusion: towards a democratic rationalism

To conclude, neither 'objectivism' nor irrationalism have any role to play in the process that will move us towards an inclusive democracy. As I tried to show in this chapter, democracy is incompatible with 'objectivist' types of rationalism, similar to the ones we inherited from the Enlightenment. Furthermore, democracy is even less compatible with irrational systems claiming esoteric knowledge, whether from mystical experience, intuition, or revelation. Democracy is only compatible with a democratic rationalism, namely, a rationalism founded in democracy as a structure and a process of social self-institution, as we defined it above.

Therefore, if our aim is to reach a synthesis of the autonomous-democratic, libertarian socialist and radical Green and feminist traditions, I think that our starting point should be the fact that the social imaginary or creative element plays a crucial role with respect to social change. This implies that the project for democracy may be grounded only on our own conscious choice between the heteronomous and the autonomous tradition.

I think that this way of thinking avoids the traps of both objectivism and relativism. Thus, it does not fall into objectivism because the liberatory project is not 'objectivized': democracy is justified not by an appeal to objective tendencies with respect to natural or social evolution, but by an appeal to reason in terms of *logon didonai*, which explicitly denies the idea of any directionality as regards social change. Furthermore, it avoids relativism because it explicitly denies the view that all traditions, as in this case the autonomy and heteronomy ones, have equal truth values. In other words, taking for granted that autonomy and democracy cannot be 'proved' but only postulated, *we* value autonomy and democracy more than heteronomy because, although both traditions are true, still, it is autonomy and democracy which *we* identify with freedom and *we assess freedom as the highest human objective.*

Notes

1. Cornelius Castoriadis, 'The era of generalized conformism', lecture given at Boston University on 19 September 1989 in a symposium under the general title 'A metaphor for our times'.
2. Paul Feyerabend, *Farewell to Reason* (London: Verso, 1987), p. 306.
3. For a definition of the liberatory project in terms of social and individual autonomy, see Cornelius Castoriadis, *L'Institution Imaginaire de la Société* (Paris: Seuil, 1975), Ch. 2 (English translation: *The Imaginary Institution of Society* (Cambridge, MA: MIT Press, 1987)).
4. Murray Bookchin, *The Philosophy of Social Ecology, Essays on Dialectical Naturalism* (Montreal: Black Rose Books, 1995), p. 129.
5. See D.W. Hamlyn, *The Theory of Knowledge* (London: Macmillan, 1970), and Frederick Copleston, *A History of Philosophy* (London: Search Press, 1976).
6. Frederick Copleston, *A History of Philosophy*, Vol. IV, p. 17.
7. D.W. Hamlyn, *The Theory of Knowledge*, pp.132–6.
8. Thomas Kuhn, *The Structure of Scientific Revolutions* (University of Chicago Press, 1970), pp.191–8.
9. M. Bookchin, *The Philosophy of Social Ecology*, pp. 114, 130.
10. See I. Lakatos's 'Falsification and the methodology of scientific research programmes' in *Criticism and the Growth of Knowledge*, Lakatos and Musgrave (Cambridge: Cambridge University Press, 1970), pp. 93–103.
11. H. Katouzian, *Ideology and Method in Economics* (London: Macmillan, 1980), p. 53.
12. Lakatos and Musgrave, *The Growth of Knowledge*, p.100.
13. Lakatos and Musgrave, *The Growth of Knowledge*, p. 103.
14. P. Feyerabend, 'Consolations for the specialist' in *The Growth of Knowledge*, Lakatos and Musgrave, pp. 197–231.
15. P. Feyerabend, 'Consolations for the specialist', p. 215.
16. P. Feyerabend, *Farewell to Reason*, p. 9.
17. D.W. Hamlyn, *The Theory of Knowledge*, p. 140.
18. M. Masterman, 'The nature of a paradigm' in *The Growth of Knowledge*, Lakatos and Musgrave, pp. 59–91.
19. T. Kuhn, *The Structure of Scientific Revolutions*, p. 175.
20. See, e.g. Kuhn's postscript in later editions of *The Structure of Scientific Revolutions* and also his contribution in *The Growth of Knowledge*, Lakatos and Musgrave.
21. M. Blaug, *The Methodology of Economics* (Cambridge: Cambridge University Press, 1980), p. 30.
22. P. Feyerabend, *Science in a Free Society* (London: Verso, 1978), p. 66.
23. T. Kuhn, *The Structure of Scientific Revolutions*, p. 94.
24. P. Feyerabend, *Farewell to Reason*, p. 8.
25. For a discussion of the 'scientific' character of economics see, e.g., T.W. Hutchison, *Knowledge and Ignorance in Economics* (Oxford: Basil Blackwell, 1977); Daniel Bell and Irving Kristol, *The Crisis in Economic Theory* (New

York: Basic Books, 1981); Homa Katouzian, *Ideology and Method in Economics* (London: Macmillan, 1980); Warren J. Samuels (ed.) *The Methodology of Economic Thought* (New Brunswick and London: Transaction Books, 1980).

26. Lucien Goldmann, *Immanuel Kant* (London: New Left Books, 1971), p. 19.

27. L. Goldmann, *Immanuel Kant*, p. 53.

28. Murray Bookchin, 'Recovering evolution: a reply to Eckersley and Fox', *Environmental Ethics*, Vol. 12 (1990), p. 2.

29. Murray Bookchin, *The Philosophy of Social Ecology*, p. 129.

30. M. Bookchin, *The Philosophy of Social Ecology*, p. 25.

31. C. Castoriadis, *L'Institution Imaginaire*, pp. 49–50.

32. C. Castoriadis, *Philosophy, Politics, Autonomy* (Oxford: Oxford University Press, 1991), pp. 104–5.

33. Barry Hindess and Paul Q. Hirst, *Pre-Capitalist Modes of Production* (London: Routledge & Kegan Paul, 1975), pp. 313–23. See also Antony Cutler, Barry Hindess *et al., Marx's Capital and Capitalism Today* (London: Routledge & Kegan Paul, 1977), Ch. 4.

34. Karl Marx, Preface to the first German edition of *Das Capital* (Moscow: Progress Publishers/Lawrence & Wishart, 1965), pp. 8–10.

35. Vladimir Lenin, 'What the friends of the people are', in *Reader in Marxist Philosophy*, H. Selsam and H. Martel (eds) (New York: International Publishers, 1963), pp. 196–7.

36. C. Castoriadis, *L'Institution Imaginaire*, pp.76–84.

37. Karl Marx, *Theses on Feuerbach*, in Karl Marx and Friedrich Engels, *The German Ideology* (Moscow: Progress Publishers, 1968), p. 667.

38. Louis Althusser, *Reading Capital* (London: New Left Books, 1970).

39. Gregor McLennan, *Marxism and the Methodologies of History* (London: New Left Books, 1981/1987), p. 22.

40. George Lukacs, *History and Class Consciousness* (London: Merlin Press, 1971), p. 1.

41. G. McLennan, *Marxism and the Methodologies of History*, p. 15.

42. C. Castoriadis, *L'Institution Imaginaire*, pp. 13–20.

43. Quoted in G. McLennan, *Marxism and the Methodologies of History*, p. 167.

44. George Lukacs, 'Technology and social relations', *New Left Review*, No. 39 (1966), p. 33.

45. Peter Binns, 'The Marxist theory of truth', *Radical Philosophy*, No. 4 (Spring 1973), p. 5.

46. P. Binns, 'The Marxist theory of truth', p. 8.

47. Anthony Collier, 'Truth and practice', *Radical Philosophy* (Summer 1973), p. 10.

48. Leszek Kolakowski, *Marxism and Beyond*, p. 59, quoted in 'Truth and practice', A. Collier, p. 10.

49. C. Castoriadis, *L'Institution Imaginaire*, pp. 40–5.

50. See, e.g. Paul Sweezy, 'Toward a critique of economics' in his *Modern Capitalism and Other Essays* (New York: Monthly Review Press, 1972).

51. For a critique of this position, see G. McLennan, *Marxism and the Methodologies of History*, p. 15.

52. See Leszek Kolakowski, *Main Currents of Marxism* (Oxford: Oxford University Press, 1981), Vol. 1, p. 181.

JUSTIFYING AN INCLUSIVE DEMOCRACY

53. In Lenin's *Materialism and Empiriocriticism*, the account of knowledge given by the author is too close to simple empiricism, as G. McLennan points out in *Marxism and the Methodologies of History*, p. 11.
54. See Michio Morishima and George Catephores, *Value, Exploitation and Growth* (London: McGraw-Hill, 1978), p. 297.
55. Max Weber, *The Methodology of Social Sciences* (Illinois: Glance, 1949), Ch. 1.
56. For a further critique of this solution, from a different viewpoint, see Leszek Kolakowski, *Main Currents of Marxism*, Vol. 1, pp. 315–16.
57. Leszek Kolakowski, *Main Currents of Marxism*, Vol. 1, pp. 322–4.
58. G. McLennan, also, agrees with this classification: 'As it affects substantive issues in historical materialism Althusser's project can be described as "rationalism"'; G. McLennan, *Marxism and the Methodologies of History*, p. 28.
59. L. Althusser, *Reading Capital*, pp. 52–6.
60. L. Althusser, *Reading Capital*, p. 59.
61. G. McLennan, *Marxism and the Methodologies of History*, p. 27.
62. G. McLennan, *Marxism and the Methodologies of History*. See also P. Binns, 'The Marxist theory of truth'.
63. P. Binns, 'The Marxist theory of thruth', p. 8.
64. C. Castoriadis, *L'Institution Imaginaire*, pp. 57–8.
65. C. Castoriadis, *L'Institution Imaginaire*, pp. 72–3.
66. C. Castoriadis, *L'Institution Imaginaire*, p. 90.
67. C. Castoriadis, *L'Institution Imaginaire*, pp. 184–90.
68. Louis Althusser and Etienne Balibar, *Reading Capital* (London: NLB, 1970), p. 180.
69. See Roy Bhaskar, *A Realist Theory of Science* (Leeds: Leeds Books, 1975); Gregor McLennan, *Marxism and the Methodologies of History*; and for a post-Marxist critique of this approach, see Nikos Mouzelis, *Post-Marxist Alternatives, The Construction of Social Orders* (London: Macmillan, 1990).
70. R. Bhaskar, *A Realist Theory of Science*, p. 250.
71. R. Bhaskar, *A Realist Theory of Science*, p. 248.
72. G. McLennan, *Marxism and the Methodologies of History*, p. 32.
73. Mouzelis, criticizing realist Marxism from a different perspective, argues that Marxist theory is unable to overcome the dilemma 'essentialism or empiricism' irrespective of the epistemological position adopted; N. Mouzelis, *Post-Marxist Alternatives*, p. 29.
74. See, for instance, Albert Bergesen, 'Deep ecology and moral community' in *Rethinking Materialism*, Robert Wuthnow (ed.) (New York: Erdmanns, 1995).
75. See M. Bookchin, *The Philosophy of Social Ecology*.
76. M. Bookchin, *The Philosophy of Social Ecology*, p. 20.
77. M. Bookchin, *The Philosophy of Social Ecology*, p. 17.
78. M. Bookchin, *The Philosophy of Social Ecology*, p. 31.
79. M. Bookchin, *Remaking Society* (Montreal: Black Rose Books, 1989), p. 25.
80. M. Bookchin, *The Philosophy of Social Ecology*, p. xii.
81. M. Bookchin, *The Philosophy of Social Ecology*, p. xi.
82. C. Castoriadis, *Philosophy, Politics, Autonomy*, pp. 268–9.
83. See, e.g. Stuart A. Kaufmann, *The Origins of Order: Self-organization and Selection in Evolution* (Oxford: Oxford Univeristy Press, 1993).

84. C. Castoriadis, *Philosophy, Politics, Autonomy*, pp. 104–5.
85. C. Castoriadis, *Philosophy, Politics, Autonomy*, p. 34.
86. Peter Marshall, *Nature's Web* (London: Simon & Schuster, 1992), p. 426.
87. M. Bookchin, *The Philosophy of Social Ecology*, p. 79.
88. See for instance, John M. Gowdy, 'Progress and environmental sustainability', *Environmental Ethics*, Vol. 16, No. 1 (Spring 1994).
89. For the non-neutrality of technology, see Frances Stewart, *Technology and Underdevelopment* (London: Macmillan, 1978).
90. Amnesty International, *A Glimpse of Hell* (London: Cassell/Amnesty International UK, 1996).
91. Karl Polanyi, *The Great Transformation* (Boston: Beacon Press, 1957), Chs 14–15.
92. Konstantinos Kavoulakos, 'The relationship of realism and utopianism in the theories of democracy of Jürgen Habermas and Cornelius Castoriadis', *Society and Nature*, Vol. 2, No. 3 (1994), p. 74. See also N. Bobbio, 'Science, power and freedom', *Eleftherotypia*, 18 Sept. 1995.
93. See J. Gowdy, 'Progress and environmental sustainability'.
94. See C. Castoriadis, 'The era of generalized conformism'.
95. Cornelius Castoriadis, 'The West and the Third World', lecture in Heraklion (Crete), March 1991, in *The Broken World*, Cornelius Castoriadis (Athens: Upsilon Books, 1992), p. 79.
96. For a classic description of the medieval free cities, see Pëtr Kropotkin, *Mutual Aid* (London, 1902) CBS. V & V.
97. Murray Bookchin, personal communication to author (24/2/1994).
98. Murray Bookchin, *From Urbanization to Cities* (London: Cassell, 1995), pp. 111–16.
99. See Sam Dolgoff (ed.) *The Anarchist Collectives: Workers' Self-management in the Spanish Revolution 1936–39* (New York: Free Life Editions, 1974).
100. This should not be misunderstood, as some deep ecologists do at the moment, to mean that society will change just by changing our values, or 'imaginary significations' at the individual level. The change in values has a social significance, as far as radical social transformation is concerned, if it is the outcome of a collective struggle, as part of a comprehensive political programme that explicitly questions the institutional framework and the dominant social paradigm.
101. C. Castoriadis, *Philosophy, Politics, Autonomy*, pp. 36–8.
102. 'What is potential in an acorn that yields an oak tree or in a human embryo that yields a mature, creative adult is equivalent to what is potential in nature that yields society and what is potential in society that yields freedom, selfhood, and consciousness', Murray Bookchin, *The Modern Crisis* (Montreal: Black Rose Books, 1987), p.13.
103. C. Castoriadis, *Philosophy, Politics, Autonomy*, p. 88.
104. M. Bookchin, *The Philosophy of Social Ecology*, pp. 157–70.
105. See, e.g., Shlomo Avineri (ed.) *Karl Marx on Colonialism and Modernization* (New York: Anchor Books, 1969), p. 13; and Anthony Brewer, *Marxist Theories of Imperialism* (London: Routledge & Kegan Paul, 1980), p. 18.
106. See G.P. Maximoff (ed.) *The Political Philosophy of Bakunin* (New York: The Free Press, 1953), p. 145. See also M. Bookchin, *The Philosophy of Social Ecology*, p. xvi.

107. M. Bookchin, *Ecology of Freedom* (Montreal: Black Rose Books, 1991), p. 274.

108. See, for instance, the criticisms raised against dialectical naturalism by eco-socialists such as David Pepper (David Pepper, *Eco-Socialism: From Deep Ecology to Social Justice* (London: Routledge, 1993), p. 165); and Andrew Light (Andrew Light, 'Rereading Bookchin and Marcuse as environmental materialists', *Capitalism, Nature, Socialism*, No. 3 (March 1993), and Andrew Light, 'Which side are you on? A rejoinder to Murray Bookchin', *Capitalism, Nature, Socialism*, No. 14 (June 1993)). See also the criticisms raised by deep ecologists like Robyn Eckersley (Robyn Eckersley, 'Divining evolution: the ecological ethics of Murray Bookchin', *Environmental Ethics*, Vol. 11, No. 2 (Summer 1989)).

109. The debate between Bookchin and Fox/Eckersley is a clear example of incommensurability. See R. Eckersley, 'Divining evolution: the ecological ethics of Murray Bookchin'; and M. Bookchin, 'Recovering evolution: a reply to Eckersley and Fox'.

110. P. Feyerabend, *Farewell to Reason*, p. 75.

111. Cornelius Castoriadis, 'The end of philosophy?' in *The Talks in Greece* (Athens: Upsilon, 1990), p. 23.

112. Herbert Marcuse, *Soviet Marxism* (London: Routledge, 1958), p. 145.

113. Vladimir Lenin, *What Is to Be Done?* (Moscow: Progress Publishers, 1967): cf. pp. 30–2.

114. H. Marcuse, *Soviet Marxism*, p. 147.

115. C. Castoriadis, *The Talks in Greece*, p. 126.

116. Cynthia Farrar, referring to the thought of the sophist philosopher Protagoras. See her article, 'Ancient Greek political theory as a response to democracy' in *Democracy, the Unfinished Journey, 508 BC to AD 1993* John Dunn (ed.) (Oxford: Oxford University Press, 1992), p. 24.

117. C. Castoriadis, *Philosophy, Politics, Autonomy*, p. 21.

118. Mogens Herman Hansen, *The Athenian Democracy in the Age of Demosthenes* (Oxford: Blackwell, 1991) p. 64.

119. Cornelius Castoriadis, 'The problem of democracy today', *Democracy and Nature*, Vol. 3, No. 2 (1996), p. 23.

120. Murray Bookchin, *Re-enchanting Humanity* (London: Cassell, 1995), p. 249.

121. Hannah Arendt, *The Human Condition* (Chicago: The University of Chicago Press, 1958), p. 18.

122. Paul J. Achtemeier (ed.) *Harper's Bible Dictionary* (San Francisco: Harper & Row, 1985), p. 481.

123. Quoted in Fritjof Capra, *The Tao of Physics* (London: Fontana, 1983), p. 126.

124. 'It may well be, however, that the tradition of democracy in the post–Greek world had its obscure roots among the Catharists': George Woodcock, 'Democracy, heretical and radical', *Our Generation*, Vol. 22, Nos 1–2 (Fall 1990–Spring 1991), pp. 115–16.

125. Peter Marshall, erroneously identifying *Nomos* (i.e. the laws of the *polis*) with custom and convention, points out that 'The Cynics of the third century came even closer to anarchism ... they alone rejected *Nomos* in favour of *Physis*; they wished to live purely "according to Nature".... since the Greek *Polis* was based on the rule of custom or convention, by rejecting *Nomos*, the

Cynics denied the right of established authority to prescribe the limits of their actions': Peter Marshall, *Demanding the Impossible* (London: HarperCollins, 1992), p. 68.

126. G.E.R. Lloyd, 'Democracy, philosophy and science in Ancient Greece' in *Democracy*, John Dunn (ed.) p. 55.

127. John Prescott, Labour deputy leader, to Michael Heseltine in the Commons, 29 Jan. 1996 (*The Guardian*, 30 Jan. 1996).

128. C. Castoriadis, *L'Institution Imaginaire*, p. 106.

129. Thanasis Kalomalos, 'The crisis of Left politics and Karl Marx', *Society and Nature*, Vol. 2, No. 1 (1993), p. 175.

130. C. Castoriadis, *L'Institution Imaginaire*, pp. 97–109.

131. C. Castoriadis, *L'Institution Imaginaire*, p. 103.

132. P. Feyerabend, *Farewell to Reason*, p. 59.

133. Even Feyerabend, a strong supporter of relativism, does not go as far as to adopt philosophical relativism; P. Feyerabend, *Science in a Free Society*, pp. 82–3.

134. C. Castoriadis, 'The era of generalized conformism'.

135. Arne Naess, 'Deep ecology and ultimate premises', *The Ecologist*, Vol. 18, Nos 4/5 (1988).

136. C. Castoriadis, 'The crisis of Marxism and the crisis of politics', *Society and Nature*, Vol. 1, No. 2 (1992), p. 209.

137. C. Castoriadis, 'The crisis of Marxism and the crisis of politics', p. 209.

138. According to Naess, the father of deep ecology, 'The higher the self-realization attained by anyone the broader and deeper the identification with others', Arne Naess, *Ecology, Community and Lifestyle* (Cambridge: Cambridge University Press, 1989), p. 196.

Epilogue

The collapse of 'actually existing socialism' led the Left to abandon any idea of a free society which, as I tried to show in the preceding chapters, is incompatible with the market economy and liberal democracy. This particularly applies to the various forms of 'radical' democracy that are advocated by the Left and the mainstream Greens who propose various combinations of the market economy with liberal 'democracy' with the aim of enhancing the civil society. The market economy is adopted because it has supposedly proved its 'efficiency' over planning, whereas the liberal democracy is embraced because it supposedly secures individual autonomy.

In fact, as shown in the preceding chapters, neither of these suppositions is valid. The market economy and the consequent growth economy are far from efficient in securing human welfare, either in terms of satisfying even the basic needs of the majority of the world population, or in terms of meeting the requirements of quality of life for everybody – apart perhaps from the 1 per cent or so of the world population which constitutes the 'overclass'. Also, liberal democracy has led to the present concentration of power in the hands of elites who control political power with the help of the mass media, which play a crucial role in manufacturing consent and legitimizing the choices of the elites.[1]

Furthermore, as the book has attempted to demonstrate, the Left's proposals for the enhancement of the civil society are utterly utopian in the present context of the internationalized market economy. As long as political and economic power is concentrated, through a system that has built-in mechanisms to enhance this concentration further, there is no arrangement from within the system to force radical decentralization in the direction desired by the supporters of the civil-societarian approach. And, as I have tried to show, the acceleration of internationalization leads to significant changes in the economic and political structures, which only further the concentration of economic and political power. In fact, the present degree of internationalization of the market economy implies not only that the model of the market economy that has the best chance of being universalized will be the most competitive one, but also that the type of civil society which will eventually prevail will be the one most compatible with this model. As we have seen in the preceding chapters, this is the model which imposes the fewest social controls on markets, that is, the most marketized one.

To put it simply, on the basis of present trends, the type of economy and society that will become universal is not the 'social market' and/or corporatist models of Germany and Japan, on which civil societarians placed their hopes after the collapse of the Scandinavian model. The world seems to be moving to a new, even cruder, world order than the present one, which has little to do with the pious hopes of the civil-societarian Left for a more democratic world where the various elites will be much more accountable to the civil society than at present. This new world order implies that, at the centre, the model that has the greatest chance of being universalized is the Anglo-Saxon model of massive low-paid employment and underemployment, with poverty alleviated by the few security nets that the '40 per cent society' will be willing to finance, in exchange for a tolerable degree of social peace which will be mainly secured by the vast security apparatuses being created by the public and private sectors. As regards the periphery, parts of it will continue with their present 'in-dustrialization', creating the illusion of economic development, whereas in fact they will be merely providing the location for cheap (in terms of labour costs) and dirty (in terms of environmental costs) production so that the growth economy in the centre and its bad copy in the periphery may be reproduced.

The development of this new world order cannot be attributed to the 'greed' of neoliberals or the 'betrayal' of social democrats. Within the present institutional framework, the policy options of the elites (either of the neoliberal or social-democratic variety) are severely restricted. Within an internationalized market economy, the introduction of effective social controls to protect the underclass and the marginalized, or to preserve the environment, will create serious comparative disadvantages for the nation-state or economic bloc that will embark on such policies. In this context, with crude dilemmas such as that of 'jobs or the environment' emerging all the time, not only the privileged '40 per cent society' but even parts of the underclass and the marginalized could be easily persuaded that the only realistic policies are the ones followed by their elites. And in a sense these policies are indeed realistic. In other words, *within the constraints imposed by the institutional framework* of the internationalized market economy, the elites are right in stressing that 'there is no alternative'.

This means that the lists of institutional arrangements proposed by the civil societarian 'Left' today in order to impose effective social controls on the national or international markets, which, they hope, under the pressure of an enhanced 'civil society' will one day become a reality, represent nothing more than the wishful thinking of a demoralized 'Left' that has abandoned any vision of a radical transformation of society. The only feasible controls today are, as it has been argued in this book, those of a regulatory character, mostly in the interest of those controlling the economy, whereas any effective social controls in the interest of the rest of society are not feasible any more, within the context of an internationalized market economy. This is why the various versions of 'radical' democracy are much more unrealistic than the proposal for an inclusive democracy presented in the preceding chapters.

This book has one aim and one ambition. The aim is to show that the way out of the present multidimensional crisis can only be found from without rather than from within the present institutional framework. The ambition is to initiate a discussion concerning the need for a new liberatory project and the strategies for implementing it.

Note

1. For an excellent description of this process, see Edward S. Herman and Noam Chomsky, *Manufacturing Consent, The Political Economy of the Mass Media* (New York: Pantheon Books, 1988).

Select Bibliography

Albert, M. *Capitalism Against Capitalism* (London: Whurr, 1993).

Albert, M. and Hahnel, R. *Looking Forward: Participatory Economics for the Twenty-First Century* (Boston: South End Press, 1991).

Allen, G. *et al.* (eds) *Community Education* (Milton Keynes: Open University Press, 1987).

Allen, J. and Massey, D. (eds) *Restructuring Britain: The Economy in Question* (London: Sage Publications, 1988).

Althusser, L. and Balibar, E. *Reading Capital* (London: New Left Books, 1970).

Amin, S. *Accumulation on a World Scale* (New York: Monthly Review Press, 1974).

Amsden, A.H. *Asia's Next Giant: South Korea and Late Industrialization* (Oxford: Oxford University Press, 1989).

Anderson, A. *Hungary 56* (London: Solidarity, 1964).

Anderson, P. 'The affinities of Norberto Bobbio', *New Left Review*, No. 170 (July/August 1988).

Anderson, P. and Camiller, P. (eds) *Mapping the West European Left* (London: Verso, 1994).

Anderson, P. and Davey, K. 'Communitarianism', *New Statesman & Society* (3 March 1995).

Anderson, V. *Alternative Economic Indicators* (New York: Routledge & Kegan Paul, 1991).

Arendt, H. *The Human Condition* (Chicago: The University of Chicago Press, 1958).

Arendt, H. *On Revolution* (Harmondsworth: Penguin, 1990).

Argy, V. *The Postwar International Money Crisis* (London: Allen & Unwin, 1981).

Aristotle, *The Athenian Constitution*, John Warrington (ed.) (London: Heron Books, 1934).

Aristotle, *Politics*, John Warrington (ed.) (London: Heron Books, 1934).

Armstrong, P. *et al.*, *Capitalism Since World War II* (London: Fontana, 1984).

Arrow, K.J. 'Problems mount in application of free market economic theory', *The Guardian* (4 Jan. 1994).

Atkinson, A. *et al.*, *Income Distribution in OECD Countries* (Paris: OECD, 1995).

Atkinson, D. *The Common Sense of Community* (London: Demos, 1994).

Auerbach, P. *et al.*, 'The transition from actually existing capitalism', *New Left Review*, No. 170 (July/August 1988).

Avineri, S. (ed.) *Karl Marx on Colonialism and Modernization* (New York: Anchor Books, 1969).

Bachrach, P. *The Theory of Democratic Elitism* (Boston, 1967).

Bahro, R. *The Alternative in Eastern Europe* (London: Verso, 1978).

Bairoch, P. *The Economic Development of the Third World Since 1900* (London: Methuen, 1975).

Baldelli, G. *Social Anarchism* (New York: Penguin, 1972).

Baran, P.A. *The Political Economy of Growth* (New York: Modern Reader, 1957).

Barr, N. *The Economics of the Welfare State* (London: Weidenfeld & Nicolson, 1987).

Barratt-Brown, M. *Models in Political Economy* (London: Penguin, 1984).

Bell, D. and Kristol, I. *The Crisis in Economic Theory* (New York: Basic Books, 1981).

Benello, C.G., Swann, R. and Turnbull, S. *Building Sustainable Communities* (New York: Bootstrap, 1989).

Bergesen, A. 'Deep ecology and moral community' in *Rethinking Materialism*, Robert Wuthnow (ed.) (New York: Erdmanns, 1995).

Berlin, I. *Four Essays on Liberty* (Oxford: Oxford University Press, 1969).

Bernstein, H. (ed.) *Underdevelopment and Development* (Harmondsworth: Penguin, 1973).

Berry, T. *The Dream of the Earth* (San Francisco: Sierra Club, 1988).

BFI, *Film and Television Handbook 1993* (London: British Film Institute, 1993).

Bhaskar, R. *A Realist Theory of Science* (Leeds: Leeds Books, 1975).

Biehl, J. *Rethinking Ecofeminist Politics* (Boston: South End Press, 1991).

Biehl, J. 'Ecology and the modernization of fascism in the German ultraright', *Society and Nature*, Vol. 2, No. 2 (1994).

Binns, P. 'The Marxist theory of truth', *Radical Philosophy*, No. 4 (Spring 1973).

Birch, A.H. *The Concepts and Theories of Modern Democracy* (London: Routledge, 1993).

Blackaby, F. (ed.) *De-Industrialization* (London: Heinemann, 1979).

Blackburn, R. 'Fin de siècle: socialism after the crash', *New Left Review* (Jan./Feb. 1991).

Blaug, M. *The Methodology of Economics* (Cambridge: Cambridge University Press, 1980).

Bleaney, M. *The Rise and Fall of Keynesian Economics* (London: Macmillan, 1985).

Bookchin, M. *Post-Scarcity Anarchism* (London: Wildwood House, 1974).

Bookchin, M. 'Municipalization: community ownership of the economy', *Green Perspectives* (Feb. 1986).

Bookchin, M. *The Modern Crisis* (Montreal: Black Rose Books, 1987).

Bookchin, M. 'Recovering evolution: a reply to Eckersley and Fox', *Environmental Ethics*, Vol. 12 (1990).

Bookchin, M. *Remaking Society* (Montreal: Black Rose Books, 1990).

Bookchin, M. and Foreman, D. *Defending the Earth, A Debate Between Murray Bookchin and Dave Foreman* (Montreal: Black Rose Books, 1991).

Bookchin, M. *The Ecology of Freedom: The Emergence and Dissolution of Hierarchy* (Montreal: Black Rose Books, 1991).

Bookchin, M. 'Libertarian municipalism: an overview', *Society and Nature*, Vol. 1, No. 1 (1992).

Bookchin, M. *Urbanization Without Cities* (Montreal: Black Rose Books, 1992).

Bookchin, M. 'The ghost of anarcho-syndicalism', *Anarchist Studies*, Vol. 1, No. 1 (Spring 1993).

Bookchin, M. *Which Way for the Ecology Movement?* (Edinburgh: AK Press, 1994).

Bookchin, M. *From Urbanization to Cities* (London: Cassell, 1995).

Bookchin, M. *The Philosophy of Social Ecology* (Montreal: Black Rose Books, 1995).

Bookchin, M. *Re-enchanting Humanity* (London: Cassell, 1995).

Bookchin, M. 'Communalism: the democratic dimension of anarchism', *Democracy and Nature* (formerly *Society and Nature*), Vol. 3, No. 2 (1996).

Bornstein, M. *Comparative Economic Systems* (Homewood, ILL: Richard Irwin, 1985).

Bosanquet, N. *After the New Right* (London: Heinemann, 1983).

Boswell, J. *Community and the Economy, The Theory of Public Co-operation* (London: Routledge, 1990).

Bowles, P. and Dong, X.-Y. 'Current successes and future challenges in China's economic reforms', *New Left Review*, No. 208 (Nov./Dec. 1994).

Bowring, F. 'André Gorz: ecology, system and lifeworld', *Capitalism, Nature, Socialism*, No. 24 (Dec. 1995).

Boyer, R. *La théorie de la régulation* (Paris: Editions La Découverte, 1986).

Brammal, C. and Jones, M. 'Rural income inequality in China since 1978', *Journal of Peasant Studies*, Vol. 21, No. 1 (Oct. 1993).

Brecher, J. and Costello, T. *Global Village or Global Pillage: Economic Restructuring from the Bottom Up* (Boston: South End Press, 1994).

Brewer, A. *Marxist Theories of Imperialism: A Critical Survey* (London: Routledge & Kegan Paul, 1980).

Brewer, P. *Feminism and Socialism: Putting the Pieces Together* (Sydney: New Course, 1992).

Brown, A.A. and Neuberger, E. *International Trade and Central Planning* (Berkeley: University of California Press, 1968).

Brown, L.S. *The Politics of Individualism* (Montreal: Black Rose Books, 1993).

Buzgalin, A. and Kolganov, A. 'Russia: the rout of the neo-liberals', *New Left Review*, No. 215 (Jan./Feb. 1996).

Campbell, M. *Capitalism in the UK* (London: Croom Helm, 1981).

Capra, F. *The Tao of Physics* (London: Fontana, 1983).

Carley, M. and Christie, I. *Managing Sustainable Development* (Minneapolis: University of Minnesota Press, 1993).

Carter, A. *The Political Theory of Anarchism* (London: Routledge & Kegan Paul, 1971).

Carter, A. *Authority and Democracy* (London: Routledge & Kegan Paul, 1979).

Carter, A. *Marx: A Radical Critique* (Brighton: Wheatsheaf, 1988).

Castoriadis, C. *Workers' Councils and the Economics of a Self-Managed Society* (London: Solidarity, 1972).

Castoriadis, C. *The Ancient Greek Democracy and its Significance for us Today* (Athens: Upsilon, 1986) (in Greek).

Castoriadis, C. *The Imaginary Institution of Society* (Cambridge: Polity Press and Cambridge, MA.: MIT, 1987).

Castoriadis, C. *Political and Social Writings* (Minneapolis: University of Minnesota Press, 1988), Vols 1–2.

Castoriadis, C. 'An interview', *Radical Philosophy*, Vol. 56 (Autumn 1990).

Castoriadis, C. *The Talks in Greece* (Athens: Upsilon, 1990) (in Greek).

Castoriadis, C. *Philosophy, Politics, Autonomy* (Oxford: Oxford University Press, 1991).

Castoriadis, C. *The Broken World* (Athens: Upsilon, 1992) (in Greek).

Castoriadis, C. 'The crisis of Marxism and the crisis of politics', *Society and Nature*, Vol. 1, No. 2 (1992).

Castoriadis, C. *Les Carrefours du Labyrinthe IV* (Paris: Seuil, 1996).

Cecchini, P. *1992: The European Challenge* (London: Wildwood House, 1988).

Chase-Dunn, C.K. (ed.) *Socialist States in the World System* (London: Sage Publications, 1982).

Chomsky, N. *The Chomsky Reader*, James Peck (ed.) (London: Serpent's Tail, 1987).

Chomsky, N. *Deterring Democracy* (London: Verso, 1991).

Chomsky, N. *The Prosperous Few and the Restless Many* (Berkeley, CA: Odonian Press, 1993).

Chomsky, N. 'Rollback IV', *Z Magazine* (May 1995).

Chomsky, N. 'On "theory" and "post-modern cults" ', *Upstream Issues* (1996).

Chomsky, N. and Herman, S. *Manufacturing Consent, The Political Economy of the Mass Media* (New York: Pantheon Books, 1988).

Clark, J. (ed.) *Renewing the Earth: The Promise of Social Ecology* (London: Green Print, 1990).

Clark, J. 'The politics of social ecology: beyond the limits of the city'. Unpublished paper presented at the International Social Ecology Conference, Dunoon, Scotland (14–19 Aug., 1995).

Clark, J. 'The spirit of hope', *Delta Greens Quarterly*, No. 39 (Summer 1995).

Clunies-Ross, T. and Hildyard, N. 'The politics of industrial agriculture', *The Ecologist*, Vol. 22, No. 2 (March/April 1992).

Collier, A. 'Truth and practice', *Radical Philosophy* (Summer 1973).

Common, M. *Environmental and Resource Economics* (London: Longman, 1988).

Conyon, M.J. 'Industry profit margins and concentration: evidence from UK manufacturing', *International Review of Applied Economics*, Vol. 9, No. 3 (1995).

Copleston, F. *A History of Philosophy* (London: Search Press, 1976).

Crump, J. 'Markets, money and social change', *Anarchist Studies*, Vol. 3, No. 1 (Spring 1995).

Cumings, B. 'The abortive abertura', *New Left Review*, No. 173 (Jan./Feb. 1989).

Cutler, A., Hindess, B., Hirst, P. and Hussain, A. *Marx's Capital and Capitalism Today* (London: Routledge & Kegan Paul, 1977).

Deane, P. *The Evolution of Economic Ideas* (Cambridge: Cambridge University Press, 1978).

Devall, B. *Simple in Means, Rich in Ends: Practising Deep Ecology* (London: Green Print, 1990).

Dobson, A. *Green Political Thought* (London: Routledge, 1990, 1995).

Dobson, R.V.G. *Bringing the Economy Home from the Market* (Montreal: Black Rose Books, 1993).

Dolgoff, S. (ed.) *The Anarchist Collectives: Workers' Self-management in the Spanish Revolution 1936–39* (New York: Free Life Editions, 1974).

Douthwaite, R. *The Growth Illusion* (Devon, UK: Resurgence, 1992).

Doyal, L. and Gough, I. *A Theory of Human Need* (London: Macmillan, 1991).

Dryzek, J. 'Ecology and discursive democracy', *Capitalism, Nature, Socialism*, Vol. 3, No. 2 (June 1992).

Dunn, J. (ed.) *Democracy, the Unfinished Journey, 508 BC to AD 1993* (Oxford: Oxford University Press, 1992).

Eckersley, R. 'Divining evolution: the ecological ethics of Murray Bookchin', *Environmental Ethics*, Vol. 11, No. 2 (Summer 1989).

Ehrlich, P. *The Population Bomb* (New York: Simon & Schuster, 1990).

Ekins, P. (ed.) *The Living Economy* (New York: Routledge & Kegan Paul, 1986).

Ekins, P. *Local Economic Mutual Self-reliance* (London: TOES Publication, 1988).

Ekins, P. *Trade for Mutual Self-reliance* (London: TOES Publication, 1989).

Ekins, P. and Max-Neef, M. (eds) *Real Life Economics: Understanding Wealth Creation* (London: Routledge, 1992).

Ellman, M. *Socialist Planning* (Cambridge: Cambridge University Press, 1979).

Ellman, M. 'The increase in death and disease under "Katastroika"', *Cambridge Journal of Economics*, No. 18 (1994).

Ely, J. 'Libertarian ecology and civil society', *Society and Nature*, Vol. 2, No. 3 (1994).

Emmanuel, A. *Unequal Exchange, A Study of the Imperialism of Trade* (New York: Monthly Review Press, 1972).

Engels, F. *The Role of Force in History* (New York: International Publishers, 1968).

Engels, F. *Anti-Dühring* (London: Lawrence & Wishart, 1969).

Etzioni, A. *The Spirit of Community* (New York: Simon & Schuster, 1994).

Etzioni, A. 'Common values', *New Statesman & Society* (12 May 1995).

European Commission, *The Challenges Ahead – A Plan for Europe* (Brussels, 1979).

European Commission, *Treaty on European Union* (Maastricht, 1992).

Eurostat, *Poverty in Figures* (Luxembourg: Office for Official Publications of the European Communities, 1990).

Eurostat, *A Social Portrait of Europe* (Luxembourg: Statistical Office of the European Communities, 1991).

Eurostat, *Basic Statistics of the Community* (Luxembourg: Statistical Office of the European Communities, 1992).

Fagerberg, J. *et al.*, 'The decline of social-democratic state capitalism in Norway', *New Left Review*, No. 181 (May/June 1990).

Feyerabend, P. *Against Method* (London: Verso, 1975).

Feyerabend, P. *Science in a Free Society* (London: Verso, 1978).

Feyerabend, P. *Farewell to Reason* (London: Verso, 1987).

Fotopoulos, T. *Dependent Development: the Case of Greece* (Athens: Exantas Press, 1985, 1987) (in Greek).

Fotopoulos, T. *The Gulf War: the First Battle in the North–South Conflict* (Athens: Exantas, 1991) (in Greek).

Fotopoulos, T. 'Economic restructuring and the debt problem: the Greek case', *International Review of Applied Economics*, Vol. 6, No. 1 (1992).

Fotopoulos, T. 'The economic foundations of an ecological society', *Society and Nature*, Vol. 1, No. 3 (1993).

Fotopoulos, T. *The Neoliberal Consensus and the Crisis of the Growth Economy* (Athens: Gordios, 1993) (in Greek).

Fotopoulos, T. 'The end of socialist statism', *Society and Nature*, Vol. 2, No. 3 (1994).

Fotopoulos, T. 'The crisis of the growth economy, the withering away of the nation-state and the community-based society' in *Education, Culture and Modernization*, ed. P. Alheit *et al.* (Roskilde, Denmark: Roskilde University Centre, 1995).

Fox Piven, F. 'Is it global economics or neo-laissez-faire?', *New Left Review*, No. 213 (Sept./Oct. 1995).

Frank, A.G. *Capitalism and Underdevelopment in Latin America* (New York: Modern Reader, 1967, 1969).

Frank, A.G. 'Is real world socialism possible?', *Society and Nature*, Vol. 2, No. 3, (1994).

Frank, A.G. 'Development, democracy, and the market', *Society and Nature*, Vol. 3, No. 1 (1995).

Friedman, M. and Friedman, R. *Free to Choose* (Harmondsworth: Penguin, 1980).

Galbraith, J.K. *The Culture of Contentment* (Harmondsworth: Penguin, 1993).

Gamble, A. 'Class politics and radical democracy', *New Left Review*, No. 164 (July/Aug. 1987).

Gellner, E. *Nations and Nationalism* (Oxford: Blackwell, 1983).

Glynn, A. 'Social democracy and full employment', *New Left Review*, No. 211 (May/June 1995).

Glynn, A. and Sutcliffe, B. *British Capitalism, Workers and the Profits Squeeze* (Harmondsworth: Penguin, 1972).

Goldmann, L. *Immanuel Kant* (London: New Left Books, 1971).

Goodman, A. and Webb, S. *For Richer, For Poorer* (London: Institute of Fiscal Studies, 1994).

Goodway, D. (ed.) *For Anarchism: History, Theory and Practice* (London: Routledge, 1989).

Gorz, A. *Capitalism, Socialism, Ecology* (London: Verso, 1994).

Gough, I. *The Political Economy of the Welfare State* (London: Macmillan, 1979).

Gowan, P. 'Neo-liberal theory and practice for Eastern Europe', *New Left Review*, No. 213 (Sept./Oct., 1995).

Gowdy, J.M. 'Progress and environmental sustainability', *Environmental Ethics*, Vol. 16, No. 1 (Spring 1994).

Green, D.G. *Reinventing Civil Society* (London: IEA, 1993).

Green, F. *et al.*, 'Income inequality in corporatist and liberal economies: a comparison of trends within OECD countries', *International Review of Applied Economics*, Vol. 8, No. 3 (1994).

Greenpeace/*The Guardian*, 'A report into the environmental forces shaping our future', *The Guardian* (2 June 1994).

Gribbin, J. 'Climate and ozone', *The Ecologist*, Vol. 21, No. 3 (May/June 1991).

Guehenno, J.-M. *The End of the Nation-State* (Minneapolis: University of Minnesota Press, 1995)

Habermas, J. 'Three normative models of democracy', *Constellations*, Vol. 1, No. 1 (1994).

Hamlyn, D.W. *The Theory of Knowledge* (London: Macmillan, 1970).

Hansen, M.H. *The Athenian Democracy in the Age of Demosthenes* (Oxford: Blackwell, 1991).

Hawkins, H. 'Community control, workers' control and the cooperative commonwealth', *Society and Nature*, Vol. 1, No. 3 (1993).

Haworth, A. *Anti-Libertarianism, Markets, Philosophy and Myth* (London: Routledge, 1994).

Hayek, F. *Individualism and Economic Order* (London: Routledge & Kegan Paul, 1945, 1949).

Hayes, M. *The New Right in Britain* (London: Pluto Press, 1994).

Heffer, E. 'A rallying call for Eurosocialists', *The Guardian* (1 Nov. 1990).

Held, D. (ed.) *Prospects for Democracy* (Cambridge: Polity Press, 1993).

Held, D. *Democracy and the Global Order* (Cambridge: Polity Press, 1995).

Henderson, H. 'Shifting gears', *Resurgence* (May-June 1993).

SELECT BIBLIOGRAPHY

Henderson, J.M. and Quandt, R. *Microeconomic Theory, a Mathematical Approach* (New York: McGraw-Hill, 1958).
Hindess, B. and Hirst, P. *Pre-Capitalist Modes of Production* (London: Routledge & Kegan Paul, 1975).
Hirst, P. *Associative Democracy: New Forms of Economic and Social Governance* (Amherst: University of Massachusetts Press, 1994).
Hirst, P. and Thompson, G. *Globalization in Question* (Cambridge: Polity Press, 1996).
Hodgson, G. *The Democratic Economy* (Gretna, LA: Pelican, 1984).
Hodgson, G. *Economics and Institutions* (Cambridge: Cambridge University Press, 1988).
Hutchinson, T.W. *Knowledge and Ignorance in Economics* (Oxford: Blackwell, 1977).
Hutton, W. *The State We're In* (London: Jonathan Cape, 1995).
Ietto-Gillies, G. 'Some indicators of multinational domination of national economies', *International Review of Applied Economics*, Vol. 3, No. 1 (1989).
International Labor Organization (ILO), *Yearbook of Labor Statistics* (Geneva: ILO, various years).
International Monetary Fund, *International Financial Statistics* (various years).
Jacobs, M. *The Green Economy* (London: Pluto Press, 1991).
Jessop, B. *et al.*, 'Popular capitalism, flexible accumulation and left strategy', *New Left Review* (Sept./Oct. 1987).
Johnson, C. *The Economy Under Mrs. Thatcher, 1979–1990* (Harmondsworth: Penguin, 1991).
Kalomalos, T. 'The crisis of left politics and Karl Marx', *Society and Nature*, Vol. 2, No. 1 (1993).
Katouzian, H. *Ideology and Method in Economics* (London: Macmillan, 1980).
Kaufmann, S.A. *The Origins of Order: Self-organization and Selection in Evolution* (Oxford: Oxford University Press, 1993).
Kavoulakos, K. 'The relationship of realism and utopianism: the theories of democracy of Jürgen Habermas and Cornelius Castoriadis', *Society and Nature*, Vol. 2, No. 3 (1994)
Kemp, P. *et al.*, *Europe's Green Alternative: A Manifesto for a New World* (London: Green Print, 1992).
Kenwood, A.G. and Lougheed, A.L. *The Growth of the International Economy, 1820-1980* (London: George Allen & Unwin, 1983).
Kohler, H. *Welfare and Planning* (New York: Wiley & Sons, 1966).
Kolakowski, L. *Main Currents of Marxism* (Oxford: Oxford University Press, 1981).

368

Kole, K. *et al.*, *Why Economists Disagree* (London & New York: Longman, 1983).

Kropotkin, P. *Mutual Aid* (Boston: Extending Horizons, 1914).

Kropotkin, P. *Selected Writings on Anarchism and Revolution* (Cambridge, MA, and London: Massachusetts Institute of Technology, 1970).

Kropotkin, P. *The Conquest of Bread* (Harmondsworth: Penguin, 1972).

Kropotkin, P. *Fields, Factories and Workshops Tomorrow* (London: George Allen & Unwin, 1974).

Krugman, P. 'The myth of Asia's miracle', *Foreign Affairs* (Nov.-Dec, 1994).

Kuhn, T.S. *The Structure of Scientific Revolutions* (Chicago: University of Chicago Press, 1970).

Lakatos, I. *Criticism and the Growth of Knowledge* (Cambridge: Cambridge University Press, 1970).

Lang, T. and Hines, C. *The New Protectionism: Protecting the Future Against Free Trade* (London: Earthscan, 1993).

Lenin, V. *The State and Revolution* (Moscow: Foreign Languages Publishing House, 1917).

Lenin, V. *What Is to Be Done?* (Moscow: Progress Publishers, 1967).

Lepage, H. *Tomorrow, Capitalism, The Economics of Economic Freedom* (London: Open Court, 1982).

Light, A. 'Rereading Bookchin and Marcuse as environmental materialists', *Capitalism, Nature, Socialism*, No. 3 (March 1993).

Light, A. 'Which side are you on? A rejoinder to Murray Bookchin', *Capitalism, Nature, Socialism*, No. 14 (June 1993).

Lipietz, A. *Miracles and Mirages* (London: Verso, 1987).

Little, I.M.D. *Economic Development: Theory, Policy and International Relations* (New York: Basic Books, 1982).

Lukacs, G. 'Technology and social relations', *New Left Review*, No. 39 (1966).

Lukacs, G. *History and Class Consciousness* (London: Merlin Press, 1971).

Lutz, M.A. and Lux, K. *Humanistic Economics* (New York: Bootstrap, 1988).

Maddison, A. *Phases of Capitalist Development* (London: Oxford University Press, 1982).

Mandel, E. 'In defence of socialist planning', *New Left Review*, No. 159 (Sept./Oct. 1986).

Marcuse, H. *Soviet Marxism* (London: Routledge, 1958).

Marshall, P. *Demanding the Impossible* (London: HarperCollins, 1992).

Marshall, P. *Nature's Web, an Exploration of Ecological Thinking* (London: Simon & Schuster, 1992).

Martin, T. 'The end of sovereignty', *Democracy and Nature* (formerly *Society and Nature*), Vol. 3, No. 2 (1996).

Marx, K. *Critique of the Gotha Programme* (Moscow: Progress Publishers, 1937).

Marx, K. *Pre-capitalist Economic Formations* (London: Lawrence and Wishart, 1964).

Marx, K. Preface to the first German edition of *Das Kapital* (Moscow: Progress Publishers/Lawrence & Wishart, 1965).

Marx, K. *A Contribution to the Critique of Political Economy* (London: Lawrence & Wishart, 1971).

Marx, K. *The Revolutions of 1848* (Harmondsworth: Penguin, 1973).

Marx, K. and Engels, F. *Manifesto of the Communist Party* (Moscow: Progress Publishers, 1952).

Marx, K. and Engels, F. *Selected Works* (Moscow: Progress Publishers, 1968).

Marx, K. and Engels, F. *The German Ideology* (Moscow: Progress Publishers, 1968).

Mathyl, M. 'Is Russia on the road to dictatorship?' *Green Perspectives*, No. 34 (Dec. 1995).

Matthews, N. 'Why has Britain full employment since the war?', *Economic Journal*, Vol. 78, No. 3 (1968).

Maximoff, G.P. (ed.) *The Political Philosophy of Bakunin* (New York: The Free Press, 1953).

McGowan, P.J. and Kurdan, B. 'Imperialism in world system perspective', *International Studies Quarterly*, Vol. 25, No. 1 (March 1981).

McKercher, W. 'Liberalism as democracy: authority over freedom', *Democracy and Nature* (formerly *Society and Nature*), Vol. 3, No. 2 (1996).

McLaughlin, A. 'What is deep ecology?', *Capitalism, Nature, Socialism*, Vol. 6/3, No. 23 (Sept. 1995).

McLennan, G. *Marxism and the Methodologies of History* (London: New Left Books, 1981, 1987).

Miliband, R. 'Fukuyama and the socialist alternative', *New Left Review*, No. 193 (May/June 1992).

Miller, D. *Market, State and Community: Theoretical Foundations of Market Socialism* (Oxford: Clarendon Press, 1989).

Morishima, M. and Catephores, G. *Value, Exploitation and Growth* (London: McGraw-Hill, 1978).

Morrison, R. *Ecological Democracy* (Boston: South End Press, 1995).

Mouffe, C. (ed.) *Dimensions of Radical Democracy* (London: Verso, 1992, 1995).

Mouzelis, N. *Post-Marxist Alternatives, The Construction of Social Orders* (London: Macmillan, 1990).

Mouzelis, N. 'Four problems regarding modernisation', *To Vima* (25 July 1993).

Mouzelis, N. 'The future of the welfare-state', *Eleftherotypia* (1–2 Jan. 1994).

Naess, A. *Ecology, Community and Lifestyle* (Cambridge: Cambridge University Press, 1989).

Naess, A. 'Deep ecology and ultimate premises', reprinted from *The Ecologist* in *Society and Nature*, Vol. 1, No. 2 (1992).

Nove, A. 'The Soviet economy: problems and prospects', *New Left Review*, No. 119 (Jan./Feb. 1980).

Nove, A. *The Economics of Feasible Socialism* (London: Allen & Unwin, 1983).

O'Connor, J. 'Capitalism, nature, socialism', *Society and Nature*, Vol. 1, No. 2 (1992) (reprinted from *Capitalism, Nature, Socialism*).

O'Connor, J. 'Socialism and ecology', *Society and Nature*, Vol. 1, No. 1 (1992) (reprinted from *Our Generation*).

O'Connor, J. 'Democracy and ecology', *Capitalism, Nature, Socialism*, Vol. 4, No. 4 (Dec. 1993).

OECD, *Economic Outlook* (various years).

Olson, M. *The Rise and Decline of Nations* (New Haven, CT: Yale University Press, 1988).

Panic, M. *European Monetary Union* (London: St Martin's Press, 1993).

Paparregopoulos, K. *History of the Greek Nation* (Athens: Seferlis, 1955), Vols 1–7 (in Greek).

Pepper, D. *Eco-Socialism: From Deep Ecology to Social Justice* (London: Routledge, 1993).

Pepper, D. *Modern Environmentalism* (London: Routledge, 1996).

Phillips, D. *Abandoning Method* (San Francisco and London: Jossey-Bass, 1973).

Plumwood, V. 'Feminism, privacy and radical democracy', *Anarchist Studies*, Vol. 3, No. 2 (Autumn 1995).

Polanyi, K. *The Great Transformation, the Political and Economic Origins of Our Time* (Boston: Beacon Press, 1944, 1957).

Polanyi-Levitt, K. (ed.) *The Life and Work of Karl Polanyi* (Montreal: Black Rose Books, 1990).

Pollert, A. (ed.) *Farewell to Flexibility?* (Oxford: Blackwell, 1991).

Pollin, R. 'Financial structures and egalitarian economic policy', *New Left Review*, No. 214 (Nov./Dec. 1995).

Pollin, R. and Alarcon, D. 'Debt crisis, accumulation and economic restructuring in Latin America', *International Review of Applied Economics*, Vol. 2, No. 2 (June 1988).

Prokopiou, A. *Athens* (London: Elek Books, 1964).

Ramaswamy, V. 'A new human rights consciousness', *IFDA Dossier* 80 (Jan.–March 1991).

Richards, V. *Lessons of the Spanish Revolution* (London: Freedom Press, 1972).

Robertson, J. *Future Wealth* (London: Cassell, 1990).

Robertson, J. 'Economics of local recovery', *Society and Nature*, Vol. 1, No. 1 (1992).

Sachs, J. 'What is to be done?', *The Economist* (13 January 1990).

Samuels, W.J. (ed.) *The Methodology of Economic Thought* (New Brunswick and London: Transaction Books, 1980).

Sayers, S. 'Moral values and progress', *New Left Review*, No. 204 (Mar./Apr., 1994).

Seabrook, J. *The Myth of the Market* (Devon: Green Books, 1990).

Selsam, H. and Martel, H. (eds) *Reader in Marxist Philosophy* (New York: International Publishers, 1963).

Shragge, E. *Community Economic Development* (Montreal: Black Rose Books, 1993).

Shulman, A.K. (ed.) *Red Emma Speaks* (New York: Vintage Books, 1972).

Skinner, B.F. *Walden II* (New York: Macmillan, 1976).

Smith, A. *The Wealth of Nations* (Harmondsworth: Penguin, 1970).

Smith, D. *In Search of Social Justice* (London: The New Economics Foundation, 1995).

Smith, R. 'The Chinese road to capitalism', *New Left Review*, No. 199 (May/June 1993).

Stewart, F. *Technology and Underdevelopment* (London: Macmillan, 1978).

Stubbs, R. and Underhill, G.R.D. *Political Economy and the Changing Global Order* (London: Macmillan, 1994).

Sweezy, P. *The Theory of Capitalist Development* (New York: Monthly Review Press, 1942).

Sweezy, P. *Modern Capitalism and Other Essays* (New York: Monthly Review Press, 1972).

Taylor, J.G. *From Modernization to Modes of Production, A Critique of the Sociologies of Development and Underdevelopment* (London: Macmillan, 1979).

Taylor, M. *Community, Anarchy, and Liberty* (Cambridge: Cambridge University Press, 1982).

Teune, H. *Growth* (London: Sage Publications, 1988).

Thirlwall, A.P. *Balance of Payments Theory* (London: Macmillan, 1980).

Thurow, L. *Head to Head: The Coming Economic Battle Among Japan, Europe and America* (Brealy, 1992).

Trainer, T. *Abandon Affluence!* (London: Zed Books, 1985).

Trainer, T. *Developed to Death* (London: Green Print, 1989).

Trainer, T. 'A rejection of the Brundtland Report', *IFDA Dossier* 77 (May–June 1990).

Trainer, T. *The Conserver Society* (London: Zed Books, 1995).

Trainer, T. 'What is development?' *Society and Nature*, Vol. 3, No. 1 (1995).

Trotsky, L. *The Revolution Betrayed* (New York: Merit, 1965).

UN Development Program, *Human Development Report* (New York: Oxford University Press, 1992 and 1996).

Vallianatos, E.G. 'Subversive theory: ecology, gaiocentric sustainable development and the third world', *Society and Nature*, Vol. 3, No. 1 (1995).

Voulgaris, Y. *Liberalism, Conservatism and the Welfare State, 1973–1990* (Athens: Themelio, 1994) (in Greek).

Wade, R. *Globalization and Its Limits: The Continuing Economic Importance of Nations and Regions* (University of Sussex: Institute of Development Studies, 1994).

Wainwright, H. *Arguments for a New Left, Answering the Free Market Right* (Oxford: Blackwell, 1994).

Wallerstein, I. *The Modern World System* (New York: Academic Press, 1974).

Wallerstein, I. *The Capitalist World Economy* (Cambridge: Cambridge University Press, 1979).

Weber, M. *The Methodology of Social Sciences* (Illinois: Glance 1949).

Weiss, L. and Hobson, J. *States and Economic Development: A Comparative Historical Analysis* (Cambridge: Cambridge University Press, 1995).

Whiteside, K.H. 'Hannah Arendt and ecological politics', *Environmetnal Ethics*, Vol. 16, No. 4 (Winter 1994).

Wolff, E. 'How the pie is sliced: America's growing concentration of wealth', *The American Prospect* (Summer 1995).

Woodcock, G. 'Democracy, heretical and radical', *Our Generation*, Vol. 22, Nos 1-2 (Fall 1990-Spring 1991).

World Bank, *Development and the Environment* (Oxford: Oxford University Press, 1992).

World Bank, *World Development Report* (various years).

World Bank Group, *Learning from the Past: Embracing the Future* (Washington, DC: World Bank, 19 July 1994).

World Commission on Environment and Development, *Our Common Future* (New York: United Nations, 1987).

Worldwatch, *Poverty and the Environment* (Washington, DC: Worldwatch Institute, 1989).

Yakovlev, A., *The Fate of Marxism in Russia* (Yale: Yale University Press, 1993).

Young, A. 'Lessons from the East Asian NICs: a contrarian view', *European Economic Review*, Vol. 38, Nos 3/4 (April 1994).

Name Index

The following index includes references appearing in the text but not those appearing in the endnotes.

Albert, M. 97, 254, 263
Alexander the Great 193
Althusser, L 159, 321, 325, 326
Arendt H. 173, 185, 195, 210, 237, 344
Aristotle 184, 186, 189, 190, 210
Arrow, K. 248
Auerbach, P. 254

Bacon, F. 308
Bakunin, M. 74, 178, 342
Baldelli, G. 264
Basso, R. 172
Beetham, D. 176
Bell, D. 33–4
Benello, C.G. 342
Bentham, J. 177
Bergson, H. 317
Berkeley, G. 308
Berlin, I. 177
Berry, T. 235
Bhaskar, R. 327
Biehl, J 212, 279
Binns, P. 322, 326
Blair, T. 22
Blaug, M. 313
Bleaney, M. 23
Bobbio, N. 199
Bodin, J. 195
Bookchin, M. 8–9, 11, 66, 179, 181, 184, 185, 198, 206, 227, 230, 231, 234, 235, 247, 254, 278, 286, 291, 307, 310, 318–19, 328–9, 330, 339, 343, 345
Brown, S. 182, 183, 201, 238, 342
Buchanan, J.M. 33, 34
Buchanan, P. 100
Bucharin, N. 324

Carnap, R. 310
Carter, A. 9, 263
Castoriadis, C. 180, 182, 185, 200, 209, 253, 286, 319, 321, 322–3, 326, 329, 333, 336, 342, 343, 345, 346, 347, 348–9
Chenery, H. 124
Chomsky, N. 159, 210–11, 262
Chuang Tzu 344
Cimon 192
Clark, D. 226
Clark, J. 235–7, 276, 330
Cleisthenes 188, 189, 190, 191
Clinton, B. 39, 122
Collier, A. 323
Comte, A. 310
Corridan, P. 322
Cumings, B. 83

Descartes, R. 308, 317
Dryzek, J. 200
Dunn, J. 195, 196

Einstein, A. 311
Engels, F. 18–19, 178, 324
Esteva G. 133
Etsioni, A. 228

Feyerabend, P. 312, 327, 341
Fotopoulos, T. 261, 282
Freud, S. 181
Friedman, M. 178

Galbraith, J.K. 37
Godwin, W. 342
Goldman, E. 178, 238
Goldmann, L. 316–17
Goldsmith, J. 100

Gorbachev, M. 76
Gorz, A. 234–5
Guehenno, J.-M. 54
Gunder Frank, A. 101, 103, 104, 135

Habermas, J. 159, 200, 201, 332
Hansen, M.H. 176, 179, 192, 208, 209, 210, 230, 298, 343
Harding, N. 174
Hayek, F. 33, 252
Hawkins, H. 233, 255, 284
Hegel, G.W.F. 316, 328, 334, 348
Heidegger, M. 317
Held, D. 161, 205
Herodotus 344
Hess, K. 232
Hindess, B. 320, 322
Hirst, P. 47, 49, 50, 161, 203, 320, 322
Hitler, A. 22
Hobbes, T. 177, 195
Hume, D. 308, 317
Huntingdon, S.P. 34
Hutton, W. 37, 38, 99, 249

Jefferson, T. 195
Jevons, S. 123

Kagarlitsky, B. 82
Kant, I. 309, 316, 348
Kaser, M. 81
Katouzian, H. 311
Keynes, J. M. 249
Khor, M. 215
Kohl, H. 98
Kolakowski, L. 178, 323
Kolko, G. 85
Korsh, K. 322
Kropotkin, P. 7, 11, 69, 232, 342
Kuhn, T. 309, 313, 314, 320, 327, 340

Lakatos, I. 311, 312, 313, 314
Leibniz, G.W. 308, 317
Lenin, V. I. 74, 174, 197, 320, 342
Lewis, A. 124
Lipietz, A. 127
Locke, J. 177, 198, 231, 317
Lukacs, G. 322

Madison, J. 195
Malthus, T. 118, 119

Mandel, E. 251
Mao Tse Tung 78
Marcuse, H. 341
Marshall, P. 276, 330, 342, 345
Martin, T. 173, 185
Marx, K. 8, 14, 65, 123, 124, 173, 187, 197, 232, 259, 319, 320, 323, 325, 342, 348
Masterman, M. 313
Maxwell, K. 311
McKercher, W. 178
McLennan, G. 321, 322, 328
Menger, C. 123
Miliband, R. 199
Mill, J. S. 177
Miller, D. 202
Mises, L. von 16, 252
Moggridge, D. 20
Montesquieu, C.L. 231
Morrison, R. 279–81
Mouffe, C. 201
Myrdal, G. 124

Naess, A. 348
Newton, I. 311
Nurkse, R. 124

O'Connor, J. 163, 200
Ostrom, E. 215

Paparregopoulos, K. 191, 193
Parekh, Bhikhu 182, 184
Pareto, V. 250
Pepper, D. 282
Pericles 188, 190, 191, 192, 193, 209
Phillip of Macedonia 193
Pierson, C. 202
Pinochet, A. 83
Pirenne, H. 8
Plato 319
Plechanov, G. 324
Plumwood, V. 212
Polanyi, K. 7, 10, 12, 14, 19, 20, 24, 27, 44, 104, 332
Popper, K. 310–11
Proudhon, P.J. 232, 259

Reagan, R. 34, 83
Ricardo, D. 118
Rosenstein-Rodan, P. 124

Rousseau, J.-J. 231

Sachs, J. 80, 82
Sale, K. 280
Saltykov, B. 75
Satterthwaite, D. 120
Sayer, D. 322
Schelling, F. 317
Schlick, M. 310
Simon, J. 121
Skinner, B.F. 261–2
Smith, A. 65, 118, 195, 248
Solon 188, 189
Spinoza, B. de 308
Stalin, J. 78
Strange, S. 48

Taylor, M. 226
Thatcher, M. 34, 36, 44
Thompson, G. 47, 49, 50, 161
Thucydides 179, 190

Trainer, T. 113, 119, 277
Trotsky, L. 79

Volcker, P. 42
Volsky, A. 82
Voltaire, F. 231

Walras, L. 123
Walzer, M. 159–61
Weber, M. 325
Whiteside, K.H. 214
Witte, S. 81
Wolff, R. 308
Woodcock, G. 344
Woolacott, M. 147

Yakovlev, A. 78

Zyuganov, G. 82

Subject Index

The following index includes references to subjects, publications and organizations discussed in the text, but the notes at the end of the chapters have not been indexed.

aboriginal 194
actually existing socialism
  achievements of 75–6
  central planning in 63, 71, 103, 263
  collapse of 3, 34, 41, 45, 74, 76–8, 103,
    145, 165, 199, 239, 357
  competitiveness and 101–2
  democracy and 174, 175, 208, 337
  ecological crisis in 66
  growth economy and 62, 64, 173–4,
    279–80
  internationalization and 29
  Marxism and 63
  social democracy and 45, 52, 74, 86,
    100, 102
affinity groups 236, 276
agora 209
Albania 79
anarchism/anarchists 69, 151, 163, 175,
  177, 182, 183, 232, 338, 344, 348
Anglo-Saxon model 116, 142, 204, 205,
  358
anthropocentrism 153
APEC 43
'appropriate development' approach 150,
  151, 155–6
Arendt, H
  on Greek gods 344
  on representative democracy 195
  on the 'communistic fiction' 173, 237
  on the concept of rule 185
  on the social realm 210
Aristotle
  on election by voting 184
  on ostracism 190
  on property as the cause of social
    conflict 186
  on Solon's reforms 189

  on the meaning of the public realm 210
ASEAN, Association of South East Asian
  Nations 43
Asiatic mode of production 123
assembly/assemblies
  community 230, 244, 248, 255–69,
    293, 296, 298, 299
  confederal 230, 233, 255–69,
  in Athens 188–92, 209, 298, 335
  in Swiss cantons 208
  minority 233
  National 184
  neighbourhood 230, 285, 298
  popular 236, 278, 343, 344
  regional 233, 255–69,
  student 212
  tribal 336, 344
  workplace 247–8, 255–69, 283, 293
associationalism 203–4
Australia 30, 87, 112
autonomy
  classical meaning of 179
  community and 226
  cultural 51, 55
  democracy and 165, 180, 350
  democratic rationalism and 348, 349
  dialectical naturalism's 'objectivism'
    versus the project of 330–1
  ethical values and 345, 348
  freedom as 176, 178, 180, 181, 182,
    343
  heteronomy versus 334, 335, 338, 339,
    343
  incompatibility with dogmas 343, 344,
    348
  individual and collective 55, 68,
    179–83, 201, 207, 226, 233, 234,
    242

individualistic conception of 182, 183, 201
irrationalism and 348
liberalism and 201
libertarian socialism and 74
national 52, 128
of European regions 97
politics and 346
project of 144, 286, 306, 332–3, 335, 336, 339, 349
relativism and 347, 348, 349, 350
science and 149, 349
self-management and 247
self-reliance and tradition of 241

Bakunin, M.
on freedom 178
on human nature 342
on the proletarian state 74
Beveridge Report 24
bio-regionalism 69, 236
Bookchin, M.
on a non-hierachical interpretation of nature 339
on a non-teleological view of evolution 328–9
on consensus decision-taking 231
on dialectical 'objectivity' 318–19
on dialectical versus analytical logic 319
on dialectics as a method 307
on lifestyle strategies 278, 291–2
on modern technology and confederal organization 234
on party cadres 286
on secular and religious themes in Athens' festivals 343
on self-managed enterprises 247
on the Anglo-Saxon meaning of autonomy 179
on the emergence of the idea of dominating nature 66
on the fact/value dichotomy 310
on the idea of a nation 9
on the interaction between ideological and material factors 181
on the meaning of citizenship 235
on the meaning of community 227
on the meaning of state 184
on the meaning of the public realm 206
on the nature–society dualism 330
on the non-statist character of Athenian democracy 185
on the political institutions of a confederal organization of society 230
on the relation of market economy to the rise of nation-state 11
on the relationship of needs to scarcity 198
on the sharing character of a confederal society 254–5
Bretton Woods 27, 28, 33
Britain
as the marketization barometer 24
Community Economic Development in 229
crime explosion in 147, 345
economic concentration in 70
effect of statism on cost of production in 31
electorate structure change in 38
Eurodollar market and effect on exchange controls of 29
film industry in 40
'forty per cent society' in 37–8
free trade adoption by 16, 18
General Strike (1926) in 20
Gold Standard adoption by 16
income inequality in 44, 95
job insecurity in 147
'mad cow disease' in 149–50
positivism in 308
poverty in 131
privatization in 25, 90
social spending in 26, 91
tax load redistribution in favour of the rich in 36
Tory nationalism in 52
trade union membership decline in 37
trickle-down effect in 113
British Institute of Economic Affairs 164
Brundtland Report 151–2
Buddhism 344, 349
Bulgaria 77, 131
budget deficit policies 22, 23
Burma 131

Caja Laboral Popular 294
Canada 30, 35, 43, 112, 281
capital

accumulation of 25, 75, 118, 124, 126, 210, 211
China and Western 85
competitiveness of 43, 145
concentration of 36, 237
East Europe and Western 78, 80, 81
European 92, 93, 95, 96, 164
flight of 23, 42, 98
freedom/mobility of 19, 32, 42, 43, 44, 94, 96, 228
Gorz's 'transcending' of 235
hegemony of 34
internationalization of 124
markets liberalization 29, 35, 41, 42, 87
movement of 17, 41, 42, 43
multinational 244
socialization of 202, 229, 282
US and Japanese capital in competition with European 96, 164
capitalism
civic 164
collectivist 240
'greening' of 100, 151–2
historical role of 124–6, 134, 315
market economy and 4–6
models of national 97
'popular' 36, 238
primacy of the individual and 71
realm of freedom and 199
social democracy and 86–7
stakeholder 97, 217
capitalist
concentration of power 70, 71, 75
culture 154
development 34, 125, 127, 128, 295
economic 'democracy' 135, 238–9
economic incentives 77
elite 15, 21, 79, 210, 239
growth economy 62–7, 70, 77, 100–2, 114, 133, 172–3
ideology 111, 160
market economy 79, 83
mode of production 4, 66, 125–7, 333
property relations 6, 279–80
world economy 4
Carter, A.
on authority 263
on nation-states in the Middle Ages 9
Castoriadis, C.
on Althusserian Marxism 326

on democracy as a regime 200
on irrationalism 348–9
on Marxist methodology 322–3
on objectivist rationalism 319, 326
on politics as a technique and as a praxis 347
on postmodern conformism 347
on public space 209
on the historical occurrence of the autonomy project 332
on the idea of autonomy as an end in itself 182
on the impossibility of grounding democracy on closed systems 343
on the impossibility of scientifying politics 342
on the lack of a genuine theory of natural evolution 329
on the movement to establish democracy 286
on the non-evolutionary character of democracy and philosophy 336
on the non-statist character of the Athenian democracy 185
on the relation of individual to collective autonomy 180
on the revolutionary and the traditional elements in Marx 321
on the source of laws in the Judeo-Christian tradition and in Athens 343
on workers' councils 253
Catharists 345
Cecchini Report 93
Chaeronea, battle of 193
chaos theory 305
Chicago School 33
China
communist party of 111
dual economy in 84
economic growth of 72, 84
explosion of geographical disparities in 84–5
family planning in 120–1
foreign investment in 80, 84
socialist market economy in 83–4
unemployment in 84
Chomsky, Noam
on B.F. Skinner 261
on freedom in the USA 210–11

on postmodern theorizing 159
Christianity 343–5, 349
citizenship
    Athenian 187, 192, 208
    community and 217
    cultural 217
    democratic conception of 216–17
    eco-communitarian view of 235
    economic 216
    instrumentalist view of 218
    liberal conception of 182, 217
    Marxist conception of 217
    political 216
    social 216
    socialist conception of 182, 217
    stakeholder capitalism and 217
city/cities
    free medieval 7, 9, 244, 333, 337
    mega 116, 244
    movement from tribes to 336
    regional governments 51, 173, 225, 228
    states in Greece 175, 185, 187, 190
civil societarian
    approach 158–64, 203, 205, 251
    Left 47, 72, 176, 234, 253, 280, 357
civil society
    associated networks of 160, 161, 203
    competitiveness and 161–2
    concentration of power and 163
    defined 159
    European 53
    Habermasian view of democracy and
        200
    internationalization and 116, 161, 162,
        164, 276, 357
    neoliberalism and 161
    proposal for an inclusive 160
    'radical' democracy and 200, 239
    state and 162
class
    communitarianism as a movement of the
        middle 227
    growth economy and 111
    in classical Athens 189–90, 195
    industrialism and 279
    Marxist analysis of 4, 5, 78, 89, 124–5
    merchant 8
    middle 37, 112, 132
    project for inclusive democracy and
        282, 286

regulation approach and 127–8
scarcity and 197
science 320, 323, 324
structure in the internationalized
    economy 37–8
state as an instrument of 163
traditional politics and new structure of
    38–9, 87
working 15, 26, 34, 36–7, 38, 144, 199
Clintonomics 22
Cold War 77
collectivism 179, 180, 181, 183
colonialism 111, 134, 154, 338, 339
Comecon 80–1
commodity
    liberalization of markets for 41, 44, 87
    neoliberal turning of labour into a 35
    rationality 235
    relations 234, 251
communism 71, 158, 197, 238
communitarianism
    as a 'third' way 228
    cultural 227
    democratic 228
    economic 228
    religious 227
community
    André Gorz versus 234
    appropriate size of 244
    citizenship and 217
    culture 229
    environment and 215
    equality and 187, 226
    inclusive democracy and 182, 224
    John Clark versus a democracy based on
        235
    Kuhn and scientific 313–14
    liberalism and 8
    marketization and 11, 12, 55, 225
    meaning of 225–7
    money, markets and 8
    movements 225, 227
    nation-state versus 11
    ownership of resources 216, 245–7
    proposals 225–7
    self-determination and 136, 178
    self-reliance 134, 241–5, 268, 288
    TNCs and 135
    totality and 317
    trade and 228

transitional strategy and 289–300
values 55, 158, 225, 227, 242
Community Economic Development 229, 276, 283
Community Land Trusts 229, 293
community-oriented models
versus worker-oriented models 253–4
competitiveness
Asian Tigers and 115
civil society and 161–2, 229
economic blocs and 43
environment and 164
European Union's declining 92
German 98
growth and 64, 103
in an internationalized market economy 31, 87
in the Triad 95, 144
Keynesianism and 145
Maastricht Treaty and 94
Single Market Act and 92–3
social wage and 91
socialist statism and 101–2
state's role on 39
concentration
growth economy and power 67–73, 103, 116, 126, 130, 152, 157, 174
in agriculture 150
market 68
of capital 36, 94
of cultural power 40
of economic power 64, 67–70, 73, 100–4, 124, 142, 157–8, 243, 284
of income and wealth 70, 71, 120, 276
of political power 21, 52, 64, 71, 72, 172, 173, 196, 336
of power 55, 66, 122, 128, 133, 154, 163, 165, 171, 192–3, 226
of production 68, 111
of social power 204
confederal
allocation of resources 248–69
democracy 214, 215, 227, 230–3
economy 214, 226, 234, 237–47
welfare system 292
confederal municipalism 254, 276, 278, 284
confederalism 230, 241
consumerism 34, 73, 77, 82, 144, 147
controls on markets

capital and exchange 21, 28, 29, 32, 35, 41, 42, 93
civil societarians and 48, 160, 161, 162, 201, 206, 276, 358
Hayek and 252
homogenization of 49, 98
in Germany 97, 204–5
in Sweden 88
internationalization and 42, 49, 99, 358
market efficiency and 164
marketization and 7, 14, 45, 50, 67–8, 172, 183
neoliberals and 33–4, 35, 150
price and wage 22, 23, 27
regulatory 5, 15, 46, 48, 359
social (broad sense) 6, 46, 164
social (narrow sense) 6, 9, 12, 13, 15, 18, 22, 27, 46–7, 158
co-ops 200, 203, 204, 245, 246, 278, 290, 293, 294, 295, 296, 297
Co-op Atlantic 281
cosmopolitan model 161, 205–6
cost of production
economic blocs and 43
social wage and 145
statism's effect on the 31
trade-led growth and 31
crime
against property 345
expansion of prison population and 147
in Russia 82
in UK 147
crisis
cultural 40, 242
ecological 66–7, 116, 129, 149–51, 158, 215, 279, 340, 348
economic 141–3, 157
fiscal 34
Great Depression 22
identity 146
ideological 148–9
in the North and the South 110
Left's way out of the 158–64
of 'politics' 143–6
of socialist statism 73–4, 102
of the Rhine model 97–8
oil 32–3
Right's way out of the 157–8
social 26, 136, 146–8, 158
'stagflation' 32, 33, 93

Cuba 131
cultural
  autonomy 51, 55, 97
  citizenship 216, 217
  Communitarianism 227
  crisis 40, 242
  homogenization 40
  identity 4, 40, 55, 200, 208
  imperialism 40
  nationalism 40
  needs 111, 132
  power 40
  values 154
culture
  alternative 25, 277
  capitalist 154
  citizenship and 217
  community 229
  dependency 292
  film 40
  hire-and-fire 35
  homogenization of 332
  market 154
  marketization of 40, 158
  of individualism 144
  socialization and 181
  white 154
currency
  demotic 290
  Euro- 32
  'Euro' 43, 45, 173
  instability 88
  nation-state and national 16, 290
  reserve 50
  speculation 42
Cynics 345
Czech republic 80

death rates 85, 121
decentralization
  ecological crisis and 215
  economic democracy and 242
  from North to South 69, 113
  of information 103, 294
  of production 69, 243, 248
  physical versus institutional 69
  remaking society versus 225
  self-reliant versus dependent 243–4
  social democratic consensus and 104
  socialist versus market 78

transitional strategy for a radical 289
deep ecology 140, 151, 152–5, 156, 275,
  276, 279, 330, 340, 348
Delian League 191
democracy
  as a process 200, 343
  as a rule 175, 185, 231
  as a set of procedures 200
  associative/associational 203–4
  Athenian/classical 182, 184, 185–94,
    208, 210, 213, 216, 218, 334–6
  autonomy and 180
  capitalist growth economy and 172–3
  citizenship and 216–17
  community and 182, 225
  confederal 230–7
  cosmopolitan model of 161, 205
  deliberative 202–3
  development and 132–6
  direct 163, 186, 188, 189, 195, 199,
    207–10, 230, 331, 344
  ecological 213–16, 278–81, 284, 287
  economic 186–8, 190, 191, 193, 194,
    196, 203, 209–11, 237–69, 282
  employee 296
  foundation of 342–5
  freedom and 182, 231, 344
  Habermasian conception of 200
  household 213, 258, 291
  human rights and 231
  inclusive 55, 111, 136, 154, 165, 176,
    186, 194, 202, 206–16, 226, 286
  irrationalism and 349–50
  liberal 53, 55, 135, 143–5, 156, 157,
    175–7, 182–4, 192, 194–6, 357
  market 135
  marketization and 172
  Marxist/Leninist 196–9
  meaning of 175–6
  parliamentary 3, 71, 143, 208, 335, 336
  people's 175
  planning and 253, 255
  political 77, 135, 176, 186, 188, 190,
    192, 193, 207–8, 237
  radical 199–206, 224, 357–9
  rationalism and 350
  red-green 200
  relativism and 347
  religion and 343–5

representative 162, 163, 171, 184, 195, 196, 203, 210, 276
scarcity and 198
social 45, 48, 52, 62, 63, 74, 85, 86–8, 91, 96, 100–4, 144, 145, 196
social realm 211–13, 337
socialist 196
socialist growth economy and 174
soviet 71, 174, 175, 208
statist/state 3, 55, 159, 177, 178, 185, 186, 195, 197, 231, 232
transitional 282–300
workplace 77, 176, 202, 203, 292, 295, 337
democratization
  double 205
  in the periphery 82–3
  of the civil society 276
  of the household 212
  of the state 199, 201
demos
  autonomy and 179
  community and 226
  Credit Unions supported by the 290
  currency controlled by the 290
  enterprises owned by the 291, 293
  equality and 186
  means of production owned by the 211, 240, 256
  paedeia and 216
  social self-institutioning and the 179
  state versus the 186
  tax system controlled by the 290
  welfare controlled by the 292
demotic
  bank 293–5, 299
  credit card scheme 290
  credit unions 290
  currency 290, 299
  economic sector 292, 293
  economy 292–8
  enterprises 247, 291, 293–8
  ownership of the means of production 186, 240, 247, 288, 289, 297
  tax system 290
  welfare system 292, 299
Denmark 18, 91
dependency development paradigm 116–17, 123–7
Depression

Great 20–2, 28, 82, 148
  of 1873–76 18
deregulation 35, 88, 150, 200
development
  'appropriate' 155–7
  capitalist 34, 125, 127, 128, 295
  classical approaches to 117–23
  Community Economic 229, 276, 283
  defined 117
  democracy versus 132–6
  ecological dimension of 129–31
  growth economy and 116–17
  intensive versus extensive 77, 84, 114, 115
  Kropotkin on 69
  local/community 290, 293, 294
  Marxist/dependency approaches to 123–7
  orthodox approaches to 124–5
  peripheral 127, 133, 134, 243–4
  population problem and 121–2
  regulation approach to 127–9
  sustainable 151–2, 154
dialectical naturalism
  directionality versus teleology in 326, 328–33, 339, 350
  law of increasing complexity and 329
  on autonomy versus heteronomy 338–9
  potentiality and 318, 329, 338, 339
discourse theory 200
distribution of income
  effect of marketization on 141, 157
  in actually existing socialism 75
  in an inclusive democracy 248, 264, 267–8, 291
  in classical Athens 192, 193, 209
  orthodox economics efficiency and 250
  social democracy and 86
dominant social paradigm
  defined 180
  growth economy and 214
  in a Marxist society 180
  in actually existing socialism 173, 174
  inclusive democracy and 213, 275, 284, 343
  socialization and 181
domination
  freedom and 178
  over Nature 67, 111, 148, 153
  rational 333

social 67, 206
sources of 67
drugs 82, 227, 345

ecclesia 185, 189, 190, 191, 207, 256, 343, 344
eco-fascism 119, 153, 236–7, 330
eco-feminism 212, 348
eco-Marxism 66
eco-socialism 150–1, 159
economic blocs 42–3, 52, 205
economic democracy
 as an element of social democracy 196
 maldevelopment in the South and 133
 citizenship and 216
 civil societarian concept of 203, 239
 community and 240
 defined 186–7, 238–41
 direct democracy and 210
 ecological democracy and 215
 freedom of choice and 238, 249, 251–69
 greens' concept of 239
 in aboriginal American communities 194
 in an inclusive democracy 209–11, 255–69
 in classical Athens 176, 186, 188–94, 210
 in the Spanish civil war 335
 industrial revolution and 13
 market democracy and 135, 337
 neoliberal concept of 238
 preconditions of 237–55
 scarcity and 238
 state socialist concept of 239
 transitional strategy for 289–300
economic growth
 as a liberal and socialist objective 63
 concentration and 124
 in actually existing socialism 62, 64
 in Asian Tigers 115
 internationalization and 93
 limits of 148
 mercantilists and 118
 Nature and 148
 neoclassicals and 123
 poverty and 151
 Progress and 52, 65, 71, 73, 100, 140, 148, 152, 242

social democratic consensus and 29
 trickle-down effect and 112
efficiency
 definitions of 64, 102, 103, 256
 employee democracy and managerial 296
 information flow 78
 internationalization and 93
 marketization and 3, 46
 massification of production and 68
 neoclassical approach and 123
 social control and 164
 socialist growth economy and 75–7, 103
 socialist statism and 101
 technology and 68, 101, 155
EFTA 29
Egypt 9
elections contesting 283, 284, 285, 293
elitism 183
Emilia-Romana 294
empiricism 306–11, 316, 318, 319, 322, 324–6
Employee Stock Ownership Plan (ESOP) 295
enclosure(s)
 in the South 154
 movement in England 119
 of communal lands in Western Europe 12
 of upper classes today 37
energy
 consumption levels 142, 143
 efficient use of 152
 local sources of 241, 242
 nuclear 143
 programmes in an inclusive democracy 290, 291
 renewable forms of 215, 216
Engels, F.
 empiricist tendency in the writings of 324
 on freedom 178
 on nation-states 18–19
England
 emergence of economic liberalism in 15–16
 enclosure movement in 119
 marketization in 10, 12, 15, 16, 18

Enlightenment 65, 73, 140, 148, 152, 332, 333, 350
environmentalism 40, 150–51
epistemological fallacy 320, 322
equilibrium
    tendencies 124, 142
    theory of general 248–9
ethics
    anarchist 342
    Christian 344
    democratic 178, 339
    'objective' 180, 318, 339
    socialist 100
'Euro' 43, 45
Euro-centrism 123, 153, 182
Euro-dollar market 29, 32
Europe
    autonomy project in medieval 333
    capitalist market economies in East 79–83
    concentration of power in Eastern 21
    democratization of Eastern 83
    development of modern 'democracy' in 183–4
    economic systems in Western 7
    enclosure movement in Western 12
    expansion of exports in 28
    human rights in 331
    idea of growth formulated in 14
    import penetration in 28, 41
    Latinamericanization of Eastern 81
    liberalization of commodity markets in 43
    market economy's emergence in 5, 12
    marketization in Eastern 51
    marketization of central 80
    Mediterranean 43, 243
    municipal confederacies in 9
    neoracism in 55
    new protectionism in 99
    of regions 51, 55
    post-Maastricht 96, 145
    profitability in OECD 32
    rationalism's emergence in 308
    social democratic parties in 39, 74
    social market in 97–100
    socialist movement's emergence in 73
    socialist growth economy in Eastern 74, 79

trend towards a federal state in Western 51, 53
European Commission 52, 92, 172
European Economic Community (EEC)
    liberalization of markets and the 29
    poverty in the 112
European Monetary Union (EMU) 44, 98
European Union (EU)
    common currency in the 43
    convergence within the 95–6
    declining export share of 92
    falling competitiveness of 92
    inter-regional and intra-regional trade 99
    loss of state's economic sovereignty within the 42
    Mondragon and Spain's integration into 297
    neoliberal marketization within the 43, 45, 51, 94
    proposals for political integration within the 51–3
    social market in the 97–100
    social wage in the 91, 94
    trade with ex-Comecon countries 80
    wage differentials in the 43
evolution
    as ethical Progress 332
    dialectics and 319, 345
    economic 5, 320
    natural 328, 329
    social 73, 125, 149, 180, 307, 315, 328, 329, 332, 339, 343, 345
    towards democracy 331, 333, 336, 337, 350
exports growth 28, 30, 41, 69, 95, 189

falsificationism 308, 311, 312
farmers/peasants
    concentration in 150
    dependence on agro-chemical TNCs 131, 150
    enclosure movement and 119
    GATT and 242
    in China 85
    intensive 149
    'mad cow disease' and British 149–50
    modern agribusiness and 242, 286
    new class structure and 286
feminism 39, 212, 218, 345, 348, 350

fertility rates 120, 121, 122
feudalism 7, 9, 10, 12, 148
film industry 40
flexible labour markets 34–6, 43, 44, 94,
    95, 141, 142, 147
Food and Agriculture Organization (FAO)
    131
foreign investment 80, 98, 135
'forty per cent society' 37–40, 47, 72, 95,
    110, 112, 132, 142, 144, 338
France
    Gold Standard adopted by 16
    marketization in 18
    pre-war Popular Front Government in
        23
    social liberalism in 38, 162
    trade openness in 50
Frankfurt school 332
freedom
    anarchist conception of 178
    as the highest human objective 350
    civil societarian conception of 199, 201
    classical Greek meaning of 179
    compatibility with socialist statism of
        181–2
    compatibility with liberal individualism
        of 181–2
    concentration of power and 183
    defined in terms of autonomy 179–80,
        342
    democracy and 180, 194, 231, 342
    directionality towards 331
    expansion of ideals of 337
    fiscal 95
    foundation of 342
    from want 13
    human nature and 342
    individual and collective 179, 181
    individualistic conception of 178
    liberal conception of 177, 194, 231
    Marxist conception of 178
    negative and positive conception of
        177–8
    of capital 19, 94
    of choice 198, 237, 238, 249, 252, 254,
        255–7, 259, 261, 269, 298
    of contract 16
    of labour 95
    of trade 19
    political and economic 210–11

    potentiality for 333, 338, 339
    realm of 159, 173, 197–9
    scarcity and 198, 269
    socialist conception of 178, 232

GATT/WTO 6, 29, 35, 41, 172, 242
Germany
    Gold Standard adopted by 16
    Nazi statism in 22, 23
    protectionism in 18
    Rhineland model of stakeholder
        capitalism in 97–8, 204, 217, 225
    trade openness in 50
glasnost 79
globalization versus internationalization
    46–50
Gold Standard
    as one of the foundations of a self-
        regulating market 16
    central banks and 16
    European Monetary Union and 43, 45
    protectionism and 19
    statism and collapse of 20
Greater London Council 163
Greece
    ancient 175, 194, 336, 344
    modern 30, 38, 43, 112, 144, 292
Green movement 39, 51, 66, 96, 99, 151,
    162, 276, 307, 357
greenhouse effect 120, 149, 152
'greening' capitalism 100, 152
Group of 7
    break of Comecon ties by the 80
    carbon dioxide emissions by the 130
    concentration of power in the 172
    export share in the 69
    growth of imports in the 41
    Lille jobs summit (1996) of 142
    manufacturing employment in the 37
    unemployment in the 35
growth economy
    Asian Tigers and 114–16
    causes of fall of socialist 73–9
    classical theories on the 117–19
    concentration of power in a 67–73,
        100, 111–12, 126, 154
    defined 3
    democracy and capitalist 33, 172–3
    democracy and socialist 173–4
    development and 113, 116–17

ecological crisis and 66–7, 126, 129, 149–51, 153, 158, 214
emergence of 14, 62, 65
Euro-centric character of 153
Far Eastern 'socialist' 83–4
growth ideology and 62, 65–7
growth society and 147
industrialism and 280
inequality and 48
internationalization of 30, 31, 41, 46, 134
market economy and 17, 48, 55, 332
principles of organizing production in a 101–2
Progress and 123, 148, 243
prospects of Eastern European 76, 79–83
reproduction of 46, 48, 53, 72, 115, 130, 148
socialist ethics and 103–4
spreading in the South of the 69, 110–14, 124, 126, 133, 135
steady-state economy versus 152–3
types of 62, 63–5
growth ideology
crisis of 148
defined 65
ecological crisis and 66
economic theory and 118
rise of 65, 214
market economy and 62, 118
Marx and 123, 199
socialist growth economy and 65
South and 111
guilds 7
Gulf War 51

Haiti 135
Hayek, F.
neoliberal insurrection of 33
on the information problem in planned economies 252
heteronomy
autonomy as a rupture with the tradition of 331, 335
forms of 334, 337
Gorz on 234
historical societies and 330, 332
history as the struggle between autonomy and 338

interaction of autonomy with 334–5
qualitative difference between autonomy and 334
relativism and 347, 350
scientification of the liberatory project and 341
social 'evolution' and 329–30, 334
social possibility for 338
hierarchical
co-ops in Mondragon 237
conception of politics 346
division of labour 243
interpretation of Nature 339
organization of production 101, 155
organization of radical movements 346
patterns of power concentration 66
relations 4, 146, 207, 215, 288, 348
society 26, 66, 67, 71, 72, 73, 116, 140, 148, 288, 315, 349
structures 40, 78, 101, 102, 150, 185, 227, 242, 263, 266, 293, 341
Holland/Netherlands
free trade policies adopted by 16, 18
trade openness in 50
Hong Kong 114
human nature
anarchist view of 342
freedom and 180
liberal view of 194
Hungary 80, 81

Iberian Anarchist Federation (FAI) 236
identity
crisis of 146
cultural 4, 40, 55, 208
movements 55
national 53
idealism 181, 235
ideology
capitalist 160
growth 62, 63, 65–7, 83, 111, 116, 118, 123, 134, 148, 154, 214, 279
liberal/neoliberal 66, 111, 135
nationalist 11, 160, 217
of dominating Nature 111, 154, 213
social democratic 40
republican 159
socialist 66, 111, 159
imaginary
element in History 326, 329, 336, 350

institutions 134, 332
significations 65, 135, 148, 333, 335
IMF 45, 79, 100, 172, 225
imperialism 18, 20, 40, 125, 127
import penetration 28, 31, 41
incentives
    material versus ideological 78, 102
    soviet absence of work 77
    tax cuts as 36
incommensurability
    between conceptions of objectivity 319
    between orthodox and Marxist
        economics 315, 340
    between paradigms 308, 314
    between social and deep ecology 340
index of desirability 263–5
India 120, 121, 122, 249
individualism
    actually existing socialism and 102
    collectivism versus 180–3
    existential versus instrumental 182, 183
    freedom and 178–9, 181
    libertarianism and liberal 182, 231, 342
    methodological 324
    neoclassical economics and 123
    neoliberalism and culture of 144
    New Right and 33
industrial revolution 8, 12, 13, 15, 24, 62,
    65, 73, 104, 118, 280
industrialism 8, 70, 155, 278–80
inequality
    as condition for the reproduction of the
        growth economy 72, 142
    economic democracy and 209, 288
    crime and 346
    equal rights and 232
    in actually existing socialism 75
    in an inclusive democracy 211, 263,
        267
    in Britain 95, 113
    in China 72, 84, 85
    in classical Athens 186, 192, 193, 194,
        196
    in OECD countries 157
    in Russia 76
    in the household 212
    in the South 113
    in USA 141, 158, 211
    increase in global 142, 158
    industrial revolution and 9

maldevelopment and 134, 249, 250
marketization and 9, 44, 113, 158, 250
infant mortality 113, 131–2
information
    decentralization of 103, 294
    feedback in an inclusive democracy
        247, 257
    flow efficiency 78, 252, 253
    revolution 33, 36
    system 248
intermediate goods 266
International Labor Organization (ILO)
    142
internationalization
    as the cause of statism's collapse 28–33
    capital markets and 41–2
    civil society and 161–2, 276
    commodity markets and 41
    concentration and 116, 357
    confederalism versus 52
    defined 46
    European integration and 91–2
    globalization versus 46–50
    information revolution and 36
    marketization and 4, 96
    nation-state and 3, 50–1, 54
    neoliberalism and 41, 104, 228
    politics and 144, 276
    representative democracy and 276
    social controls and 4, 161
    trade and 99
internationalized market economy
    Asian Tigers and 115
    capital markets in the 35
    civil societarian approach and 161–2,
        202–3, 205
    class divisions within the 37
    commodity markets in the 35
    communitarianism and 229
    Community Economic Development
        (CED) and 230
    conditions for the success of an 44
    decentralization within the 243
    East Europe and 75, 76, 78, 80
    ecological crisis and 216
    economic blocs and 42
    first attempt for an 17, 44
    Gold Standard and 17
    Habermasian view of democracy and
        200

in west Europe 92
institutionalization of 29
liberal and neoliberal forms of 49
loss of state's economic sovereignty in
    the 42
new protectionism and 99
North–South divide and 131
radical democracy approaches and
    204–6, 224
role of state in an 46
Russia's integration into the 81
social controls within an 46, 49, 161,
    358
social expenditure and 91
social liberalism and 88
stakeholder capitalism and 218–19
statism and 115
irrationalism 40, 306, 330, 340, 343,
    347–9
Italy 43, 144, 294

Japan
    Anglo-Saxon model and 358
    Asian Tigers and 115
    competitiveness of 92
    export share of 92
    hegemony of US dollar and 28
    growth decline in 115
    Kohsetsushi of 294
    Rhineland model and 99
    Seikatsu of 281
    trade openness in 50
    unit labour cost in 98
job complexes 262, 263
job insecurity 75, 141, 147
Jordan 131

Kantianism 183, 309, 316, 321, 326
Kenya 131
Keynesianism
    European versus national 92, 96
    neoclassical trend versus 27
    social democracy and 74–5
Kohsetsushi 294
Korea (South) 69, 114, 243
Kropotkin, Pëtr
    on ethics 342
    on pre-market economy markets 7
    on state versus free towns 11

on the 'consecutive development of
    nations' 69
on voluntary agreements 232

labour theory of value 261
Labour Party of Britain 22, 89, 227
laissez-faire 115, 118, 232
Laos 63, 83, 111
Left
    civil societarian 47, 74, 158–64, 357,
        358
    collapse of actually existing socialism and
        the 357
    decline of the 34
    libertarian socialism and the 74, 253
    Marxist 197
    New 86, 145
    Old 25
    politics 145
    socialist statism and the 74
    vision of 'radical' democracy 224, 357
Lenin, V.
    on democracy 174, 197
    on objectivity 320
    on socialist consciousness 342
    on the proletarian state 74
Leninism 85, 101, 144, 175, 305
liberal
    approach on the collapse of actually
        existing statism 76
    conception of citizenship 217
    conception of democracy 194–6
    conception of freedom 177, 196, 232
    conception of human rights 217, 232
    definition of development 117
    environmentalism 150, 313
    individualism 182, 183, 232, 342
    internationalized market economy 3,
        17, 49
    nationalism 18
    Old Right versus neoliberal New Right
        33
    oligarchy 54, 83, 176, 202, 336
    phase of marketization 11, 15, 44, 47,
        172
    philosophy 177, 195, 232
liberalism
    anarchism/libertarianism and 182–3
    concentration of power and 71
    democracy and 195–6

economic 8, 15–17, 18, 201
environmentalism and 151
instrumental 201
laissez-faire versus 39
national 18
political 71, 201
pure 20, 47
social 41, 47, 85–91, 143, 162
socialism and 63, 151, 179, 180, 200, 228, 319
liberalization
cultural homogenization and market 40
distribution of income and 141
international borrowing and market 42
of capital markets 35
of commodity markets 43
of labour markets 34–5, 43, 141
Right's proposals for further 157–8
Russian market 82
libertarian
concept of freedom 178
ecology 276
ethics 342
individualism 181–2, 238
municipalism 291
conception of politics 186
socialism 74, 151, 253, 286
society 260
tradition 218, 345, 350
lifestyle strategies 276–8, 346
Lille jobs summit of G7 (1996) 142
localism 12, 54, 156, 227
Lubeck 185

Maastricht Treaty 6, 45, 53, 92, 93, 94, 95, 96, 98, 145
maldevelopment 134, 246, 249, 250, 288
Mantineia, battle of 193
marginalist revolution 123
market(s)
bond 42
capital 6, 29, 35, 41, 42, 43, 87, 93
'democracy' 135
deregulation of 35, 40, 88
Euro-dollar 29, 32
European 6, 40, 91
financial 32, 35, 47, 99
flexible/free 17, 18, 36, 44, 94, 96, 124, 142

labour 12, 13, 14, 16, 17, 27, 32, 34, 35, 43, 45, 97, 98, 141
liberalization of 35, 141, 157, 158
local versus national 8, 10, 11, 291, 297
mechanism 14, 16, 20, 21, 71, 72, 76, 104, 134, 248–50, 259
money 27, 88
'nationalization' of 10, 11, 54
pre-'market economy' 7–8
regulated versus self-regulated 7, 8, 10, 12, 13, 15, 16, 24, 39, 44, 45, 47, 97
social 97–100
social controls on 7, 9, 11, 13, 15, 18, 22, 27, 34, 42, 44, 46, 98, 99, 150, 162
socialism 202, 203
sovereignty 173
trade and 8
values 55, 146, 242
market economy
André Gorz and 234
as a system 3, 7, 10, 14, 111
capitalism and 6
civil societarians and 160, 162, 164
communitarianism on the 228
competitiveness and 102
concentration and 69, 73, 156, 158, 183
culture and 7, 154
defined 4–5
East European 75, 76, 79–83
economic democracy and 337
emergence of 7, 10–14, 19, 104, 172, 210
employment and 141
freedom of choice in a 249
general equilibrium in the 248–9
Great Depression and 20, 22–4
grow-or-die dynamic of 29, 52, 62, 65, 83, 84, 99, 110, 128
growth economy and 55, 62, 64, 100
growth ideology and 62, 65
hierarchical society and 71
industrialism and 12
internationalization of 29, 31, 32, 33, 41, 44, 46, 48, 53, 87, 92, 96, 128, 144, 228
John Clark and 237
'maldevelopment' and 134
nationalized industries and 102

nationalism and 19
nature and 150, 153, 155, 158
openness of 49
orthodox economics paradigm and 124
orthodox economists and 249
planned economy and 64
price distortions in a 252
protectionism and 19, 99
self-managed enterprises and 246
social controls on the 5–6, 49, 50
social crisis and 146
social struggle in a 15
socialism and 100, 251
'socialist' 6, 64, 78, 79, 83–5
South and 69, 110, 111, 119, 133, 134,
   135, 142
stakeholder 218, 225
state and 39, 46, 47, 51
technology and 155
market-oriented models 251–2
marketization
colonialism and 111, 134, 154
community values and 55, 158, 225,
   242
concentration of economic power and
   68, 252
defined 7
democracy's incompatibility with 172
Eastern European 51
emergence of 10
environment and 130, 164
European Union and 94
industrialism and 8
inequality and 44, 157, 158
insecurity and 147
internationalization and 4, 28, 44, 48,
   52, 337
liberal phase of 14–21
nation-state and 11
neoliberal phase of 33–45
New Right and 157
North–South divide and 128, 132
not an evolutionary process 10
of communications 40
of culture 40, 158
of labour 12, 15, 147
of land 12, 15
of society 13, 41, 44, 55, 158
peripheral 142
protectionism and 17–18

Rhine model and 97
social controls and 67
social crisis and 146
Stalinist Russia and 21
statist phase of 21–33
trade and 10, 17
trickle-down effect and 113
Marx, Karl
Eurocentrism of 123
on economic growth 65, 123
on human rights 232
on spreading of capitalism 124
on the 'science' of socialism 319, 320,
   323, 325, 342
on the ancient Greek city 187
on the nation-state 8, 173, 197
on the value of commodities 259
Polanyi and 14
progress and 347
Marxism
actually existing socialism and 63
Anglo-American 324
as 'science' of socialism 148, 154, 321,
   323, 324, 341, 346
as method 322
as philosophy 321, 322
concentration of power and 71
instrumentalist 183
liberalism and 319
positivistic 323, 324
realist 326
social ecology and 307
socialist statism and 74, 102, 151
structuralist 321, 325–26
materialism 181, 214
dialectical 306, 321, 323
historical 326
mercantilism 10, 11, 12, 117, 118
MERCOSUR 43
methodological monism 327
Mexico 43, 133, 243
Middle Ages
markets in the 7–8
nation-states in the 9–10
minorities 26, 37, 211, 231, 233, 249,
   287, 331
Mises, Ludwig von
on central banks 16
on planned economies 252

mixed economy 26, 39, 48, 49, 72, 75, 78, 251
mobility
    of capital 42, 43, 93
    of labour 15, 43, 248
Mondragon 237, 246, 247, 291, 294, 296, 297
money
    community and 8
    demotic 290
    inclusive democracy and 268, 282
    liberalization/deregulation of markets for 42, 88
    marketization of 12
    needs versus wants backed by 249–50, 256
    speculative 35
    statism's controls on markets for 27
    vouchers versus 257, 261
Multi-/Trans-national Corporations 29, 32, 47, 48, 68–70, 88, 96, 99, 114, 135, 225, 243
muslim fundamentalism 348

NAFTA 41, 42, 49, 99
nationalized enterprises 25, 29, 246
nation-state(s)
    civil society and 239
    economic sovereignty of 4, 28, 32, 42, 173
    emergence of 3, 8–10, 183
    internationalization and 46–56
    market economy and 8–10, 11, 13, 18, 99
    nationalism and 11, 19, 51
    politics and 53–5
    regional differences and 43
    relations between confederations and 284
    today's significance of 47–8, 50–4, 88
    world system and 126
nationalism
    cultural 40
    in Eastern Europe 51, 82
    internationalism versus 51
    liberal 18
    market economy and 16, 19
    modernity and 19
    protectionism and 17–19
NATO 51

nature
    democracy and 154, 213–16
    first and second 215, 329
    free 329
    growth ideology and 111, 153, 199, 213
    instrumentalist view of 67, 153, 214
    society and 52, 63, 66, 67, 73, 148, 330
needs
    basic 64, 89, 90, 111, 136, 143, 217, 249, 254, 256–8, 290, 292, 299, 357
    consumer 82
    cultural 111, 132
    local 289
    non-basic 225, 254, 259–62
    'objective' 117, 156, 198, 256
    satisfiers and 256–7
    scarcity and 198, 238
neo-classical school 27, 123, 124, 125
neo-Darwinian synthesis 329
neoliberal
    character of EU 91–7
    internationalized market economy 47, 48, 51, 131, 146, 157, 235
    movement 33–6
    phase of marketization 33–45, 243, 250
    policies 35, 36, 38, 41, 45, 80, 95, 349, 358
neoliberal consensus
    at the cultural level 40
    at the economic level 39
    at the ideological level 40
    at the political level 39
    at the social level 39
    civil societarian approach and 162
    European Federation and 52
    European Union and 53, 91, 94
    'forty per cent society' and 39–40
    in Sweden 87–8
    marketization and 44
    not a conjunctural phenomenon 45, 49
    post-modernist movement and 41
    social crisis and 146
    social liberalism and 87
    socialist statism and 80–6
    social democrats and 86, 145
neoliberalism
    adoption by international institutions 45, 125

civil society and 161
community values and 55, 144
laissez-faire versus 39
neoclassical economics and 125
not a conjunctural phenomenon 45
post-modernism and 148
rise of 33–6
underclass and 144
neo-Malthussians 119
Nepal 131
New Age 236, 278
'New' North and South 132, 136
new social movements 74, 201
New Zealand 30, 112
North–South
    Asian Tigers and 114–16
    concentration and 142, 157, 225
    conventional approaches on
        development of 117–29
    democracy and 132–6
    development problem and 110
    'forty per cent society' and 72, 132
    historical gap between 69
    irrationalism and 348
    market/growth economy and 111–14,
        116, 133, 135
    'new' 113, 131–2, 136
    population pattern in 119–23
    poverty in 112, 119
    trickle-down effect and 113, 122
    widening gap between 112, 157
Norway 30, 86, 87, 112

objectivism
    basic needs and 156
    irrationalism and 348, 349
    liberal individualism and 342
    liberatory project and 340
    post modern subjectivism/relativism
        versus 305–6, 348, 350
    scientific 326
objectivity
    dialectical 316–20
    dialectical naturalism and 328–40
    Marxist 320–28
    notion of 314
    of the liberatory project 340–50
    orthodox 306–12
    realist 326–8
    scientific 310

versus intersubjectivity 312–16
OECD
    concentration of production in 112
    distribution of GDP in 31
    growth rates in 30
    liberalization in 36
    on Comecon fragmentation 81
    on inequality 158
    on the Anglo-Saxon model's superiority
        142
    profitability in 32
oil crisis 32, 33
oligarchy
    economic 135, 210
    in Athens 187–9, 196
    liberal 54, 83, 202, 336
    political 176, 208, 335
openness
    financial 32, 50
    trade 32, 49, 50
orthodox development paradigm 124–5
ostracism 190
overclass 37, 147, 286, 357
ownership of productive resources
    allocation versus 245
    control versus 245
    demotic 186, 240, 245–7, 289, 297
    private/capitalist 6, 13, 66, 70, 79, 239,
        245, 288
    social 6, 84, 199, 202, 246, 247, 251
    state/socialist 70, 79, 84, 174

paedeia 209, 214, 216, 231, 234
paradigm
    democratic 213, 275, 282
    dependency 125–6
    dominant social 63, 173, 174, 180, 181,
        214, 284, 343
    ecological 140, 150
    incommensurability 308, 314, 315, 319,
        326, 340
    Marxist 125–6, 315
    orthodox 124, 315
    scientific 313–14
Parisian sections 209, 332, 335, 348
Peloponnesian War 188, 193
perestroika 78–9
Persian Wars 191, 192–3
philosophy
    as a closed system 321

democracy and 336, 344
Kant's 316
liberal 177
Marxism-as 321, 322
New Right's versus Old Right's 33
of economic liberalism 8
of history 181, 326
of liberal nationalism 18
of positivism 309
of science 306, 310, 312, 316, 319, 323
of social ecology 339
political 319
physiocrats 117, 118
planability 76, 77
planning
central 21, 63, 64, 67, 71, 84, 115, 250–1, 261
centralized versus decentralized 250–1, 253
democratic 225, 234, 237, 238, 244, 247, 252, 254–69, 298
family 120, 121
indicative 35, 92, 250
participatory 251–5
Plataia, battle of 190
Poland 79, 80, 82, 131, 281
Polanyi, Karl
Marx and 14
on marketization of land, labour and money 12, 14
on Nazi versus Western statism 24
on pre-'market economy' markets 7
on the '100 years peace' 19
on the Great Depression 20
on the institutions for a self-regulating market 44
on the market economy 10, 44, 104, 332
the Great Transformation and 27
polis
as a form of social self-instituting 342, 343, 344
autonomia versus eleutheria in the 179
democratic education in the 209
oikos and 212
religion and the 343
sovereignty of the 185
politics
a new kind of 276–89
as technique 346

autonomy and 342
classical conception of 185, 216, 347
crisis of traditional 143–6
crisis of Left 145
deliberative 200
end of 53–6
hierarchical conception of 346
libertarian definition of 185
Marxist 346
of individualism 238
republican 159
science and 342, 346
socialist 305
statecraft versus 173, 347
Portugal 30, 43, 112
positivism 306, 308, 310, 311, 318, 319, 323, 324, 326
postmodernism
general relativism in 148, 347, 348
neoliberal consensus and 41
on History 347
subjectivism and 305
poverty
as development and as underdevelopment 130
determinants of 121
environment and 151
growth and 151
in Britain 37, 131
in Russia 82
in the European Union 95
in the South 112, 129
in the USA 112, 131
overpopulation and 119, 121
Reaganomics and 164
power
concentration of 9, 21, 66, 67–73, 152, 154
cultural 40
democracy as equal sharing of 171, 175, 180, 185, 186, 342, 344
dual 84, 284, 291
economic 4, 23, 34, 38, 62, 68, 70, 71, 116, 189, 196, 209, 210, 239–40, 337
financial 289, 290
freedom and 183
inclusive democracy and 206–18, 231, 238–41, 267

political 52, 111, 163, 171, 172, 183, 189, 195, 196, 207, 336
relations 4, 66, 177, 185, 207, 313
rights and 232–3
social 72, 73, 191, 204, 340
state 15, 162, 163, 198, 231
system of balance-of 19, 45
structures in modern hierarchical societies 116, 230, 279, 284
taxing 290, 299
to determine production 291
working class 15, 26, 34, 37
praxis 241, 322, 325, 346–7
private property
Aristotle on social conflict related to 186
crime against 346
definition of freedom and 178
economic power and 239
private versus public realm 179, 194, 195, 210, 212
privatizations 25, 36, 80, 81, 82, 87, 89, 293
production
decentralization of 69, 243, 268
diversification of 68, 70
massification versus de-massification of 68
mode of 4–5, 123, 125, 126, 187
progress
as an evolutionary process 329, 330, 331, 333, 338, 347
as development of productive forces 65, 71, 73, 100, 183, 243
ethical 332
science and 148
profitability
decline in the 1970s 32–3
hierarchy and 245
increase in the 1980s 36
market concentration and 68
protectionism
in the Asian Tigers 115
nationalism and 18
'new' 99–100
rise of 17–19
statism and 19–21
types of 17
public utilities 18, 22, 89–90

race/racism 4, 208, 231, 233, 267, 331
rationalism
democratic 149, 306, 349–50
empiricism/positivism versus 308–11, 316, 318, 322, 323, 325
multi-dimensional crisis and 148, 149
'objectivist' 149, 326
rationing 117, 131, 249, 259, 260, 261
Reaganomics 164, 350
realm
ecological 206
economic 5, 196, 206
of freedom 159, 173, 197, 198, 199, 269, 287
of necessity 197, 198
political 206, 207, 210
private 179, 194, 210, 212, 213
public 159, 171, 173, 176, 179, 195, 206, 210, 211, 212, 284
social 26, 206, 210, 211, 212, 213, 214, 215, 286, 288
regulation approach to development 116, 127–9
relativism
democratic 347–8
general 148, 306, 347, 348
Marxist 'philosophical tendency' and 321
philosophical 347
political 347
'realist' Marxism and 326, 327
religion 7, 121, 340, 348
democracy and 343–4
old hierarchical societies and 71, 148
representatives versus delegates 184, 207, 230
republicanism 159, 160, 195, 200, 206, 230
revolution
American 231
commercial 11
English 231
French 184, 231
industrial 8, 12, 13, 15, 24, 62, 65, 73, 104, 118, 280
information 33, 36
Kuhnian 313
marginalist 123
Russian 20
socialist 23, 126, 197

Rhineland model 97, 141
Right
  economists of the 252
  'libertarian' 183
  nationalist 47
  New 33, 74, 157, 158
  Old 33
  proposals to deal with the crisis 157–8
  protectionist 99–100
  shift to the 37, 38, 145
rights
  animal 276, 277
  civic 187, 188, 190, 191, 192, 298
  economic 173, 182, 232
  holistic view of 232
  human 173, 194, 331
  in an inclusive democracy 232
  liberal versus socialist conception of
    231–2
  minorities' 233, 331
  political 94, 182, 187, 191, 192, 217,
    231
  property 183
  social 99, 182
  women's 331
Romania 131
Rome Treaty 91–2
rotation of work 262
Roosevelt's New Deal 22
Russia
  'democratization' of 83
  Latinamericanization of 45, 81–2
  nationalism in 51
  Stalinist 21

safety nets 36, 47, 90, 91, 116, 292
scarcity
  class dictatorships and 197
  communistic fiction and 198
  economic realm and 197–8
  inclusive democracy and 225, 238, 252,
    254
  post-scarcity 198, 224, 255, 269
science
  actually existing socialism and Marxist
    174
  autonomy tradition and 349
  credibility crisis of 148–9
  growth ideology and 65, 148
  liberatory project and 279, 319, 326

  'neutrality' of 155, 310
  New Right and economic 33, 40, 123
  politics and 73, 341, 342, 347
  problem of knowledge in Marxist theory
    of 321, 323
  problem of method in orthodox
    philosophy of 312, 316
  traditions in the philosophy of 306,
    307, 310
scientific research programmes (SRP) 312
scientism 148, 306, 309, 340, 345, 347,
  348
Second International 87
Seikatsu 281
seisachtheia 189
self-managed enterprises 246–7, 251
self-organization theory 329
self-reliance
  autonomy and 241
  central planning and 243
  community 241–5
  comparative advantage and 68
  conditions for the increase in 289–92,
    295
  defined 241
  ecological society and 242
  economic 11, 95, 97, 102, 133–4, 289
  economic democracy and 244
  GATT and 242
  implications of the trend away from
    241–2
  marketization and 102, 249
  self-sufficiency versus 268
  viable size for 244
shareholders versus stakeholders 204
Singapore 114
Single Market Act 45, 53, 92, 94
slavery 9, 179, 187, 192, 193, 194, 334
Slovakia 80
Social Charter 94
social democracy
  collapse of Swedish 87–8
  competitiveness and 102, 144
  decline of the EU 91–7
  defined 74
  demeaning of the content of 86–7
  neoliberalism and 86, 145
social democratic consensus
  at the economic level 25, 86
  at the ideological level 27

at the political level 25
at the social level 26
causes of collapse of 104
European Keynesianism and 92, 93
growth economy and 29
internationalization and 29, 96
neoliberal consensus and 39, 45, 91,
    141
neoliberal critique of 33–4
not a conjunctural phenomenon 24
Polanyi and 27
post-war boom and 25
wage and price controls and 27
social ecology 150, 151, 276, 330, 339,
    340, 348
social legislation 15, 18, 20
social liberalism
    from social democracy to 85–91
    in France 162
social protection 97
social versus natural sciences 306, 309,
    315, 316, 328
social wage 26, 36, 86, 91, 94, 145
socialization 181, 215, 277, 285
socialism 4, 68
    eco-socialism 150, 151
    guild 204
    in one country 103
    liberalism and 15, 63, 199, 228
    libertarian 74, 151
    market 202, 203
    Marxist-Leninist 144
    nation-state and 8, 202
    planning and 71, 251
    power relations and 174
    scientific 323, 341
    statist/state 181, 182, 183, 203, 295,
        334
socialist
    conception of democracy 196
    conception of freedom 178, 232
    conception of human rights 217, 232
    enterprises 293, 295
    ethics 100
    growth economy 62–7, 70, 71, 74,
        78–80, 100–2, 111, 115, 116, 174,
        243
    ideology 66, 111, 159
    market economy 6, 78, 79, 83–5, 251
    movement 65, 73, 165, 333, 341

planning 246, 253, 255
project 103, 145, 251, 305, 324, 341
socialist statism
    causes of the failure of 100–4
    crisis of 73–4
    defined 15
    East European 21, 75
    economic democracy and 210, 239
    freedom and 182
    growth ideology and 66
    main historical forms of 74
society
    anarchist 69, 236
    autonomous 179, 180, 233, 334, 337,
        340, 343
    capitalist 150
    class 85, 323
    commercial 12, 13
    communist 197
    community-based 233, 234, 235, 254,
        278
    confederal 214, 215
    conserver 155
    consumer 66, 214, 337, 346
    decentred 200
    democratic 198, 206, 207, 233, 254,
        283, 339, 340, 343
    ecological 215, 254, 281, 328, 329
    economy and 116, 145, 183, 214, 217,
        241, 310, 358
    free 198, 329, 330, 331, 332, 333, 337,
        339, 340, 357
    growth 147, 148
    heteronomous 334, 337, 338, 339
    hierarchical 26, 66, 67, 71, 72, 116,
        148, 185, 349
    industrial 25, 154, 155
    libertarian 259
    market 4, 104, 202
    marketless 225, 255, 282
    Marxist 180
    moneyless 225, 281, 282
    multi-communal 182
    nature and 213, 214, 215, 330, 345
    non-society 147
    non-statist 232
    organic 13
    post-industrial 68, 70, 144, 235, 253
    primitive 13
    religious 180

scarcity versus post-scarcity 206, 225, 238, 254, 269
single-nation 86
state and 341, 342
stateless 226, 239, 281, 282
tribal 180
'two-thirds' versus '40 per cent' 38, 39, 47, 48, 83, 86, 95, 110, 132, 142, 276, 358
Solidarity, Polish 158, 159, 281
sovereignty
 Athenian versus European conception of 184
 collective 54
 market 173
 of Parliament 184
 of polis 185
 of the nation-state 3, 4, 28, 42, 48, 173
 supranational 173
Soviet Union see USSR
Spain 38, 43, 144, 281, 293, 297
Spanish collectives 208, 333, 335
spiritualism 199, 235, 236, 344, 348, 349
Sri Lanka 131
'stagflation' crisis 33, 93
stakeholder capitalism 99, 217, 225
Stalinism 21, 83, 178, 250, 341
state
 as a class instrument 163
 as necessary evil 338
 bourgeois versus proletarian 74, 197
 civil society and 160, 161, 162, 199–200, 239
 confederations versus the 11, 19, 52, 299
 democracy and the 197
 'democratization' of 199, 201, 283
 economic role of the 20–3, 25–7, 29, 32, 39, 48, 50, 51, 141, 172
 emergence of 9
 globalization thesis and the 46
 human rights and 232
 in the Middle Ages 9–10
 intervention(-ism) 22, 23, 27, 86, 93, 118, 202
 market and 8–10, 11, 25
 minimal 157
 monopoly of violence of the 47, 51
 nationalism and the 11, 19

separation of economy from the 183, 194, 205
separation of society from the 177, 182, 184, 195, 341
social role of the 96, 164
supranational 51
statism
 as a transitional phenomenon 44
 Bretton Woods system and 27
 civil society and 38, 161
 collapse of 28–33
 cost of production and 31
 defined 3
 dialectic of 251
 during World War II 24
 flexible currencies and 27, 28
 'forty per cent society' and 38
 Gold Standard and 20, 27
 international 53
 internationalization and 28–33, 46
 Keynesian 124
 Nazi versus Western 23–4
 Polanyi and 24, 44
 pre-war 22–4
 protectionism and 19–21
 social democratic 33, 34
 Stalinist Russia and 21
 unemployment and 25–6, 34
steady-state versus growth economy 111, 136, 152, 153
Stoics 345
structuralist approaches to development 124–5
subjectivism 305
surplus
 agricultural 21
 economic 9, 118, 124, 126, 127, 163, 187, 188, 192
 labour 84
 trade 80
sustainable development approach 150–2
Sweden 22, 38, 86, 87, 88
Swiss cantons 208, 334, 347
Switzerland 30
Syria 131

Taiwan 114, 243
Taoism 344, 345, 348
tax(-es)
 as cost of production 31–2

cuts for the rich 36
demotic system of 290
disparate effect of 38
evasion 35, 90
power in a transitional strategy 290
progressiveness of income 86, 189
technical progress 118, 123, 259
technology
  confederalism and 234
  direct democracy and 230
  ecological crisis and 154–5, 331
  efficiency and 68
  homogenization of 331
  in actually existing socialism 101
  in an inclusive democracy 265–7
  'neutrality' of 101, 155, 331
teleology 326, 328
Thailand 114, 243
Thatcherism 37, 164, 350
Third World 29, 74, 113, 119, 125, 132,
    135, 155, 215
torture 331, 332
totality 127, 252, 316, 317, 318
trade
  Bretton Woods and 27–8
  expansion of international 17, 18, 28
  flexible currencies and 27
  foreign 10, 42
  free 15, 16, 17, 18, 19, 31, 43, 242, 243
  'greening' of 100
  in classical Athens 189, 192
  in Middle Ages 8
  internationalization and 28–30
  intra-regional versus inter-regional 99
  local 8, 10
  national (internal) 10, 11, 16
  openness 32, 50
  speculative capital movements versus
      movements related to 42
  statism's controls on 21
  TNCs' control of 135
  welfare state and 87
  within the Comecon region 81–2
  within the G7 countries 69
transitional strategy 275, 281, 282–5, 289,
    291, 292, 299
Triad 47, 48, 49, 69, 72, 89, 92, 95,
    141–2, 144, 157
trickle-down effect 48, 113, 122, 151, 250
truth theories 308

uncertainty principle 305
underclass 37, 38, 89, 144, 146, 151, 276,
    277, 286, 358
unemployment
  as an incentive 77
  general equilibrium and 249
  Gold Standard and 20
  in China 84–5
  in Germany 98
  in Japan 115
  in Sweden 88
  in the G7 35
  in the neoliberal phase 35
  in the statist phase 24–5
  in the USA 35, 98, 141, 147
  in theory 75
  low-paid employment versus open 142
  open versus disguised 75, 78
  prospects for 95, 141
  'stagflation' and 33
  structural 35
UNICEF 131
unions
  civil society and 158, 160, 162
  in a transitional strategy 283
  in Britain 37, 163
  in Sweden 88, 162
  in the USA 37
  legislation against 15, 23
  neoliberal consensus and 40
  social democratic consensus and 26, 34
United Nations 45, 46, 51, 158, 205
UN Human Development Report 142
universality of welfare state 47, 90, 91
USA
  as a reserve currency country 50
  film industry of the 40
  income inequality in the 37, 141, 158
  NAFTA and 42, 144
  positivism in the 308
  prison population in the 147
  trade openness in the 41, 50
  unemployment in the 35, 98, 141
US Labor Department 141
USSR/Soviet Union 76, 77, 79, 81, 337
utopia 345, 346
utopianism 156, 340, 345

values
  community 55, 158, 225, 227, 242

cultural 68, 73, 154, 156–7
democratic 233, 345
dominant social 63, 156
ecological 153, 237, 332
human 153, 177
individualistic 145
market 55, 146, 242
'rationing' 259
'universal' 78
Vienna Circle 310, 317
Vietnam 6, 63, 79, 83, 111, 131
violence
physical 120, 285
economic 9, 120, 285, 299
state's monopoly of 47, 51
vouchers
basic 257–8
non-basic 258–61

wage differentials 43, 127, 293
Walden II 261–2
welfare state
Asian Tigers and 115
Beveridge Report and 24
communitarianism and 225–7
crisis of social democratic politics and 145
demotic welfare system versus 292

dependence on 33
European Union and 52, 93, 95
expansion of 26, 31
financing of 35, 86
'forty per cent society' and 86
neoliberal consensus and 24, 36, 38, 87
neoliberal theorists on 33–4
'safety net' versus 47, 292
state commitment to 38, 196
social democratic consensus and 25, 86
social liberalism and 87
trade and 87
universality of the 90
Westphalian system of nation-states 51
worker-oriented models 253, 255
World Bank 30, 45, 79, 82, 84, 100, 112–14, 121, 125, 129, 130, 131, 172, 225, 244
World Conference on Population (1994) 120
worldview 197, 313, 314, 315, 316, 317, 321, 326, 340, 348
World War I 19, 21
World War II 21, 74, 111

Yugoslavia 79, 146